DEMOLITION AGENDA

Also by Thomas O. McGarity

Pollution, Politics, and Power
Freedom to Harm
The Preemption War

DEMOLITION AGENDA

How Trump Tried to Dismantle American Government, and What Biden Needs to Do to Save It

Thomas O. McGarity

THE
NEW
PRESS

NEW YORK
LONDON

Requests for permission to reproduce selections from this book should be made through our website: https://thenewpress.com/contact.

Published in the United States by The New Press, New York, 2022
Distributed by Two Rivers Distribution

ISBN 978-1-62097-639-5 (hc)
ISBN 978-1-62097-640-1 (ebook)
CIP data is available

The New Press publishes books that promote and enrich public discussion and understanding of the issues vital to our democracy and to a more equitable world. These books are made possible by the enthusiasm of our readers; the support of a committed group of donors, large and small; the collaboration of our many partners in the independent media and the not-for-profit sector; booksellers, who often hand-sell New Press books; librarians; and above all by our authors.

www.thenewpress.com

Book design and composition by Bookbright Media
This book was set in Times New Roman

Printed in the United States of America

10 9 8 7 6 5 4 3 2 1

CONTENTS

DEMOLITION AGENDA

had an ace in the hole. It pointed out that in the fine print of the loan agreement that Jennifer (and all of her co-plaintiffs) had signed, there was a clause agreeing to resolve any disputes through private arbitration, rather than by suing Wells Fargo in a court of law. Moreover, the contract barred class actions in arbitration or in court. Therefore, the class action had to be dismissed. Flabbergasted, Jennifer wondered how a clause in an account that she had authorized could bar a lawsuit based on the company's creation of fake accounts that she had not authorized. Yet several courts had already dismissed similar class-action and individual lawsuits against Wells Fargo based on similar arbitration clauses.

Despite their ubiquity in consumer contracts, take-it-or-leave-it arbitration clauses are unfair to consumers. The arbitration procedures are conducted behind closed doors pursuant to rules mandated by the arbitrators without the right of judicial review. Arbitrators have an incentive to side with the companies because the companies are repeat players and usually choose the arbitrator or have veto power over the choice. Consumers who do go through arbitration in disputes involving financial products obtain relief only about 20 percent of the time. Because arbitrations are carried out in total secrecy, none of the facts about the company's misconduct are likely to see the light of day. This secrecy eviscerates accountability and destroys the tendency of successful lawsuits to deter unlawful conduct. Worst of all, like Jennifer Zeleny, most consumers are unaware of the fact that the fine print in consumer contracts that they sign (or click on) often contains arbitration clauses.[4]

Forced arbitration clauses deprive victims of corporate misconduct of their constitutional right to a trial by jury. In the Supreme Court's questionable logic, that is not a problem, because citizens can waive their constitutional rights in contracts into which they freely enter. It takes a considerable perversion of reality, however, to conclude that consumers who sign or click on multiple pages of indecipherable fine print in a contract over which no negotiation is possible have freely given up their right to a jury trial. Everybody knows that no one reads lengthy consumer contracts. One study found that only 13 percent of consumers who were asked to read arbitration clauses realized that they prohibited class-action lawsuits. Nevertheless, the Supreme Court applied a 1925 statute that was intended to apply to contracts between corporations of equal bargaining strength to create a presumption that consumers who click "agree" on purchases have agreed to arbitrate any disputes. It took only a slight additional step for the Court to conclude that the same presumption applied to clauses that limited class actions in arbitration, thereby limiting arbitration to individual claims by individual consumers. This effectively insulated companies from accountability for irresponsible products and actions that didn't do *enough* damage to any individual that a plaintiff's lawyer would be willing to take on the burden of expensive litigation. As Judge Richard Posner famously explained, "The realistic alternative to a class action is not 17 million individual suits, but zero individual suits, as only a lunatic or a fanatic sues for $30."[5]

Congress recognized the unfairness of arbitration clauses in consumer financial contracts. The Dodd–Frank Wall Street Reform and Consumer Protection Act of 2010 created the Consumer Financial Protection Bureau and empowered it to write regulations prohibiting or otherwise regulating such clauses if such action was "in the public interest and for the protection of consumers," a broad standard aimed at protecting vulnerable consumers.[6]

In July 2017, the bureau, then headed by Barack Obama appointee Richard Cordray, issued a regulation prohibiting the use of arbitration clauses containing class-action waivers in contracts for most consumer financial products. In a massive document, consuming 224 triple-columned pages in the *Federal Register* (the daily compendium of federal notices), the bureau spelled out the basis for its determination that class-action-limiting arbitration clauses should be banned.[7] Since

Congress had explicitly invited the agency to come up with an arbitration regulation, the ruling was certain to survive judicial review.

Concerned that their clients might suddenly be faced with a spate of class-action suits, lobbyists for the financial industry and the U.S. Chamber of Commerce made a beeline to Republican offices on Capitol Hill, urging their occupants to nullify the new regulations under an obscure law called the Congressional Review Act. Enacted in 1996 during a massive deregulatory push in Congress inspired by Newt Gingrich's Contract With America, the Act allows Congress to overturn major federal regulations within sixty days of promulgation by passing a joint resolution of disapproval signed by the president. A special provision in the law simplifies the process by preventing filibusters in the Senate. The lobbyists succeeded, and the bureau's arbitration rule died before it protected a single consumer.[8]

Courts have dismissed many claims like Jennifer's on the basis of arbitration clauses that bar class actions. For example, a federal court in Mississippi relied on an arbitration clause to dismiss Gwendolyn Byrd's class-action lawsuit against Wells Fargo, even though she was legally blind and counted on sales personnel to read her the relevant sections of the contract. No matter—she had signed the contract.[9] And now, anyone who signs or clicks on consumer financial contracts containing forced arbitration clauses will suffer the same fate.

The neutering of the Consumer Financial Protection Bureau and the related demise of the arbitration rule were two small items on a much larger agenda pursued by President Donald Trump, his political appointees, and the Republican leadership in Congress. Much has been written about the Trump administration's revolving cast of cabinet members and agency heads, many of them deeply unqualified for their posts. What has gone less noticed is the vigor with which the Trump administration attempted to dismantle a host of agencies and regulatory programs that Congress put in place over the course of many decades to protect consumers, workers, communities, children, and the environment, in pursuit of a comprehensive demolition agenda.

From the Environmental Protection Agency to the Department of the Interior, the Department of Transportation, and the Consumer Financial Protection Bureau, the Trump administration employed an unprecedented set of strategies to disempower, muzzle, and undermine the agencies that Congress had created to regulate big business and protect citizens. Long-serving agency heads were dismissed. Unqualified appointees, often from the industries their agencies were meant to regulate, were placed in charge. The work of career civil servants was buried, removed from government websites, and unfairly discredited.

The Trump administration pulled back the EPA's attempts to protect neighbors of large power plants from emissions of mercury and other hazardous air pollutants, the Department of the Interior's attempts to protect the oceans from spills like the Deepwater Horizon blowouts, the Department of Transportation's attempts to require better brakes on "high-hazard" trains, and the Consumer Financial Protection Bureau's attempts to protect vulnerable low-income workers from payday lenders. Under the direction of Trump appointees, the agencies authorized dangerous activities ranging from the Keystone XL pipeline to drilling for oil and gas in the Alaska National Wildlife Reserve. And what rules remained in play were laxly enforced, including those protecting miners, consumers, travelers, students, and the environment.

Conservative academics, think tanks, activists, and politicians have been advocating a demolition agenda for decades with generous support from wealthy donors and corporations. These "free-market fundamentalists" are deeply suspicious of all governmental programs that intrude on "economic freedom." They would like to return the American economy to the halcyon days at the end of the nineteenth century, before Congress created regulatory agencies to protect vulnerable citizens from polluters, profiteers, and plunderers. They formed a natural alliance with the less ideological business wing of the Republican Party, represented by the Chamber of Commerce, the National Association of Manufacturers, and the Business Roundtable, to resist attempts to interfere with the free market, scorning consumer and environmental protections and advocating for deregulation and the dismantling of key agencies over the course of four decades beginning in the late 1970s.[10]

In the 2016 elections, Donald Trump's populist appeal to disaffected white workers, rural Americans, and leaders of the religious right delivered the White House and both houses of Congress to the Republican Party. Although these constituencies were not directly burdened by federal regulation, populist activists and conservative media pundits had instilled in them a great distrust of the federal government and distaste for federal regulations—even those that demonstrably benefited them.

As President Trump took the oath of office in January 2017, the Republican Party consisted of a volatile mix of free-market fundamentalists, Trumpian populists, and pragmatic businesspersons who were comparatively apolitical but highly protective of their enterprises. The groups had many areas of disagreement. The business Republicans were not enamored with restrictions on immigration, which provided a continuous supply of cheap labor, and both free-market fundamentalists and business Republicans strongly opposed raising tariffs on imported goods. Cosmopolitan business Republicans and free-market fundamentalists did not necessarily share the populists' social agenda in areas like abortion, gay marriage, and gun ownership. But all three groups strongly agreed that government regulation of business was highly undesirable.

This consensus formed the basis for a demolition agenda that called for dismantling, disabling, or radically changing the direction of the federal agencies that were responsible for implementing protective federal programs. Although this demolition agenda grew out of "regulatory reform" initiatives dating back to the Carter administration, it encompassed far more radical projects aimed at, in the words of Trump advisor Steve Bannon, "deconstructing the administrative state."[11] Complaining that "an ever-growing maze of regulations, rules, restrictions has cost our country trillions and trillions of dollars, millions of jobs, countless American factories, and devastated many industries," Trump promised in late 2017 to bring about "the most far-reaching regulatory reform in American history."[12] But demolition, not reform, was the order of the day.

The assault on federal agencies during the Trump administration was all about implementing this demolition agenda. And Trump's appointees in most departments and agencies strived mightily to fulfill that promise. The Trump administration's assault was more aggressive and in many ways more successful than previous assaults. It focused not just on rolling back regulations, but also on crippling and dismantling the agencies themselves, in some cases effectively neutering them, in others putting in place unqualified leadership or issuing presidential mandates that prevented agency staffs from effectively implementing statutory directives. The return of the House of Representatives to Democratic control in the 2018 elections effectively stymied efforts to destroy the core of the protective edifice—the protective statutes that Congress had enacted over many decades to protect us from irresponsible corporate products and activities. But much damage had already been done, and it continued until the day that Trump reluctantly departed the White House without conceding defeat. The protective edifice is weaker now than it was at the outset of the Trump administration. It may not survive the next assault.

PART I

THE PROTECTIVE EDIFICE
AND THE DEMOLITION CREW

CHAPTER 1

THE PROTECTIVE EDIFICE

When I was thirteen years old in 1962, my father (a Presbyterian minister) told me that the family would be moving to Port Neches, Texas. Knowing that I would not be enthusiastic about leaving my friends and familiar surroundings, he tried to soften the blow by pointing out that we would be living right next to the city park, and the park bordered the Neches River, where there was a boat ramp and a rock wall from which I could go fishing. As soon after the move as I had access to my rod and reel and tackle box, I headed to the river and began to cast my favorite spinner lure into the water and retrieve it, all to no avail. An elderly fellow nursing a flask watched for a time with an amused look on his face before asking: "Son, what are you doing?" I said that I was hoping to catch a fish, and I asked him if he knew what kind of lure or bait would work. He replied: "Son, there ain't no fish in that river, and there ain't been for years." Disappointed, I returned to my new home and put away my fishing equipment.

I later discovered that if one were so inclined, one could fish the river for alligator gar, a Jurassic-era species that can breathe air when the water lacks sufficient oxygen to support fish. But most people were afraid to eat them because of the pollution that came from several petroleum refineries, petrochemical manufacturing plants, synthetic rubber plants, and the city's own barely functioning sewage treatment system. Port Neches was located in the middle of one of the most highly concentrated petrochemical complexes in the world. The fractionating towers and massive flares at a string of plants that ran parallel to and a block away from the high school and junior high lit up the night, and the acrid air when the wind was out of the southeast, which it often was, would sting my eyes as I rode my bike to school.

The next summer, I learned of a nearby 280-acre lake where one could rent a boat and fish for bass. As I rode my bike along the two-lane highway to the lake, I crossed Jefferson Canal, which emitted visible fumes as it transported chemical-laden wastewater to the river. After crossing over the Orange Bridge, which cut a high arc over the river so that oceangoing oil tankers could pass beneath on their way to the refineries in Port Neches, Groves, and Beaumont, I took the first road after the bridge to Bailey's Fish Camp. I paid my five dollars, and I caught a couple of eating-sized fish. But they had strange-looking tumors on their sides, and my mother refused to serve them to the family.

The plants and refineries in Port Neches may have polluted the air and the water, but they paid their workers well. In the summer after my freshman year of college, I was lucky enough to secure a job as a day laborer along with several other college kids at one of the refineries. When we not infrequently wound up with oil and grease on our arms and hands, we were instructed to use a solvent from a spigot attached to one of the thousands of pipes called the "benzene line." Benzene circulated at room temperature, was an excellent solvent, and was as safe as water, we were told, so long as you didn't drink it. Years later, scientists discovered that benzene caused leukemia in workers exposed to it.

I burden you with this bit of personal history to provide an example of the dark side of free markets. The refineries and chemical plants in Port Neches produced (and continue to produce) valuable products that we all use on a daily basis. The gasoline, diesel, and jet fuel from the refineries power the automobiles, trucks, and planes that transport millions of Americans and the goods that they rely on in their daily lives. The synthetic rubber plants that were built during World War II to provide rubber for the tires of military vehicles when supplies of natural rubber from the Pacific islands were unavailable continue to supply rubber for millions of automobile tires.

The jobs in the plants were good-paying union jobs with benefits. At the same time, there were no laws or regulations in place in the late 1960s to protect the workers from the risks posed by benzene, to shield the town's residents from the chemicals the plants emitted into the air, or to guard the environment from the pollutants that they discharged into the water and disposed of on the land. Free-market fundamentalism may have sounded good in theory, but people suffered considerably from its prescriptions in the real world.

In 1970, President Richard Nixon signed a reorganization plan that created the Environmental Protection Agency (EPA), and Congress created the Occupational Safety and Health Administration (OSHA). During the next few years, Congress passed the Clean Air Act, the Clean Water Act, the Resource Conservation and Recovery Act, and the Occupational Safety and Health Act. Over the fierce opposition of the affected companies, the EPA and OSHA put into place regulations, standards, and permits that required the plants to install pollution control equipment and implement operational changes that brought about dramatic reductions in the risks that they posed to their workers, their neighbors, and the environment. By 2016, one could catch croaker, redfish, and speckled trout from the river at City Park, and they were all edible. The air was still laden with photochemical oxidants in the summer, but the levels of hazardous chemicals were down. The workers were protected by OSHA's benzene standard, which traveled all the way to the Supreme Court and back before it finally went into place. And both the Jefferson Canal and Bailey Lake, which was adjacent to a chemical dump, became Superfund sites that were being remediated.[1]

With the election of Donald J. Trump, however, things began to move in the opposite direction. On the day before Thanksgiving in 2019, two massive explosions at the TPC plant (known as Neches Butane when

I lived there) injured three workers, blew out doors and windows of nearby houses and businesses, and caused the forced evacuation of thousands of residents. The unit that exploded produced butadiene, a carcinogenic chemical used to make synthetic rubber. Lingering chemicals in the air caused a voluntary evacuation of fifty thousand residents later in the week. It was one of a number of "significant incidents" that occurred at Gulf Coast petrochemical plants in 2019. Coincidentally, it happened one week after the Trump administration's EPA gutted the Obama administration's risk management rule, which was aimed at preventing such disasters.[2]

The protective edifice that President Trump wanted to demolish consists of the foundational laws that Congress has enacted over the years and the agencies that Congress has created to implement those laws by issuing regulations, imposing permit requirements, and enforcing the laws and regulations. Although these laws and the agencies they created had many goals, the overarching purpose was to protect vulnerable people, places, and species from polluters, profiteers, and plunderers.

The agencies that make up the protective edifice include the Environmental Protection Agency, the Fish and Wildlife Service, the Bureau of Reclamation, the Bureau of Safety and Environmental Enforcement, and the Office of Surface Mining Reclamation and Enforcement in the Department of the Interior; the Occupational Safety and Health Administration and the Mine Safety and Health Administration in the Department of Labor; and the National Highway Traffic Safety Administration, the Federal Railroad Administration, and the Pipeline and Hazardous Materials Safety Administration in the Department of Transportation. Most of these agencies came into existence during the public interest era of the late 1960s and early 1970s.

The financial meltdown of 2008 inspired Congress to create the Consumer Financial Protection Bureau and empower it to protect consumers from unfair, deceptive, or abusive practices of financial institutions. It further assigned to that agency the responsibility for implementing the Truth in Lending Act of 1968, the Fair Credit Reporting Act of 1970, and the Fair Debt Collection Practices Act of 1977. The massive Deepwater Horizon oil spill in April 2010 inspired President Barack Obama to create the Bureau of Ocean Energy Management and the Bureau of Safety and Environmental Enforcement in the Department of the Interior to ensure that environmental considerations played a role in managing offshore oil and gas leasing and to ensure that offshore oil platforms were operated safely. A series of outbreaks of foodborne illness culminating in a recall of a half-billion eggs in August 2010 provided the impetus needed to pass the Food Safety Modernization Act of 2010, which assigns to the Food and Drug Administration responsibility for protecting consumers from contaminated food.

Crises inspire legislative action. But when the need to regulate is less apparent to ordinary folks, it is far more difficult for the government to reduce newly arising risks. This pattern is well known to students of the policymaking process as a typical governmental response to the "collective action" problem. The costs of complying with consumer and environmental protection regulations are borne directly by the companies subject to their requirements or restrictions, but the benefits of the protections they provide are spread across large segments of the public. The prospective beneficiaries of a new regulatory program are diffuse and unorganized, and no match for the organized opposition of the prospective subjects of the program, even when its overall benefits are likely to outweigh the costs by a substantial margin.[3]

Climate change is a good example. It poses serious risks to the planet, but we continue to debate the nature of those risks. During the first two years of the Obama administration, Congress nearly enacted legislation creating a cap-and-trade program for reducing emissions of greenhouse gases, but climate change skeptics and the companies that funded them prevailed. The EPA spent the remainder of the Obama administration attempting to adapt a statute from the early 1970s to global warming.

Of course, not all companies are polluters, profiteers, or plunderers. Many companies want to do right by their customers and care a great deal about their images as good stewards of shared resources. Congress has recognized, however, that without a firm edifice of laws setting out the rules of the marketplace and attentive agencies to administer and enforce those laws, competitive pressures drive all companies to reduce costs. And this provides an incentive to avoid their responsibilities to their customers, their workers, their neighbors, and the planet, in a race to the bottom.

When the government protects the public from the risk of a terrorist attack or a wildfire, the benefit is obvious and appreciated by everyone. But we also face risks from a number of products and activities that are remote or unquantifiable, but no less dangerous. Less visible, but still apparent to the perceptive observer are the health and aesthetic protections that government provides when it limits emissions of pollutants that cause smog and reduce visibility in national parks. The risks posed by massive trucks on the interstate highways are readily apparent, but the limitations that government imposes on the hours that truck drivers may be on the road to ensure that they remain alert are invisible. We trust the local police to protect our homes from the risks posed by burglars, but we also depend on federal agencies to protect our homes from the risks posed by nearby natural gas pipelines and chemicals in the plywood that makes up the walls.

The probability that a worker will contract cancer after being exposed to a carcinogen in the workplace is low, but the consequences are very real to workers and their families who must watch them suffer and die. The same is true for the communities like Port Neches that border chemical plants that emit toxic chemicals and sometimes explode. The protection that the government provides by banning carcinogens, limiting workplace exposures, and requiring pollution controls and risk management plans is critical to our health and safety, but largely invisible. The rivers, lakes, and streams that meander across our lands and the oceans on our borders provide habitat for thousands of marine and aquatic species, some of which have visible economic value and many of which are literally invisible. But many of those waters would be as polluted as the Neches River of the 1960s if it were not for the mostly invisible work of the Environmental Protection Agency and the state agencies that it oversees.

Not all of us regularly visit our national parks, national monuments, and national wildlife refuges, but most of us value their existence and are not enthusiastic about leasing out pristine publicly owned lands for mineral extraction. We don't lose sleep over the risk that real estate development in the habitat of the greater Houston toad may cause it to become extinct, but the same laws that protect the toad also protect more visible bald eagles and polar bears.

People with money have been making loans to people who need money since money was invented. And the potential abuses that can arise out of that relationship have been known since biblical times. The Old Testament is full of commands against usury,[4] but payday lenders do not think twice about extracting usurious sums for small payday loans. The Consumer Financial Protection Bureau used its newly acquired powers to take on payday lenders during the Obama administration, but the effort attracted little public attention. Money lending is not the only way that companies prey on vulnerable consumers. For-profit educational institutions entice prospective students to sign up for degree programs with promises of great jobs that don't materialize, leaving the students on the hook for government-backed loans. These abusive practices are all too real to the vulnerable victims, but the government programs that protect them from unscrupulous business practices are nearly invisible.

We depend on these largely invisible government protections in virtually every aspect of our daily lives, but we take for granted the laws and the civil servants in the government agencies that provide those protections. How often when we board an airplane do we think about the thousands of hours that the airline safety experts at the Federal Aviation Administration spend overseeing the design and maintenance of the aircraft? We acknowledge and appreciate the visible protection provided by the police and the military, but we are mostly unaware of the thousands of civil servants in the federal government who devote some or all of their careers to writing and enforcing the regulations that protect our health, our homes, our communities, our safety where we work and when we travel, our environment, our shared public resources, and our pocketbooks.

The scientists, engineers, economists, and other professionals who make up the civil service play essential roles in deciding whether to ban or otherwise regulate carcinogens, how best to protect the habitats of endangered species, what disclosures will be most helpful to student borrowers, and thousands of other issues that regulatory agencies must resolve. These civil servants provide a vital public service for which they receive modest compensation and are the targets of scurrilous attacks from right-wing demagogues. They are, however, protected by civil service laws dating back to the post–Civil War years that prevent them from being fired arbitrarily, grant them due process protections, and empower them to bargain collectively through unions.

Although the Constitution has almost nothing to say about who should work for the federal government, the United States has a long history of independent civil servants working to advance the public interest as articulated in the laws Congress enacts. For the first forty years of the nation's existence, the civil service consisted largely of "upper class white men, with fathers handing their positions down to their sons." That changed dramatically during the presidency of

Andrew Jackson, the first populist president. Jackson converted a system based on inherited entitlement to one based on political patronage. During much of the nineteenth century, most federal jobs were doled out to political favorites who promised to return a percentage of their pay to their political patrons. The workforce turned over with changing administrations.[5]

A growing economy and the recognition that professionals with expertise were needed to address the negative side effects of the laissez-faire regime that emerged during the last quarter of the nineteenth century brought about demands for civil service reform. Congress responded with the Pendleton Act of 1883, which created a merit-based civil service system in which most federal employees are hired on the basis of their qualifications and can be fired only for good reasons. Before they can be let go, they are entitled to due process, including a hearing and an appeal to the Merit Systems Protection Board.[6]

The goal was "neutral competence" in the federal workforce. The Hatch Act of 1939 rounded the circle by prohibiting federal employees from engaging in most political activities. All the while, political appointees who served at the pleasure of the president remained at the top of the agencies. In 1978, Congress moved slightly in the opposite direction by creating the senior executive service (SES), a category of high-level civil servants who received higher pay and could receive bonuses, but were subject to being summarily transferred to different positions within the agency. This allowed political appointees to put favored SES employees in positions of power and transfer disfavored SES employees to "Siberia" where they had few responsibilities.[7]

The vast majority of civil servants are people who could make more money in the private sector, but elect public service "out of conviction and dedication, maybe even old-fashioned patriotism." Although the civil service is vastly underappreciated by the American public, we might ask ourselves whether we want neutral professional scientists and engineers or some politician's cousin deciding how to keep our air clean and our water pure.[8]

The protective edifice is built on the belief that government can and should protect vulnerable people, places, and species from the vicissitudes of the marketplace. When provided adequate resources, regulatory agencies have the expertise to fashion science-based standards that protect us without slowing down the economy or putting people out of work. In many cases, the regulated companies prefer clear and detailed rules articulated by a regulatory agency over broad statutory commands because they need the certainty of clear rules to plan for future products and activities. When regulation does result in economic damage and job loss, we have often come up with programs to ease the suffering. In sum, we have discovered that "[g]iving up a little liberty is something we agree to when we agree to live in a democratic society that is governed by laws."[9] As we shall see in the next chapter, however, there are still many powerful economic actors out there who would like to demolish the protective edifice or at least render it far less effective.

CHAPTER 2

THE DEMOLITION CREW

In December 1946, an Austrian political economist named Friedrich August von Hayek penned a letter to fifty-eight conservative scholars and intellectuals from the United States and Europe inviting them to an all-expenses-paid ten-day gathering at the Pelerin Palace, a luxurious resort atop Mont Pelerin in the Swiss foothills, with sweeping views of beautiful Lake Geneva against a backdrop of the snow-covered Alps. Hayek had just published a bestselling 1944 book titled *The Road to Serfdom*, which was an unabashed celebration of the virtues of capitalism and a polemic against government regulation. The ambitious goals of the meeting were to discuss the possibility of forming a society of thinkers who were willing to advance economic liberty against the undesirable intrusion of government into private economic arrangements, to "formulate a statement of common principles" for the organization, and ultimately to come up with "a programme which has a chance of gaining general support."[1]

The meeting took place between April 1 and April 10, 1947. The thirty-nine participants from ten countries were mostly academic economists, but the gathering included a smattering of academics from law, history, political science, and philosophy, as well as three journalists. The travel, lodging, and dining expenses were covered by several Swiss banks and a small foundation established by William Volker, the owner of a successful Kansas City dry goods business. An ambitious young University of Chicago economist named Milton Friedman made his first trip to Europe to attend the meeting. The congregants were not men of the people; they were in fact quite elitist, and they shared Hayek's willingness to sacrifice democracy, at least temporarily, for economic freedom.[2]

The assembled luminaries agreed on the advisability of creating an international institution with the goal of educating the world about the virtues of free markets and the dangers of government intervention. After some debate, they selected the decidedly nonideological name Mont Pelerin Society for the permanent group. The Society met again in Switzerland two years later and annually thereafter as it evolved into "a sort of international 'who's who' of free-market-oriented conservatives." The society is still alive and well. It has no fixed residence, it lacks an endowment, and it does not pay its officers. It remains a home for the "free marketeers" throughout the world who share a belief in free-market fundamentalism.[3]

Free Marketeers

Free-market fundamentalism is the near-religious belief that unimpeded free markets are the best way to allocate society's resources. Free marketeers believe that government should be limited to the minimal functions of protecting private property, enforcing contracts, maintaining order, and providing for the common defense. Erstwhile "public" goods, like public lands, primary and secondary education, and free-access highways, must be privatized and treated as commodities to be bought and sold in the marketplace. The goal of free marketeers is to move the American political economy back to the laissez-faire benchmark of the last quarter of the nineteenth century, where Social Darwinism validated hard work and self-reliance, and government policies tolerated large disparities in wealth. To accomplish this goal, free marketeers hope to eliminate all laws that impede the exercise of private property rights and freedom of contract—a demolition agenda.[4]

The "idea brokers" for free-market fundamentalism were the think tanks that sprang up in Washington, D.C., during the 1970s with major financial support from conservative foundations, wealthy donors, and corporations. The free-market think tanks provided intellectual firepower for the demolition agenda. Their economic and policy expertise lent credibility to their prescriptions, and they were adept at what consumer advocate Michael Pertschuk characterized as "the dehumanization of pain, suffering, and economic injury" so that the policymakers and the public focused on the economic cost of regulations and not their benefits. They excelled at packaging ideologically driven policy prescriptions and marketing them to policymakers, the media, and the general public. And, unlike political action committees, they were not generally required to disclose the sources of their tax-deductible donations.[5]

Although they were supposed to be fountainheads of new ideas, the free-market think tanks mostly just reframed free-market fundamentalism for general consumption by policymakers and the public. At the same time, they played an important role in destroying public trust in government and in the capacity of regulatory agencies to protect the public. The most prominent think tank proponents of the demolition agenda were the American Enterprise Institute, the Heritage Foundation, the Cato Institute, and the Mercatus Center at George Mason University. The network of conservative think tanks carefully coordinated with one another to stay "on message" during their continuing assaults on the protective edifice.[6]

The "storm troopers" for free-market fundamentalism were conservative advocacy groups located primarily in Washington, D.C. They lobbied Congress and the federal agencies, filed lawsuits challenging agency actions, and served as go-to spokespersons for reporters eager to report "both sides" of controversial issues involving federal regulation. One of the oldest, Grover Norquist's Americans for Tax Reform, was created in 1985 to drum up support for President Ronald Reagan's Tax Reform Act of 1986, and it soon turned into the headquarters of Norquist's "Leave Us Alone Coalition." As a self-proclaimed libertarian, Norquist was not concerned about abortion and homosexuality, and he did not attend church regularly. But he was able to form a coalition with the religious right to fight regulatory programs that they both opposed. As a highly visible fiscal conservative, Norquist was also a favorite of the Tea Party, and from 2000 to 2018 he served on the board of the National Rifle Association. He was therefore in a perfect position to bring together free marketeers and populists from the religious right and the white working class. For decades, Norquist hosted a weekly gathering of 150 free-market advocates, including congressional staffers, sympathetic media pundits, scholars from conservative think tanks, right-wing activists, leaders of the religious right, and K-street lobbyists, to plot strategy and coordinate messaging.[7]

Other prominent activists pursuing free-market policies included the Competitive Enterprise Institute, a comparatively small free-market advocacy group that specialized in attacking consumer and environmental regulation; the Heartland Institute, the nation's premier climate change–denying organization; the Club for Growth, a national network of more than 250,000 members with a reputation as a "bureaucrat slayer"; and the Pacific Legal Foundation, a legal group devoted to using the courts to debilitate government institutions that place constraints on free markets and property rights.[8]

The members of the Mont Pelerin Society could not have maintained their habit of meeting annually at commodious locations without the support of foundations created by wealthy individuals. Conservative foundations, including the Lynde and Harry Bradley Foundation, the Smith Richardson Foundation, and the three foundations controlled by Richard Mellon Scaife, devoted hundreds of millions of dollars to support free-market think tanks and advocacy groups.[9] But no one was more influential than two well-heeled brothers from Wichita, Kansas, named Charles and David Koch.

Under Charles's direction, Koch Industries, a huge international conglomerate, became the second-largest privately owned company in the United States. It also became a poster child for rogue corporations that did not allow protective regulations to stand in the way of corporate profits. As the consumer and environmental movements were in ascendance in the late 1960s and early 1970s, the brothers decided to devote the bulk of their philanthropic efforts to advancing free-market fundamentalism. Charles co-founded the Cato Institute with businessman and Libertarian Party leader Edward Crane in 1977. The Koch brothers were also major contributors to the Mercatus Center. By 2016, the Koch brothers had spent hundreds of millions of dollars creating and supporting at least fifty-three free-market fundamentalist centers and endowing chairs at universities throughout the country. The output of all of these entities complemented the parallel efforts of Koch Industries to reduce taxes and resist federal regulation.[10]

Many of the wealthy financiers and industrialists who funded the think tanks and activist groups that disseminated free-market fundamentalism have passed on, but they continue to have an outsized influence on public policy.[11] The free-market think tanks they created provide the intellectual firepower behind today's demolition agenda. And the free-market activist groups they assisted provide the boots on the ground to advance free-market thinking in the media, on Capitol Hill, and in the agencies during the Trump administration.

Business Republicans

These wealthy donors also had considerable assistance from the companies that stood to gain a great deal from the successful implementation of the demolition agenda. The Republican Party has always been a home for businesspeople who believe in civic responsibility but resist what they believe to be needless government regulation. Pillars of their communities in small towns across the heartland, these "business Republicans" join the Rotary Club and the local Chamber of Commerce, participate in charitable fundraising drives, and contribute their time and resources to improving their communities. But they generally oppose government action to protect their customers, their workers, or their neighbors from their risky products and activities. Though they may not be ideologically opposed to regulation, they know that regulations impose costs, not all of which can be passed on to consumers.

At the national level, business Republicans are represented by several organizations, including the U.S. Chamber of Commerce, the Business Roundtable, and the National Association of Manufacturers.[12] Since 1912, the U.S. Chamber of Commerce has viewed itself as a beacon for free enterprise. It started out as a nonpartisan advocate for business-friendly policies, but it reacted to Congress's creation of protective regulatory agencies in the early 1970s by adopting a strategy of determined resistance. It seized the offensive in the late 1990s under the leadership of Tom Donohue, a former trucking industry lobbyist and a prolific fundraiser. By the onset of the Trump administration, the Chamber had become, in Donohue's words, "the biggest gorilla in this town—the most aggressive and vigorous business advocate our nation has ever seen." Its power derived from its ability to mobilize local businesspersons from every congressional district to call, email, and visit their representatives in Congress, to attack federal regulatory agencies, and to support aggressive exploitation of public resources.[13]

The Business Roundtable was created in the early 1970s by the CEOs of the Exxon Corporation and the Alcoa Corporation to defend large companies from the perceived threat to corporate America posed by the growing number of regulatory agencies. The key to its success was its ability to summon the CEOs of major corporations to meetings with powerful politicians and agency heads.[14]

The National Association of Manufacturers was created in 1895 to fight labor unions in the manufacturing sector and to promote the export of goods manufactured in the United States. A political power-house during the Reagan administration, it became less influential in the 2000s as manufacturing became a less significant contributor to the economy and public policy issues divided its members. But it regained its prominence as President Trump attempted to fulfill his promise of returning manufacturing jobs to America. It currently represents four-teen thousand member companies in every industrial sector.[15]

Business Republicans support policies that are best for American businesses, not necessarily those best for the American public or the planet. Mitt Romney was the prototypical business Republican candi-date when he ran for president in 2012. He ran as a successful conserva-tive businessman, but he struck voters as someone who could not relate to the struggles of everyday people, and he ultimately lost the race to Barack Obama.[16]

Trumpian Populists

Free marketeers and the business Republicans launched several assaults on the protective edifice during the Reagan administration, the Gin-grich Congress of the mid-1990s, and the George W. Bush adminis-tration. But they encountered strong public support for the agencies that protected people from irresponsible corporate behavior, and their efforts were largely unsuccessful. What changed between the end of the Bush administration and the beginning of the Trump administration was the advent of a robust populist movement in the wake of the 2008 financial meltdown. Working folks, farmers, and religious conserva-tives across the country were outraged by the irresponsible conduct of Wall Street bankers and the fact that they were not being punished, but were instead being bailed out with taxpayer dollars. As the Obama administration focused on passing the Affordable Care Act, a coordinated campaign by conservative media outlets, well-financed activist groups, and opportunistic religious leaders refocused this public outrage away from the banks and toward the federal agencies that were allegedly weighing down the economy.[17]

Donald Trump appeared to be a successful businessman like Mitt Romney. But unlike Romney, Trump's populist appeals to the fears, prejudices, and resentments of many rural Americans, white working-class males, and conservative Christians added a whole new constituency to the Republican base. And these "Trumpian populists" accounted for the different outcome in the 2016 elections.

The first manifestation of the conservative populist movement that provided the extra support necessary to elect Donald Trump was the Tea Party, which sprung up early in the Obama administration with the help of conservative activist groups funded by many of the same wealthy individuals and foundations that supported the free marketeers. Tea Party funders also included reclusive hedge-fund manager Robert Mercer and his daughter Rebecca, the Richard and Helen DeVos Foundation, and big tobacco companies. Two prominent Tea Party organizers, Americans for Prosperity and FreedomWorks, were "grasstops" organizations that appeared to be spontaneous uprisings but were actually supported by corporate interests desiring lower taxes and less regulation. The Heritage Foundation created an advocacy organization called Heritage Action to assist Tea Party activists and ensure that they directed their energy against federal agencies.[18]

At the training sessions that FreedomWorks conducted across the country for Tea Partiers, its campaign director focused on fiscal responsibility and deregulation, and he urged participants to stay away from social issues like abortion and gay rights. They got the message. The motto of the Tea Party Patriots, another prominent Tea Party group, was: "Fiscal responsibility, limited government, and free markets." Americans for Prosperity hired dozens of organizers in many states and drew big crowds for rallies at gas stations with the promise of half-price gasoline. It also bussed Tea Partiers to Washington, D.C., where it provided free box lunches and glossy signs for planned protests featuring 1776-era costumes and "Don't Tread on Me" flags. Fox News bolstered the fledgling movement with round-the-clock coverage that, in turn, obliged CNN and the big three networks to cover Tea Party rallies. The efforts were successful as the Tea Party played a prominent role in turning the House of Representatives over to the Republican Party in 2011.[19]

The power of the Tea Party began to wane after the 2012 elections, in which President Obama retained the presidency and the Democrats retained control of the Senate. By 2016, support for the Tea Party had plummeted from 30 percent of Americans to 15 percent. But the cultural resentment and distrust in government upon which it had thrived were picked up by Donald Trump as he deftly co-opted the Tea Party in 2016. Trump's populist demands for lower taxes and less federal regulation appealed to a dwindling Tea Party movement, even though Trump did not stress fiscal responsibility. Trump broadened his appeal to include white working-class and rural Americans and conservative Christians by taking sides in the culture wars (abortion, gay rights, guns) and by nationalist appeals to limit immigration and raise tariffs. By early 2018, voters who had previously identified with the Tea Party now identified with Trump. And they were joined by millions of white Americans who saw themselves as victims of economic and cultural forces that were leaving them behind and who responded to Trump's promise to return them to their previous dominant social status.[20]

Tensions and the Tie That Binds

Through the years, tensions have arisen among the free marketeers, the business Republicans, and the Trumpian populists over matters about which they disagree. To the chagrin of free marketeers, business Republicans generally support government action to enhance infrastructure and protect domestic companies from foreign competition.[21] Free-market fundamentalists do not share Trumpian populists' support for Social Security and Medicare or their vehement opposition to abortion and gay marriage.[22] While free marketeers oppose corporate subsidies, Trumpian populists are willing to provide tax breaks to corporations to keep them from sending jobs overseas and to pay billions of dollars to farmers to offset the effects of retaliatory tariffs.[23] Free-market fundamentalists strongly oppose the restrictions on immigration that Trumpian populists strongly support.[24]

Trumpian populists strongly oppose government bailouts of corporations that business Republicans favor.[25] At the same time, business Republicans are appalled by the extreme rhetoric and intransigence of the Trumpian populists and their tendency to go off half-cocked.[26] Business Republicans do not share the Trumpian populists' animosity to immigrants; many companies support liberal immigration policies as a source of cheap labor.[27] They are also disinclined to share the Trumpian populist position on cultural issues and race.[28] White working-class Trumpian populists want higher wages and safe workplaces. The Business Republicans who run the corporations want low wages and resist safety requirements to keep costs down.[29]

Despite these significant differences, however, the three disparate groups find common ground in their mutual disregard for regulatory agencies. Like the free marketeers, the leaders of Trumpian populist groups are committed Hayekians, hoping to minimize the role of government in business and in the everyday lives of people. Fox News

pundits and talk radio hosts are adept at framing government bureaucracy as a common devil that both business Republicans and Trumpian
populists should fear. The three groups also agree on the desirability of
appointing judges who oppose abortion and take a dim view of regulatory agencies.[30]

The 2016 Elections

During the 2016 campaign, Donald Trump pitched his message to
Trumpian populists through the adept use of cable news coverage, his
own incessant posts to social media, and dozens of rallies around the
country. Rather than propose a plan for making the country better, however, Trump made populist appeals to the grievances of white workers,
rural Americans, and conservative Christians with rhetoric that lacked
any pretense of civility. This strategy worked in part because public
trust in the mainstream media was at an all-time low. Breitbart News
and the Mercer-funded Government Accountability Institute were
major progenitors of the Trumpian populist narrative that the nation
was in steep decline because the federal government had grown too big
and too intrusive. The religious right brought a prodigious get-out-the-
vote machine consisting of seventy-five "faith-oriented" nonprofits and
pastors of thousands of churches. And they broadcasted in hundreds of
programs on Christian radio and television networks. Trump paid very
little attention to business Republicans and free marketeers, but they
had little choice but to go along with his antics in the anticipation of
broad deregulatory initiatives upon his election.[31]

Trump's margin of victory in the Electoral College came from dozens of mostly rural counties in swing states that had gone for Obama in
the previous election. In a clear demonstration that Trump had co-opted
the Tea Party, 83 percent of the voters who identified with the Tea Party
voted for Trump. Fully 81 percent of evangelicals voted for Trump, a

PART II
DEMOLITION STRATEGIES

CHAPTER 3

APPOINTING TOXIC LEADERS

Prominent religious right pollster George Barna called President Donald Trump "God's Wrecking Ball," and that wrecking ball was aimed directly at what he believed to be worthless federal regulatory agencies.[1] To bring the agencies to heel, the Trump administration employed several strategies. At the outset of his presidency, Trump appointed toxic leaders, most of whom were wholly unqualified to manage their agencies. When many of them went down in flames, Trump replaced them with competent but deeply conflicted experts from the regulated industries and the law firms that represented them. These leaders quickly set about the task of dismantling their agencies through reorganizations and reassignments that by design resulted in a mass exodus of competent civil servants, and by persuading Congress and the courts to restructure their agencies in ways that would render them less effective. This chapter will focus on the people Trump put in charge of the agencies. Subsequent chapters will explore a number of other demolition strategies that the Trump administration and its allies in Congress employed to dismantle government agencies, roll back regulations, allow more destructive use of federally owned resources, ease enforcement, and make it more difficult for the government to function in the future.

In speech after speech, candidate Donald Trump promised to appoint "the best people" to run the government agencies. Far from fulfilling that promise, however, President Trump created a government run by the worst people—a kakistocracy of cabinet secretaries and agency heads composed of former politicians, cronies, wealthy ideologues and incompetents. To fill the critical mid-level positions in the agencies, Trump relied heavily on personnel from the Heritage Foundation, Americans for Prosperity, and the regulated industries themselves.

Almost 25 percent of Trump's appointees to regulatory positions involving environmental issues, for example, had ties to energy companies, and almost 50 percent had no regulatory experience. Senate Majority Leader Mitch McConnell (R-Ky.) rushed through many of their confirmations before they had submitted the required financial disclosure documents. By early 2019, more than one hundred former Heritage Foundation employees or interns were serving or had served in the Trump administration. Soon after his inauguration, Trump signed an ethics executive order requiring all of his appointees to pledge to refrain from engaging in any lobbying activities before their agencies for five years after leaving the government, but the White House granted waivers to virtually anyone who requested one.[2]

The Trump administration got off to a bad start during the transition between the election and the inauguration. Trump believed that the transition team headed by former New Jersey governor Chris Christie was a waste of time because he didn't need any advice on how to run the executive branch. Presidential advisor Steve Bannon declared that he (Bannon) used Christie's multi-volume transition plan for toilet paper. Within the agencies, hundreds of employees prepared briefing materials to introduce the new leaders to the programs for which they would soon be responsible, but few of the new arrivals seemed interested in what the bureaucrats had to say.[3]

Trump's choice of Scott Pruitt to be the administrator of the Environmental Protection Agency (EPA) offers a prime example of the toxic leaders that Trump assembled at the outset of his administration. The son of a Kentucky restaurant owner, Pruitt had been a talented baseball player in high school, but he was not good enough to win a starting position at the University of Kentucky. He transferred to (and graduated from) Georgetown College, a small Baptist school, and he then attended the University of Tulsa School of Law. In 2011, Pruitt became Oklahoma's attorney general. A vociferous foe of government regulation, Pruitt was also a darling of the energy companies; he was subsequently elected head of the Republican Attorneys General Association, a group that assisted energy companies in their legal challenges to federal regulations. He also dissolved the attorney general's environmental protection office and opened a new office dedicated to fighting federal agencies. In preparing letters to federal officials, Pruitt sometimes cut and pasted passages from energy industry documents onto official state letterhead.

Free-market advocates and Trumpian populist groups joined business Republicans in supporting Pruitt during his bruising confirmation battle. Koch Industries spent $3.1 million on lobbying the federal government during the first three months of the Trump administration, much of which was devoted to ensuring Pruitt's confirmation. Environmental groups strongly opposed the appointment. Protesters interrupted the confirmation hearings and packed the committee chairman's Senate office, arguing that Pruitt was unfit to lead that important agency. Hundreds of current EPA employees urged senators not to confirm Pruitt. But it was all to no avail. In mid-February, the Senate confirmed him in a 52–46 vote.[4]

Once in office, Pruitt remained true to his anti-regulatory roots. He hired committed pro-business advocates to mid-level positions throughout the agency, where they were well positioned to advance the Trump administration's demolition agenda. So many Pruitt appointees had served as aides to Senator James Inhofe (R-Okla.), the Senate's strongest climate change denier, that they became known to the career staff as the "Inhofe infantry." Pruitt also drew liberally on the Heritage Foundation, Americans for Prosperity, and the National Association of the residence was not available for other guests during his absence. The EPA had to reimburse the owners $2,400 after EPA security officers broke down the front door when Pruitt, who was napping one after-noon, did not respond to the doorbell. And the building's owner had to change the locks on the doors of the townhouse when Pruitt failed to leave after his lease expired.[10]

Pruitt was not shy about asking federal employees to run personal errands for him during working hours. On one occasion, he sent an aide on a failed mission to purchase a "Trump Home Luxury Plush Euro Pillow Top" mattress for him from the Trump International Hotel. On another, he had an EPA employee drive him around town to find a spe-cial Ritz-Carlton moisturizing lotion. With the help of the head of the EPA's policy office, Pruitt lined up a contracting job for his wife with a conservative advocacy group. The fundamental problem, according to an anonymous staffer, was that Pruitt was "not a billionaire" like some of the other cabinet members, but "sincerely thinks he is."[11]

During the early summer of 2018, rarely a day passed without some new report of Pruitt's misbehavior. By July 2018, more than sixteen federal inquiries were pending into his lavish spending, mismanage-ment, conflicts of interest and corruption. Although several Trumpian populist groups rallied to his defense, Republicans in Congress soon grew tired of the constant drip-drip of reports of Pruitt's indiscretions. In early July 2018, the White House demanded his resignation. In the end, Pruitt was more committed to power and the accoutrements of power than he was to the demolition agenda.[12]

Another prominent example of the toxic agency heads that President Trump appointed was first interior secretary—Ryan Zinke. A fifth-generation Montanan, Zinke played football at the University of Ore-gon, where he also studied geology. He then joined the navy and became a Navy SEAL. But he got into trouble for traveling back to Montana at government expense to work on a house that he was remodeling. After leaving the navy, he served in the Montana Senate for four years before winning the 2014 election for Montana's only seat in the U.S. House of Representatives.

Zinke considered himself a Theodore Roosevelt Republican, and he strived mightily to project a public image of a cowboy determined to bring some common sense to Washington. On his first day as secretary, he rode a horse named Tonto through the streets of D.C. with an escort of park police on horseback. He installed an arcade game called Big Buck Hunter in the department's cafeteria, and a special flag flew over the department's headquarters whenever he was on the premises. But he brought very little else to the job. His short political career had hardly prepared him for the role of protector of millions of acres of federal land, even larger expanses of coastal waters, and endangered species. One former high-level department employee described Zinke as "all hat and no cattle."[13]

Like Pruitt, Zinke filled the department's mid-level positions with ideologues from conservative think tanks and advocacy organizations and with former energy executives and lobbyists who embraced the demolition agenda. A career civil servant reported that these political appointees were only interested in "their checklist for dismantling regulations and weakening environmental and land use protections." Zinke also shared Pruitt's penchant for traveling in style, often with his wife, at government expense. In October 2018, the department's inspector general reported that Park Service security guards had accompanied Zinke and his wife on their vacation to Greece and Turkey at a cost to taxpayers of $25,000. Zinke also entered into an arrangement with the president of Halliburton, a company that did a great deal of business with the department, to build a brewery on land that Zinke owned in Montana. By the time that President Trump fired him in mid-December 2018, Zinke was the target of eighteen separate federal investigations.[14]

A series of additional appointments confirmed the pattern. To head the Office of Management and Budget (OMB), which sets agency budgets and reviews all major regulations, President Trump appointed a congressman from South Carolina named Mick Mulvaney. A free-market fundamentalist to the core, Mulvaney was one of the founders of the House Freedom Caucus, a group of Trumpian populist Republicans who made life extremely difficult for the House Republican leadership. At OMB, Mulvaney headed up the Trump administration's efforts to reduce spending, cut regulations, and reorganize the executive branch. In the summer of 2017, Trump appointed Mulvaney to serve concurrently as the acting director of the Consumer Financial Protection Bureau, an agency that Mulvaney had vigorously opposed as a congressman. Mulvaney took a meat axe to the bureau. He bypassed the merit-based civil service system to bring in a dozen inexperienced but highly compensated political appointees to ensure that the career staff abided by his new goal for the agency of "regularly identifying and addressing outdated, unnecessary, or unduly burdensome regulations."[15]

Appointing Elaine Chao, a consummate corporate and government insider, to be secretary of transportation was the opposite of draining the swamp. For starters, she was the wife of Senate Majority Leader Mitch McConnell. She had been a White House fellow during the Reagan administration and deputy transportation secretary under President George H.W. Bush. Under George W. Bush, she had served eight years as an employer-friendly secretary of labor. When Republicans did not occupy the Oval Office, she was a fellow at the Heritage Foundation and a frequent contributor to Fox News. She had close ties to the corporate world as a member of the boards of the News Corporation, Northwest Airlines, and the scandal-ridden Wells Fargo Corporation. During her tenure as secretary of transportation, the department rescinded requirements that high-hazard trains install special braking systems, weakened standards for storing natural gas, and lengthened the hours that truck drivers could be on the road without a rest break. According to Neil Eisner, a well-respected administrative lawyer who oversaw the regulation-writing process at the Department of Transportation for more than thirty years, industry influence on regulations was "probably more powerful" during the Trump administration "than it has ever been."[16]

Secretary Chao seemed to have little regard for conflicts of interest. She was on the job for more than two years before selling her interests in a large manufacturer of road construction materials that could benefit from the decisions of the department's Federal Highway Administration. Soon after she became secretary, Chao assigned to her aide, Todd Inman, the specific task of working with her husband's office to facilitate requests from Kentucky local governments for grants from the department. Among other things, Inman helped his hometown of Owensboro, Kentucky, obtain an $11 million grant, for which McConnell took credit in a meeting with local business and political leaders just days after announcing his bid for reelection in 2020. After the *New York Times* published a lengthy investigative report on the maritime shipping company that Chao's father created and her sister ran, the department's inspector general concluded that Chao had used her government staff on several occasions to advance her family's business interests. Near the end of the Trump administration, however, the Justice Department concluded that although the inspector general's report may have raised "ethical or administrative" issues, any transgressions did not warrant criminal prosecution. Despite the scandals, Chao remained in office until January 2021, when she resigned, ostensibly to protest President Trump's role in fomenting the January 6 assault on the Capitol.[17]

During his brief presidential run in 2016, former Texas governor Rick Perry promised to abolish three executive branch departments, but in a famous lapse of memory in a primary debate, he could not remember the name of one of them—the Department of Energy. He was therefore the obvious pick to head that department. Perry had a degree in animal science from Texas A&M University. His Obama administration predecessors, Dr. Ernest Moniz and Dr. Steven Chu, had headed MIT's physics department and received the Nobel prize in physics, respectively. But they lacked Perry's experience competing on *Dancing with the Stars*. Perry endeared himself to his boss when he proclaimed on Fox News that Donald Trump was God's "chosen one" to lead the nation at this juncture in the nation's history.[18]

Perry was contemptuous of Democratic politicians who wanted to commit the nation to greenhouse gas reduction goals, telling Fox News that they lived in a "fantasy world." To run the office in charge of setting energy-efficiency standards and developing renewable energy, Perry appointed a young critic of renewable energy who had run an advocacy group created by Koch Industries to promote fossil fuels to low-income and minority groups. To no one's surprise, Perry presided over the weakening of many of the department's energy-efficiency standards and its failure to update many others. Perry resigned in December 2019 as Congress was investigating his role as one of the "three amigos" who had made overtures to the government of Ukraine during the time that President Trump was urging that nation's president to launch an investigation into Hunter Biden's business dealings.[19]

Trump's pick to head the Department of Education, Betsy Prince DeVos, was born rich and married richer. Both the Prince and DeVos family dynasties were generous supporters of the religious right, free marketeer think tanks, and populist activist groups. DeVos had a sheltered childhood in Holland, Michigan, as the daughter of the founding owner of a successful machine and auto parts manufacturing company. A devoted member of the Calvinist Reformed Church in America, she attended Calvin College, a conservative religious school. After graduation, she married fellow Calvin College graduate Dick DeVos, whose father had created a successful mass-marketing scheme called Amway. Flush with Amway profits, the DeVos family invested heavily in groups that opposed the federal agencies that protected consumers from scam artists and pyramid schemes.

A political junkie, Betsy was actively involved in national politics beginning in the mid-1970s, devoting her time especially to advancing the cause of creating charter schools and destroying teachers' unions, even as her own children attended private religious schools. Like other Trump appointees, she had financial investments in some of the industries that she would be regulating. For example, she invested money in a debt-collection company and a charter school operator. The program that her family pushed through the Michigan legislature produced huge returns for the wealth hedge funds and large financial institutions that invested in charter schools, but the students received subpar educations from an educational system journalist Anne Nelson described as "deeply dysfunctional."[20]

DeVos revealed at her confirmation hearing that she knew vanishingly little about federal education programs. Her speculation that Wyoming school teachers should be armed to protect students from grizzly bears drew national ridicule. It took Vice President Mike Pence's tie-breaking vote to confirm DeVos to be the Trump administration's secretary of education.[21]

In the volatile Trump administration, where high-level officials came and went with surprising regularity, Secretary DeVos was a pillar of stability. Relying heavily on recommendations from the Heritage Foundation and activist religious groups, DeVos brought in a cadre of ideologues and former employees of for-profit education companies whose views were mostly antithetical to the goals that Congress had set for the department. Her special assistant, Robert S. Eitel, had been the chief attorney for Career Education Corporation, a company that had

and he had a deep understanding of administrative procedure. Environmental groups correctly worried that he would prove far more adept at chipping away at the protective edifice than Pruitt had been, because Wheeler was careful to deregulate in ways that would survive judicial review.

The EPA's new deputy administrator, Doug Benevento, had worked for a major utility company and a law firm representing industry clients against the EPA. To head the EPA office in charge of administering the Superfund program for cleaning up contaminated chemical waste sites, President Trump appointed Peter C. Wright, a longtime attorney for Dow Chemical, a company responsible for toxic wastes at 187 proposed and final Superfund sites. David Fischer had worked for the American Chemical Council, the chemical industry's trade association, before heading the EPA office in charge of regulating toxic chemicals. The head of the air office, Bill Wehrum, had been a $2 million-a-year partner at a law firm that was one of the country's fiercest challengers of environmental regulations. Wehrum had sued the EPA many times on behalf of clients, including the American Petroleum Institute and Koch Industries. He knew exactly which buttons to push to accomplish the demolition agenda in the EPA's air programs.[26]

At the Department of the Interior, Trump elevated Deputy Secretary David Bernhardt to replace Ryan Zinke. A native of the oil and gas hub of Rifle, Colorado, Bernhardt grew up hunting and fishing on nearby public lands. He dropped out of high school but later obtained a graduate equivalent degree and graduated from the University of Northern Colorado and George Washington University's National Law Center. Bernhardt worked for a few years in the offices of Representative Scott McInnis (D-Colo.) and for another three years at a large Washington, D.C., law firm. During the George W. Bush administration, Bernhardt held a number of high-level positions in the Department of the Interior, winding up as the department's solicitor, a position in which he became intimately familiar with the department's statutes and with how to negotiate the bureaucratic byways to ensure that deregulation went smoothly. Returning to his law firm at the end of Bush's second term, he spent the next eight years as an attorney and lobbyist for a number of large energy and mineral development companies with interests in public lands. An unlikely candidate for draining the swamp, Bernhardt had so many potential conflicts of interest that he carried around a list of them on an index card to remind himself whom to avoid.[27]

In July 2018, Bernhardt hired William Pendley to be acting director of the Bureau of Land Management, the entity responsible for managing activities such as oil and gas leasing on federal lands. Pendley had been the president of the Mountain States Legal Foundation, a militantly anti-regulatory organization that had for decades opposed environmental protections and restrictions on private development of federal lands. Pendley's recusal list was even longer than Bernhardt's; it included nearly sixty companies, organizations, and individuals that Pendley had represented while at Mountain States. Pendley continued to carry out the Trump administration's demolition agenda as acting director long after the 210 days allowed by the Vacancies Reform Act had expired. In late September 2020, a federal judge in Montana concluded that Pendley's remaining in the acting position beyond the 210 days was unlawful, and he ordered Pendley to cease exercising the authority of the director.[28]

After Rick Perry resigned at the Department of Energy, President Trump appointed Deputy Secretary Dan Brouillette to succeed him. Brouillette had a long history in and out of government, including stints as a lobbyist for Ford Motor Company and as an executive at an organization that made loans to servicemen and veterans. If Perry was a show horse, Brouillette was a work horse. Having served as an assistant energy secretary during the George W. Bush administration and deputy secretary for two years, he knew the department inside out. He was a moving force behind the department's extensive efforts to bail out coal companies and owners of aging coal-fired power plants. Brouillette believed that climate change was "something we need to work on," but only if it did not impede the Trump administration's goal of "energy dominance." He filled the upper reaches of the department with former energy industry lobbyists.[29]

President Trump's initial preference for secretary of labor was Andrew Puzder, the CEO of the company that owned the Carl's Jr. and Hardee's fast-food chains. Puzder's company was perennially in trouble with the Labor Department's Wage and Hour Division for failing to pay employees what they were entitled to under federal law. When the media revealed that he had employed an undocumented immigrant as his housekeeper and had not paid the required federal taxes, he withdrew. President Trump then played it safe by appointing a prominent Hispanic Republican, Alexander Acosta, to be labor secretary. But when a federal judge found that Acosta had violated the law when he was U.S. attorney for Florida by striking a deal with billionaire sex-trafficker and child molester Jeffrey Epstein that allowed Epstein to escape prosecution, Acosta resigned in July 2019.[30]

President Trump quickly nominated Eugene Scalia, son of recently deceased Supreme Court Justice Antonin Scalia (a conservative icon), to succeed Acosta. Scalia had briefly served as solicitor of labor during the George W. Bush administration, before becoming a partner in a large law firm where he represented business interests in disputes with the Department of Labor and various other federal agencies. The appointment was welcomed by the *Wall Street Journal*'s editorial page and the U.S. Chamber of Commerce, but labor representatives accurately predicted that Scalia would not aggressively protect workers. Both Acosta and Scalia filled the department's leadership with former lobbyists and ideologues who, in addition to having deep industry ties, shared a common disdain for federal worker protections. For example, the head of the Mine Safety and Health Administration, David Zatezalo, had most recently been the CEO of Rhino Resources Partners, a coal-mining company with holdings in several basins throughout the country and a history of serious safety violations.[31]

President Trump appointed Jeff Rosen, a high-powered attorney who represented major clients like General Motors before agencies, to be deputy secretary of transportation. Rosen was a strong proponent of imposing additional analytical requirements on regulatory agencies and increasing the stringency of judicial review of agency rules. To head the agencies within the department that were responsible for protecting travelers, President Trump relied mostly on former executives of the industries the agencies regulated. For example, his appointee to head the Federal Aviation Administration, Steve Dickson, had spent twenty-seven years as an executive with Delta Airlines.[32]

By the end of his first two years in office, Trump had appointed 281 former lobbyists to positions in the administration, four times the number that President Obama had appointed during his first six years in office. The administration also hired 125 people from conservative think tanks. And thirty-five Trump political appointees had worked at Freedom Partners and other groups affiliated with the Koch Brothers. They were all loyal to the president, and they were all committed to the demolition agenda.[33]

CHAPTER 4

DISMANTLING AGENCIES

President Donald Trump brought in toxic leaders to tear down the protective edifice, but the administration had no plan for replacing it. The goal was not to make government more effective at achieving the protective purposes of the laws that Congress had enacted over the years. The Trump administration had no clear legislative agenda, and it did not expend political capital pursuing comprehensive amendments to those statutes. It was content to render the government ineffective by hamstringing the departments and agencies that were struggling to implement the laws.[1] Close presidential aide Steve Bannon explained that President Trump's attacks on civil servants were nothing personal: "It's just the natural process of how one looks to dismantle part of a massive bureaucracy."[2]

A prime target of the Trump administration was the Consumer Financial Protection Bureau, a new agency that Congress had created in the wake of the 2008 financial meltdown to protect ordinary folks from predatory lenders, abusive bill collectors, unscrupulous for-profit trade schools, and a host of other scammers. In addition to its all-out assault on that bureau, the administration worked to quietly dismantle other agencies through reorganizations and relocations of critical personnel.

Over the strenuous objections of the Heritage Foundation, the U.S. Chamber of Commerce, and the financial services industry, Congress in 2010 created the independent Consumer Financial Protection Bureau (CFPB). The bureau was headed by a director appointed to a five-year term by the president, who could fire the director only for "inefficiency, neglect of duty, or malfeasance in office." The bureau was not reliant on Congress for funding, because the director could request such funding as he or she deemed "reasonably necessary to carry out" the bureau's functions from the Federal Reserve Board, which collected fees from the financial institutions that it oversaw. The bureau's rulemaking activities were not subject to review by the White House, but the statute subjected its rules to a possible veto by a two-thirds vote of a simultaneously created Financial Stability Oversight Council, which included the treasury secretary, the Fed chairman, and an "independent" member with expertise in insurance. In short, Congress structured the agency so that it would be immune to lobbying efforts by companies that were subject to its rulemaking, supervision, and enforcement powers.[3]

The CFPB has three broad responsibilities. First, it writes rules for financial institutions within its jurisdiction, implementing the nineteen statutes that it administers. In particular, the Dodd–Frank Act authorizes the bureau to issue rules prohibiting unfair, deceptive, or abusive practices in the provision of consumer financial products and services. Second, it must enforce the rules and punish those who violate those rules. Third, it has "supervisory" power over large financial institutions, which means that its inspectors have continuing access to company books and records to ensure that they are complying with the laws that the bureau administers.[4]

As the CFPB aggressively exercised its regulatory authority during the Obama administration, companies unsuccessfully challenged its regulations in court. The financial services industry and its Republican allies also launched vigorous attacks on the new agency, aiming to cripple it before it wrote too many regulations. Hundreds of industry lobbyists worked overtime to delay or roll back the dozens of regulations that the CFPB was required to write. The Mercatus Center, the Cato Institute, and the Heritage Foundation published criticisms of the agency in right-wing media, including the *Washington Times*, the *Daily Caller*, and *Breitbart News*.[5]

The Consumer Financial Protection Bureau's first director, Richard Cordray, was a centrist attorney with an impressive resume (Rhodes Scholar and five-time champion on *Jeopardy*) who had been a hard-charging advocate for consumers as attorney general of Ohio before being defeated in the 2010 election. Cordray hired the best people he could find. The fact that the statute allowed high-level officials to receive higher salaries than most civil servants helped, but Cordray also recruited people from high-paying jobs in financial services companies and law firms who wanted to protect consumers from irresponsible banks.[6]

During the Cordray years, the bureau was an aggressive protector of consumers from fraud, misrepresentation, and abuse by banks, payday lenders, debt collectors, and shady financial institutions. It adopted an "evidence-based" approach to rulemaking under which it used its information-gathering power and the analytical capabilities of its professional staff to study the relevant markets and evaluate the costs and benefits of alternative regulations. The quantitative analyses were supplemented by qualitative insights derived from supervisory examinations, consumer complaints, and other sources. This meant that it took years to complete a regulatory initiative.

Nevertheless, the CFPB issued several important regulations to protect consumers during Cordray's tenure. One important regulation required mortgage lenders to document that borrowers had the ability to make the monthly payments on their loans before they committed themselves to home mortgages. Another limited the "incentive" payments that banks and mortgage companies could pay to employees and brokers for talking consumers into mortgage loans they could not afford. The industry complained bitterly, but it complied with the new requirements without the precipitous decline in loan availability that it had predicted. By 2016, the number of home loans was back up to 2007 levels, but now predatory lenders could not pressure desperate borrowers into taking out loans they couldn't afford.[7]

One of Cordray's first actions was to create a highly successful online portal where consumers could lodge complaints and companies could respond. If they could not reach an accommodation, consumers could tell their stories of alleged deception or abuse in a database that could be accessed by any member of the public with a computer or a smartphone. By 2016, the agency staff had fielded more than 650,000 complaints, and consumers had published 7,000 narratives online detailing what they thought were abusive lending practices. In addition to providing a "public bullhorn" for consumers, the database provided information for setting agency priorities.[8]

During the 2016 election season, the Republican Party put a target on the bureau's back. Its platform called the CFPB a "rogue agency" that the party hoped to abolish or at least scale back considerably. Candidate Donald Trump complained that the bureau had made it "very hard for bankers to loan money for people to create jobs," and "that has to stop." By the time that President Trump assumed office, conservative think tanks had published articles and books declaring that the 2008 financial meltdown had been caused by excess government regulation. This revisionist history would have been laughable but for the fact that it came from otherwise credible places like the American Enterprise Institute. Through dint of constant repetition, it became an article of faith for Trumpian populists and, of course, for the financial sector.[9]

With Donald Trump in the White House and both houses of Congress under Republican control, the Republican leadership had a unique opportunity to clip the bureau's wings. FreedomWorks argued that Congress should eliminate it and return its powers to the old-line banking agencies and the states. Senator Ted Cruz (R-Tex.) and Representative John Ratcliffe (R-Tex.) introduced bills in the Senate and the House to do just that. But the proposal went nowhere because the agency was popular with ordinary folks who had been on the receiving end of unfair and abusive practices by financial institutions.[10]

Less than two weeks after his inauguration, President Trump signed an executive order directing the secretary of the treasury to prepare a report detailing the extent to which existing laws and regulations promoted certain "core principles" for regulating the financial system, and making recommendations for improvement. The report that the Treasury Department published in June 2017 concluded (without supporting evidence) that the Consumer Financial Protection Bureau had "hindered consumer access to credit, limited innovation and imposed unduly high compliance burdens . . . on small institutions." The conclusion that the bureau had hindered access to credit was, however, belied by the fact that consumer lending had increased at a substantial pace during the previous five years.[11]

Because CFPB was an independent agency, Cordray remained as director after Trump's inauguration. Many of President Trump's closest advisors and the editorial board of the *Wall Street Journal* urged him to fire Cordray and let the courts decide whether he had that power under the Constitution. Anxious to avoid a lengthy legal battle, however, Trump was persuaded that Cordray would be resigning voluntarily to run for governor of Ohio. Trump wasn't interested in making Cordray a martyr by firing him just as Cordray initiated a campaign to head a key battleground state. There was also the uncomfortable fact that 80 percent of Democrats and 66 percent of Republicans supported what the bureau was doing. With Cordray remaining in place as director, the CFPB continued to write regulations and bring enforcement actions at a torrid pace, earning the wrath of the financial services industry in the process.[12]

President Trump's political instincts paid off when Cordray announced in mid-November of 2017 that he would be leaving the bureau at the end of the month. Tweeting that the bureau was "a total disaster," Trump relished the opportunity to appoint a new director to a five-year term. But Cordray had other things in mind for the succession. Just before he departed, Cordray appointed Leandra English to be the bureau's deputy director. The Dodd–Frank Act specified that when the director was unavailable, the deputy director would become the acting director. Trump countered by appointing Mick Mulvaney, the head of the Office of Management and Budget, to be the bureau's acting director that same day. The Vacancies Reform Act of 1998 allowed the president to fill a vacancy in an "executive agency" upon the resignation of an official requiring Senate confirmation, with another officer in any executive branch agency who had been confirmed. Mulvaney showed up at the office the following Monday bearing donuts for the staff. At about the same time, English sent an email to the staff claiming that she had the authority to run the agency. Mulvaney then sent an email instructing the staff to ignore English's message. English then requested a temporary restraining order against Mulvaney, but the Trump-appointed judge denied her request. To the consternation of consumer advocates, Mulvaney became the de facto agency head for the next seven months.[13]

As a congressman, Mulvaney had proclaimed that he did not "like the fact that [the bureau] exists." As its acting director, he set about systematically dismantling the young agency. A White House official told *Politico* that Mulvaney's mission was "to blow that [agency] up." Calling the bureau "far too powerful," Mulvaney urged Congress to amend the Dodd–Frank Act to require congressional approval for all new regulations, make the director subject to removal by the president, and make the bureau's funding subject to the annual appropriations process. Consumer groups were aghast that the head of the new agency would advocate such drastic and debilitating changes. Even some industry advocates recognized that his suggestions would bring an end to rulemaking by the agency, something they did not support. It was hard for Mulvaney to make the case that the agency was doing a great deal of damage to the financial services industry as banks were making record profits and the mortgage market was doing splendidly.[14]

The single-director institutional structure that had been the target of fierce criticism from the financial services industry and congressional Republicans now worked in their favor as Mulvaney sent the CFPB in a radically different direction without having to consult with a multi-member board. According to a bureau spokesperson, Mulvaney was "committed to fulfill the Bureau's statutory responsibilities, but go no further." In reality, the bureau began to shirk its responsibilities while at the same time promoting free markets and guarding the contract rights of lenders, loan servicers, and bill collectors. The first thing Mulvaney did upon taking over was to place a thirty-day freeze on hiring, writing new regulations, and initiating new enforcement actions. Next, he ordered the staff to survey financial firms to obtain their views on the bureau's investigative processes, its enforcement procedures, and the conduct of its supervisory examiners. He then put a freeze on the agency's collection of the private financial data that it used to determine whether financial institutions were taking advantage of their customers.[15]

Mulvaney made his contempt for the agency clear when he asked the Federal Reserve Board for no additional monies for the second quarter of 2018, indicating that he would not be replacing all of the employees who were leaving the agency in droves. He further ordered the staff to cease implementing three recently issued regulations governing payday loans, prepaid cards, and mortgage disclosures. And he changed the agency's mission statement to shift its emphasis from protecting and empowering consumers to ensuring that consumer financial markets work by "regularly identifying and addressing outdated, unnecessary, or burdensome regulations."[16]

Mulvaney made several organizational changes that reduced the agency's effectiveness. He moved the Office of Fair Lending and Equal Opportunity into the Office of the Director to bring it under his direct control, and he stripped it of its enforcement and supervisory powers in flat violation of a Dodd–Frank Act requirement that the office oversee the enforcement of laws meant to ensure fair, equitable, and nondiscriminatory access to credit. He also demoted the Office for Students and Young Consumers, which was responsible for protecting college students and servicepersons from unscrupulous loan companies, and he moved it into the Office of Financial Education. That precipitated protests by consumer groups outside the building and the resignation of the bureau's student loan ombudsman, who accused Mulvaney of abandoning the bureau's legal duty to protect student borrowers. Mulvaney then created a separate Office of Cost Benefit Analysis and placed it directly beneath the director to elevate the status of economic analysis in the agency and to ensure that agency enforcers did not proceed against financial institutions if the benefits to consumers did not outweigh the cost to the scofflaws. Finally, Mulvaney rolled back the bureau's supervisory powers.[17]

Mulvaney stressed that all of these changes were meant to make the bureau "more efficient, effective, and accountable." While they did make the professional staff more accountable to the director, they made the bureau far less efficient and effective in pursuing its statutory mandates. Career civil servants complained that they were spending more time on busy-work than on protecting consumers and pursuing scofflaws. Many of the CFPB's career professionals had been attracted to the new agency out of a commitment to help consumers in their struggles against sophisticated lenders and disreputable bill collectors. They were shocked when Mulvaney's political underlings began to overrule staff recommendations and push the bureau in a deeply deregulatory direction. Those who could find acceptable jobs elsewhere left, accusing the new leadership of "repeatedly undercut[ting] and undermin[ing] career

CFPB staff working to secure relief for consumers." During Mulvaney's tenure, the bureau lost 11 percent of its staff. Morale among the remaining staff was at an all-time low.[18]

Although Mulvaney's attempts to dismantle the CFPB were music to the ears of the payday lenders, irresponsible bankers, and scammers who had been the targets of its actions under Cordray, Mulvaney's turnaround ran directly contrary to polls indicating that the public strongly supported the agency and its protective mission. In a poll conducted at the end of 2016, prospective Trump voters by a two-to-one margin wanted Congress to leave the Consumer Financial Protection Bureau alone or strengthen it. Although many respondents to an April 2017 poll had not heard of the bureau, when they were told what it did, 70 percent said they supported it. And in a February 2018 nationwide poll of likely voters, 63 percent opposed the Trump bureau's efforts to roll back regulations, and only 27 percent supported them.[19]

In July 2018, President Trump appointed Kathleen Kraninger, a graduate of Marquette University and Georgetown Law School, to a five-year term as the bureau's director. Kraninger was Mulvaney's deputy at the OMB, but she lacked any relevant experience in financial regulation or consumer protection. Like Mulvaney, she was an enthusiastic free marketeer. When asked whether there were any issues on which she disagreed with Mulvaney, she could not think of any. Mulvaney stayed on as acting director until Kraninger was confirmed in December 2018 by a party-line vote of 50 to 49.[20]

Kraninger took up where Mulvaney left off. Early in her tenure, she announced that the agency's top priority would be consumer education so that people could "help themselves" by avoiding deals that looked too good to be true and by bargaining for better terms and conditions in consumer contracts. Writing regulations was a lower priority, followed by supervision and enforcement. Critics charged that Kraninger was trying to shift responsibility from the professionals that Congress had charged with protecting consumers to the consumers themselves. After she had been in office for a year, she told a gathering of bankers that they were "really helping drive the agenda" at the bureau.[21]

When Richard Cordray left the bureau, it was fighting for its life with the financial services industry and the Chamber of Commerce over whether its structure was unconstitutional. They argued that limiting the president's power to fire the director only for "inefficiency, neglect of duty, or malfeasance in office" (for cause) was inconsistent with the Constitution's vesting of executive power in the president of the United States and the president's responsibility to "take care that the Laws be faithfully executed." To implement this power and fulfill this responsibility, they maintained, the president needed to have the ability to fire the heads of regulatory agencies at will. They further argued that the "for cause" limitation violated the constitutional principle of separation of powers.[22]

Acting Director Mulvaney and Director Kraninger initially defended the agency, but in September 2019 Kraninger ordered the bureau's attorneys to align it with the challengers seeking its demise. When the Supreme Court agreed to resolve the issue, the Trump administration refused to defend the bureau's independence. The Supreme Court therefore asked former Solicitor General Paul D. Clement to file an amicus brief defending the constitutionality of the CFPB's structure.

Then, in a 5–4 opinion split along party lines, the Supreme Court in June 2020 agreed with the challengers and the Trump administration that granting the director the power to write and enforce regulations without fear of removal by the president violated the principle of separation of powers. According to the ruling, multi-member independent agencies, like the Federal Trade Commission, were nonpartisan in the sense that they contained members from both political parties, and members served for staggered terms that allowed the president to change the balance of power within a single presidential term. But "an independent agency led by a single Director and vested with significant executive power" had "no basis in history and no place in our constitutional structure." The "for cause" provision in the statute was therefore unconstitutional. To the great relief of consumer advocates, however, the rest of the statute empowering the bureau to regulate remained in effect, because Congress would have wanted the bureau to fulfill its responsibilities even if its director were subject to removal by the president.[23]

With the active encouragement of the Trump administration, the Supreme Court had eviscerated the CFPB's power to protect consumers independent of a president who was more interested in protecting big banks and payday lenders. While the ruling came too late for President Trump to fire Director Cordray, he could now fire Director Kraninger if she ever refused one of his directives. Of course, the Court's ruling also meant that President Biden could fire her before her five-year term ended in 2023. She jumped first, resigning on the day Biden was inaugurated. The financial services industry promised to continue its efforts to further dismantle the bureau.[24]

When Congress refuses a president's request to cut an agency's budget, one way to get rid of unwanted civil servants is to reassign them to busy-work jobs where they cannot use their skills to pursue disfavored goals. Another is to relocate an entire office containing uncooperative civil servants out of Washington, D.C., to some city far away—a strategy that federal employees refer to as being sent to "the turkey farm."[25] Since civil servants who have purchased homes, have spouses with jobs in Washington, and have enrolled their children in local schools are generally reluctant to pull up roots, many will retire or resign, leaving political appointees with positions to be kept vacant or to fill with new hires who meet their ideological criteria. Because reassignments and relocations are always disruptive, they also slow down the office's production of regulations, analyses, or whatever else it does. The Trump administration employed both of these dismantling strategies with alacrity.

Complaining that "30 percent of the crew" at the Department of the Interior was not "loyal to the flag," Secretary Ryan Zinke created a board consisting of political appointees to reassign members of the department's 227 senior executive service employees to new positions. In what became known around the department as the "Thursday Night Massacre," the board reassigned twenty-seven scientists and technical experts from jobs in which they were using their skills to protect the nation's natural resources to jobs where, in many cases, their expertise was not needed. Many of the reassigned specialists believed that their reassignments were related to the fact that they were working in the areas of climate change, energy, and resource conservation. After the massacre, career civil servants kept their heads down and avoided promotions out of fear that they would rise to a level where their increased visibility would get them reassigned to some far-off locale.[26]

The Environmental Protection Agency employed the same strategy to remove Dr. Ruth Etzel as the head of the EPA's Office of Children's Health Protection. In late September 2018, the agency's deputy chief of staff placed Etzel on administrative leave, forcing her to clean out her office and surrender her identification card without an opportunity to bid her staff farewell. Dr. Etzel was a well-known and highly respected pediatrician who had worked at the U.S. Public Health Service and the World Health Organization for thirty years prior to joining the EPA in 2015. The agency provided no reasons for the sudden action beyond a vague reference to Etzel's poor leadership.[27]

Etzel claimed that she was put on leave because the Trump administration was unhappy with her aggressive advocacy for children's health. Her office had strongly resisted an effort by the EPA's Office of Pesticide Programs to weaken a standard prohibiting children under the age of eighteen from applying certain toxic pesticides to crops in the field. Three weeks before she was placed on leave, Etzel had unsuccessfully pressed the deputy chief of staff to set up a meeting with Acting Administrator Andrew Wheeler to discuss a multi-agency strategy for reducing children's exposure to lead, a potent neurotoxin. And she noted that every agency budget proposed by the Trump administration had called for drastic cuts in her office. Administrator Wheeler responded with a photo op placing him with a group of school children and a diesel-powered school bus proclaiming that "children's health is a top priority at EPA." Etzel was ultimately assigned to a non-leadership position in an unrelated office.[28]

President Trump preferred to rule by edict. In the case of the regulatory agencies, this meant issuing a plethora of executive orders on a wide range of topics, from writing regulations to issuing permits, that in many cases radically changed the ways the agencies did business. In early March 2017, Trump signed an executive order directing the Office of Management and Budget to come up with a plan to reorganize the federal government and eliminate unnecessary agencies. That office in turn issued a memorandum requiring departments and agencies to come up with reorganization plans as part of their budget submissions.

Interior Secretary Ryan Zinke responded in January 2018 with a plan for the most ambitious reorganization in the department's 168-year history. He hoped to divide the surface area of the country into twelve regions based on a complex combination of state boundary lines and watersheds and move the headquarters of the department's major bureaus out of Washington, D.C., to the various regions. Thousands of the agency's employees would then have to move to the regional offices or resign. Zinke estimated that the plan would eliminate four thousand positions from the department's payroll, representing a 12 percent reduction in the department's budget. Although the industries that extracted billions of dollars' worth of coal, oil, gas, and other minerals from federal lands thought it was a great idea, Western governors weren't keen on it because it would have moved personnel from the western state capitals to the regional offices. The Trump administration came to an end before Zinke's grand plan went into effect.[29]

One aspect of the reorganization plan that did survive was a project to move the Bureau of Land Management's headquarters from D.C. to Colorado. That bureau was responsible for all mineral leasing on federal lands and in federal waters. Ninety-five percent of the bureau's nine thousand employees already worked in the field, and the plan was to move around 300 of the 360 D.C. positions to a new bureau headquarters in Grand Junction, Colorado, and various other offices in the western United States. Since the Grand Junction office shared a building with Chevron, an oil and gas trade association, and an independent natural gas exploration company, fossil fuel interests would have easy access. Half of the bureau's environmental review experts would be scattered throughout several western states, making it considerably more difficult for the bureau to assess the environmental impacts of proposed energy development projects on federal lands. The Government Accountability Office subsequently found that the bureau did not provide an adequate opportunity for employees and the public to participate in the relocation decision.[30]

Conservative think tanks had been advocating such a move for years, as a way to bring decision making closer to the people who were affected by the decisions. Of course, it was also a way to get rid of troublesome agency employees without violating the civil service laws. At a February 2020 campaign rally in Colorado, President Trump boasted that the BLM move was part of his "historic regulatory reduction campaign." The strategy worked, as longtime civil servants at the bureau had to make agonizing choices about whether to seek other employment or move their children away from their friends and grandparents and leave aging parents to fend for themselves. Morale at the bureau hit rock bottom. The move also had a chilling effect on the hundreds of the department's remaining D.C. employees, who worried that if they got crossways with upper-level political appointees, they could find their headquarters moved to the western United States. A spokesperson for the largest federal employee union accurately predicted that the BLM would lose a great deal of institutional memory. Experts calculated the relocation cost at around $100,000 per employee.[31]

As the move began in January, protesters in Grand Junction provided an "unwelcoming committee" to greet the transferred employees. Even though the department had offered employees a relocation bonus of 25 percent of their salaries to agree to relocate, only forty-one people made the move. A total of 287 employees retired or found other jobs in Washington, D.C. The reorganization effectively decapitated the agency responsible for protecting public lands from the extractive industries that rely on easy access to public resources for their profits.[32]

Although the attempts to dismantle the regulatory agencies were only partially successful, they served the Trump administration's goal of disrupting the day-to-day business of writing and enforcing protective regulations. Career employees knew that if they failed to adhere to the Trump administration's deregulatory policies, they could suffer the same fate as Ruth Etzel or the Bureau of Land Management's unfortunate Washington, D.C., staff. They also discovered that Trump appointees at the heads of the agencies had other strategies for avoiding their expert advice.

CHAPTER 5

DENIGRATING EXPERTISE

As tens of millions of Americans sheltered in place and the economy spiraled into a recession in March 2020, President Donald Trump understood that an effective treatment for COVID-19 would greatly facilitate efforts to reopen the economy. His first instinct was to bypass the drug-approval process at the Food and Drug Administration by giving the power to authorize clinical testing of coronavirus-fighting drugs to a Trump-appointed panel consisting of a scientist, a hospital administrator, a doctor, and a person with regulatory affairs expertise.

When this turned out to be unlawful, Trump picked up on a suggestion by his friend Larry Ellison, the CEO of Oracle, that two related anti-malarial drugs called chloroquine and hydroxychloroquine might be the magic bullet that the president craved. Ellison promised to develop an app that doctors administering the drugs could use to feed information to the government on how patients were progressing under the drugs. And Bayer, which had discovered the drugs, promised to donate three million doses of chloroquine to the federal government's Strategic National Stockpile for rapid distribution to COVID-19 patients. Two Trumpian populist advocacy groups, Job Creators Network and Physicians for Reform, launched a social media campaign urging Trump to make the drugs available to COVID-19 patients as soon as possible.[1]

Sensing Trump's eagerness to make the drugs available to the public, an assistant secretary in the Department of Health and Human Services directed Dr. Rick Bright, the head of the department's Biomedical Advanced Research and Development Authority, to have his team

"take a look" at chloroquine. The career scientists in that agency, which
partners with private companies to develop drugs, expressed concern
that not a single clinical study supported the efficacy of that drug
against COVID-19. But when President Trump convened a March 18
meeting with public health officials that included Health and Human
Services Secretary Alex Azar, Food and Drug Administration Commissioner Stephen Hahn, Centers for Disease Control Director Robert Redfield, and National Institute of Allergy and Infectious Diseases
Director Anthony Fauci to discuss the possibility of speeding up the use
of those drugs, Azar did not mention the scientists' concerns. Instead,
he presented options for getting the two drugs rapidly approved for
COVID-19. Trump wanted to promote the drugs to the public as a "shot
of inspiration," and he urged the FDA to promote the drugs as well.
Hahn, Redfield, and Fauci, however, strongly discouraged Trump from
promoting the drugs until randomized clinical trials had shown them to
be effective against COVID-19 and safe for patients to use. Neither of
the two small studies upon which supporters based their claims came
up to the standards that the FDA applies to approve a new use for an
existing drug.[2]

Ignoring the experts, Trump announced at a press conference the
following day that hydroxychloroquine could be a "game-changer" in
treating people suffering from COVID-19. He promised that the FDA
would be making the drug available "almost immediately" because it
had gone through the FDA process and "it's been approved." The FDA
had been "so great" to reduce the approval process "from many months
to immediate." It looked to be a stunning deregulatory coup for the
Trump administration, except that it never happened. Since the FDA
had already approved chloroquine and hydroxychloroquine for treating
malaria, lupus, and rheumatoid arthritis, doctors could prescribe them
to treat COVID-19 without prior FDA approval. But the FDA had definitely not approved the drugs for COVID-19. Dr. Fauci stepped to the

microphone to caution the public that controlled clinical testing would be necessary before anyone could know whether the drugs would be effective for this new disease. And the FDA quickly issued a press release emphatically denying that it had approved the drugs for treating COVID-19.[3]

Trump was apparently suggesting that doctors begin to prescribe the drugs right away for the unapproved "off-label" use because they were already on the market and relatively inexpensive. He asked doctors, "What the hell do you have to lose?" In fact, thousands of people who were taking the drugs to treat lupus and rheumatoid arthritis had a lot to lose if there was a run on the drugs and they could not get their prescriptions filled. After the president's endorsement, there was in fact a huge increase in demand for the drugs that sent prices through the roof. Doctors were even prescribing the drugs prophylactically to their families and patients who did not show symptoms of disease.[4]

None of this stopped Trump from continuing to advocate the two drugs as magic bullets in an effort to calm the public and revive the equity markets. As if on cue, Fox News hosts began relentlessly pushing the drugs. By the end of March, Fox commentators had mentioned the drugs more than five hundred times.[5]

On March 23, the White House directed HHS Secretary Alex Azar to take whatever action was necessary to make hydroxychloroquine available to the American public through the Strategic National Stockpile. Azar then told the department's Biomedical Advanced Research and Development Authority to establish within the next two days a "Nationwide Expanded Access Investigational New Drug" protocol to make the drugs available throughout the country to doctors who participated in Mr. Ellison's promised phone app. Under the guise of a scientific study, this would make the drugs available for treating COVID-19 patients outside of a hospital setting and without close doctor supervision. The Research and Development scientists at Health and Human Services were reluctant to implement the Azar directive because of the lack of scientific data showing that the drugs would work against COVID-19, and because of the risk that they would cause dangerous irregular heart rhythms and death, known side effects of the drugs.[6]

Dr. Janet Woodcock, head of the FDA's drug-approval office, and Dr. Rick Bright, head of the Biomedical Advanced Research and Development Authority, were both longtime career civil servants. They agreed that the best way to make the drugs available to doctors throughout the country was for the Research and Development Authority to apply for an emergency use authorization to use chloroquine and hydroxychloroquine in hospitals under the direct supervision of doctors, a far more limited use than Azar's investigational new drug option. Bright submitted the application at 11:31 p.m. on March 28, and the FDA approved it thirty-two minutes later. The emergency use authorization made drugs from the National Stockpile available to hospitals, and it shielded manufacturers and doctors from liability.[7]

Although Dr. Bright and Dr. Woodcock thought they had achieved an acceptable compromise, it did not satisfy the White House's determination to distribute the tens of millions of pills that the government had been purchasing. On April 3, Trump and the FDA commissioner, Stephen Hahn, met with Fox News commentator Laura Ingraham and two of her frequent guests, Dr. Ramin Oskoui and Dr. Stephen Smith, all three of whom were strong proponents of hydroxychloroquine. While Trump listened intently, Smith presented the case for using the drug against COVID-19 based on his own experience prescribing it to his sick patients. Trump had also been hearing from his New York friends, including attorney Rudy Giuliani, that hydroxychloroquine had the potential to get Americans back to work. This sort of anecdotal evidence, with no control subjects, was not adequate for FDA scientists to approve the drugs; those patients might have gotten better anyway.[8]

At a White House briefing the next afternoon, President Trump sounded like a patent medicine salesman for hydroxychloroquine as he urged listeners to "take it," because "[i]t can clean out the lungs." Hours later, the White House instructed Dr. Bright's superior and other Health and Human Services officials to "flood NY and NJ" with hydroxychloroquine. When the deputy director in charge of the Strategic National Stockpile pointed out that the FDA's emergency use authorization for the drugs limited treatment to hospitalized patients, a Trump-appointed assistant secretary ordered him to do it anyway. Over the weekend, the stockpile rushed hydroxychloroquine to hospitals and to pharmacies for use by outpatients throughout the country in direct violation of the FDA authorization.[9]

The next day, Trump proudly announced that the government had purchased and stockpiled 29 million doses of hydroxychloroquine to be used for treating patients suffering from COVID-19 infections. He urged doctors, nurses, and first responders to take the drug to ward off the disease, even though there were no studies suggesting such a prophylactic effect. "What do you have to lose?" he asked on five separate occasions. He later announced that he was taking hydroxychloroquine prophylactically to ward off the disease. Relying on anecdotal evidence and his gut, he concluded that the risk of side effects from taking the drug was acceptable, and he urged the public to follow his lead.[10]

Things went rapidly downhill for the drugs, however, beginning in mid-April, when reports started to trickle in that they were not working and that they were actually causing harm. It soon became clear that the drugs did not operate to prevent the onset of COVID-19, as more than five dozen people who were taking them for various chronic diseases contracted COVID-19. Doctors in Wuhan, China, where the pandemic began, reported that they had tried hydroxychloroquine and did not see evidence that it was effective in relieving COVID-19 symptoms. Doctors in France halted a clinical study of the safety and effectiveness of hydroxychloroquine when electrocardiogram monitoring indicated that it was causing an irregular heartbeat in one of the patients. On April 24, the FDA issued a warning that patients taking chloroquine and hydroxychloroquine to treat COVID-19 were at risk of suffering abnormal heart rhythms and a dangerously high pulse. In mid-May, two major studies of New York patients published in the *Journal of the American Medical Association* and the *New England Journal of Medicine* found no evidence that the risk of intubation or death was lower in patients taking hydroxychloroquine. In mid-June, the FDA withdrew the emergency use authorization. By then, most doctors had quit prescribing the drugs for COVID-19, and Trump had stopped taking hydroxychloroquine.[11]

Suddenly, as if on cue again, chloroquine and hydroxychloroquine disappeared from the Trumpian populist media. The drugs sank from public view without the slightest acknowledgment that the scientists had been right all along. And the government was stuck with millions of stockpiled hydroxychloroquine pills that didn't work. The chloroquine culture war did, however, claim many victims. One of them was Rick Bright, who was relieved of his position as head of the Biomedical Advanced Research and Development Authority and transferred to an inferior position in the National Institutes of Health because he had refused to spend federal money promoting drugs that didn't cure COVID-19. He was convinced that the Trump administration had "put politics and cronyism ahead of science."[12]

Donald Trump regarded expertise as an overrated liberal virtue. In making important decisions, he was far more inclined to rely on his gut than on experts armed with data and analysis. He would much rather bowl over his opponents with histrionics than attempt to persuade them with facts and analysis. And when he needed facts for support, he could always make them up. All of this was immensely attractive to his Trumpian populist base, which regarded scientists, engineers, and other experts as elitists lacking in common sense. Like Trump, Trumpian populists approached public policy questions not by reference to statistics and scientific studies, but through anecdote and personal experience or the experience of friends and relatives.[13] Trump's disdain for expertise was reflected in the sustained attempts by his administration to bend the civil service to his will. But it also manifested itself in efforts by Trump appointees in the agencies to censor science, change the rules for using agency experts, and manipulate advisory committees.

Trashing the Civil Service

At the outset of the Trump administration, Joel Clement was responsible for the Interior Department's efforts to achieve climate change resiliency in the Arctic. An expert in forest ecology, he had worked in the department for seven years on issues at the intersection of climate science and public lands. Interior Secretary Zinke, however, was not interested in climate change resiliency in the Arctic or anywhere else. Zinke reassigned Clement to the department's accounting office, where he was supposed to be in charge of employees auditing royalty payments. Clement protested that he was wholly unqualified for his new position, and his new boss confirmed that the office had no need for an employee with his expertise.

Clement believed that he was reassigned because the department's political leaders did not agree with the department's scientists that global warming was a serious enough problem to warrant the assistance that his group had been providing to Native villages in Alaska. He further concluded that he was being punished for bringing the plight of the Native villagers to the attention of White House officials and, later, to that of the international community. Clement reported that other Department of the Interior experts were also being sidelined. Convinced that his expertise was no longer wanted, he resigned in October 2017.[14]

One of the Trump administration's most powerful demolition strategies was to undermine the capacity, credibility, and legitimacy of the civil service. President Trump and his political appointees launched a four-year war on the scientists, engineers, economists, managers, and other professionals who do the real work at the agencies that provide the protections most Americans take for granted. To him they were the "deep state" whose goal it was to frustrate his policy initiatives and ensure that he would not be reelected. He was therefore determined to make it easier to fire civil service employees. One of his early hires was James Sherk, a Heritage Foundation labor economist who had spent much of his career arguing that federal employees were grossly overpaid and offering suggestions for cutting back on their compensation and decreasing federal contributions to their health insurance and retirement pensions.[15]

On January 23, 2017, President Trump instructed all executive branch agencies to refrain from filling any vacant positions or creating any new positions, except for military personnel. At the same time, Trump told the White House Office of Management and Budget to come up with "a long-term plan to reduce the size of the Federal Government workforce through attrition." Trump was not the first president to impose a hiring freeze, but the plan to reduce the size of the workforce through attrition was unprecedented. Trump ended the hiring freeze in mid-April, but he directed the agencies to come up with plans to reduce spending on personnel on a permanent basis. Among other things, the agencies were to begin immediately to offer voluntary early retirement and voluntary separation incentive payments to their employees. In his first State of the Union address in February 2017, Trump urged Congress to pass legislation making it easier for government managers to fire civil servants. As Trump's populist base cheered, the president of the largest government employee union warned that such legislation would bring about a return to the spoils system of the early nineteenth century that politicized the federal bureaucracy.[16]

In May 2018, President Trump signed three executive orders aimed at enhancing the power of politically appointed managers over the civil service. The brainchild of James Sherk, the orders told federal agencies to provide fewer collective bargaining protections to government employees and to move more aggressively in firing employees. Critics saw the orders as an unlawful attempt to bust federal employee unions and intimidate agency employees. Conservative think tanks and Fox News pundits agreed that the orders were aimed at weakening unions, and they were delighted with that possibility. The largest federal employees' union challenged the executive orders in the D.C. federal district court, and hundreds of federal employees held a rally at the courthouse when the court heard the case in July 2018. The court concluded that some aspects of the executive orders were unlawful, and it issued an injunction prohibiting agency heads from implementing them. The D.C. Circuit Court of Appeals, however, held in July 2019 that the district court lacked jurisdiction over the action, and the orders went into effect.[17]

Determined to hit civil servants in their pocketbooks, the Trump administration and Republicans in Congress proposed a reduction in employer contributions to federal employees' retirement benefits by $145 billion, a requirement that they pay more for the same health insurance, and a pay freeze at fiscal year 2018 levels. The full Congress, however, was unwilling to enact legislation putting employees' pensions and health insurance at risk. Instead, it provided small across-the-board increases in federal pay. But Trump reduced the pay increases for fiscal year 2019 to zero under a statute empowering the president to put into place alternative compensation rates in "serious economic conditions affecting the general welfare." Trump cited the "current fiscal situation" as the reason for denying the increases, but he did not mention the $1.5 trillion tax cut he had championed that had ballooned the federal deficit. Trump also ordered agencies to hand out fewer performance-based awards and to make it more difficult to give employees the top performance rating. And in a spectacularly ill-timed move, the administration put into place restrictions on employee teleworking just two months before the COVID-19 pandemic made teleworking a safety necessity.[18]

Longtime civil servants were rightly concerned that the newcomers were bent on ridding the government of anyone who posed a threat to their demolition agenda. Most professionals in the agencies could have been making more money in the private sector, but they chose to work for their agencies because they were committed to their statutory missions. As it became clear that Trump appointees were seeking to dismantle the agencies, highly qualified and irreplaceable career employees headed for the doors, an option that the Trump appointees facilitated by offering buyouts and early retirements. By the end of 2018, nearly 1,600 civil servants had left the EPA alone, including 260 scientists, 185 environmental specialists, and 106 engineers, most of whom were not replaced. Since many of these employees had been with the agency since its beginnings in the early 1970s, the agency lost much of its institutional memory. At the end of the Trump administration, the EPA was still saddled with 600 unfilled positions. The agency will have to rebuild many of its capacities from the ground up. The Occupational Safety and Health Administration lost 6 percent of its workforce as experienced scientists, industrial hygienists, and inspectors retired or left an agency that was no longer advancing its mission. All of this was just fine with the Trump appointees, who wanted to push the agency in a radically different direction.[19]

One necessary consequence of civil service laws' providing due process protections to federal workers is that employees hired during Republican administrations can remain during Democratic administrations. Republican political appointees can "burrow in" by changing their status to permanent civil servants prior to Democratic administrations. These holdovers can become a thorn in the side of the new political appointees as they criticize regulatory initiatives internally, at conservative think tank conferences, and in right-wing media outlets. When the politics change and a new Republican administration is in place, they can offer valuable assistance to deregulatory initiatives because they know the technical and procedural ropes.

When President Trump assumed office, these "cicadas" hummed to life with ideas on how to chip away at the protective edifice. For example, Indur M. Goklany, a low-level civil servant at the Department of the Interior since the Reagan administration, stressed the uncertainties in climate science and advanced the theory, at conferences put on by the Heartland Institute and the Cato Institute, that increased levels of carbon dioxide in the atmosphere were good for the planet. At the outset of the Trump administration, he was elevated to the office of Deputy Secretary David Bernhardt, where he saw to it that departmental documents on climate change contained a cautionary note about uncertainties and referenced his "climate change is good" theory.[20]

As it became clear in late October 2020 that President Trump was probably not going to be reelected, the president fired a parting shot at the civil service with an executive order taking away due process protections from civil servants engaged in writing regulations and other policymaking functions. The executive order created a new "Schedule F" category of government employees that included "positions of a confidential, policy-determining, policy-making, or policy-advocating character not normally subject to change as a result of a Presidential transition." Schedule F employees would no longer benefit from the protections against arbitrary firing that the civil service laws provide to most civil servants, and they would no longer have the right to be represented by a union. Experts estimated that as many as 100,000 federal employees could wind up in the unprotected Schedule F category.

The order was another brainchild of James Sherk, who maintained that the president had inherent power to fire government employees without regard to the civil service laws, which, in his view, were unconstitutional. But it drew a firestorm of opposition from supporters of independent expertise in government. Had the order been fully implemented, it would have represented the most profound rearrangement of the civil service in the 140 years since Congress created it. President Biden, however, quickly rescinded the executive order before it had been implemented in any agency. But James Sherk is still advocating Schedule F, and Republicans in Congress are eager to pass legislation creating it as soon as they are back in power.[21]

Manipulating Science

The Trump administration adopted several strategies for ensuring that scientific facts and analysis did not get in the way of the demolition agenda. In the past, career scientists had faced few constraints on how they weighed scientific evidence. The Trump administration, however, achieved its desired deregulatory outcomes by imposing restrictions on how staff scientists analyzed and synthesized available scientific information. For example, EPA Administrator Scott Pruitt in April 2018 proposed a "transparency rule" that excluded from consideration peer-reviewed scientific studies if the authors did not make all of the underlying "dose response data . . . publicly available in a manner sufficient for independent validation." The rule operated as an enforceable exclusion on any research for which underlying data could not be produced. The Department of the Interior proposed a similar limitation on the scientific evidence that its scientists could consider.[22]

Although data transparency is generally a desirable scientific practice, the proposal ignored the fact that, in the kinds of epidemiological studies the EPA relies on to formulate protective standards, scientists generally agree to keep personal information about the subjects confidential. If strictly applied, for example, the new rule would have prevented the EPA from relying on the ongoing "Six Cities" study, the basis for decades of protective ambient air quality standards. The editors of top scientific journals, including *Science* and *Nature*, objected to the proposal, noting that "in not every case can all data be fully shared." By forcing agency scientists to ignore legitimate scientific studies, the transparency rule would have made it harder for the EPA to tighten air quality standards and take other protective actions based on epidemiological data.[23]

The final transparency rule was issued as a "midnight regulation" in January 2021. It was modified to say that the EPA would give studies for which underlying data were unavailable less weight, but the rule was expanded beyond the use of epidemiological studies in writing regulations, to discourage the use of such studies in disseminating "influential scientific information," including on the agency's website. Before the rule went into effect, however, a federal district court in Montana held that the EPA lacked authority to issue such a substantive regulation pursuant to its "general housekeeping" authority under the Administrative Procedure Act. At the Biden administration's request, the court vacated the entire rule, and it never went into effect. Both the EPA and the Department of the Interior officially revoked their transparency policies, but the model remains available for future Republican administrations.[24]

One important way in which government agencies protect the public is by disseminating information about the risks posed by corporate products and activities so that people can protect themselves or demand that the government protect them. The Trump administration, however, prevented the dissemination of scientific information that might lead to demands that it take protective action. For example, Trump-appointed officials at the EPA removed a climate change website that the agency had been curating for twenty years, and several other agencies made

scientific data related to climate change less accessible on their websites. The Department of the Interior canceled a National Academy
of Sciences contract to look into the health risks that mountaintop-
removal mining posed to neighboring communities, when it looked
as if the study might conclude that the health risks were significant.
And a renowned scientist at the Department of Agriculture resigned
because the department tried to bury his pathbreaking study showing
that increased levels of carbon dioxide in the atmosphere were causing
declining levels of nutrients in rice. Scientists throughout the government complained that President Trump's political appointees were trying to impede the dissemination of research that came to conclusions
that were inconsistent with the administration's policies.[25]

Agencies often appoint scientific advisory committees to draw on the
expertise of highly credentialed researchers who frequently hold presti-
gious positions at major universities and corporations. Serving without
pay or with modest stipends, these scientists and engineers "provide
an important vehicle for providing decisionmakers with robust, professional, and up-to-date scientific advice," according to the Union of
Concerned Scientists. In addition to helping agencies get the science
right, these advisory committees can serve as a brake on attempts by
upper-level political appointees to politicize the science that agencies
rely on in writing regulations. For example, in May 2018, a working
group of the EPA's Science Advisory Board blew the whistle on political
intervention into several pending EPA actions, including the economic
analysis for a proposal to allow increased greenhouse gas emissions
from power plants, a review of the Obama administration's limitations
on emissions from motor vehicles, and a proposal to repeal the Obama
administration's requirements for "glider" trucks.[26]

Agency administrators can, however, manipulate the scientific advice
that they receive from scientific advisory committees by appointing
members who share their policy views. Trump appointees employed

this practice frequently throughout the government to stack scientific advisory committees with scientists from the extreme fringe of scientific opinion on important issues, including the extent to which humans contributed to climate change, the risks posed by pollutants, and the need to protect threatened species. In a brutal break with tradition, the administration cleared out dozens of existing science advisors and replaced them with scientists more to its liking, often finding these new advisors in the regulated industries. The Government Accountability Office found that in selecting appointees to two of the EPA's most important advisory committees, the Trump administration did not solicit staff evaluations as required by the EPA's own advisory committee handbook.[27]

Without consulting the agency's scientists or its Scientific Advisory Board, EPA Administrator Pruitt in late October 2017 issued a novel directive prohibiting any scientist with an EPA grant from serving on an EPA advisory committee. The Department of Labor adopted a similar policy for its advisory committees in late 2020. Court documents later revealed that Republican politicians working with representatives of various industries had come up with the unprecedented exclusionary policy. Academics with EPA grants had been providing independent advice to the EPA since its inception because they were often leaders in their fields who were conducting cutting-edge research and were familiar with the newest developments. Since the EPA was one of the largest funders of environmental research, the action had the effect of purging the EPA's scientific advisory committees of some of the most prominent environmental scientists in the country. At the same time, Pruitt imposed no such restrictions on scientists who worked for or consulted with EPA-regulated *industries*. The net result was to stack advisory committees in favor of the very industries the agencies were designed to regulate.[28]

Industry trade associations and Trumpian populist activist groups enthusiastically supported the move. But the D.C. Circuit Court of Appeals in April 2020 held that Pruitt had arbitrarily and capriciously issued the directive without a "reasoned explanation" for why the agency was deviating from its previous practice. President Biden's EPA returned to the competitive process for filling advisory committee positions that the agency had employed prior to Pruitt's ill-considered intervention.[29]

Rejecting Expert Advice

The hydroxychloroquine saga was a good example of President Trump's prioritizing his anecdote-based gut feelings over scientific inquiry. It was also indicative of a broader tendency throughout the Trump administration to devalue expertise and reject the advice of government experts. For example, upper-level political appointees in the Department of the Interior ignored a warning from its endangered species expert in the field that excluding 3.5 million acres from the endangered spotted owl's previously designated critical habitat in Oregon would probably cause the species to go extinct.[30]

EPA Administrator Scott Pruitt rivaled President Trump in his dismissal of advice from experts. Instead of allowing regulatory projects to percolate through the agency, he relied on the political appointees whom he had brought in from Oklahoma and from conservative think tanks, along with a network of industry lobbyists, to prioritize and craft his deregulatory initiatives. Agency experts with decades of experience with the legal and technical requirements for successful regulatory action were either frozen out of decision-making meetings or ignored when they were allowed to participate. Pruitt was known to demote agency employees who questioned his actions on legal or technical grounds. For example, when an operations officer complained to the White House and Congress about what he called Pruitt's "chronic abuse of taxpayer dollars," he was locked out of his office and put on administrative leave without pay. Not surprisingly, the agency's civil servants reported that morale had sunk to the lowest levels since the Reagan administration. Pruitt's refusal to involve the staff frequently resulted in aggressive proposals for repealing and revising regulations. But because the proposals lacked scientific, technical, and legal justification, they were vulnerable to judicial reversal.[31]

Secrecy was the order of the day for Pruitt. He so intensely distrusted civil servants that career staffers had to be escorted into his inner sanctum. He insisted that they leave their cell phones at the door, and he prohibited note taking at some meetings. In September 2017, Pruitt arranged to have a contractor install a secure phone booth in his office at a cost of $43,000 so that he could make phone calls without being overheard. The Office of Management and Budget later determined that the telephone booth expenditure was unlawful. Six EPA employees were either reassigned or fired when they objected to Pruitt's lavish security demands. Pruitt's allies in the conservative think tanks and advocacy groups argued that his obsession with secrecy was a rational reaction to the fact that the EPA was "stocked with leftists" who were unsympathetic to his deregulatory agenda.[32]

A good example of Pruitt's willingness to reject expert advice from the staff was his determination that air quality in the Racine, Wisconsin, area complied with the national ambient air quality standards for ozone. During the Obama administration, the EPA had determined that air quality in that area did not meet—or, in technical parlance, "attain"—the standards. Consequently, any major new source of pollutants contributing to the high ozone levels was required to install top-of-the-line pollution-control technology and to purchase offsetting emissions reductions from other sources in the area. But President Trump and Republican Governor Scott Walker had recently announced a huge deal with the Taiwan-based electronics company Foxconn to build a giant flat-screen factory near Racine that was supposed to create 13,000 jobs. Designating the Racine area "nonattainment" would probably kill the deal. So political appointees at the EPA directed the scientists to come up with an analysis that justified designating the Racine area "attainment" while the surrounding areas remained nonattainment. Finding "no sound technical basis" for that move, the scientists patched together a support document out of bits and pieces of information taken out of context, but they correctly worried that it would mislead the public. The plant that Foxconn built was far less extensive than originally promised, and it employed only around 1,500 workers. But the air in Racine remained polluted.[33]

Disregard for the expertise of career civil servants was rampant throughout the Trump administration, especially in the office of Secretary of the Interior Ryan Zinke. According to one high-level career official, the members of Zinke's inner circle spent their time on the sixth floor of the department's Washington, D.C., headquarters "trying to figure out how they were going to kick through the Heritage Foundation's agenda." As Trump appointees at the Department of Energy made decisions that affected millions of people throughout the country, they kept the career staff out of the loop. According to the *New York Times*, the Consumer Financial Protection Bureau's acting director, Mick Mulvaney, was convinced that at least 1,600 of the bureau's 1,700 employees wanted to block Trump's initiatives. To avoid that result, he assigned to each of the career associate directors a politically appointed "policy associate director" to ensure that the career staffers adhered to the Trump administration's new deregulatory policies.[34]

Many civil servants retired or left the government out of frustration over not being able to play their assigned roles in protecting the public and the environment. Others were fired or eased out of office by transfers to distant locations or less desirable jobs. Over 11,000 federal employees left during the first six months of 2017 without being replaced. For those who remained, morale sank to all-time lows as they were forced to undo regulations that they had spent years crafting during previous administrations. By the end of the Trump administration, every regulatory department and agency other than the Departments of Homeland Security, Veterans Affairs, and Defense had suffered a loss of staff. And Trump's assault on the civil service made government service much less attractive to young professionals who might have migrated in that direction. To Donald Trump, this mass exodus represented a significant victory over the "deep state," which he advertised to the delight of his populist base.[35] Career civil servants were the cement that held the protective edifice together. They were therefore targets of the demolition agenda. As a result, the protective edifice was severely damaged in ways that will take decades to repair.

CHAPTER 6

STEPPING ON THE BRAKE

At the end of the Thanksgiving holiday in 2002, Cullum Owings and his brother Pierce were on their way back to Washington and Lee University. A senior business major with plans to join the Peace Corps, Cullum was driving along Interstate 81 in Rockbridge County, Virginia, on the busiest traffic day of the year when traffic slowed and then came to a stop. About a half-mile behind their stopped car, a fully loaded tractor trailer was barreling toward them at seven miles per hour over the speed limit. When he realized that the truck was moving too fast to stop before colliding with his vehicle, Cullum attempted to steer his car into the median, but the truck was coming too fast. The speeding truck crushed the boys' vehicle against a stone embankment, trapping both of them in the car. Miraculously, Pierce suffered only minor injuries, but Cullum was badly injured. By the time rescuers freed the boys, Cullum was gone.[1]

Determined to ensure that Cullum did not die in vain, his parents co-founded Road Safe America to advocate for regulations to protect travelers from speeding trucks. The organization's first major initiative was to persuade the Federal Motor Carrier Safety Administration to write regulations requiring newly manufactured trucks to contain speed-limiting software. To garner support for the petition, Steve Owings appeared on the *Today* show, MSNBC, and numerous local news shows across the country. Road Safe America and the American Trucking Association agreed to support regulations requiring mechanisms capping truck speeds at 65 miles per hour to be installed on all trucks manufactured since 1992.[2]

In September 2016, the National Highway Traffic Safety Administration and the Federal Motor Carrier Safety Administration published a proposal to require speed limiters in new heavy trucks and asked for comments on whether the speed limit should be 62, 65, or 68 mph. The agencies predicted that fuel cost savings alone would justify installing the devices. Supporters argued that the regulation would reflect simple physics. The slower a truck is moving at the time of a collision, the fewer people will be killed or injured. Truckers opposing the proposal argued that forcing them to go under highway speed limits (which in some states are as high as 80 mph) would cause traffic congestion, which might result in more accidents.[3]

The agencies were prepared to finalize the "killer truck" regulations in the summer of 2017, but they were stymied by an executive order that President Trump had signed in January 2017 requiring them to identify two rules to repeal to offset the regulation's costs. Despite overwhelming support for the proposal, the Department of Transportation in March 2018 moved the proposal to its inactive agenda, signaling that the proposal was effectively dead.[4]

The first order of business for the incoming Trump administration was to stop the regulatory agencies from writing new regulations. President Trump easily accomplished this with a temporary freeze on new regulations and with the ham-fisted executive order that stymied the FMCSA speed-limiter rule. During the first two years of the Trump administration, agencies issued far fewer significant regulations than the previous two administrations had.[5] When the agencies did begin to write new regulations, often because they were required by statute, they were nearly always so weak that they had the potential to yield only modest benefits.

The Freeze on Regulation

Shortly after the inauguration, Reince Priebus, the new White House chief of staff, sent a memo to all federal agencies putting a freeze on all regulations until a Trump-appointed agency head approved their issuance. The memo resulted in scores of withdrawals ranging from a proposed increase in campground fees for public land in Richland County, North Dakota, to a rule governing inspections of airline fuselages for cracks. In some cases, the freeze had unintended consequences. For example, a Federal Aviation Administration regulation authorizing drones to be flown out of eyesight got caught in the freeze, to the great chagrin of the drone manufacturing industry. Many of the regulations caught in the freeze remained frozen for the duration of the Trump administration.[6]

The 2-for-1 Executive Order

Within a week of his inauguration, President Trump signed an executive order titled "Reducing Regulation and Controlling Regulatory Costs" that required executive branch agencies to identify at least two existing regulations to repeal for every new regulation that they proposed. Furthermore, the agencies had to ensure that any new costs associated with the new regulation were offset by the elimination of costs associated with repeals of two or more existing regulations. New *deregulatory* rules, however, were exempt from the requirements because they supposedly imposed negative costs.[7]

Proponents of the executive order in conservative think tanks and activist groups praised it as a way to force agencies to engage in a retrospective look at their regulations. They argued that previous administrations had burdened the national economy with too many rules, and the executive order would force agencies to begin the process of reducing those regulatory burdens. The U.S. Chamber of Commerce predicted that the executive order would "drive growth and jobs." Business Republican groups stressed that it was more important that the agency offset costs imposed by new regulations than it was to come up with two arbitrary regulations to repeal.[8]

Public interest groups, labor unions, and administrative law scholars found much to dislike in the executive order. It was inconsistent with agency statutes, which allowed (and often required) agencies to write regulations without any mention of repealing existing regulations. Since most of the capital costs of complying with regulations occur when they are first issued, it would also be difficult for their repeal to result in large cost savings. And by transforming a single rulemaking exercise into three, the executive order tripled the workload for agency staffs aiming to issue new rules at a time when the Trump administration was doing its best to cut agency budgets. Finally, the executive order focused exclusively on regulatory *costs* without any regard for the *benefits* provided by the regulations' protections. It could preclude agencies from writing regulations that might have considerable net benefits and cause the agencies to repeal regulations with net benefits just to obtain the cost reductions necessary to justify the new regulations. Despite these powerful critiques, the executive order remained in effect for the entire Trump tenure.[9]

Failures to Regulate

The "two-for-one" executive order and the general reluctance of Trump's appointees to plow new regulatory ground caused the agencies to forego many opportunities to protect health and safety, natural resources and the environment, and consumers' pocketbooks.

Health Protections. The EPA had an opportunity to protect millions of Americans from premature death and lung disease during its five-year

review of the national ambient air quality standards for particulate matter. The EPA's staff experts concluded, based on studies published since
the EPA last tightened the standards in 2012, that tightening them further would prevent over twelve thousand premature deaths every year.
In addition, two recent studies by Harvard University and University
of Sienna epidemiologists found that significantly more deaths from
COVID-19 occurred in areas with high particulate-matter concentrations than occurred in areas with lower levels. But EPA Administrator
Andrew Wheeler elected to ignore the staff assessment and the recent
COVID-19 studies. In December 2020, the EPA published Wheeler's
final decision to retain the existing standards.[10]

The coal and electric power industries were delighted with the decision. Environmental groups accused Wheeler of rushing out his determination to prevent the incoming Biden administration from tightening
the standards for another five years. If that was the strategy, it apparently failed. On January 20, 2021, President Biden signed an executive order instructing the EPA to review the particulate-matter decision
immediately with an eye toward reversing Wheeler's determination.[11]

Safety Protections. The heavy truck speed-limiter proposal was not
the only opportunity the Trump administration missed to protect travelers on the nation's highways. For many years the National Transportation Safety Board has recommended that the Federal Motor Carrier
Safety Administration and the Federal Railroad Administration require
drivers of semi-trucks and engineers of trains to undergo testing for
sleep apnea. People suffering from that condition endure blocked air
passages during sleep, causing victims to experience sleep loss and
loss of concentration and situational awareness while awake. More than
20 million Americans are estimated to suffer from undiagnosed sleep
apnea. And the safety board estimated that sleep apnea can increase
the risk of a motor vehicle accident by up to seven-fold. Simple and
inexpensive tests exist to identify persons suffering from sleep apnea,

and inexpensive treatments such as CPAP machines are readily available to treat it. The Federal Aviation Administration requires airline pilots to be tested for sleep apnea before flying commercial airplanes. Sleep apnea tests for drivers and engineers would therefore seem like a no-brainer.[12]

In March 2016, the Federal Railroad Administration and the Federal Motor Carrier Safety Administration published a notice asking whether they should write regulations requiring the tests. The American Trucking Association strongly objected to the idea, arguing that the risk of liability already provided companies with an incentive to voluntarily test for sleep apnea. Yet while the agencies were deciding how to proceed, two more train wrecks, in Hoboken and Brooklyn, in which trains ran off the end of the tracks, suggested that sleep apnea was still causing accidents. The Hoboken crash killed a bystander and caused $6 million in property damage. The Brooklyn crash injured one hundred people and did $5 million in property damage. The Trump administration, however, was unimpressed. In August 2017, the agencies terminated the initiative.[13]

Worker Protections. On a late summer afternoon near Dallas, Texas, twenty-five-year-old Roendy Granillo was installing hardwood floors in a house under construction when his hands started cramping up and he began to feel ill. He had no access to water, and he was not provided a break as he continued to lay flooring. A few minutes later, his co-workers found him lying unconscious on the floor he had installed, and they called an ambulance. When he arrived at the hospital, his temperature was 110 degrees. Soon thereafter, he went into cardiac arrest and died. The official cause of death was heat stroke.[14]

It is no secret that workers who are exposed to excessive heat will suffer from nausea and headaches, and in the absence of intervention they can die from heat stroke. Between 1992 and 2016, heat killed almost eight hundred workers and injured nearly seventy thousand.

In recent years, climate change has greatly added to the risk of heat-related disease in a wide variety of workplaces. Farm workers who must work outside during the summer when the crops are ready for harvest are especially vulnerable to heat-related diseases, and they are often the least likely to complain, because they fear retaliation or deportation. Preventative measures, including access to drinking water, rest breaks, and working in the shade, are quite feasible, but many employers are apparently unwilling to implement such sensible measures without the impetus of an enforceable regulation. Yet despite several recommendations by the National Institute for Occupational Safety and Health, the Occupational Safety and Health Administration has consistently declined to promulgate a standard protecting workers from heat.[15]

In July 2018, 130 public interest and worker safety organizations petitioned the agency to issue a heat standard. They wanted it to require employers whose employees were regularly exposed to heat to produce written plans for addressing heat alerts, provide hourly rest breaks of varying lengths depending on weather conditions, and provide personal protective equipment such as clothing that breathes easily to dissipate heat. The Trump administration, however, did not take heat seriously as a workplace safety issue, and OSHA ignored the petition.[16]

Community Protections. In January 2014, ten thousand gallons of two highly toxic chemicals from a Freedom Industries above-ground storage tank spilled into the Elk River 1.5 miles upstream from the drinking-water intake for the city of Charleston, West Virginia. Over the next few days, nearly six hundred people sought help in emergency rooms, and thirteen were hospitalized. Around 300,000 residents in nine counties could not use tap water for drinking, showers, or washing clothes and dishes for several days. Responding to a lawsuit by environmental groups, the Obama administration agreed to write long-delayed regulations requiring facilities that store or handle hazardous substances, including in above-ground storage tanks, to formulate plans to protect surrounding communities from catastrophic spills. When the Trump administration reneged on that agreement, environmental groups returned to court in March 2019. The EPA responded the following September with a lengthy publication in the *Federal Register* concluding that spill-prevention regulations were not necessary because other programs the EPA administered under other laws adequately protected communities from such spills. The problem with that conclusion was that the Clean Water Act said that the EPA "shall" promulgate spill-prevention regulations, language that did not permit the EPA to shift that responsibility to other programs that were not designed to prevent the hazardous-substance spills. The Trump administration was simply not interested in protecting communities like Charleston when regulations would force chemical companies to do a better job of preventing spills.[17]

Environmental Protections. More than five thousand slaughterhouses in the United States process more than 8 billion chickens, 100 million pigs, and 30 million cattle every year. The enormous amount of wastewater that these facilities produce contains blood, grease, and fats, which in turn contain high levels of organic nitrogen, phosphorus, and ammonia that can stimulate fish-killing algae growth and otherwise befoul rivers and lakes. The average slaughterhouse discharges more pollution than a town of fourteen thousand people, making slaughterhouses the nation's largest industrial source of nitrogen pollution.

In October 2019, the EPA denied a long-standing demand by environmental groups to update its 2004 standards for slaughterhouses to reflect modern cleanup technologies. The groups argued that many companies had cleaned up their effluent to levels far lower than the existing standards. The EPA therefore had a statutory duty to update the standards to reflect the "best available technology." The Trump EPA thought otherwise. The environmental groups sued the EPA in December 2019, but the lawsuit went unresolved until the conclusion of the Trump administration.[18]

Public Resource Protections. The Endangered Species Act provides powerful protections for species that are on the Department of the Interior's lists of threatened and endangered species. Because the protections frequently restrict the use that farmers, ranchers, and developers can make of their land, the Trump administration was extremely reluctant to add species to the lists. While the Obama administration listed an average of forty-nine new species as threatened or endangered per year, the Trump administration listed fewer than twenty-five new threatened or endangered species during Trump's four-year term. The Center for Biological Diversity called it "a moral failure of epic proportions."

In February 2020, the center filed a lawsuit challenging the department's failure to come to a decision on listing more than two hundred extremely vulnerable species. Environmental groups also filed separate lawsuits challenging the Trump administration's failure to protect individual species. Among other failures, the Trump administration failed to protect grizzly bears and red and gray wolves from hunters, Beluga whales from seismic mineral testing, wolverines from habitat loss, northern spotted owls from logging, the Tiehm's buckwheat flower from lithium exploration, sea turtles from long-line fishermen, the Mount Graham squirrel from second-home builders, monarch butterflies and rusty patched bumblebees from global warming, burying beetles from hydraulic fracking, and the greater Houston toad from urban development. While the lawsuits were often successful, the Trump administration's refusal to protect vulnerable species persisted until the very end.[19]

Pocketbook Protections. By the end of the Obama administration, almost 40 percent of the regulations required by the Dodd–Frank Act remained to be written. The big banks had recovered from the recession and were bigger than ever, and they were back to some of their old abusive practices.[20] Because the head of the Consumer Financial Protection Bureau served for a five-year term, the bureau did not become a part of the Trump administration until Obama appointee Richard Cordray resigned in November 2017. He continued to push the agency to write new regulations until the day he left, not the least of which was the arbitration rule described in the introduction to this book.

Neither Mick Mulvaney, who became acting director, nor Kathy Kraninger, who took over in December 2018, were much interested in writing regulations to protect consumers. Immediately after taking over, Mulvaney placed a freeze on all new regulations, and the freeze remained in place for much of his tenure. When Kraninger became the bureau's director, the agency had not yet met 20 percent of the Dodd–Frank Act's deadlines for issuing new regulations. Very little had changed by the time she left in January 2021.[21]

One of the most serious derelictions of the agency's duty to protect consumers was its failure to protect college and trade-school students from overly aggressive loan servicers. As the cost of a college education has spiraled upward since the 1980s, more and more students from low- and middle-income families have taken out student loans to finance the cost of their post-secondary educations. For-profit colleges rely on loans provided by the federal government to such students to sustain their business model. By 2020, more than 44 million borrowers owed an average of $35,000 each on student loans, for a total of more than $1.6 trillion. The burden of student loans is not evenly distributed across borrowers: while 66 percent of white students take out student loans, 90 percent of African American and 72 percent of Latinx students take out such loans. Half of all college students are women, but they account for 66 percent of all student loans. The students with the most debt are from rural areas.[22]

Many students enter their first jobs so deeply in debt that they cannot seriously consider getting married, purchasing a house, having children, or changing jobs. In one survey of student loan debtors, one-third of the respondents reported that their monthly student loan bill was

higher than their rent. A surprising number of people in their sixties
are still paying student loans and are worried that they will never be
able to retire. At least one million borrowers per year default on their
student loans. Consequently, around 11 percent of student loan debt is
delinquent, a rate that exceeds the delinquency rate for mortgages, car
loans, and credit cards.[23]

The Department of Education is responsible for the overwhelming
majority of those loans, with a student loan portfolio of around $1.2 tril-
lion. The department contracts out the job of servicing 80 percent of
its loans to three companies, all nonbank entities subject to the department's contract administration and the Consumer Financial Protection
Bureau's regulatory authorities. Student loan servicers communicate
with borrowers about the status of their loans, maintain loan records,
counsel borrowers on selecting repayment plans, process payments,
and contact students who are delinquent in their payments.

Former students who get behind in their payments often receive phone
calls from loan servicers threatening to garnish their wages, place liens
on their houses, withhold tax refunds, offset Social Security benefits,
or worse. Collection efforts can become so aggressive that they violate
the Dodd–Frank Act's prohibition on abusive tactics. Irresponsible loan
servicers file hundreds of lawsuits and secure default judgments against
borrowers without producing paperwork demonstrating that they have
the right to collect. The department's inspector general found that
servicers frequently miscalculated the amounts owed, leading to payments that were too high or too low. Student loan servicing errors cause
improper interest capitalization that can lead to thousands of dollars
being added to the loan balance, loss of eligibility for loan forgiveness
programs, and loss of access to loan subsidy programs.[24]

By 2015, the Consumer Financial Protection Bureau had received a
sufficient number of complaints of student loan servicer malfeasance
and abuse that Director Richard Cordray was convinced it was time to

write regulations protecting student borrowers. The bureau had ample authority to issue such regulations under its power to prescribe rules to protect borrowers from unfair, deceptive, or abusive acts or practices. The bureau therefore added a student loan servicing regulation to its regulatory agenda and began the process of preparing a proposal for public comment. When he came aboard, however, Director Mulvaney thought otherwise. In May 2018, he scrapped the project.[25]

Weak Trump Regulations

On the rare occasions that the Trump administration did move forward with a regulatory initiative, it tended to write weak standards that the regulated industries could easily meet.

EPA Airplane Emissions Standards. In what appeared at first glance to be a highly unusual effort by the Trump administration to reduce greenhouse gas emissions, the EPA in August 2020 proposed standards for new passenger aircraft. Appearances, however, were deceiving. The EPA issued the proposal at the behest of the aircraft and engine manufacturing industries (primarily Boeing and General Electric). Passenger aircraft manufacturers worldwide, if they wanted to sell their planes internationally, had to demonstrate that their regulators required them to comply with standards promulgated by the United Nations' International Civil Aviation Organization. The aircraft manufacturers' production lines already easily met the Civil Aviation standards, and the EPA proposed to implement the equivalent of those standards. So the proposal was really a favor to the industry that came at very little cost. Even the National Association of Manufacturers supported it. Environmental groups and several state attorneys general complained that the manufacturers were capable of meeting far more stringent standards, and they noted that airplanes subject to the new standards were responsible for as much as 3 percent of the country's greenhouse gas emissions, by no means a trivial amount. During the Trump administration, however, the EPA was not inclined to force greenhouse gas reduction technology; the agency finalized the milquetoast regulation in January 2021.[26]

Debt-Collection Rule. By one estimate, 70 million Americans are contacted by a debt collector every year. Debt collection is an $11.5 billion industry in which 7,700 collecting agencies employ almost 120,000 people. Debt collectors come in three varieties. First, the original creditor that extended credit to the borrower may pursue an overdue payment. Second, creditors may hire third-party debt collectors, usually on a contingency-fee basis, to persuade debtors to pay. Third, creditors may sell the obligation to a debt buyer, usually for a small fraction of the value of the debt, and the buyer then pursues the debtor or sells the debt to still another buyer. Since states do not generally license debt collectors, the entities that purchase and collect debts range from big companies with large computer databases to small, specialized law firms. Unscrupulous debt collectors use small-claims courts as "debt collection mills" to fast-track "robo-signed" documents through legal processes in order to receive judgments that may then be used to garnish wages or seize debtors' assets. Companies frequently fail to document that the persons sued are in fact the debtors, or that the debtors owe the amount sought. They just hope that the debtor won't be able to afford a lawyer to contest the claim, leaving them with a default judgment.[27]

Debt-collection companies are notorious for harassing and mistreating delinquent debtors with multiple phone calls, emails, and other abusive collection techniques. But debt collectors don't stop with the debtor. They frequently pursue the debtor's family, friends, and even employers. Some companies simply report the debt to one of the three credit reporting agencies and wait for the consumers to contact them after discovering that their credit ratings have dropped. And an increasing number of debt-collection companies persuade local judges to issue arrest warrants to debtors who failed to appear at civil proceedings, thereby subjecting unsuspecting debtors to the rough equivalent of the long-ago-banned debtors' prison. When a company sells debt to another company, the debtor and his family, friends, and employer are subjected to a new round of communications. As time passes, information gets lost or garbled, and debt collectors wind up pursuing debtors who are not delinquent, who have a legitimate dispute with the original creditor, or for whom the statute of limitations has rendered the debt no longer collectable.[28]

The Consumer Financial Protection Bureau began the process of regulating debt collection during Richard Cordray's tenure, holding field hearings and soliciting public input on what a regulation should look like.[29] There was widespread agreement among consumer groups, debt-collection companies, and creditors that regulations were necessary. Debt collectors wanted regulations to provide greater certainty, because litigation across the country had resulted in conflicting court opinions on several questions, including whether debt collectors could leave messages on telephones. Consumer groups wanted the bureau to provide greater protections, such as prohibiting debt collectors from calling more than once a week and from attempting to collect "zombie debt" after time had run out under the relevant statute of limitations. But the process was in midstream when Cordray resigned.[30]

After studying the matter for much of the Trump administration, the bureau published regulations in October and December 2020 that contained some modest protections against harassing debtors and collecting zombie debt. Instead of the "bright line" limit of a single phone call per week favored by consumer groups, the bureau created a "presumption" against more than seven calls per week, which a company could rebut by showing that more calls were necessary in the circumstances. The regulations allowed companies to send unlimited emails, text messages, and social media communications to debtors, but, in a concession to consumers, each message had to give recipients the option of opting out of future messages. The regulations also prohibited companies from leaving messages with family members or co-workers. Companies still could attempt to persuade debtors to pay off zombie debt, but they could not sue or threaten a lawsuit. If the debtor paid off some of the debt, however, the company could sue to collect the remainder. Consumer groups were pleased by some aspects of the regulations, but they maintained that the new rules were far less protective than they should have been.[31]

The Trump administration was not at all interested in writing new protective regulations. The preceding examples represent just a few of the hundreds of opportunities the administration missed to protect the public from irresponsible and unscrupulous companies. The "two-for-one" executive order that President Trump signed in January 2017—requiring the repeal of two existing regulations for every new regulation proposed—discouraged new regulations.[32] And on the rare occasions that the agencies did write new regulations, they were either in response to industry demand for more certainty or carefully crafted so as to make them minimally intrusive. The free marketeers and business Republicans that President Trump appointed to the top positions in the agencies were far more interested in rolling back existing regulations than in writing new ones.

CHAPTER 7

SHIFTING INTO REVERSE

Having staunched the flow of new regulations, the Trump administration agencies turned to rolling back existing regulations, focusing especially on the products of the Obama administration. Days after his election, Donald Trump promised to cut 75 percent of all federal regulations, "maybe more." Although every president since Jimmy Carter has required agencies to "look back" at existing regulations with an eye toward revising or eliminating outdated or duplicative rules, the Trump administration's look back was far more comprehensive in scope and far more aggressive. And it was unique in its explicit determination to demolish its predecessor's legacy. Beyond that, the Trump appointees in the agencies assigned top priority to regulations identified by various industry groups as being ideal for repeal.[1]

In the process of pulling back those protections, the administration showed little regard for the procedural requirements of the Administrative Procedure Act, or for the substantive laws under which the agencies had provided those protections. And that got the agencies in trouble with the reviewing courts. For example, courts overturned many attempts to push back the starting dates for regulations that had been finalized prior to Trump's inauguration because the agencies had failed to solicit public comment on the extensions.[2]

Nevertheless, by halfway through his term, Trump's agencies had initiated the lengthy process of revoking or revising at least seventy-eight significant regulations protecting human health and safety, natural resources, and the environment, not to mention many more regulations protecting workers and consumers. The agencies often tried to hide the negative impacts of their actions by neglecting to engage with affected beneficiaries and failing to address the scientific and technical underpinnings for those regulations. These efforts, too, departed from settled administrative law and therefore fared poorly in reviewing courts.[3]

The Regulatory Reform Task Force Executive Order

In late February 2017, President Trump signed Executive Order 13777, which required each executive branch agency head to designate a "regulatory reform officer" to chair a regulatory reform task force charged with recommending regulations for repeal, replacement, or modification. To accomplish this task, the task forces were required to seek input and assistance from the businesses that were significantly affected by the regulations. It turned out that many task force members had worked for the industries demanding regulatory relief prior to joining the agencies. Others had worked for free marketeer think tanks and Trumpian populist advocacy organizations that had bitterly opposed the agencies during the Obama administration. The task forces held public meetings, but they also met behind closed doors with industry lobbyists to hear their recommendations, most of which wound up on the agencies' deregulatory agendas.[4]

Demolishing Protections Against Climate Disruption

The Republican Party at one time contained strong environmentalists, such as Senators James Buckley (R-N.Y.) and Jim Jeffords (R-Vt.), but no longer. As Fox News commentators, free market think tanks, the U.S. Chamber of Commerce, religious right preachers, and Tea Party groups made opposition to environmental regulation a litmus test for Republican politicians in the early 2010s, a deep chasm developed between Democrats and Republicans over environmental issues. By the 2016 elections, only 38 percent of Republicans and only 15 percent of conservative Republicans agreed with the basic premise that human activity caused global warming, compared to 85 percent of Democrats who believed this was the case.[5]

Donald Trump's views on climate change had opportunistically evolved to match those of his populist base. In 2009, he signed a full-page advertisement in the *New York Times* demanding "meaningful and effective measures to combat climate change." In 2012, he famously tweeted that "global warming was created by and for the Chinese in order to make U.S. manufacturing non-competitive." During the 2016 presidential campaign, Trump promised to get rid of "regulations that shut down hundreds of coal-fired power plants and block the construction of new ones." Soon after the election, Trump allowed that he had an "open mind" about climate disruption. His actions, however, were those of a president who was convinced that human activities had no effect on global temperatures. And midway through his first year, Trump declared that he was "not a believer in man-made global warming."[6]

Trump's appointees to head the agencies with the greatest power to regulate climate-altering greenhouse gas emissions were generally climate-disruption deniers.[7] Soon after the inauguration, agency websites deleted previously posted information about climate change. The Obama White House's web page on climate change was replaced with a page devoted to an "America First Energy Plan," which set out the new administration's goals for rolling back Obama administration climate change regulations and promoting fossil fuel companies. Upper-level political appointees in the Environmental Protection Agency insisted that the staff adhere to talking points that sowed doubts about the connection between human emissions of greenhouse gases and climate disruption.[8]

The clearest indication of where the Trump administration stood on climate disruption was President Trump's decision to withdraw from the Paris Climate Accords, a multinational agreement that called for voluntary reductions in greenhouse gas emissions by sufficient amounts to keep the increase in global average temperature from pre-industrial levels to well below two degrees centigrade. With presidential counselor Steve Bannon, EPA Administrator Scott Pruitt, and Competitive Enterprise Institute climate skeptic Myron Ebel standing in the background, Trump delivered a Rose Garden speech in which he declared that he was "elected to represent the citizens of Pittsburgh, not Paris."[9]

Auto Emissions Standards and the California Waiver. One of the first actions the EPA undertook at the outset of the Obama administration was to publish a formal finding that greenhouse gas emissions endanger public health and welfare. This endangerment finding provided the scientific underpinning for action under the Clean Air Act to reduce greenhouse gas emissions. When industry groups challenged the finding, the D.C. Circuit Court of Appeals held that the finding was amply supported in the voluminous record that the agency assembled. Having made that finding, the Clean Air Act then required the EPA to issue tailpipe emissions standards for automobiles at levels that were technologically feasible and not unduly costly. With no known technology for removing carbon dioxide from auto exhaust, the agency's approach involved requirements that vehicles burn less gasoline per mile traveled. The Obama-era EPA and National Highway Traffic Safety Administration, which had its own statutory obligation to increase gas mileage for fleets of motor vehicles by 2020, collaborated on the initiative, and the industry had no trouble complying with the Phase I standards issued by the agencies in April 2010.[10]

In October 2012, the agencies published Phase II regulations for model years 2017 through 2025 that reflected a deal struck between the EPA, the state of California, and the auto industry. Auto manufacturers were required to increase average mileage from 27.8 miles per gallon to 54.5 miles per gallon. The manufacturers, however, insisted on a mid-term evaluation to give the agencies an opportunity to amend the standards if they proved to be too stringent. The agencies further agreed to coordinate the evaluation and any mid-course corrections with the state of California, which the Clean Air Act empowered to promulgate more stringent standards than the EPA, if the EPA granted the state a waiver. Other states could then adopt the California standards instead of the EPA's standards.[11]

With the election of Donald Trump in November 2016, however, the auto manufacturers changed their tune and urged the incoming administration to "adjust" the requirements. Consumers were purchasing trucks and SUVs that were more profitable for the manufacturers, and that made it more difficult for the industry to meet standards based on average fuel economy across all vehicles. Seeing the writing on the wall, the outgoing Obama EPA published its mid-term determination that the agreed-upon standards for model years 2022–2025 were "appropriate" a week before President Trump's inauguration.[12]

In March 2017, President Trump announced that the EPA would be revisiting the mid-term determination, and he ordered the agency to reexamine the waiver that allowed California and twelve other states to write more stringent emissions standards and to require a certain percentage of new cars to be zero-emission vehicles. Trump declared that "the assault on the American auto industry is over." It was an odd claim, given that the federal government had recently bailed out two of the big three American car companies from bankruptcy.[13]

As staffers from the EPA and the Highway Safety Administration worked on the documents to support Trump's changes, some EPA staffers worried that the technical justifications for changing the standards provided by engineers in the Department of Transportation would not stand up to judicial scrutiny because they contained "a wide range of errors," used "outdated data," and relied on "unsupported assumptions." When the support documents containing those justifications came before the EPA's Scientific Advisory Board, which contained a large number of Trump administration appointees, it found "significant weaknesses" in the agency's technical analyses. But the scientific and engineering experts' objections and concerns were ignored by the Trump appointees at the top of the agencies. In early August 2018, the EPA and the Highway Safety Administration issued a joint proposal to freeze the standards for greenhouse gas emissions from autos, SUVs, and pickups at model year 2020 levels through model year 2026. It was a massive rollback of the Obama administration standards. At the same time, the EPA proposed to withdraw the California waiver and preempt the California emissions limitations and zero-emitting vehicle requirements.[14]

In a surprise move, Ford, Volkswagen of America, Honda, BMW, and Volvo negotiated a deal with California under which they agreed to support California in its fight with the EPA, and the state agreed to relax its standards slightly. The Trump administration struck back with a bogus antitrust investigation into the five companies, which was dropped five months later under heavy criticism from antitrust attorneys.[15]

The EPA and the highway safety agency published final regulations in September 2019 that revoked California's Clean Air Act waiver and preempted California's emissions standards. In separate regulations published in April 2020, the agencies replaced the Obama requirement that fleets of automobiles average around 54.5 miles per gallon by 2025 with an easily met requirement that they average 40 miles per gallon by 2026. By the agencies' own reckoning, the change would cause an additional 444 to 1,000 premature deaths and result in a net loss to consumers of $13.1 billion. Tucked away in the dense analysis was the agencies' conclusion that the change would result in a net reduction of

13,474 U.S. jobs, a conclusion not mentioned by EPA Administrator Andrew Wheeler and Transportation Secretary Elaine Chao as they touted how beneficial the changes would be to the auto industry. One EPA scientist left the agency with "a leaden feeling in my soul."[16]

Clean Power Plan Replacement. The Obama administration's endangerment finding also triggered the EPA's responsibility to write emissions standards for greenhouse gas emissions from new power plants and guidelines for state regulation of existing plants.[17] The EPA accomplished those tasks in August 2015 with a massive regulation called the Clean Power Plan. The standard of performance for *new* plants was based on the capability of an efficiently run modern boiler using "carbon capture" technology to remove around 16 percent of the plant's carbon dioxide emissions. The standard was, however, of little practical relevance, because no one was building new coal-fired power plants.[18]

The agency concluded that carbon capture was not yet available for retrofitting into *existing* plants. Running power plants more efficiently, however, would reduce carbon dioxide emissions per kilowatt-hour of electricity produced, and many efficiency-enhancing technologies and techniques had been adequately demonstrated. The EPA went a step further, however, to look outside the plant's physical boundaries—"beyond the fence line"—for things that companies could do to reduce emissions. For one thing, a company could shift load from coal-fired plants to low-emitting gas-fired plants that it owned. Companies with multiple power plants frequently employed this technique, called "generation shifting," to ensure that electricity was coming from the least expensive generator. Alternatively, a company could build non-emitting solar arrays or wind farms or purchase renewable power from existing facilities. The EPA gave states until August 2018 to prepare plans for complying with the guidelines, and the agency then had a year to approve or disapprove the plans. Generators had to begin making reductions by no later than 2022, and they had to meet the final goals by 2030.[19]

The publication of the regulations in October 2015 resulted in many lawsuits in the D.C. Circuit Court of Appeals. In an unprecedented move, the Supreme Court in February 2016, by a 5–4 vote, issued an order preventing the regulations from going into effect until the litigation was resolved.[20] The Court's action paved the way for the Trump administration to rewrite the regulations.

In late March 2017, President Trump signed an executive order directing federal agencies to "immediately review existing regulations" that could slow the development of domestic energy resources and to "suspend, revise, or rescind" those that "unduly burden[ed]" the development of those resources. This "energy dominance" order explicitly included the Clean Power Plan. To drive home the point that there was a new boss in town, Trump showed up at the EPA's headquarters along with a group of coal miners as props to announce the new order.[21]

The Trump administration's "Affordable Clean Energy" plan, published in early July 2019, took the position that the Clean Air Act unambiguously precluded the EPA from requiring anything beyond increasing power plant efficiency, even though the record the Obama administration had compiled demonstrated that generation shifting was a highly cost-effective way to reduce emissions. The Trump plan limited the states' toolbox of emission limitations to one of seven modest efficiency-improvement measures that the EPA specifically identified; the states were then allowed to apply other factors to soften the requirements, including cost considerations, the physical impossibility of installing a control technology, and the remaining useful life of the facility.[22]

In resting its repeal of the Clean Power Plan on the assertion that the Clean Air Act unambiguously precluded the agency from regulating beyond the fence line, the Trump administration was betting that the D.C. Circuit Court of Appeals or the Supreme Court would agree and that its interpretation would therefore be binding on all future administrations. It lost that bet in the D.C. Circuit. In a comprehensive sixty-six-page opinion, the D.C. Circuit in January 2021 thoroughly eviscerated the Trump administration's legal analysis and vacated the Trump plan. The Supreme Court, however, agreed to hear the industry's appeal. The Affordable Clean Energy plan did not go into effect, but the Trump administration successfully forestalled any federal greenhouse gas reduction requirements for existing power plants for four critical years and the time it would take for the Biden administration to put together a new plan. And if the Supreme Court agrees with the Trump administration that the Clean Air Act unambiguously precludes requirements beyond the fence line, then EPA will be prevented from taking desperately needed action to address climate disruption.[23]

Methane Emissions from Oil and Gas Production. The advent of hydraulic fracturing (fracking) technologies at the turn of the twenty-first century brought about a dramatic increase in oil and gas exploration and development. While this resulted in much greater domestic oil and gas production, it also increased emissions of methane, a potent greenhouse gas that is 28–38 times more potent in trapping heat than carbon dioxide. The Obama administration issued two regulations to reduce methane emissions from oil and gas production. In June 2016, the EPA published regulations that required oil and gas developers to lower emissions from processing and storage facilities and transmission pipelines using various available technologies. The agency estimated that the regulations would result in the reduction of the release of 300,000 tons of methane per year by 2020.[24] The following November, the Department of the Interior published a regulation establishing requirements for preventing oil and gas drilling operations on federal lands from wasting natural gas, which had the effect of reducing methane emissions by the equivalent of carbon dioxide emissions from almost a million automobiles.[25]

The Trump administration rolled back the most protective aspects of both regulations. The EPA decided that regulating methane emissions was not necessary after all, and the Department of the Interior concluded that it did not have the authority to protect the planet from climate change. The EPA's rollback was one of three regulations that Congress repealed under the Congressional Review Act after Joe Biden was elected and the Democrats assumed control of the Senate. That action made the Obama regulations immediately applicable to new oil and gas drilling operations.

A federal district court in California threw out the Interior Department's rollback in July 2020. That action brought back to life an industry challenge to the Obama regulations, and a Wyoming court in October 2020 set them aside after adopting the Trump administration's position that the department lacked authority to regulate methane emissions to reduce global warming risks. Consequently, oil and gas operators on federal lands continue to waste millions of dollars' worth of gas every year.[26]

Energy and Water Efficiency Standards. After it became clear that his deregulatory policies were doing virtually nothing to fulfill his 2016 promise to revive the coal industry, President Trump opened his 2020 campaign with the modest promise of deregulating efficiency standards for showers, toilets, dishwashers, and lightbulbs. The strategy reflected Trump's uncanny ability to appeal to a populist crowd through nostalgic invocation of a former time when regulatory agencies did not tell companies how to design appliances. The odd thing about his new obsession was that the affected industries were generally happy with the standards, many of which had been around for years, and there was no public outcry for relaxing the standards until Trump began complaining about them on the campaign trail. Nevertheless, Trump's appointees in the Department of Energy got the message and instructed their staffs to get busy relaxing the standards.[27]

"Showerheads—you take a shower, the water doesn't come out. . . .

So what do you do? You just stand there longer or you take a shower longer?" That riff, and another about toilets that had to be flushed many times, were hardy perennials on the Trump 2020 campaign trail. Like many of Trump's populist tropes, however, his complaints about showerheads and toilets had no basis in fact. Years of academic research demonstrated that modern toilet and shower appliances work just as well as or better than their counterparts of the 1960s, and they reduce water consumption by billions of gallons as well as save homeowners hundreds of dollars a year in utility bills.[28]

Since the 1990s, the Department of Energy (DOE) had enforced a standard limiting the showerhead flow rate to 2.5 gallons per minute and taken the position that the limitation applied to showerheads with multiple nozzles. Around 70 percent of the showerheads on the market used 20 percent less water than the DOE regulation allowed. To make Trump happy, the department proposed to apply the 2.5-gallons-per-minute limitation to each nozzle of multiple-nozzle showerheads, meaning that a single showerhead with multiple nozzles could use a lot more water. Consumer groups persuasively argued that the proposal would violate the statute's anti-backsliding provision. Plumbing equipment manufacturers, plumbing suppliers, and water utility companies all came out against the change because the manufacturers and suppliers were happy with the existing standards and the utility companies wanted to conserve scarce water. Trump told an adoring crowd in late October that "now you go into a shower and the water pours out." But the Energy Department did not finalize the rule until more than a month after the 2020 elections, and no manufacturer was willing to start making water-gushing multi-nozzle showerheads with the Biden administration in place. The Biden administration quickly proposed to reinstate the prior definition.[29]

President Trump had a similar personal problem with an Obama-era regulation that broadened a previous phase-out of incandescent lightbulbs to include seven categories of bulbs that were used in ceiling fans, candelabras, chandeliers, and the like in the expectation that they would be replaced with far more efficient light-emitting diodes. He thought LED light made his famous tan look orange. He was probably referring to compact fluorescent bulbs, which are a very small part of the market, not LEDs, which can emit light that is indistinguishable from that of an incandescent bulb. The Energy Department dutifully published a proposal in February 2019 to exclude many kinds of specialty bulbs from the phase-out.[30]

Consumer groups estimated that the regulations the Trump administration proposed to repeal would save enough energy to retire twenty-five large power plants. Dozens of investor-owned utility companies also weighed in against the proposal, which would have undermined their efforts to conserve electricity. In a *New York Times* op-ed, two great-grandsons of Thomas Edison, the inventor of the incandescent bulb, argued that he would have welcomed the advent of LED bulbs and would have urged the Trump administration to allow the Obama phase-out to remain in effect. Nevertheless, the Department of Energy finalized the withdrawal of the Obama phase-out in early September 2019, finding that it was not "economically justified." The same scenario played out when President Trump set his sights on the department's water conservation standards for residential dishwashers.[31]

Demolishing Health Protections

By the mid-1990s, poison control centers in the United States had received reports of more than seven thousand acute poisonings attributed to exposure to the pesticide chlorpyrifos (also known as Dursban or Lorsban), a potent bug killer closely related to the chemical warfare agent sarin. The Dow Chemical Company had received a license from the EPA's predecessor in 1965 to produce and sell chlorpyrifos. In the following years, the EPA established tolerances (acceptable concentrations of pesticides) for chlorpyrifos on various food-use crops. It then became one of the most heavily used pesticides in the country. In September 2007, after several epidemiological studies of children concluded that chlorpyrifos exposure was associated with decreased IQ and increased memory deficits, two environmental groups filed a formal petition requesting that the EPA revoke the tolerances for chlorpyrifos.[32]

In October 2015, the Obama EPA proposed to revoke all of the tolerances for chlorpyrifos. The agency could not conclude that the exposure to the pesticide from food and drinking water at the allowed levels presented a "reasonable certainty of no harm" to human beings, the test for leaving a tolerance in place under the 1996 Food Quality Protection Act. The EPA's pesticide scientific advisory panel agreed with this assessment, as did dozens of other scientists, doctors, and public health professionals.[33]

In the fall of 2017, several days after Trump's EPA administrator, Scott Pruitt, met privately with Dow lobbyists, EPA Chief of Staff Ryan Jackson ordered Wendy Cleland-Hamnet, the career employee in charge of pesticide tolerances, to ignore the agency's scientists and deny the environmental groups' petition. At the time worried that she was harming farmworkers' children, she later recalled that the day she denied the petition was "not one of my best days." Soon thereafter, she retired.[34]

In mid-April 2019, the Ninth Circuit vacated Pruitt's action and ordered the agency to rule on the environmental groups' motion. Three months later, the EPA once again denied the petition, and the environmental groups once again sought review in the Ninth Circuit. In the meantime, Hawaii and California decided to ban the use of chlorpyrifos in those states. The day the California ban went into effect, the largest manufacturer of chlorpyrifos announced that it would cease making the pesticide. Other manufacturers, however, continued to sell the product.

On President Biden's first day in office, he ordered the EPA to review the chlorpyrifos decision. And in April 2021, a three-judge panel of the Ninth Circuit ordered the EPA to revoke or modify chlorpyrifos tolerances for good. The frustrated panel noted that "EPA's egregious delay exposed a generation of American children to unsafe levels" of the neurotoxic pesticide.[35]

Demolishing Safety Protections

On July 6, 2013, a runaway train pulling seventy-two tank cars full of crude oil extracted from North Dakota shale derailed in the downtown of Lac-Megantic, Quebec. More than one million gallons of oil spilled into the streets and ignited into an enormous fireball that killed forty-seven people and destroyed forty buildings. The train's engineer had stopped the train in a town several miles away to take a rest break, and he had set the train's hand brakes to ensure that it did not roll downhill, but the brakes failed an hour after the lead engine was turned off to extinguish a minor fire. The train then rolled downhill for seven miles, gaining speed. When it came to a curve in the track in Lac-Megantic, several tank cars left the track, causing the explosion. Had the train been outfitted with electronically controlled pneumatic brakes, instead of hand brakes, it most likely would have been stopped before it reached the town.[36]

The Obama administration reacted to the Lac-Megantic tragedy by directing the Pipeline and Hazardous Materials Safety Administration and the Federal Railroad Administration to collaborate in writing a comprehensive set of regulations governing "high hazard flammable trains," or "bomb trains" in the vernacular. The controversial regulations, which were published in May 2015, required trains comprising more than seventy loaded tank cars containing flammable liquids to install electronically controlled pneumatic brakes on the locomotive and every tank car. Such braking systems tell all of the cars on the train to put on the brakes at the same time, a system that works much more quickly than conventional air brakes. The requirement was applicable to trains carrying crude oil after 2020 and to trains carrying ethanol after 2022.[37]

Unwilling to concede defeat, industry lobbyists persuaded the sponsors of the upcoming surface transportation bill to include an innocuous-looking provision that required the secretary of transportation to perform a regulatory impact analysis to determine whether the requirement was justified, and to repeal it if it was not. The analysis the Trump agencies published in December 2017 arbitrarily lowered the estimate of the number of carloads of highly flammable liquids that would be shipped over the next twenty years, resulting in dramatically lower benefits in the cost/benefit analysis, even though the use of bomb trains was rapidly increasing. With that, the Transportation Department rescinded the electronic braking requirement in September 2018 without seeking public comment as required by the Administrative Procedure Act. An administrative appeal by environmental groups was pending at the start of the Biden administration.[38]

Demolishing Worker Protections

Although conditions in meatpacking plants have improved considerably over the horrors described by Upton Sinclair in his 1905 book *The Jungle*, slaughterhouses are still dangerous places to work. Workers are still exposed to cold, wet, noisy, slippery conditions as they convert hog carcasses into pork and bacon, using saws, hooks, and knives as the carcasses move rapidly along conveyer belts. The job requires thousands of forceful slices each day by dozens of workers. On average, a worker on a meat preparation line somewhere in the United States suffers a lost limb or other serious injury every two days. Workers also suffer rapid-motion disorders, including carpal tunnel syndrome and tendinitis, at rates sixteen times those of workers in other industries. The ninety thousand pork slaughterhouse workers in the United States are generally poorly paid, non-unionized immigrants (both legal and illegal) who support their families in rural communities.[39]

In January 2018, the Trump administration's Department of Agriculture proposed to revoke the long-standing federal limit of 1,106 hogs per hour on the conveyer belts transporting hog carcasses past workers attempting to slice them into marketable portions and federal inspectors attempting to ensure that the meat does not become contaminated in the process. A coalition of food safety, worker safety, and public interest groups argued that revoking the maximum line speed would increase the risk that overtaxed workers would sustain rapid-motion injuries or accidentally injure themselves with the sharp knives that they used to slice the meat. The department responded that it had neither the authority nor the expertise to regulate slaughterhouses to protect workers. In finalizing the line-speed revocation in September 2019, the department did not consider the effects of increasing line speeds on workers.[40]

In March 2021, a federal district court in Minnesota reinstated the limitation on line speeds. Noting that the Department of Agriculture had considered worker safety in regulating line speeds in the past, the court found the Trump administration's failure to consider worker safety in the hog line-speed regulations to be arbitrary and capricious.[41] Workers in hog slaughterhouses received a reprieve, but the industry is biding its time for the next Republican administration.

Demolishing Community Protections

In April 2013, a fire at the West Fertilizer Company's plant in McClennan County, Texas, resulted in an enormous explosion that killed fifteen people, including twelve emergency responders, and injured 260 others. The explosion leveled the plant and destroyed or damaged 150 nearby buildings, including two schools and a nursing home. President Obama responded to the tragedy with an executive order requiring the EPA to come up with a plan to improve safety and security regulations for facilities that manufacture, store, and distribute toxic and explosive chemicals. The EPA published updated risk management regulations on January 13, 2017, a week before President Trump's inauguration.[42]

The new regulations added modest new investigation, disclosure, and coordinating requirements to those already imposed on the 12,500 facilities that stored hazardous chemicals in greater than specified quantities. Facility operators had to arrange for an independent third-party auditor to conduct a compliance audit after any reportable accident. To prevent future accidents, the regulations required certain "high-hazard" facilities to conduct a "root cause" analysis as part of any investigation of a catastrophic release or a near miss. High-hazard facilities also had to implement emergency response enhancements aimed at ensuring better coordination between their personnel and emergency responders. Owners of "very high-hazard" facilities had to explore the practicability of employing "inherently safer technologies," such as using less dangerous chemicals. The regulations required facilities to share basic risk information with the public, but it gave them a great deal of discretion in determining what information to share.[43]

Industry groups filed a motion to reconsider the regulations with the Trump EPA and urged it to delay the compliance deadlines. In mid-March 2017, Administrator Pruitt granted the motion to reconsider and extended the March deadlines for three months to June 2017. The agency's attempt to extend the deadlines for an additional twenty months, however, was rejected by the D.C. Circuit Court of Appeals in August 2018. Consequently, the process safety, third-party auditing, and emergency coordination requirements became immediately effective.[44] But not for long.

In December 2019, the EPA published regulations eliminating all of the Obama regulations except for a somewhat weakened version of the requirement that facilities work more closely with first responders. Several environmental groups, fifteen states, and the United Steelworkers Union challenged the rollback in the D.C. Circuit Court of Appeals. A series of deadly explosions at Texas chemical plants following the rollback, including the Port Neches explosion described in Chapter 1, highlighted the need for better federal protections, but these would not be forthcoming during the Trump administration.[45]

Demolishing Environmental Protections

Although past Republican administrations dating back to the Reagan administration had attempted to roll back environmental regulations, the Trump administration was unique in the number of regulations it targeted and the speed with which it attempted to repeal them. By the end of the Trump administration, agencies had repealed or revised more than 125 regulations and policies aimed at protecting the environment.[46]

The most consequential of the environmental rollbacks was the revision of the Obama regulation defining the "waters of the United States." Anyone who discharges pollutants into the "navigable waters" of the United States must have an EPA-issued permit. Likewise, anyone who wants to dredge or fill "navigable waters" must obtain a permit from the U.S. Army Corps of Engineers. The Clean Water Act defines "navigable waters" to mean "the waters of the United States," a circular definition that appears to eliminate the navigability requirement. The Supreme Court, however, has insisted that the concept of navigability still plays a role in limiting the permit requirements.[47]

Rivers and lakes are unquestionably navigable waters, but the EPA and the Corps of Engineers have struggled for decades to define the "waters of the United States" in a way that complies with the Supreme

Court's erratic opinions on the extent to which that phrase limited their power to protect wetlands and streams that did not flow continuously. The Supreme Court took up the issue most recently in 2006 in the *Rapanos* case, but the justices could not agree on the appropriate test to apply. Relying on Webster's Dictionary, Justice Antonin Scalia in an opinion joined by three other justices concluded that the term did not include ephemeral or intermittent streams or most wetlands. Relying on prior precedent, Justice Anthony Kennedy interpreted the term to include all waters that had a "significant nexus" to a navigable stream.[48]

During the Obama administration, the Corps and the EPA attempted to provide some certainty by providing a definitive definition of "waters of the United States" that reflected both the intent of the Clean Water Act and the relevant science. The so-called WOTUS rule that they published in June 2015 adopted Justice Kennedy's "significant nexus" test and attempted to ensure that its application reflected the best available science.[49] Industry, environmental groups, and thirty-eight states challenged the rule in various district and appellate courts. Scott Pruitt represented the state of Oklahoma in the litigation. After several courts issued orders staying the rule's application, it remained in effect in only twenty-three states and the District of Columbia.[50]

In late February 2017, President Trump signed a short executive order directing the EPA and the Corps of Engineers to review the WOTUS rule and publish a notice proposing to revise it in a manner "consistent with" Justice Scalia's extremely narrow definition in *Rapanos*. President Trump was laboring under a conflict of interest, because a narrow definition would benefit some of his golf courses that were located near or on wetlands. The American Farm Bureau Federation suggested a "rubber duck" test for navigability. It created a large flock of rubber ducks, attached to each of which was the message, "If you can't float us, it's not a WOTUS."[51]

The final WOTUS replacement rule that the Trump administration published in April 2020 rejected the significant nexus test and created a narrow definition of "waters of the United States" that looked a lot like the Scalia definition. Most lakes and ponds were covered, but artificial lakes located in upland waters were not. Most ditches were excluded, unless they were used for navigation or affected by the tides. Wetlands separated from other waters by dikes, barriers, or similar structures were included if there was a "direct hydrologic surface connection" to jurisdictional waters. Connection through groundwater, which is typical of many wetlands, did not count. Ephemeral streams that flowed only in direct response to rainfall or snowfall events were excluded, as were most intermittent streams. The EPA's Science Advisory Board criticized the agency's failure to base the definition on the multitude of scientific studies demonstrating that wetlands, ephemeral streams, and ditches were intimately connected to larger bodies of water through groundwater and intermittent surface water.[52]

Arguing that the Trump rollback endangered more that forty thousand waterways, environmental groups, Native American tribes, and more than a dozen states challenged the rollback in federal district courts throughout the country. The American Farm Bureau, the U.S. Chamber of Commerce, and the American Petroleum Institute intervened on behalf of the Trump administration to defend the rule. None of the lawsuits was resolved before the end of the Trump administration. On his first day in office, President Biden announced that the EPA and the Corps of Engineers would be reviewing and revising the Trump administration regulations, but he left the Trump rule in place in the interim. In late August 2021, a federal district court in Arizona set aside the Trump regulations, holding that the agencies had apparently disregarded some of their own scientific findings regarding the impact that polluting excluded wetlands and intermittent streams would have on larger bodies of water. In the interim, the Trump administration had allowed more than three hundred projects across the country to proceed without permits.[53]

Demolishing Endangered Species Protections

The Endangered Species Act flatly prohibits any federal agency from engaging in any action, including leasing and permitting, that is "likely to jeopardize the continued existence of any endangered species or threatened species." The statute further prohibits anyone from "taking," where "taking" is defined to mean hunting, trapping, or even harassing, animals and plants on the lists of endangered and threatened species prepared by the Department of the Interior's Fish and Wildlife Service (for terrestrial and aquatic species) and the Department of Commerce's National Marine Fisheries Service (for marine species). Fish and Wildlife maintains and periodically modifies lists of endangered and threatened species. The taking of endangered or threatened animals is permitted where it is "incidental to, and not the purpose of, the carrying out of an otherwise lawful activity."[54]

Permitting agencies must ensure that the permitted activities are "not likely to jeopardize the continued existence of" a listed endangered or threatened species or to "result in the destruction or adverse modification" of designated "habitat" that is "critical" to the species' continued existence. When an agency determines that a permitting action "may affect" a listed species or critical habitat, it must consult with the Fish and Wildlife Service. If the service determines that a proposed project is not likely to jeopardize a listed species but will result in the taking of a few members of the species, the project may not go forward unless the service issues an "incidental take" permit setting out enforceable limits on the quantity that may be taken. A negative review can delay a project or result in its disapproval.[55]

In August 2019, the Trump Fish and Wildlife Service published final regulations that profoundly affected many aspects of the implementation of the Endangered Species Act. Among other things, they reversed a decades-old presumption that threatened species were entitled to the same protections as endangered species. They also reduced the time horizon the agency used for listing threatened species, which restricted the department's ability to consider long-term trends like climate change in deciding whether to list a species. In a separate regulation published in mid-December 2020, the service limited the department's definition of "critical habitat" to exclude areas that an endangered species had abandoned but would need to survive once it recovered.[56]

Arguing that the regulations "crash[ed] a bulldozer through the Endangered Species Act's lifesaving protections for America's most vulnerable wildlife," environmental groups and attorneys general representing seventeen states challenged the regulations in federal district courts in California and Hawaii. The courts had not acted by the end of the Trump administration. The Biden administration announced in June 2021 that it would be revisiting the regulations, but the Trump regulations remain in effect, and threatened and endangered species remain at greater risk until the department completes the rulemaking process.[57]

Demolishing Public Resource Protections

Trump's Department of the Interior undertook the most radical transformation of the lands that the federal government holds in trust for Native Americans and for the American people since President Theodore Roosevelt first set out to protect that national heritage.[58] One of the department's top priorities was a rollback of President Obama's recent expansions of several national monuments in the West.

From sixty miles away, the two buttes resemble the ears of a bear emerging from the flat southeastern Utah horizon. The surrounding area is a red rock desert plateau pierced by canyons carved out over eons by tributaries of the Colorado River. The indigenous people who centuries ago named the region "Bears Ears" left behind thousands of works of art on the red cliff walls, along with many ancient ruins and hundreds of thousands of remnants of prior matrilineal civilizations that remain well preserved by the dry climate. Anglo Mormons, whose ancestors settled in the area during the nineteenth century, believed that they were destined by divine provenance to live and prosper there. In more recent times, the stark beauty of the place and the extraordinary prehistoric pueblos built into the canyon walls have attracted visitors from around the country.[59]

Beneath some of the land, however, lie shale deposits that might yield millions of barrels of oil and gas to companies with the wherewithal to drill. The land also contains deposits of uranium for future mining. Royalties from mineral extraction helped build roads, hospitals, and schools in the small towns of San Juan County—population 17,000.

The Antiquities Act, which was signed into law by President Theodore Roosevelt in 1906, allows the president to "declare by public proclamation historic landmarks, historic and prehistoric structures, and other objects of historic or scientific interest" that are located on federal land to be "national monuments." It is a crime to disturb protected parcels within the monuments without a permit.[60]

After three years of intense negotiations during which representatives of the tribes and the local Anglo community could not reach agreement, President Obama in late December 2016 issued a proclamation creating the Bears Ears National Monument. The proclamation preserved existing grazing leases and allowed new grazing leases on some of the 1.35-million-acre monument. But it prohibited any oil and gas drilling or mining for minerals on the land. It required the

Departments of Agriculture and the Interior to prepare a management plan and write regulations to ensure sound management of the lands.[61]

The proclamation was not well received by the dominant political elites of southeastern Utah. Speaker of the Utah House of Representatives Greg Hughes called the proclamation a "blatant federal land grab," an odd characterization of a redesignation of land that already belonged to the federal government, but characteristic of the paternalistic view that many Anglo Westerners take toward land that the federal government long ago took from the tribes. Although the designation was not as extensive as they had hoped, the tribes were generally pleased with the outcome.[62] Their joy would soon turn to anger.

Before a Salt Lake City crowd of mostly Anglo supporters chanting "four more years," President Trump announced in December 2017 that he had come "to take a very historic action to reverse federal overreach and restore the rights of this land to your citizens." The proclamation he signed modified the Bears Ears National Monument by dividing it into two much smaller management areas and reducing it from 1.3 million to 228,000 acres. The monument still protected the iconic buttes, but a great deal of land containing protected objects was now open for oil and gas leasing, mining patents, cattle grazing, timber production, and more destructive recreational use. In late July 2019, the Bureau of Land Management finalized a plan for the 202,000 acres that were left in the monument, allowing all-terrain vehicles to operate in some areas, permitting cattle-grazing lessees to clear vegetation by dragging a thick chain between two bulldozers, allowing construction of utility lines and cell towers within the monument, and removing five Native Americans from the management advisory board. In response to the Trump administration's actions, the World Monuments Fund in October 2019 added Bears Ears to its worldwide list of endangered cultural sites.[63]

Several tribes and environmental groups filed a lawsuit in the District Court for the District of Columbia challenging Trump's redesignation of Bears Ears and a similar redesignation that shrank the nearby Grand Staircase-Escalante National Monument to half its original size. The state of Utah and the American Farm Bureau intervened on behalf of the government. The court, however, stayed the litigation after President Biden ordered the Department of the Interior to review the Trump actions with an eye toward restoring the original boundaries of both monuments. In the meantime, the Bureau of Land Management leased out previously included land for grazing and mineral development, and hundreds of thousands of tourists swarmed the area, some of whom looted the former tribal settlements of fossils and relics.[64]

Demolishing Pocketbook Protections

From the moment Mick Mulvaney became acting director of the Consumer Financial Protection Bureau, he made it his mission to roll back every regulation to which the financial services industry objected. Kathy Kraninger, who took over in December 2018, pursued that goal with equal vigor. After the arbitration rule that Congress repealed under the Congressional Review Act (described in the Introduction), the most far-reaching financial protection regulation issued during the Obama administration was its payday lending rule.

Payday loans are loans for small dollar amounts (usually less than $500) that consumers with limited savings can take out to cope with financial shortfalls, often due to unexpected medical expenses or loss of employment. They are easily obtained in a matter of hours, either at storefront locations or online, at sky-high interest rates ranging from an average of around 400 percent to as much as 1,950 percent. Most of the 12 million annual payday borrowers are low-income workers living from paycheck to paycheck, and they use the loans to pay for necessities like groceries, rent, or electric bills.[65] Payday lenders count on borrowers' not being able to pay the full amount of the loan, plus fees and interest, at the end of the typical two-week loan period, so that they will need another loan at the same high interest rate with another fee. The bureau discovered that four out of five payday loans were rolled over, and half of those loans were rolled over at least ten times, with additional fees added each time. By 2017, there were more payday loan stores in the United States than McDonald's restaurants, and payday lending had blossomed into a $46 billion industry.[66]

The 2010 Dodd–Frank Act specifically authorized the Consumer Financial Protection Bureau to write regulations governing payday lending, and the staff spent five years assembling a massive rulemaking record, meeting with stakeholders, and preparing an extensive cost-benefit analysis to support the major rulemaking initiative. The Obama payday lending rule was finalized in October 2017. It applied to loans with terms of forty-five days or less, vehicle title loans, and some long-term installment loans. The rule contained two major provisions—the mandatory underwriting (ability to repay) requirements and payment practices rules. Under the mandatory underwriting requirements, lenders could either document that borrowers could afford to repay their loans at the outset or observe specified limitations on loan amounts and number of loan rollovers. The payment practices rule required a covered lender to give the consumer notice of its first attempt to withdraw funds from an account, and it made it unlawful for a lender to attempt to withdraw payments from borrowers' accounts for certain loans after two prior attempts had failed because of insufficient funds without a specific authorization from the consumer.[67]

On the day that the payday lending rule was to go into effect in January 2018, Acting Director Mulvaney announced that the bureau would be reconsidering the regulation. Having spent years preparing the regulations, however, few employees with expertise on the bureau's staff were willing to be part of gutting them. High-level Mulvaney appointees instructed staff economists and social scientists to research only Mulvaney's preferred changes, whether or not other options would be more efficient or effective. While the bureau staff labored, executives from two of the nation's largest payday lenders were premium sponsors for a $100,000-per-person fundraiser for the Trump reelection campaign in October 2019 featuring a keynote address by Vice President Mike Pence. So much for draining the swamp.[68]

The bureau revoked the Obama regulation's mandatory underwriting requirements in July 2020. Consumer groups challenged the action in a D.C. federal district court. The Biden-appointed acting head of the Consumer Financial Protection Bureau in late March 2021 announced that the bureau would be revisiting the payday lending rule yet again. In the meantime, however, payday lenders in most states are free to entice vulnerable people into loans they cannot afford and reap obscene profits as their customers sink deeper into debt.[69]

The Shock Doctrine During the Pandemic

While most Americans were focusing on coping with the disorienting pandemic in the spring of 2020, the Trump administration accelerated its deregulatory agenda in a classic invocation of the "shock doctrine." Free-market fundamentalist guru Milton Friedman recognized in the 1960s that natural disasters and war provide opportunities for radical change, and he recommended that free marketeers take advantage of those opportunities by pressing for deregulation and privatization to meet the emergencies. The prescription calls for a heavy dose of nationalism to mask the suffering of the victims of the lost public protections. Then, when the crisis is over, make the temporary changes permanent, with the overall result being a reduced role for government in society. With the onset of the COVID-19 pandemic, the Heritage Foundation created a seventeen-member commission to recommend deregulatory

actions to the administration, and the National Association of Manufacturers produced an "American Renewal Action Plan" with similar
recommendations.[70]

For the Trump administration, which was already advancing the
demolition agenda, the first response to the pandemic was to deny
requests to slow down the process of rolling back protective regulations.
Trump appointees in the agencies told the staffs that they would tolerate
no slippage in schedules despite the inconveniences caused by the pandemic. The agencies then took advantage of the fact that people were
preoccupied with the pandemic to rush through deregulatory changes
unrelated to the pandemic with minimal pushback. The administration
pressed ahead with regulations making it easier to get permit approvals under the National Environmental Policy Act, regulations making
it harder for the EPA to tighten ambient air–quality standards, regulations increasing allowable greenhouse gas emissions from automobiles,
regulations reducing protections for migratory birds, regulations rolling back protections from abusive payday lenders, regulations easing
requirements for permitting liquid natural gas terminals, regulations
rolling back requirements for oil and gas producers to control methane
emissions, and many others.[71]

In May 2020, President Trump signed an executive order that directed executive branch agencies to address the continuing emergency
by "rescinding, modifying, waiving, or providing exemptions from
regulations and other requirements that may inhibit economic recovery." In addition, the president ordered the agencies to review the six
hundred standards that they had temporarily suspended, modified, or
waived during the COVID-19 emergency with an eye toward making
the changes permanent. The Competitive Enterprise Institute suggested (erroneously) that the emergency order gave the agencies authority
to roll back regulations without the otherwise applicable procedural
requirements of the Administrative Procedure Act. And the adminis-

tration reached out to the institute and other conservative groups for suggestions about which regulations to roll back under cover of the crisis.[72]

To speed up deliveries of "essential goods" during the pandemic, the Federal Motor Carrier Safety Administration in mid-March 2020 suspended its regulations limiting the amount of time that drivers could be on the road in any given day for trucks carrying medical supplies, hand sanitizer, personal protective gear, and food for restocking store shelves. It was the first time that the agency had ever suspended its hours-of-service regulations on a nationwide basis. While the suspension was in effect, Amber Sahagun, a thirty-year-old mother of two, was crushed to death when the car in which she was a passenger was hit by a tractor-trailer truck carrying essential goods and being driven at a high rate of speed by an operator who had been behind the wheel for sixteen hours straight without a rest break. The motto in the industry is "If the wheels aren't turnin', nobody's earnin'."[73]

In the environmental protection arena, the Trump administration implemented special deregulatory measures, some of which responded to concerns about employee exposure to the coronavirus, but many of which were aimed at making it easier for companies to remain profitable during the accompanying recession. In September 2020, the Department of the Interior forwarded to the White House a list of fifty major energy infrastructure projects that it planned to expedite in an effort to jump-start the pandemic-stalled economy. And the Pipeline and Hazardous Materials Safety Administration extended the deadlines for compliance with a new pipeline safety regulation.[74]

To deal with a distorted market for many food items due to increased demand for retail foods and decreased demand for institutional food, the Food and Drug Administration issued a temporary rule allowing retail establishments to sell foods labeled for institutions, even though they were missing the familiar nutrition information. It also allowed food chains to make minor changes to the contents of standard menu items sold for takeout without changing the menu labels for those items. Later, it allowed food manufacturers to substitute plentiful for scarce ingredients without changing the ingredients labels, and it allowed vending machine operators to omit calorie counts. Food safety advocates worried that people with food allergies and dietary restrictions would no longer be able to trust food labels. They were alarmed when the Food and Drug Administration suggested, pursuant to President Trump's executive order, that it was considering making some of the deregulatory changes permanent.[75]

Education Secretary Betsy DeVos advanced her stymied efforts to privatize elementary and secondary schools by issuing an interim final rule diverting millions of dollars appropriated on an emergency basis for schools in high-poverty areas to well-off students attending private schools. Instead of providing computers and internet access to students from low-income families to allow them to continue learning from home, DeVos steered federal dollars to the owners of for-profit charter schools. A federal judge in Washington enjoined the department from implementing the "reverse Robin Hood" rule in August 2020.[76]

Unprecedented Rollbacks in Congress

With Republicans in control of both houses of Congress at the outset of the Trump administration, the first order of business was to roll back recently issued Obama administration regulations under an obscure statute called the Congressional Review Act, described in the Introduction, which allowed Congress to overturn regulations issued at the end of the previous administration. The Koch-funded Freedom Partners issued a "Roadmap to Repeal" containing a list of dozens of Obama administration initiatives that should be overturned. This effort was by a considerable degree the most aggressive attempt ever to use the Congressional Review Act to eviscerate protective regulations. It resulted in the elimination of sixteen regulations, including the arbitration rule featured in the Introduction.[77] Among the sensible regulations that congressional Republicans and Trump terminated were a regulation protecting streams from environmentally devastating mountaintop-removal mines in Appalachia, a rule prohibiting hunters from using inhumane tactics such as killing mother wolves and their pups in their dens with gas and using donuts and other sweet baits to set up bears for easy kills, and a requirement that Social Security Administration personnel submit records to the national firearms background-check system of any Social Security recipients who were not allowed to possess guns because of severe mental illness.[78]

All of these repealed regulations had been enacted to protect real people and the environment from the harms caused by unfettered capitalism. The most striking thing about the damage attributable to this wave of repealed regulations was its utter randomness. None of the disapprovals was the subject of congressional hearings, none was debated in committee, and few received any serious debate on the floor of the House or Senate. The Congressional Review Act repeals received a good deal of attention in the trade press, and some attention in the mainstream media, but the coverage was usually overwhelmed by President Trump's latest tweets and outrages.[79]

After his first year in office, President Trump tweeted that his administration had "terminated more UNNECESSARY Regulations in just 12 months, than any other Administration has terminated during their full term in office."[80] By that time, the administration had in fact pulled back nearly all of the outstanding Obama administration proposals and initiated the process of repealing or revising most of the significant regulations that the Obama administration had finalized. But the Trump administration had only limited success in persuading federal courts that its actions were backed up by sound legal and technical analyses. As it continued to roll back protective regulations, the administration turned its attention to doing more permanent damage to the protective edifice by changing the techniques and methods that the agencies used to write new rules.

CHAPTER 8

SOPHISTICATED SABOTAGE

The Trump administration's rollbacks of existing regulations reduced protections that Congress meant for the government to provide, and they were easily identified and subject to reversal by courts or the Biden administration, albeit with some effort. The Trump administration, however, went beyond demolishing individual regulations to meddle with the underlying methodologies and practices that the agencies employed in writing protective regulations, changing the agencies' thinking about the need for and consequences of regulations. In the words of environmental activist Brett Hartl, the Trump administration was trying to "make it systematically harder for an agency to do the right thing." This form of "sophisticated sabotage" was much less transparent than the rollbacks, and it had far more staying power.[1]

Limiting Information Flows

Government agencies have traditionally been robust sources of accurate, policy-relevant information that both public policymakers and ordinary citizens need to make sound decisions. For example, the Department of Labor's Bureau of Labor Statistics has long been a trustworthy source of information on labor markets that businesses, investors, and government agencies constantly rely on to address employment issues. In the age of the internet, government agency websites have been vital sources of useful information for the public. The Trump administration did not attempt to cut off all government-generated information;

instead, it selectively stemmed the flow of information that could be used by agencies to support additional regulation or by the public to demand more regulation.

A good example is the demise of the electronic recordkeeping rule that the Occupational Safety and Health Administration published in May 2016. The regulation required all employers in high-risk industries to provide annual injury and illness summaries to the agency, and it required large employers to provide more detailed data from their injury logs and individual injury reports in electronic format. OSHA planned to use the electronic information to target its enforcement efforts. But it also planned to make the data available on its website after removing personally identifiable information. A panel of the National Academy of Sciences concluded that the rule would create a valuable source of information that scientists could use to identify causes of workplace accidents and illnesses. Worker advocates hoped that it would encourage employers to maintain safer workplaces so as to avoid damaging their reputations.[2]

The Trump administration was unimpressed. In late July 2017, OSHA proposed to drop the requirement that employers file injury and illness reports electronically. Its primary rationale was its concern for the privacy of the injured workers. Worker advocates pointed out that the regulation specifically declined to collect personally identifiable information, and the unions were not concerned about worker privacy. The National Institute for Occupational Safety and Health urged OSHA to leave the regulation in effect because it wanted access to the information in connection with its duty to recommend topics for future OSHA regulations. Rejecting these arguments, OSHA rescinded the electronic reporting requirements in January 2019 except for summaries of the information.[3] The electronic injury and illness data remain hidden in company files, where it is available to OSHA inspectors, but virtually useless for the agency's regulation writers, and unavailable to the public.[4]

Privatizing Standard Setting

The massive Deepwater Horizon oil spill of April 2010, which allowed oil to flow into the Gulf of Mexico at a rate of forty thousand barrels per day for eighty-seven days, inspired President Obama to create a new agency called the Bureau of Safety and Environmental Enforcement in the Department of the Interior to protect the oceans from such catastrophes in the future. In April 2016, this bureau published comprehensive regulations, called the Well Control Rule, that regulated the construction and operation of offshore drilling facilities, focusing on blowout-prevention technology, well design, and other safety-enhancing features. Environmental groups were not especially happy with the Obama regulations, in part because they relied too heavily on industry standards written by the American Petroleum Institute, a private standard-setting organization that was also the chief lobbying arm for the petroleum industry. But the regulations went beyond the industry standards in important regards, and they represented an improvement over the existing regulations.[5]

In late April 2017, President Donald Trump signed an executive order proclaiming an "America-first offshore energy strategy." The president instructed the Safety Bureau to review the Obama blowout-prevention rule for consistency with the Trump administration's policy to "encourage energy exploration and production." Soon thereafter, Trump appointed Scott Angelle to head the bureau. Angelle had been on the board of a major pipeline company, and he firmly believed that the federal government and the oil and gas industry should be partners in the enterprise of extracting minerals from beneath the ocean floor.[6]

An industry wish list presented to Angelle in September 2017 formed the basis for revisions to the blowout-prevention rule that the bureau published in May 2019. The bureau revised the Obama requirements to make them no more stringent than the petroleum industry standards. For example, where the Obama rules required operators to maintain drilling pressures within a specified "safe margin," the Trump revisions allowed them to adhere to an American Petroleum Institute memorandum that allowed further drilling for an additional 300 feet when pressures exceeded the margin. The bureau's staff did not agree with the industry that the revisions provided adequate protection, but Angelle ordered the drafters to remove sentences expressing the staff's reservations from the decision memos accompanying the regulations. When a staffer asked Angelle to put his orders in writing for the record, Angelle declined, saying that a record of his command was "not important." In the end, the petroleum industry got to write the regulations governing its undersea operations.[7]

The Trump Department of Energy went a step further and wrote reliance on industry standards into its procedures for crafting new and revised appliance-efficiency regulations. In February 2019, the department proposed changes to the "process rule," which specifies how the department goes about developing testing procedures for appliances. Among other things, the department proposed to require the staff to adopt any testing procedures issued by a recognized private entity so long as they were consistent with the relevant statute. Environmental groups and state attorneys general argued that it was wrong to adopt industry testing procedures automatically because the entities that wrote those procedures were often dominated by the regulated industries, which made the procedures inherently untrustworthy. The department finalized the proposal with few changes in February 2020. State attorneys general and environmental groups challenged the changes to the process rule in April 2020, but the proceedings were stayed after the Biden administration published a proposal to revise the Trump changes. In the meantime, department experts are compelled to incorporate the industry testing procedures as they conduct their five-year updates of the department's energy-efficiency regulations.[8]

MAGA Math

The problems with attempting to assign a cost to a ton of greenhouse gas emissions, referred to as the "social cost of carbon," are manifest Unlike conventional pollutants, the emissions do not directly cause harm to the people who are exposed to them. The emissions contribute to the global problems resulting from climate disruption. In addition, the fact that the harm may manifest itself decades in the future generates philosophical debates over the extent to which those future benefits should be discounted to present value because a dollar in hand is worth more than a dollar in the future. The answers to both of these questions can make an enormous difference in a cost-benefit analysis.

An interagency working group appointed by President Obama set the social cost of carbon dioxide emissions at $36 per ton in 2015. By the end of the Obama administration, agencies had relied on this calculation more than 150 times in taking various regulatory actions. A federal court of appeals approved of the Department of Energy's reliance on the Obama social-cost estimate in upholding its energy-efficiency standards for commercial refrigeration equipment. And a January 2017 report by the National Academy of Sciences concluded that the working group's approach was appropriate.[9]

President Trump's "energy independence" executive order disbanded the interagency working group and withdrew all of the technical support documents underlying the group's estimates. With the stroke of a Sharpie pen, the initiative was dead. The president instructed the agencies to rely on a much less precautionary guidance document prepared by the Office of Management and Budget during the George W. Bush administration, and he told agencies to limit their estimates to impacts within the United States. The resulting estimate of the social cost of carbon dioxide emissions dropped from $36 per ton to $1 per ton.[10]

The Trump administration's approach, referred to as MAGA math by one critic, greatly devalued future benefits and did not comport with economic reality. Limiting the benefits to those enjoyed by people in the United States was also inappropriate for a pollutant that affects the entire world. The approach was also short-sighted. Americans will have to deal with the consequences of a more acidic ocean, the higher prices paid for food imported from countries suffering droughts, and the migration from countries to the south resulting from increased global temperatures.[11]

The Trump administration also insisted that agencies writing major regulations and deregulatory actions demonstrate to the White House Office of Management and Budget that their benefits exceeded the costs they imposed on the regulated industries.[12] Because the benefits of most existing regulations were already deemed to exceed their costs, the Trump administration needed to come up with a way to increase cost estimates or decrease benefits estimates to justify repealing them. It found a silver bullet in the previous administrations' consideration of the "co-benefits" that resulted when technologies installed to limit a target pollutant also limited nontarget pollutants. Nearly all economists believed that co-benefits should be included in the benefits attributable to government regulations, and the EPA had considered co-benefits consistently across all presidential administrations from Reagan through Obama. Former EPA Administrator William Reilly said it makes sense to take co-benefits into account because they give the agency "several bangs for the buck."[13]

The issue came up early in the Trump administration as the coal industry pressured the EPA to withdraw the Obama administration's calculations of the costs and benefits of reducing emissions of mercury and other hazardous pollutants from power plant emissions. The impact assessment estimated $6 million in health benefits attributable to reducing mercury emissions. The standards, however, would also bring about much larger reductions in emissions of particulate matter, which increased mortality rates in exposed populations. Adding in these co-benefits yielded overall benefits of somewhere between $37 billion and $90 billion. The EPA predicted that companies would spend $9.6 billion to comply with the standards.[14]

By the time that Donald Trump was inaugurated, nearly all of the nation's coal-fired power plants complied with the Obama standards or had been retired. As a practical matter, that meant that the cost of leaving the Obama-era standards in place would be virtually nonexistent. In fact, electric power companies did not want the agency to relax the standards, because they had already made the investments necessary to comply. That inconvenient fact did not, however, stop the Trump administration from reconsidering the Obama assessment. In late December 2018, the agency concluded that the costs of compliance (which the industry had already borne) exceeded the benefits. It reached this conclusion by ignoring the co-benefits of reducing particulate matter (which were by then being realized by vulnerable populations living downwind of power plants).[15]

Excluding co-benefits meant that it was no longer "appropriate and necessary" to regulate mercury emissions from coal-fired power plants. That conclusion, however, did not affect power plant emissions, because virtually all of the operating plants already complied with the standards that the Trump EPA now found to be inappropriate and unnecessary. But it did set a precedent for future EPA efforts to regulate hazardous air pollutants from other industrial sources. Failing to consider co-benefits in the future would make it harder for the EPA to justify stringent protections over industry objections that their benefits did not justify the costs they imposed.[16]

The agency's changed methodology for calculating benefits was roundly criticized by environmental groups, legal scholars, and economists. Former NYU Law School Dean Richard Revesz noted that the EPA was careful to exclude indirect benefits while including indirect costs, thus skewing the cost-benefit balance against benefits. The problem with the Trump administration's argument that the EPA could use its other authorities to achieve the co-benefits is that it doesn't always do so. At the same time that the EPA threw out the co-benefits of reduced particulate emissions in the mercury rule, it declined to tighten the national ambient air–quality standards for particulate matter. Alan Krupnick, an economist with Resources for the Future, saw the mercury proposal as a stalking horse for a broader initiative to change the way the agency thought about the benefits of environmental regulations, which would make it easier to "justify loosening many other pollution regulations."[17]

The broader initiative to which Krupnick alluded was an agency-wide attempt to write binding guidelines for conducting cost-benefit analyses in all of its regulatory programs. EPA Administrator Andrew Wheeler told attendees at a Heritage Foundation symposium that he hoped that changing the way that the agency went about calculating the costs and benefits of regulations would "lock in" the Trump administration roadblocks to future regulation. Lobbyists for a wide variety of industry groups beat a familiar path to EPA headquarters to suggest ways to "improve" cost-benefit analysis. At the top of their list was the elimination of co-benefits from regulatory impact analyses. Fortunately for them, the lead political appointee in charge of the EPA initiative was a former lobbyist for the National Association of Manufacturers.[18]

The cost-benefit guidelines that the EPA published in early December 2020 applied to analyses prepared to support regulations issued under the Clean Air Act. They did not require the EPA staff to ignore co-benefits, but they instructed the staff to clearly and specifically identify the direct benefits "arising from the environmental improvement" that the relevant EPA action addressed, and to distinguish those benefits from the co-benefits in the cost-benefit analysis. The EPA could still take co-benefits into account in future decisions, but it would have to explain why it was doing so. Administrator Wheeler hoped that the guidelines would create a "cause of action" for companies to challenge future EPA actions based on cost-benefit analyses that did not comply with the new requirements.[19]

The Biden administration issued an "interim final rule" in May 2021 rescinding the Trump cost-benefit analysis guidelines. The EPA took the position that the guidelines and their repeal came within the Administrative Procedure Act's exemption for rules of agency organization, procedure, or practice and therefore did not require public comment. Industry opponents are biding their time until the EPA prepares a cost-benefit analysis that does not comply with the Trump guidelines to challenge the rescission. The battle over cost-benefit analysis is far from over.[20]

Gutting Environmental Reviews

The National Environmental Policy Act of 1970, the "Magna Carta" of environmental law, requires federal agencies to prepare environmental impact statements detailing the environmental effects of every "major federal action significantly affecting the quality of the human environment" and available alternatives to such actions. The requirement has an indirect effect on private-sector activities that require federal approval—including oil and gas leases, pipelines, and highways—because the permitting agency is obliged to prepare an impact statement if the activity is major and has a significant impact on the environment. The statute does not, however, require that the agency reach any particular substantive outcome; the agency just has to prepare and consider the impact statement. The statute also created the Council on Environmental Quality to advise the president and oversee its implementation, but the federal courts concluded that the impact statement requirement was judicially enforceable under the Administrative Procedure Act. Federal courts decide between 100 and 150 cases under the National Environmental Policy Act every year challenging agency failures to prepare impact statements and challenging the adequacy of the impact statements that they do prepare.[21]

At the outset of the Trump administration, energy development companies and conservative activist groups lobbied the president to undertake significant reforms to the regulations that the council wrote in 1978 to govern how agencies prepared and used impact statements. Business Republicans pointed to a Montana court's injunction halting construction on the massive Keystone XL pipeline as a clear indication that the regulations should be amended to make it easier to obtain permits and to reduce the power of the courts to stop ongoing projects. Environmental groups responded that the judicial reversals showed that the Act was forcing agencies to pay attention to the environmental consequences of approving projects like the Keystone XL pipeline that could irreversibly change the planet. They pointed out that because the council's regulations excluded whole categories of projects, federal agencies prepared a total of only around five hundred impact statements per year.[22]

In a carefully staged event in Georgia, President Trump in July 2020 unveiled amendments to the 1978 regulations as "part of my administration's fierce commitment to slashing the web of needless bureaucracy that is holding back our citizens." While many of the Trump changes consisted of reshuffling requirements and eliminating obsolete provisions, some changes had the potential to bring about profound changes in the way federal agencies implemented the Act. Many of those changes were directed toward provisions in the regulations that environmental groups had successfully invoked in challenges to Trump administration energy dominance projects. For example, Mary Neumayr, head of the Trump administration's Council on Environmental Quality, acknowledged that one goal of the changes was to relieve agencies of the need to address the impact of their actions on climate change.[23]

The most significant change was the elimination of the requirement that agencies consider cumulative effects when deciding whether an action would have a "significant" impact on the environment, and when preparing impact statements. The change codified a strategy that Trump administration agencies were employing to avoid considering greenhouse gas emissions when they approved energy projects. Rather than analyze the cumulative effects of all oil and gas leases in a particular shale play, the agency would conduct a "site-specific" analysis for each lease. Since the emissions from no single lease were sufficient to cross the "significance" threshold, the agency avoided considering the cumulative effect of all of the leases in the shale play.[24]

The regulations further limited the indirect effects that impact statements had to examine to those that were "reasonably foreseeable" and that had a "reasonably close causal relationship" to the proposed action. Agencies no longer had to consider effects that were "remote in time, geographically remote, or the result of a lengthy causal chain." The obvious motivation behind this limitation was a desire to relieve agencies of their obligation to consider such indirect effects as rising sea levels and fiercer wildfires when approving oil pipelines and coal leases that would result in massive emissions of greenhouse gases when the oil and coal were burned.[25]

Another aggressive change was the limitation that the updated regulations attempted to place on the ability of courts to review challenges to agency actions that allegedly failed to comply with the National Environmental Policy Act. The new regulations required that the decisionmaker for the lead agency "certify" that he or she had considered the information, alternatives, and analysis submitted by the public during the comment period. The regulations then created a "rebuttable presumption" that the agency had considered those submissions for purposes of judicial review.[26] The clear intent was to preclude challengers from arguing in court that the agency had not considered the impact statement and/or comments. But the fact that a decisionmaker signs a boilerplate certification does not make the certification true.

Industry trade associations, the U.S. Chamber of Commerce, and conservative think tanks applauded the changes as a much-needed modernization of ancient regulations that were holding back critical energy and infrastructure projects. Environmental groups called the changes "the single biggest giveaway to polluters in the past 40 years." Rather than speeding up infrastructure projects, they predicted, the changes would only increase the controversy and litigation over such projects. Environmental justice groups warned that the effects of the changes would be felt most acutely by low-income Americans and minorities, because an agency would not have to consider the cumulative effects of multiple industrial facilities bordering a low-income neighborhood. The regulations went into effect in early September 2020, after a Virginia district court declined to issue a preliminary injunction against their implementation.[27]

Killing Compensatory Mitigation

One way to comply with an agency's environmental obligations is to mitigate unavoidable environmental damage caused by a project by acquiring and protecting otherwise unprotected land or resources in a process called compensatory mitigation. In the 1980s, compensatory mitigation became a popular vehicle for acquiring permits to develop wetlands, as developers purchased and protected equivalent wetlands in nearby locations to compensate for those that they destroyed. Mitigation became so popular that entrepreneurs developed "mitigation banks" of undeveloped resources to be sold to companies that needed to offset environmental damage caused by their projects.[28]

In November 2013, President Obama signed a presidential memorandum requiring agencies to adopt "clear and consistent" mitigation policies. The memo encouraged agencies to secure mitigation in advance of the projects needing mitigation, and it established a goal of "net benefit or, at a minimum, no net loss" for the natural resources that agencies were responsible for protecting.[29]

The Trump administration took a dim view of mitigation, equating it with extortion. President Trump's "energy independence" executive order rescinded President Obama's memorandum. Memoranda issued by the Interior Department's Bureau of Land Management and Fish and Wildlife Service in July 2018 prohibited staff from explicitly or implicitly requiring compensatory mitigation as part of the approval process for any project. And the Obama administration's goal of net benefit or no net loss was out the window.[30]

The Trump administration's position mystified many observers because compensatory mitigation had been supported by presidents of both parties in the past, and it was consistent with the emissions trading paradigm that free marketeers had advocated for decades. Many companies, environmental groups, and the conservative Western Governors Association viewed it as a common-sense tool for facilitating compromise among warring factions that allowed projects to go forward that otherwise would have wound up in court for years. The uncompromising Trump administration, however, wanted none of it.[31]

Stiffing States

Trumpian populists purport to be for states' rights because state governments are closer to the people than the distant federal government. In practice, however, they prefer the federal government when state governments are advancing policies they oppose. In this, they find common ground with free-market fundamentalists, who are agnostic about the level of government, and business Republicans, who seek out whatever government level best advances business interests on any particular issue. A good example is the Trump administration's assault on the power of states to veto federal permits under the Clean Water Act.

Under the Clean Water Act, an applicant for a federal permit to discharge pollutants into the waters of the United States must obtain from the affected state a certification that the discharge will comply with the state's water-quality standards. The certification can specify any limitations and monitoring requirements necessary to ensure that the discharge will comply with those standards. The limitations included in the certification then become requirements of the federal permit.[32]

At the beginning of the Trump administration, energy companies complained about the certification process after New York refused to certify a high-profile pipeline because of fears that it might leak into the state's rivers and streams, and the state of Washington refused to certify a massive coal terminal, citing concerns about water pollution, air pollution, and the contribution to global warming of the coal that would be shipped to China and elsewhere. Energy trade associations and the Competitive Enterprise Institute pressed the Trump administration to set deadlines for state permit reviews and to limit the scope of certification denials to impacts on state water-quality standards.[33]

In an April 2019 signing ceremony attended by hard-hatted union members in the heart of Texas oil and gas country, President Trump blamed entrenched bureaucrats and radical activists for holding up badly needed energy infrastructure projects. He then signed an executive order that required the EPA to issue regulations making it easier for companies to receive state certifications.[34]

Environmental groups viewed the executive order as an effort to cut states and local communities out of the decision-making process for pipelines and other major energy initiatives. A coalition of states argued that limiting state authority to certify federally permitted projects was inconsistent with the Trump administration's professed commitment to cooperative federalism. They pointed out that certification denials were extremely rare, and federal courts were available to overturn unjustified denials. Nor was it necessary to impose strict limits on the time states took to issue certifications, because on average it took only 132 days to process certification requests.[35]

Their pleas were unavailing. In early July 2020, the EPA published final regulations that limited the reach of state certifications to direct impacts on state water quality due to point sources. In particular, states would no longer be allowed to withhold certification based on a project's contribution to climate disruption. The regulations also allowed federal agencies to specify a "reasonable" deadline of less than one year for states to complete their certifications. Even before the EPA finalized the regulation, the Corps of Engineers announced that it would be giving states only sixty days to make their certifications except in rare circumstances. The EPA ignored the argument of state officials that firm deadlines would allow companies to simply "run out the clock" before complying with state agency demands for critical information needed to certify the projects.[36]

Several states pointed out that the agency's position was inconsistent with a 1994 Supreme Court decision holding that the scope of the certification process went beyond water quality to include water quantity. In an audacious assertion of presidential power, however, the EPA concluded that the Supreme Court majority had misinterpreted the Clean Water Act and that Justice Clarence Thomas had gotten it right in his dissent. In the battle over the "waters of the United States" described in Chapter 7, the Trump administration justified its narrow definition by emphasizing the importance of allowing states to decide how to manage land use. Yet when it came to a statutory provision that explicitly delegated to states the power to veto federally permitted projects, cooperative federalism took a back seat. Senator Sheldon Whitehouse dubbed the Trump administration's approach to state-versus-federal power as "cooperative corporatism."[37]

In May 2021, the Biden administration announced that it would be revising the Trump regulation to give more power back to the states, but it was unclear how eager the administration was to empower states to veto infrastructure projects the federal government was touting as part of the economic recovery from the COVID-19 pandemic. It did not ask the court hearing a challenge to the Trump regulation to stay its applicability. The court finally ruled in late October 2021 that the Trump regulation was invalid because it departed from the Supreme Court precedent. In the meantime, pipelines that have received federal approval and state certification under the Trump EPA regulations continue to leak oil and toxic substances into lakes, rivers, and wetlands.[38]

Unforgiving Student Loans

In May 2015, Corinthian College, a massive for-profit institution with seventy thousand students at more than one hundred campuses across the country, collapsed after the Department of Education found that it had misrepresented its job placement rates. The collapse left 350,000 students and recent graduates with credits they could not transfer to other schools and questionable degrees that employers did not respect. And thousands of those students still owed the federal government for loans that they had taken out to obtain worthless educations. During the Clinton administration, the Department of Education had written "borrower defense" regulations permitting students to refuse to repay loans that they had obtained from for-profit educational institutions that deceptively lured them into taking out those loans. The Obama administration had completely forgiven thirty thousand loans in its last two weeks, but more than one hundred thousand claims remained unsettled at the outset of the Trump administration.[39]

The Trump Education Department adopted a far more restrictive approach to loan forgiveness. A committed free-market fundamentalist, Education Secretary Betsy DeVos was a huge fan of for-profit education, and she had little sympathy for students with government loans. During her leadership, only one full-time staff position was devoted to processing loan forgiveness claims. By April 2019, nearly 180,000 claims were pending. Interest on the loans continued to accumulate, and servicers hired by the department continued to badger the students and garnish their wages and income tax returns.[40]

Secretary DeVos was determined not to allow defrauded students to achieve full loan forgiveness if they received any benefit at all from the education. She therefore had the staff conjure up a formula for leaving past students on the hook for some proportion of their loans in all but the most egregious cases. The formula based the extent of partial cancellation on the subsequent income of students who graduated from the failed institution, which the department obtained from the Social Security Administration. But a federal magistrate judge in California threw out the formula because using the Social Security data violated students' privacy rights, and she issued an injunction prohibiting the department from attempting to collect any additional payments from the Corinthian College students who had brought the case. When lawyers for the students brought to the judge's attention the fact that loan servicing companies working for the Education Department were still dunning the students, the judge fined the department $100,000 for contempt of court.[41]

Undeterred, DeVos ordered the staff to come up with a new formula based on a comparison of the median incomes of defrauded students and the median incomes of students from comparable institutions. The larger the difference, the greater the relief. Representatives of the defrauded students called the move "a slap in the face of students," who were not included in the decision-making process. Meanwhile, for-profit trade schools, many of which had substantial online presences, thrived during the COVID-19 pandemic as recently unemployed people paid for additional training with government loans.[42]

The Trump administration's efforts to hamstring future administrations by meddling with agency methodologies, formulas, and practices were less visible than its direct attempts to roll back previous regulations, but they had greater potential for permanence. Some were successfully challenged in court. Some were subject to quick reversal by the Biden administration. For example, an outrageous attempt by the Trump EPA to sneak into a final standard for new coal-fired power plants a new policy that greenhouse gas emissions of up to 3 percent of total U.S. emissions—a huge amount—were not "significant," was quickly remanded to the Biden EPA, after the Biden EPA admitted that the Trump EPA had not provided notice to the public that the agency had such a drastic limitation in mind.[43] But other sophisticated efforts to sabotage the ability of future agencies to write progressive regulations will take a great deal of time and many agency resources to reverse. The full extent to which the Trump administration was able to "lock in" roadblocks to future regulation remains to be seen.

CHAPTER 9

PROMISCUOUS PERMITTING

As a young pilot, Rick Halford used to hunt polar bears from his airplane along the shores of Alaska's Bering Sea, but he was forced to quit when the federal government banned aerial hunting in the early 1970s. He then earned a living ferrying prospectors and geologists across parts of Alaska to search for promising mineral deposits. As he learned more about what they had in mind, however, he realized that he was participating in the eventual destruction of an irreplaceable area of natural beauty and a way of life.[1]

What they had in mind became apparent in February 2011, when Northern Dynasty Minerals Ltd, a Canadian company, revealed plans to dig an enormous surface mine to extract copper, gold, and other precious metals from a large area in the headwaters of two rivers flowing into Bristol Bay. With 57 billion pounds of copper and 70 million ounces of gold, the deposit was the largest untapped reserve of both of those metals in the world. Northern Dynasty wanted to dig an open pit to a depth three-quarters as deep as the Grand Canyon and extending almost seven square miles in area. In addition to the pit, the company would construct three massive mining waste impoundments covering another 8.7 square miles of highly productive land, streams, and wetlands. The mine's full footprint would be the size of Manhattan. The company would also construct support facilities, including a major road, a power plant and associated pipelines to provide natural gas, wastewater treatment plants, housing, and other infrastructure.[2]

The rugged beauty of southwestern Alaska's Bristol Bay area, where nine rivers and hundreds of feeder streams flow out of the mountains and into the Bering Sea, is matched only by its "unparalleled ecological value." The bay and the rivers that feed it are some of the most productive fisheries in the world. Tens of millions of salmon make their annual run through the bay and up the rivers to spawn. They produce around half of the world's sockeye salmon and large harvests of coho, chum, and pink salmon, as well as several other commercially valuable species. It is one of the few places left in the world that produces such bountiful harvests. The indigenous Yup'ik, Dena'ina, and Alutiiq tribes that have inhabited the area for four thousand years are three of the last remaining "salmon cultures" in the world. In addition to feeding the tribes, the watershed generates about $480 million in direct economic benefits and provides employment to more than fourteen thousand full- and part-time employees. An important reason for the remarkable productivity of the Bristol Bay area is the purity of the water.[3]

Along with copper and gold, the Pebble deposit contains millions of tons of sulfur that could convert to sulfuric acid and poison streams, rivers, and ultimately the bay. Open pit mines are notorious for leaking toxic heavy metals and hydrocarbons into ground and surface water. Breaches of tailings impoundments are not uncommon, and when that happens, millions of pounds of toxic material are released into whatever body of water is downstream of the release.[4]

Although Rick Halford fancied himself a rugged libertarian, he began to see the virtue of protective regulation, and he went to war against the Northern Dynasty project. A wealthy Anchorage businessman who owned a local fishing camp financed a public relations and lobbying campaign against the mine. Many in the community worried that, as Northern Dynasty put in roads and pipelines to serve the project, there would be a modern-day gold rush as other companies flooded the area with prospecting projects and additional mines. In a statewide referendum on the mine, 66 percent of voters supported a requirement that the Pebble project receive legislative approval before going forward.[5]

The project did not require legislative approval, but it did need the U.S. Army Corps of Engineers to issue a permit to fill in wetlands that pervaded the area. And that required a sign-off from the Environmental Protection Agency that the project would not result in unacceptable adverse effects on the environment. The permit requirement provided a legal tool for the mine's opponents to use in their efforts to stop the project in its tracks.

Some regulatory programs erect a presumption against engaging in specified activities that could be harmful to people, places, or the environment. In order to engage in such activities, a company has to obtain a permit from a federal agency. This usually requires the company to gather sufficient information to persuade the permitting agency that the activity will not pose an unacceptable risk of harm. Agencies with responsibility for protecting the nation's natural resources grant leases, easements, and permits to exploit those resources. They take their protective responsibilities into account when deciding whether to allow development on federal land and when attaching enforceable conditions to those permissions. Companies constantly complain that the government is overly protective and dilatory in issuing permits, leases, and the like. Reacting to those complaints, the Trump administration radically changed the agencies' approach to granting permissions to discharge pollutants, build pipelines, and otherwise develop publicly owned resources. In many cases, the agencies made obtaining approvals so easy that the permits lost much of their protective function.

The impetus for the Trump administration's promiscuous permitting came from the top. Days after the inauguration, President Trump signed an executive order directing federal agencies to expedite environmental reviews and approvals of high-priority infrastructure projects including pipelines, electricity transmission lines, bridges, and highways. The so-called energy independence executive order that President Trump signed in late March 2017 instructed federal agencies to review permitting programs that hindered private-sector development of the nation's energy resources. And in August 2017, President Trump signed an executive order requiring agencies involved in permitting major infrastructure projects to complete the permitting process within two years on average, a dramatic reduction from the prior average of 4.7 years.[6]

Pebble Mine

In July 2014, scientists in the EPA's Northwest regional office concluded that there was "reason to believe" that the proposed Pebble mine "could result in significant and unacceptable adverse effects on ecologically important streams, wetlands, lakes, and ponds and the fishery areas they support." The office further concluded that techniques available to mitigate the loss of affected streams and wetlands were "unlikely to offset" the mine's impacts on the area's water resources. For the first time ever, the Obama EPA proposed to veto a disposal site even before the company applied to the Corps for a permit.[7] The Trump administration, however, was more favorably inclined toward the project.

In early May 2017, newly appointed EPA Administrator Scott Pruitt met with Tom Collier, the CEO of Pebble Limited Partnership, a subsidiary of Northern Dynasty Corporation, to discuss the project. Hours later, Pruitt ordered the EPA staff to withdraw the proposed adverse effects determination. In early July 2017, the agency published a formal proposal to withdraw the Obama administration determination. The move was roundly condemned by Native American groups who depend on salmon for their livelihoods, commercial and recreational fishing companies, and environmental groups.[8]

In late December 2018, Northern Dynasty filed a formal application with the Corps of Engineers for a mine with a much smaller footprint than that in its original plan. The draft environmental impact statement that the Corps of Engineers circulated in February 2019 did not consider the possibility that the project would expand to develop more of the massive deposit in the future. It also failed to analyze the "worst case" spill scenario that the EPA had evaluated in its assessment. And it took different approaches toward evaluating the toxicity of mine tailings and toward predicting the project's effect on salmon spawning. Consequently, the Corps concluded that the project "would not be expected to have measurable effects" on overall salmon populations, though it was possible that fishermen would have to fish in different locations.[9]

Nobody believed that the company would stop once it had mined out all of the precious metal from the limited area specified in the application, after having spent tens of millions of dollars on roads, a power plant, and other infrastructure. Pebble's CEO candidly admitted that expanding the mine made sense to him. Even with the reduced footprint, the facility would have to reliably treat around 13,000 gallons of wastewater per minute, 5,000 gallons of which would have to be managed in perpetuity along with more than a billion tons of tailings.[10]

On June 26, 2019, on his way to a G-20 summit, Trump met aboard Air Force One with Alaska governor Mike Dunleavy, a strong supporter of the mine. The next day, EPA General Counsel Matthew Leopold, acting as administrator for the recused Andrew Wheeler, summoned staff to a video conference to tell them that the decision had been made to withdraw the proposed "unacceptable adverse effects" determination, and that there would be no further consideration of the matter. An EPA scientist who was on the call recalled that "[w]e were told to get out of the way and just make it happen." In August 2019, the EPA withdrew the Obama administration's proposed preemptive veto of the permit.[11]

Events took an ominous turn for the company in August 2020, however, when Donald Trump, Jr., an avid sportsman who had attended a bachelor party for his brother near Bristol Bay, tweeted his opposition to the project. A week later, Fox News pundit Tucker Carlson announced that he and a number of other "very conservative Republicans" opposed the mine. The president promised to take a "look at both sides" of the issue when it came up for decision. It was a classic example of advocates' using Fox News and the president's relatives to bring a president with few real convictions around to their point of view.[12]

The project suffered another body blow the next month when an environmental group whose members had posed as potential investors in a meeting with Northern Dynasty officials revealed tapes of the officials boasting that the mine would probably be operating for 120 years beyond the twenty years specified in its permit application. Northern Dynasty's CEO bragged that the company had access to the White House chief of staff any time it wanted, but it preferred to allow Alaska's governor to do the talking for the company. The day after the media revealed the contents of the tape, the CEO resigned. Finally, in late November 2020, the Corps dealt a fatal blow to the project, declaring it to be "contrary to the public interest." Northern Dynasty and the state of Alaska appealed the denial to an appellate entity within the Corps. But after Joe Biden promised to protect Bristol Bay from the proposed mine, prospects for the project were extremely dim.[13]

Dakota Access Pipeline

During the Obama administration, a consortium called Energy Transfer Partners proposed a 1,200-mile-long pipeline to ship 500,000 gallons of crude oil daily from the Bakken oil shale play in North Dakota across South Dakota and Iowa to Patoka, Illinois. The pipeline was essentially completed except for a segment that was to pass beneath Lake Oahe, a reservoir created by a dam on the Missouri River that extends from North Dakota into South Dakota and borders the Standing Rock and

Cheyenne River Sioux Reservations to the east. The Dakota Access pipeline was designed to cross the lake a half-mile to the north of the Standing Rock Reservation and seventy-three miles to the north of the Cheyenne River Reservation. Lake Oahe had special significance to the tribes because it inundated 160,000 acres of land that used to belong to them. The tribes relied on water from the lake for drinking water and for irrigating crops. Moreover, the waters were deemed sacred to both tribes and were used in religious rituals. And Energy Transfer Partners had a history of leaks and spills from its many pipelines.[14]

A group of Sioux youth that had originally formed to stem a wave of teenage suicides became deeply concerned about the possibility that a leak from the pipeline would pollute the sacred waters. They created a "prayer camp" near the pipeline route where they received training in civil disobedience from environmental activists. Over time, the young people attracted the support of tribal elders, who concluded that they were the Seventh Generation that, according to a tribal prophesy, would rise up to restore balance and order to the world. As news of the camp spread through social media, the group grew into a congregation of more than ten thousand indigenous people, climate change activists, and representatives of Black Lives Matter. Their cause received international attention when the Corps of Engineers withdrew permission for the protesters to be on the land and occupiers were maced by state police and threatened by attack dogs. As military veterans and movie stars joined the assembly, it became impossible for the Obama administration to ignore their plea.[15]

The project required an easement from the Corps of Engineers to cross Lake Oahe. The Obama administration in early December 2016 agreed that the Corps would not grant the easement until it had prepared an environmental impact statement for the portion of the pipeline that crossed the lake. President Trump, however, had other plans for the pipeline. He had owned stock in Energy Transfer Partners (which he sold during the summer of 2016), and the CEO of that company had contributed $250,000 to Trump's inauguration.[16]

Four days after the inauguration, President Trump signed a memorandum instructing the Corps "to take all actions necessary and appropriate to . . . review and approve" the right of way "in an expedited manner" along with "such conditions as are necessary or appropriate." The memo further ordered the Corps to rely on the abbreviated environmental assessment that it had prepared before agreeing to prepare a full-fledged impact statement. Complying with the memo, the Corps in early February 2017 determined that the environmental assessment would suffice, and that granting the easement would not significantly affect the environment. It then issued the easement on February 8, 2017.[17]

By then, most of the protesters had left the prayer camp because of the threat of spring floods with the snow melt. The police cleared out the bulk of the remaining protesters in early February. The protests, however, continued in Washington, D.C., where hundreds of pipeline opponents set up a ceremonial teepee camp near the Washington Monument and held cultural workshops. Oil began flowing through the pipeline in early May 2017.[18]

The Standing Rock tribe challenged the Trump administration's action in the District Court for the District of Columbia. The court in mid-June 2017 rejected many of the tribe's claims, but concluded that the Corps had not sufficiently responded to the tribe's assertion that the Corps' assessment of spill risks contained methodological and data flaws. The court, however, decided not to vacate the easement, noting that the company had already completed the segment underlying the lake. In October 2017, the court concluded that the Corps would likely be able to fix the problems with its analyses and that those analyses would probably not persuade the agency to change its mind. It therefore decided to allow the pipeline to continue transporting oil while the Corps worked on correcting the analyses.[19]

The Corps filed a lengthy report with the court in August 2019 containing its responses to the court's remand. Among other things, the Corps found that the segment of the pipeline underlying Lake Oahe would not have a significant impact on the environment, so a full-fledged environmental impact statement was not required. The tribes called the response a "sham" and asked the court to vacate the easement. At the same time, the company announced plans to double the pipeline's capacity to 1.1 million barrels per day. In March 2020, the court agreed with the tribes that the Corps had still not adequately addressed the controversy over the pipeline's leak-detection system, Energy Transfer Partners' safety record, the impact of harsh North Dakota winters on responses to spills, and the assessment's failure to conduct a worst-case analysis. A full-fledged environmental impact statement was therefore required.[20]

Then, in early July 2020, the court sent shock waves through the petroleum industry when it vacated the easement because the Corps had still not prepared an adequate impact assessment and ordered the company to shut down the pipeline and empty all the oil it contained within thirty days. At that point, oil had been flowing through the pipeline for three years. The court was not swayed by the company's argument that a shutdown would deprive state, local, and tribal governments of much-needed taxes and royalties. Nor did it shed any tears over the company's prediction that it would lose as much as $2 billion over the eighteen months that it would take the Corps to prepare an impact statement. It was the first time a court had ever shut down a major pipeline because a federal agency had violated the National Environmental Policy Act. And the decision seriously undermined the conventional wisdom that developers were in the clear after completing a project, even if permitting agencies violated environmental laws in the process. But, as the

court noted, "if you can build first and consider environmental consequences later, NEPA's action-forcing purpose loses its bite."[21]

The Trump administration joined Energy Transfer Partners in appealing the court's holding to the D.C. Circuit and in filing an emergency
request for a stay of the court's order. The court of appeals granted the
stay until it could decide the merits of the appeal. In the meantime, the
company's CEO, Kelcy Warren, contributed $10 million to President
Trump's campaign in the hope that Joe Biden would not be elected and
change the government's position on the easement. In January 2021,
the court of appeals affirmed the district judge's decision to vacate the
easement, but it held that he should not have ordered a shutdown without first engaging in a four-part balancing test. It therefore remanded
the case to the lower court to decide anew whether to halt the flow of
oil through the pipeline pending the Corps' preparation of an impact
statement. The district court in May 2021 declined to stop oil from
flowing through the pipeline while the Biden administration completed
the impact assessment. In the end, it appears that the company suffered
few consequences from the Trump administration's failure to follow
the law.[22]

Oil and Gas Leasing

The Department of the Interior's Bureau of Land Management is
responsible for managing federally owned lands, which make up more
than 10 percent of the nation's surface area and contain 30 percent
of the nation's mineral resources. Its statutory goal is to "sustain the
health, diversity, and productivity of public lands for the use and enjoy-
ment of present and future generations." Consistent with that mission,
the bureau conducts quarterly offerings of federal land to be leased for
energy and mineral development, livestock grazing, and timber har-
vesting. According to the U.S. Geological Service, around one-quarter

of all U.S. carbon dioxide emissions come from fossil fuels extracted from federal lands.[23]

The Coal Leasing Moratorium. Noting that coal companies could make a winning bid on a coal lease for as little as a dollar per ton of coal, Obama administration Interior Secretary Sally Jewell decided to re-examine a number of issues, including whether the coal leasing program was consistent with the administration's climate change objectives. In January 2016, she ordered the bureau to prepare a programmatic environmental impact statement to help the department decide how to modernize the coal leasing program. As in the past, the agency declared a moratorium on new leases (with a few exceptions) pending the completion of the impact statement. The moratorium was expected to last for three years. It lasted just over a year.[24]

Candidate Donald Trump promised to "rescind the coal mining lease moratorium" as part of his commitment to end the "war on coal" and "put our coal miners and steel workers back to work." His March 2017 "energy independence" executive order told the department to revise or rescind the moratorium. The next day, Interior Secretary Ryan Zinke ordered the bureau to cease work on the impact statement and to proceed with the coal leasing program as quickly as possible. The action, however, had little immediate impact on energy independence, jobs, or the environment, because coal companies were not much interested in applying for new leases at the time. Power plant demand for coal had plummeted because of cheap natural gas and renewable energy, and companies had withdrawn applications for leases for 930 million tons of coal. The market had briefly declared its own moratorium. Toward the end of the Trump administration, however, the Interior Department issued leases for more than four thousand acres, and it was considering lease applications for thousands of additional acres containing at least one billion tons of coal. Secretary Deb Haaland, a Biden appointee, revoked the Trump rollback of the Obama moratorium, and the department resumed the Obama administration's reassessment of the coal leasing program. But its attempt to reinstate the Obama moratorium was foiled when a federal district judge held that the department could not indefinitely put off lease sales.[25]

A Fire Sale. Companies were still interested in leasing public land for oil and gas development at the right price, and the Trump administration was happy to oblige. In an unprecedented fire sale, the Trump Bureau of Land Management made millions of acres of onshore public lands available for leasing, three times the acreage offered by the Obama administration, and it sold leases for development on much of that land.[26] At the behest of oil and gas drillers, the Trump bureau changed its approach to oil and gas leasing from offering small clusters of land likely to contain rich deposits to offering vast areas containing thousands of acres for lease to speculators. Upper-level officials at headquarters sent out a memo instructing the local offices to skip environmental assessments for individual projects whenever possible. Some of the lands opened for leasing were within a mile of popular national parks and monuments, like the Canyonlands and Arches National Parks and the Bears Ears National Monument in Utah. The National Park Service, which was also housed in the Department of the Interior, urged the bureau not to lease parcels adjoining the scenic Hovenweep National Monument in southeastern Utah, but the bureau ignored its plea and sold leases to drill for as low as $3.00 an acre.[27]

It might have made sense to open up more federal lands to drilling if Americans needed the fuel, but hydraulic fracturing technology had resulted in a glut of both oil and gas on the market. There was no reason to make additional land available to an industry that was already swimming in leases. But when companies could purchase leases that were good for ten years for as little as $1.50 per acre, they frequently did so just to preserve the option to drill when the price of oil increased. In some Western states, sales of these "noncompetitive" leases made up a majority of the purchases. These speculative leases locked up millions of acres of federal land for a decade, making it difficult to use the land for wildlife conservation zones or recreational uses.[28]

Outraged environmental and Native American groups challenged nearly all of the major lease sales in court, and they prevailed much of the time. The courts were quite receptive to arguments that the bureau had failed to consider the environmental impacts of the greenhouse gas emissions that would result from burning the oil and gas that the wells produced. In one case, a district court in Montana overturned 287 leases on 150,000 acres of federal land in a single ruling. In response to the losses, Secretary David Bernhardt reluctantly agreed to begin considering so-called downstream emissions, but he insisted that the department would not make that information an important aspect of the decision-making process. Although they could slow down the leasing process, the challenges could not stop the leasing once the bureau started writing adequate environmental documents. The fire sales continued in earnest during the lame-duck period between the 2020 election and President Biden's inauguration. Unlike regulations that can be repealed or rewritten, lawfully issued leases last as long as the lessee continues to extract minerals from the land.[29]

Arctic National Wildlife Refuge. The Alaska National Interest Lands Conservation Act of 1980 established the Arctic National Wildlife Refuge to preserve the unique wildlife, wilderness, and recreational values of a pristine 20-million-acre wilderness in northwestern Alaska. The largest of the nation's wildlife refuges, this unparalleled property "extends for 200 miles from the Arctic coast, across the tundra plain, over the glacier-capped peaks of the Brooks Range, and into the spruce and birch boreal forests of the Yukon River basin." Around 160 rivers and streams flow through the refuge, but not a single road disturbs the permafrost. The refuge is home to forty-five species of land and marine mammals and more than two hundred species of birds from six continents. The Porcupine herd of around 200,000 caribou migrates to the refuge's northern coastal plain each year to give birth to its young.[30]

The land encompassed by the refuge has been inhabited by the Inupiat indigenous population to the north and the Gwich'in population toward the south. For millennia, both peoples have depended on the Porcupine caribou herd for sustenance. But they were at odds over the extent to which the area should be developed. The Inupiats generally favored development because it would bring revenue and jobs to their villages. The Gwich'ins generally opposed development for fear that it would disturb the migration patterns of the Porcupine herd.[31]

The 1980 act deferred any decision about whether and how to develop the vast 1.5-million-acre coastal plain at the northern end of the refuge, but it allowed the Department of the Interior to authorize *exploration* for oil and gas on the sensitive coastal plain, so long as it was performed in a manner that avoided significant adverse impacts on fish, wildlife, and other resources. But the act prohibited any oil and gas *leasing* on the plain unless specifically authorized by an act of Congress.[32]

Oil and gas companies and the Alaska congressional delegation spent four decades trying to persuade Congress to relax the leasing ban, and their efforts finally paid off with the election of Donald Trump. Senator Lisa Murkowski (R-Alaska) provided the deciding vote for the president's Tax Cuts and Jobs Act in December 2018 after the Republican leadership added a rider that eliminated the leasing ban. Disguised as a revenue-raising action, the bill directed the department to conduct lease sales covering 400,000 acres in 2021 and again in 2024. The Trump administration then made opening up the area a centerpiece of its "energy dominance" agenda, despite polls showing that 70 percent of U.S. voters opposed drilling in the refuge.[33]

Without staff input, upper-level political appointees in the Bureau of Land Management put nearly all of the refuge's sensitive coastal plain up for grabs in August 2020. As many as four airstrips and well pads,

175 miles of roads, a seawater treatment plant, and a barge landing and storage site would be permitted. The program did establish buffer zones around polar bear dens and timing limitations to reduce disruptions during caribou calving season. But flatly denying that there was a "climate crisis," the accompanying impact statement dismissed the impact on climate disruption with a sleight-of-hand reference to a highly debatable assumption that oil produced from the area would simply displace oil drilled elsewhere. At the same time, the statement predicted that the drilling and associated global warming could cause the extinction of up to 69 of the 157 bird species found in the Arctic Refuge.[34]

The bureau then expedited the bidding process on two-thirds of the area in anticipation of conducting an auction in early January before the incoming Biden administration could block it. The lease sale on January 6 attracted modest bids from two small companies and a much larger bid from the Alaska Industrial Development and Export Authority, a state-owned entity that had never purchased an oil lease before but hoped to sell the leases to oil companies in the future. The total came to only $14.4 million for around 553,000 acres, a great disappointment for proponents of energy development in the Arctic Refuge. No major oil companies entered the bidding, perhaps because the six largest U.S. banks and the five largest Canadian banks refused to finance any development in the refuge. On inauguration day, President Biden signed an order imposing a temporary moratorium on any lease-related activity in the refuge, but the Trump administration had already conveyed the leases to the purchasers the day before, and they were legally binding. The Biden Interior Department briefly suspended the leases in June 2021 to give the department time to determine whether they were lawfully granted.[35]

The new owners of the leases still have to obtain individual permits from the Bureau of Land Management to drill on the leased land, and those permits will be subject to legal challenges. The lawsuits against the leasing action could result in a court order setting them aside. In any event, the 2017 tax law that authorized the leasing also required the bureau to conduct a second lease sale in 2024. If companies do begin pumping oil a decade from now, they may well be providing fuel for a dwindling fleet of gas-burning cars as the nation moves to all-electric vehicles.[36]

Tongass National Forest. When we think about the rainforests that play such a profound role in protecting the planet by sequestering greenhouse gases, we usually focus on the tropical forests of the Amazon River basin, the Congo River basin, and large portions of Southeast Asia. But there is a vast rainforest in southeastern Alaska that sequesters the equivalent of 8 percent of U.S. carbon dioxide emissions. Millions of the giant spruce and hemlock trees that fill this place were there when the United States purchased the Alaska territory from Russia in 1867, and some were there when William the Conqueror invaded England in 1066. Most of the Alaskan rainforest is now located within the boundaries of the Tongass National Forest. Created in 1907 by President Theodore Roosevelt, it is the nation's largest national forest and the world's largest intact temperate rainforest. This vast 17-million-acre expanse of glaciers, dramatic fjords, and tree-laden peninsulas and islands is home to humpback and orca whales, beavers, bears, wolves, five species of salmon, and one of the largest concentrations of bald eagles on Earth. It provides critical habitat to several endangered species, and around 40 percent of West Coast salmon spawn in Tongass rivers.[37]

At the very end of the Clinton administration, the U.S. Forest Service, a division of the Department of Agriculture, issued regulations designating 9.3 million of the forest's 16.8 million acres of public land as "roadless areas." That designation meant that neither the Forest Service nor companies in the private sector could build new roads, reconstruct existing roads, or engage in timber harvests in those areas, except for stewardship purposes. As a practical matter, designation as a roadless area also meant that mineral development was precluded. The primary benefits of roadless areas are recreational and ecological. The logging industry, the oil and gas and mining industries, and several states challenged the so-called Roadless Rule in court, but they were unsuccessful.[38]

In early 2018, the state of Alaska petitioned the Forest Service to write a regulation exempting Tongass from the roadless area rule. The once powerful logging industry was in decline, and state politicians were eager to remove restrictions on development in an area brimming with possibilities. The Forest Service agreed to initiate a rulemaking to consider several options for opening up some or all of the roadless areas in Alaska to logging and mineral development. It took the first step in that direction in August 2018 when it announced that it was preparing an impact statement detailing the environmental consequences of such a broad exemption.[39]

Those consequences would be considerable. Clear-cutting old-growth trees would adversely affect salmon, deer, and bear populations, all of which were essential to the area's recreational value and to the livelihoods of the region's Native American tribes. It would also destroy the forest's capacity to absorb the carbon dioxide emissions of 10 million automobiles. In a world where the tropical rainforests in Brazil were burning away due to government neglect, it made no sense at all to begin the destruction of the world's largest temperate rainforest. Exempting Tongass from the roadless area rule would also open the area up to oil, gas, and mineral extraction, activities with a huge potential to alter the pristine character of the forest and the rivers and streams that flowed through it.[40]

After meeting with Alaska's Republican governor, Mike Dunleavy, President Trump in early August 2019 ordered Agriculture Secretary Sonny Perdue to grant the exemption before the end of the year. In mid-October of that year, the Forest Service published a proposal to grant the exemption as dictated by the president.[41]

Environmental groups, outdoor sporting groups, and many local businesses opposed the move. Critics noted that once the Forest Service removed acreage from the roadless area, it would have to incur the $30 million annual cost of building and maintaining access roads, reforestation, and providing other services. They pointed to studies showing that there were more than enough "young growth" trees that had grown up in areas that loggers had clear-cut decades ago to meet any foreseeable demand. If the government insisted on opening up the Tongass for logging, it should limit it to those areas. Very limited harvests of old-growth trees could be allowed to meet specialty needs like piano sounding boards.[42]

The Trump administration, however, was not interested in limited-use compromises. The final impact statement that the Forest Service unveiled in September 2020 found that excluding the entire national forest from the roadless area rule would not significantly affect the environment. Critics pointed out that the statement ignored the agency's own scientific findings on the effect of logging on climate change. Nevertheless, the Forest Service finalized its proposal to exempt all of Tongass from the roadless area rule in late October 2020.[43]

Several environmental groups and tribes challenged the action in an Alaska federal district court. More important, the Biden Forest Service proposed to end all old-growth logging in Tongass, except for totem poles, canoes, and the like, and it proposed to limit road development on nine million acres in the forest. It was not likely that the Forest Service would hold any timber sales until it acted on the proposal. But the environmental impact statement is available to justify the next Republican administration's attempt to withdraw Tongass from roadless area protection.[44]

———————

The Trump administration assigned a high priority to speeding up permitting of large-scale activities that had the potential to increase the production and use of fuels and other products. The president signed numerous executive orders requiring agencies to expedite the permitting and leasing of public lands, and the White House pushed the agencies to follow up on those orders. When companies were having trouble getting their projects approved, they could count on sympathetic receptions at the White House and in the offices of Trump appointees in the agencies. These rushed approvals, however, had the potential to cause enormous harm to the environment and to waste precious publicly owned resources. They therefore encountered intense opposition from environmental groups and Native American tribes. Nearly all of the significant approvals wound up in court where judges appointed by both Republican and Democratic presidents forced the agencies to toe the line procedurally and to follow the requirements of the statutes under which they allowed the activities to proceed.

Some of the most controversial projects, like the Pebble Mine, that attracted opposition from across the political spectrum were never approved. Some wound up in litigation that lasted past the end of the Trump administration and were therefore subject to reversal by the Biden administration. But a valid lease or permit is a property right that cannot be taken away without due process of law and payment of just compensation. The thousands of permits and leases that agencies did grant during the Trump administration will therefore be in effect until they expire. Thanks to the persistent efforts of the environmental groups and the tribes, pristine places like the Arctic National Wildlife Refuge and Bristol Bay dodged many very powerful bullets, but many less iconic places will suffer degradation into the indefinite future. By the end of the Trump administration, the Department of the Interior had leased more than 4 million acres in Western states and 1 million acres in Alaska for oil and gas drilling. The largest developers stockpiled a "huge inventory" of leases and drilling permits that will probably last through the end of the Biden administration.[45] The Dakota Access Pipeline continues to transport oil, putting the sacred waters through which it flows at risk of spills. The oil will be refined and burned to the planet's detriment.

CHAPTER 10

FAILURE TO ENFORCE

As Southwest Flight 1380 prepared for takeoff at New York's LaGuardia Airport on the morning of April 18, 2018, Jennifer Riordan was looking forward to seeing her husband, her eleven-year-old son, and her fourteen-year-old daughter at their home in Albuquerque, New Mexico.[1] She buckled up in a window seat and settled in for the flight to Dallas next to two grandparents from Texas who were returning from their first trip to New York City. The plane had reached its cruising altitude and was flying over Pennsylvania when the passengers heard a loud "pop" followed by screams and the sound of rushing air. The aircraft shuddered and veered hard to the left as the pilot struggled to gain control. The pilot later offered that it felt like the airplane had been "T-boned by a Mac Truck." As she regained some control over the airplane and radioed air traffic control for permission to make an emergency landing in Philadelphia, passengers donned the oxygen masks that had descended throughout the cabin. Everyone on board seemed OK, except for Jennifer Riordan.

The loud popping sound was caused by the aircraft's now-mangled left engine as a fan blade sheared off and sent shrapnel flying through the air, destroying a critical inlet on the left wing and knocking out the window next to Jennifer. The pressure differential forced her head and upper torso through the window where the temperature was minus fifty degrees and the wind was blowing at around five hundred miles per hour, while the rest of her body remained belted to her seat. Two flight attendants and a couple of passengers struggled mightily to bring

Ms. Riordan back into the plane. Once that was accomplished, a nurse and a doctor tried to revive her, but without success. When the plane safely landed in Philadelphia, all of the passengers except for Jennifer breathed a sigh of relief.

As investigators began to look into what went wrong on Flight 1380, they soon discovered that the accident was not unprecedented. In August 2016, an almost identical mishap had occurred on a Southwest 737 jet when a fan blade separated from the same model engine and damaged the wing of the plane as it flew over Mississippi, but it fortunately did not blow out a window. After that incident, the Trump Federal Aviation Administration did not issue an emergency order requiring owners of aircraft with the same engine to inspect for cracks indicating metal fatigue in the fan blades. Relying on information supplied by the engine's manufacturer, agency officials recognized that the engines had been propelling passenger planes through the air for almost 300 million hours over the previous two decades without a similar incident. They concluded that the risk of another engine blade malfunction fell into the "low-risk" category that did not warrant immediate action. Instead, the agency's Trump-appointed leaders began the lengthy process of proposing and accepting public comment on a regulation requiring airlines to inspect Boeing 737 engines with an advanced ultrasound device. This slow response troubled some career civil servants in the agency who worried that the leaders were deferring too much to the companies that were assembling and maintaining engines.

Although the European Union's aviation safety agency issued a final regulation requiring enhanced inspections of the blades of similar engines within nine months, the American agency did not get around to finalizing its proposal before the accident that killed Jennifer Riordan. In the meantime, Southwest conducted visual inspections of fan blades. It visually inspected blade number 13 on Riordan's plane ten months before the mishap on Flight 1380. But a visual inspection was not nearly as likely to detect a crack as would an ultrasound machine. Following recommendations from the engine's manufacturer, Southwest started making ultrasound inspections in December 2017, but had not gotten around to inspecting Riordan's plane. The Federal Aviation Administration issued an emergency order a few days after Jennifer Riordan's death requiring all airlines flying Boeing 737 planes with the same engine to inspect for cracks in the rotor blades using ultrasound.

Jennifer Riordan's death inspired the Department of Transportation's inspector general to conduct an audit of the aviation agency's Dallas division, which was charged with inspecting Southwest's operations for compliance with the agency's regulations and directives. In February 2020, the inspector general reported that the Dallas office routinely allowed Southwest "to fly aircraft with unresolved safety concerns." The agency's oversight of Southwest was "ineffective" because it relied too heavily on the company's assurances that repeated violations presented a "low risk," instead of "requiring the airline to comply with its regulatory requirements." Significantly, the inspector general noted that during the Trump administration, the agency had moved from strict enforcement of its regulations to a more collaborative "compliance assurance" program, but it concluded that the agency had not succeeded in "navigating the balance between industry collaboration and managing safety risk" at Southwest.[2]

The aviation agency was not the only agency that emphasized "compliance assurance" over strict enforcement during the Trump administration. That was, in fact, the approach employed by all Republican administrations going back to Ronald Reagan. Upper-level Trump appointees preached that the agencies were partners with the regulated companies in pursuit of statutory goals. Agency inspectors were supposed to assume that companies were operating in good faith and help them return to the straight and narrow when they inadvertently strayed.

Notices of violation were to be followed by earnest discussions about how the violators could avoid future violations. Fines, orders, and jail sentences were reserved for incorrigible scofflaws who were unwilling to change their ways after repeated warnings. The problem with this approach was that it didn't work. As a result, too many Jennifer Riordans and their families suffered needless pain.

Enforcing Planet Protections

Since 1975, the National Highway Traffic Safety Administration has prescribed how many miles per gallon an auto manufacturer's fleet of new vehicles must average over the upcoming model year. Companies can meet the standard by designing more efficient cars, by selling more high-mileage cars and fewer gas guzzlers, or by purchasing credits from companies that have kept their averages below their targets. The Energy Conservation Act further requires the agency to collect a "civil penalty" from companies that fail to meet their prescribed targets. Congress set the civil penalty at $5.00 for every tenth of a mile per gallon over the target multiplied by the number of vehicles in the company's annual fleet. The goal was to set the civil penalty high enough to inspire manufacturers to meet mileage requirements with a resulting decrease in gas consumption and greenhouse gas emissions.[3]

Congress later recognized that civil penalties established in many regulatory statutes remained at their original levels despite the fact that inflation had effectively reduced their power to bring about compliance. The Federal Civil Penalties Inflation Adjustment Improvements Act of 2015 required federal agencies to "catch up" by adjusting "civil monetary penalties" for inflation. The Traffic Safety Administration complied with that mandate in December 2016 by increasing the civil penalty to $14.00 per tenth of a mile per gallon over the standard beginning with model year 2019.[4]

The Trump administration, however, was not as keen on compliance as the Obama administration. In July 2019, the administration formally repealed the penalty adjustment. It concluded that the penalty adjustment statute did not apply to the "civil penalties" mentioned in the Energy Conservation Act because they were not really "civil monetary penalties," but rather a component of a complex cap-and-trade regime, the purpose of which was not to penalize violations of the law but to incentivize fuel-economy increases. Recognizing that this rationale was not entirely persuasive, the agency also found that the increase from $5.50 to $14.00 was not warranted because of the impact on the economy if auto manufacturers were forced to pay higher penalties for breaking the law.[5]

Fifteen state attorneys general and several environmental groups challenged the rollback in the Second Circuit Court of Appeals. The court in August 2020 held that the Energy Conservation Act fines were indeed "civil monetary penalties" and that the agency did not have the authority to adjust them downward. Undeterred, the agency on January 14, 2020, issued an "interim final rule," without allowing public comment, delaying the "applicability" of the $14.00 adjustment until the 2022 model year. The Trump administration decided to give auto manufacturers a reprieve because the auto industry said that it had already "locked in" its production plans on the assumption that the fines would be only $5.50 per tenth of a mile per gallon. In other words, the auto manufacturers had already calculated the extent to which they planned to break the law, and it would be unfair to upset their expectations.[6]

Enforcing Worker Protections

Ray Hatfield was an experienced miner with twenty-three years under his belt when he took a new job at the R&C Mine Number 2 near Pikeville, Kentucky, manning the huge conveyer belt that moved coal from the interior of the underground mine to the surface. As he was shoveling coal that fell off the belt, his clothing got tangled in bolts on a roller shaft, and he was pulled into the rapidly moving belt and instantly killed. It was five days after his forty-third birthday. Investigators later determined that the death was preventable; the operator had not installed adequate guarding around the conveyer belt, and it lacked an effective program to ensure that employees turned off machines before working near them. The operator owed $92,000 in unpaid fines as a result of numerous prior citations for safety violations from the Mine Safety and Health Administration, and it received five more citations for the conditions that led to Ray's death. That fatality was one of many preventable deaths that occurred on the Trump administration's watch, and it was a good example of the carnage that can result when an industry can break the rules with impunity because the government doesn't enforce the law.[7]

During the Trump administration, the Mine Safety and Health Administration continued to inspect every underground mine four times per year as required by statute, but the agency shifted its emphasis to voluntary "compliance assistance" programs. Instead of cracking down on mining companies that fostered unsafe conditions, the agency sent inspectors to mines to conduct safety-training exercises. While performing this educational function, however, inspectors were prohibited from issuing citations for safety violations that they observed. Coal mine fatalities in 2017 were double those in 2016 before declining slightly in 2018. The United Mine Workers union blamed the increase on the administration's conciliatory approach to enforcement.[8]

The Occupational Safety and Health Administration can impose civil penalties for violations of occupational safety and health standards and for violations of the Occupational Safety and Health Act's "general duty clause." That clause requires every employer to furnish each employee a place of employment that is "free from recognized hazards that are causing or are likely to cause death or serious physical harm." The statute, however, provides ridiculously small penalties for employers who put their employees' lives at risk. The penalty for a "serious" violation—one where there is a "substantial probability that death or serious physical harm could result"—is a meager $7,000 per offense. Penalties for "willful violations" cannot exceed $70,000 per incident, even when death results. In the real world, however, OSHA penalties rarely come close to those amounts. The median penalty that OSHA levied for violations that resulted in the death of a worker was $7,761, about the cost of a funeral. Criminal penalties are also a joke; a scofflaw can spend more time in jail for killing an endangered toad than for creating conditions that result in a worker's death.[9]

With the advent of the Trump administration, OSHA enforcement slowed to a trickle. The Trump administration suspended new OSHA hires in 2017, and it adopted new hiring procedures that slowed down the process of bringing on replacements. By the time that the COVID-19 outbreak made hiring even more difficult in early 2020, OSHA employed only 862 inspectors, the lowest number in its fifty-year history. That represented one inspector for every 79,262 workers. With that tiny inspectorate, OSHA had the capacity to inspect each workplace under its jurisdiction just once every 165 years. On top of that, Labor Secretary Eugene Scalia shifted enforcement discretion from career investigators to Trump-appointed departmental officials who took a more lenient approach.[10]

The Trump OSHA adopted the "compliance assurance" approach favored by Republican administrations. The assumption was that employers would naturally want to protect their valuable employees from disease and injury so that penalties should be imposed only on the rare scofflaw. Worker advocates pointed out, however, that nearly 75 percent of OSHA citations were for "serious" violations, which means that the employer knew or should have known of a hazard threatening death or serious bodily injury but failed to correct it. Past experience convinced them that without the threat of an enforcement action, employers would cut corners to save money.[11]

The Trump administration discarded several Obama administration enforcement policies. For example, during the Obama administration, OSHA posted on its homepage a box labeled "Workplace Fatalities" that included every fatality report that it received, including the name of the deceased worker, the identity of the employer, and the circumstances surrounding the death. OSHA did this to honor their passing and to remind viewers that more than 4,500 workers were killed in U.S. workplaces every year. It also discouraged employers from allowing their workplaces to become death traps. The agency also issued press releases publicizing its major enforcement actions against lawbreakers where it assessed a fine of more than $40,000.

These "shaming" strategies worked. Obama OSHA head David Michaels heard from attorneys for employers that their clients were more concerned about winding up in a press release than about paying fines. A Duke University researcher found that once a violation showed up in an OSHA press release, OSHA violations by similar businesses within a three-mile radius of the site fell by 75 percent for the next three years. After the U.S. Chamber of Commerce complained about the program, the Trump administration buried the fatalities report deep on the website, and it omitted the identities of the victim and the employer. It did not issue its first press release until April 2017, and they came out only sporadically after that.[12]

Enforcing Health Protections

By any measure, enforcement efforts by the Food and Drug Administration, the agency charged with protecting public health from unsafe food, drugs, and medical devices, dropped dramatically during the Trump administration. An analysis of FDA enforcement data undertaken by *Science* magazine found that warning letters demanding quick corrections were down by one-third during the first two years of the Trump administration. Actions in court for injunctions to get dangerous products off the market also fell by 26 percent during the same period.[13]

Enforcing Safety Protections

The Pipeline and Hazardous Materials Safety Agency is responsible for the safety of over 2.7 million miles of pipelines containing oil, compressed gas, and other hazardous materials. To enforce its regulations, the agency has only 188 pipeline inspectors; there are also 340 state inspectors. These 528 inspectors have an average of 5,000 miles of pipeline for each inspector, not to mention the 148 liquified natural gas plants and 7,574 hazardous liquid breakout tanks for which they are also responsible. When inspectors found violations during the Trump administration, the agency rarely assessed civil penalties, even after explosions that caused a great deal of damage. In a classic expression of the Republican "compliance assurance" rationale for failing to prosecute lawbreakers, Administrator Skip Elliott reasoned that "[i]t is not as though we are going to inspire further carefulness with punitive measures." Small wonder that 35 percent of the agency's career staff believed that its leaders were unduly influenced by the pipeline industry.[14]

Enforcing Animal Welfare Protections

When inspectors for the United States Department of Agriculture discovered raccoons panting and drooling in 100-degree heat at an Iowa animal farm with a history of violations, they issued a warning to the company to take better care of its animals. The Department of

Agriculture is responsible for enforcing the animal welfare statutes that Congress has enacted since the 1960s to protect animals from inhumane treatment. The burden of enforcement falls on the two hundred employees in the Animal Care Division who are responsible for inspecting more than ten thousand businesses, research labs, and show-horse facilities. While most companies make every effort to ensure their animals are fed and receive humane treatment, there are notable exceptions. When the Animal Care Division uncovers mistreatment, it can issue citations and, if necessary, seize the mistreated animals.[15]

After three warnings, the inspectors confiscated ten of the raccoons, and they were planning to return for the rest when upper-level officials in Washington, D.C., told them to stop seizing animals and to return the ones they had already seized. It turned out that the owners of the farm had complained to a trade association called the Calvary Group, which in turn had contacted members of President Trump's agricultural advisory committee, who had communicated their displeasure to Agriculture Secretary Sonny Perdue. Soon thereafter, the order to stop the seizure went down the chain of command. A veterinarian who oversaw animal welfare inspections in twenty-seven states between 2014 and 2018 complained that USDA management during the Trump administration had "systematically dismantled and weakened the inspection process." Consequently, "untold numbers of animals . . . experienced unnecessary suffering."[16]

Enforcing Environmental Protections

In response to criticism that the Environmental Protection Agency was rolling back environmental regulations, Administrator Scott Pruitt said that he was placing more emphasis on enforcement. But he wanted the states to assume more responsibility for policing violations of federal environmental laws. Critics argued that states lacked adequate resources to take over federal enforcement responsibilities. And cutting back on federal enforcement would be a signal to the states that they were free to deemphasize enforcement. Despite Pruitt's verbiage, enforcement suffered greatly during his tenure.[17]

The EPA replaced its National Enforcement Initiative with a National Compliance Initiative that emphasized less-punitive tools like compliance advisories, voluntary audits, and engagement with industry trade associations. The agency also initiated a program to allow new owners of oil and gas drilling facilities to self-report air pollution violations resulting from leaks in storage tanks. If the companies then agreed to correct the problems on a flexible timeline, the EPA waived all or nearly all of the penalties. An attorney for compliant companies worried that their competitors would "cheat, get caught, and then . . . request compliance assistance instead of enforcement."[18]

The changed enforcement culture had a predictable effect on both the morale of career enforcement officers and the conduct of regulated companies. The officers lost confidence that their investigations and recommendations would be supported by upper-level political appointees. Companies were more inclined to resist enforcement efforts, and they asked upper-level officials to re-open past cases to allow them to argue for different outcomes. The change also had a noticeable effect on the quantity of enforcement actions that the EPA brought. During the Trump administration, the EPA brought fewer than half as many enforcement actions annually as did the Obama and George W. Bush administrations. The agency also referred fewer cases to the Justice Department than the previous two administrations had, and the number of felony prosecutions was sharply down.[19] The Trump administration, however, wanted to bring about systemic changes in the way that the government enforced the environmental laws.

The vast majority of the enforcement actions that the EPA brings are settled. The violator typically agrees to take corrective action to prevent future violations and to pay a civil penalty for past violations. Beginning in the early 1980s, the EPA and the Justice Department began to add a third element to settlement agreements, called supplemental environmental projects—projects that "secure environmental or public health benefits in addition to those achieved by compliance with applicable laws." They were nearly always accompanied by a reduction in the civil penalty that the violator would otherwise have paid. The supplemental projects have proven popular with violators seeking reconciliation with the victims of their unlawful actions or restoration of tarnished public images, with local communities that benefit from projects, with groups seeking environmental improvement, and with career EPA enforcement officials.[20]

Supplemental projects can bring about pollution reduction in ways that the EPA is not otherwise empowered to demand, giving the EPA and violators an opportunity to experiment with new pollution-reduction techniques and technologies. And they have a unique ability to respond to the individual circumstances of affected individuals and communities. By forcing a dialogue between violators and the victims who are the beneficiaries of the projects, these projects can achieve restorative justice for the victims and the polluter. When, as is often the case, the victims are members of low-income and minority communities, supplemental projects can advance environmental justice.[21]

Despite their overall popularity, the Trump administration decided to abolish supplemental projects. In a lengthy memo circulated in March 2020, Assistant Attorney General Jeffrey Bossert Clark declared that henceforth the Environment and Natural Resources Division attorneys could no longer include them in settlements. The action had a predictably chilling effect on settlement negotiations. Ultimately, more money went to the Treasury to make minuscule contributions to reducing the deficit, and less money was spent on improving affected neighborhoods and the environment. The Biden Justice Department, however, withdrew the Clark memo soon after the inauguration, finding it "inconsistent with longstanding [department] policy and practice."[22]

Enforcing Public Resource Protections

The 2010 Deepwater Horizon blowout and massive oil spill killed millions of birds that migrate to the Gulf of Mexico for part of the year. British Petroleum pleaded guilty to violating the Migratory Bird Treaty Act and agreed to pay $100 million to the American Wetlands Conservation Fund to restore migratory bird habitat. That powerful federal statute makes it a crime to "pursue, hunt, take, capture, or kill" any migratory bird. The statute does not define the word "take," but the Department of the Interior for decades interpreted the word to include an "incidental take," which "results from human activity when taking the bird is not the purpose of the activity." The department had on many occasions prosecuted companies whose activities had resulted in the death of migratory birds, even though they did not mean to kill them. At the very end of the Obama administration, the department's solicitor wrote a memorandum formalizing the "longstanding interpretation" that the statute prohibited "incidental take."[23]

President Trump's Deputy Interior Secretary David Bernhardt, a former coal industry lobbyist, and Deputy Solicitor Daniel Jorjani, a former Koch Industries executive, disagreed. Over the objections of Justice Department attorneys and the department's scientific staff, Jorjani penned a December 2017 memorandum concluding that incidental taking did not violate the statute. After that, the department refused to prosecute companies that did not capture or kill migratory birds intentionally.[24]

In the past, the incidental take provision provided a strong incentive to oil companies not to maintain open waste pits that kill hundreds of thousands of birds every year, to electric companies not to erect power lines with an insufficient distance between wires to protect birds, and to wind power companies not to erect turbines in migratory bird flight paths. Under the Trump administration, those incentives disappeared. During the first two years that the Trump policy was in place, dozens of efforts to protect migratory birds from human activities were canceled. Several environmental groups and state attorneys general filed a lawsuit in the Southern District of New York seeking an order setting aside the interpretation as inconsistent with the statute.[25]

Worried that a subsequent administration could rescind the Trump memo, the department published a January 2020 proposal to codify the Trump position on incidental takings into a formal regulation that could be reversed only by another formal rulemaking. The environmental impact statement that accompanied the proposal predicted that the change would negatively impact migratory birds and that the impact would get worse as companies realized that they could no longer be prosecuted for inadvertently killing migratory birds. But it predicted that the regulation would save energy companies lots of money.[26]

In August 2020, the New York court delivered a stunning defeat to the department with a comprehensive point-by-point rejection of Jorjani's memorandum. The court vacated the memorandum and held that the statute's prohibitions continued to apply to incidental takes of migratory birds. Unperturbed, the department in early January 2021 published a final rule adopting the Jorjani memorandum's conclusion that incidental takes were not covered by the Migratory Bird Treaty Act. The preamble "respectfully disagree[d]" with the district court's opinion and referred to a 2015 Fifth Circuit Court of Appeals holding that the statute did not prohibit incidental takes. But in September 2021, the Biden administration rescinded the Trump administration regulation and promised to vigorously enforce the statute's ban on unintentional takes of migratory birds.[27]

Enforcing Pocketbook Protections

The Consumer Financial Protection Bureau is responsible for enforcing more than eighteen consumer protection statutes. Having uncovered a violation, the bureau can seek civil and criminal penalties, and it can also require the perpetrator to make restitution by returning the money that it misappropriated from the victims. Under Director Richard Cordray, an Obama appointee, the bureau brought more than two hundred enforcement actions that resulted in companies' returning more than $12 billion of purloined funds to cheated consumers. It ordered Bank of America and Citibank to refund $727 million and $700 million, respectively, to consumers for worthless add-ons to their credit cards. The agency forced TransUnion and Equifax to return $17.6 million in monthly payments for worthless credit-related products. It halted an illegal debt-collection lawsuit mill. It levied fines of $24 million and $21.9 million against Honda and Toyota for engaging in discriminatory lending practices. And it stopped a scam operation from tricking students into paying extra fees for loans while representing itself as an agency of the Department of Education.[28]

This all changed when President Trump asked free marketeer Mick Mulvaney to run the Consumer Financial Protection Bureau on an acting basis. Rather than "pushing the envelope," Mulvaney directed the bureau's staff to "focus on quantifiable and unavoidable harm to the consumer," filing lawsuits only as a last resort. The bureau's enforcement emphasis shifted from suing violators to collaborating with them to achieve settlements. After halting all new enforcement actions, Mulvaney personally reviewed more than 125 active enforcement investigations to ensure that the agency was "not getting in the way of the proper functioning of the financial services and capital markets."[29]

Mulvaney required all enforcement actions to come to him for approval through Associate Director Eric Blankenstein. Blankenstein believed that the bureau was unconstitutional, but he was willing to take a hefty $260,000 paycheck from the government to protect the financial services industry from high fines. He later became embroiled in controversy when the *Washington Post* reported that he had made racist remarks on his blog, but Mulvaney kept him on anyway. Political appointees micromanaged every stage of enforcement cases to ensure that career attorneys were not overly aggressive. The number of enforcement actions dropped dramatically from forty-eight during Cordray's last year to eleven during Mulvaney's entire tenure. All of this precipitated a mass exodus of experienced enforcers and supervisors who wanted no part of an agency that was no longer interested in ensuring compliance with the law.[30]

In July 2018, Kathy Kraninger took over where Mulvaney left off. In her first speech as director of the CFPB, Kraninger said the agency would focus on working with violators to bring them into compliance, rather than filing lots of enforcement actions, and she left Eric Blankenstein in charge of enforcement. Her top priority was consumer education. The agency would put its resources into pamphlets and websites urging consumers to save money, balance budgets, and avoid scam artists, not into aggressively policing financial instruments for fraud and putting scam artists out of business. In January 2020, Kraninger issued a policy statement announcing that the bureau would not generally prosecute "abusive" practices if the target had made "good faith" efforts to comply with the law.

By 2019, enforcement was down 80 percent from 2015 levels. The number of enforcement actions ticked upward in 2020, especially in the lame-duck months after the 2020 election, but many of those actions had been initiated during the Cordray years. During the Mulvaney/Kraninger years, the bureau brought only one enforcement action against a major bank and no actions against lenders for discriminatory lending practices. Discrimination against minorities in the provision of financial services did not disappear with the election of Donald Trump, but the victims of unlawful discrimination could no longer count upon the federal government to protect them.[31]

On those rare occasions when the bureau did decide to prosecute violations, both Mulvaney and Kraninger adopted a policy of basing penalties on the violator's ability to pay. This often meant that the agency sought much lower penalties than the staff professionals recommended. A three-year prosecution of a group of payday lenders for unlawfully threatening debtors with prison if they did not pay what they owed ended with an agreement under which the economically marginal payday lenders paid no fines. The policy also meant that the bureau rarely sought restitution for bilked consumers. When the bureau charged a large payday lender, Enova International, with unlawfully extracting funds from the bank accounts of almost seven thousand consumers, the company agreed to pay a fine of $3.2 million and pay $1.6 million in restitution to the bilked consumers, but Kraninger overruled the bureau's technical staff and career attorneys to remove the restitution remedy from the settlement. During 2020, the bureau ordered a total of $700 million in restitution, a fraction of the $5.6 billion that the agency ordered in 2015 under Cordray. Consumer groups called it the "Kraninger discount."[32]

Military bases are fertile sources of financially inexperienced service members who have regular paychecks, bank accounts, and pensions. Because service members relocate frequently, they are prime targets for predatory lenders, scammers, and disreputable loan servicers. It is therefore not surprising that the streets near military installations are lined with shops of payday lenders, rent-to-own companies, and "buy here pay here" auto dealers. Predatory lending and abusive debt-collection practices aimed at service members are not just bad for them; they also reduce military preparedness when soldiers' minds are on economic troubles rather than their jobs. Heavy debt can also cause soldiers to lose their security clearances. Congress therefore enacted the Military Lending Act of 2006, which gives the Consumer Financial Protection Bureau supervisory and enforcement powers to prevent predatory lenders from taking advantage of active-duty service members. During the Cordray years, the bureau helped service members recoup around $120 million in restitution from unlawfully administered mortgages, credit cards, student loans, payday and car-title loans, and other financial scams.[33]

That all changed when Mick Mulvaney took over. Overruling career staff, Mulvaney pulled examiners from military lending establishments, claiming that the bureau never had authority to supervise these companies. Mulvaney failed to consult with the Department of Defense, which was "baffled" by the decision. When she took over the directorship, Kathy Kraninger endorsed the Mulvaney position, despite the fact that no company had ever questioned the bureau's supervisory authority over military loans. As a result, the bureau protected service members only when someone filed a complaint. The bureau filed a total of two enforcement actions against violators of the Military Lending Act during the Mulvaney and Kraninger years.[34]

Easing Enforcement During the Pandemic

Like all organizations, federal agencies were thrown off-stride by the COVID-19 pandemic. Relaxation of some regulations was necessary to meet the exigencies of the situation. For example, it made a great deal of sense for the Centers for Medicare and Medicaid Services to allow hospitals to treat more patients in temporary facilities than they would in non-emergency times. And it was sensible for the Mine Safety and Health Administration to suspend the requirement for routine gatherings of mineworkers for on-site discussion of safety matters.[35] But the

Trump administration went far beyond these sensible accommodations to give companies free passes to violate protective regulations.

In May 2020, President Trump signed an executive order directing regulatory agencies to exercise their discretion not to file enforcement actions when companies had "attempted in reasonable good faith" to comply with the relevant legal requirements. An accompanying memorandum from the head of the Office of Management and Budget urged the agencies to apply the "rule of lenity" in enforcement actions by reading ambiguities in statutes and regulations in favor of the "targeted party." Some of the memo's suggestions addressed basic issues of due process and fairness that agencies had been addressing all along. But many of the suggestions were simply restatements of demands made by right-wing think tanks and activist groups. The executive order and OMB memo set the stage for a full-scale relaxation of enforcement throughout the federal government.[36]

EPA Enforcement. After receiving pleas from the American Petroleum Institute for regulatory relief during the pandemic, the EPA on March 26, 2020, issued an enforcement policy memorandum in which it promised not to seek penalties for violations of routine compliance monitoring and associated activities if the source demonstrated that the reason for the violations was the COVID-19 outbreak. With respect to other violations, including those creating an acute risk or an imminent hazard to human health or the environment, the EPA would decide whether to seek penalties on a case-by-case basis. The policy contained everything on the American Petroleum Institute's wish list.[37]

An Associated Press analysis found that the EPA and state environmental enforcers granted more than three thousand pandemic-related waivers from monitoring requirements. Companies undertook 40 percent fewer smokestack-monitoring tests in March and April compared with the previous year. The EPA's inspector general found that the policy "threaten[ed] the Agency's overall mission to protect human health and the environment." In a remarkably salient study, American University researchers found that concentrations of fine particulate matter and ozone in counties with more industrial facilities subject to the EPA's enforcement policy had increased during the time that the policy was in effect and that there was a 19 percent increase in COVID-19-related death rates in those counties compared to counties with fewer such industrial facilities. Since refineries and chemical plants often operate in the vicinity of low-income residents, the monitoring policy disproportionately harmed them. Under pressure from Senate Democrats, the EPA terminated the policy at the end of August 2020. But by then, much of the damage was done.[38]

FDA Enforcement. The Food and Drug Administration was fairly diligent in its enforcement against companies making unsupported claims that their unapproved products inhibited COVID-19 or assisted in the recovery of persons suffering from the disease. By early April, it had sent warning letters to twenty-one companies telling them to stop advertising bogus products on the internet or face monetary penalties, seizures, or injunctive relief. The agency, however, cut back on inspections of farms and food production facilities. It announced in mid-March that its inspectors would no longer be conducting in-person inspections until it was safe to do so. It would, however, continue to make "for cause" inspections in the case of suspected foodborne disease outbreaks. Consequently, inspections declined from an average of nine hundred per month to just eight in April. The number of recalls of potentially contaminated or mislabeled food fell from 173 in February to 70 in April. This reduction in enforcement reduced the incentive for food manufacturers to comply with the law that the potential for a fine and bad publicity provided. The agency reinitiated on-site inspections in July 2020.[39]

Financial Protection Enforcement. With the pandemic wreaking havoc on the economy, complaints to the Consumer Financial Protection Bureau for unfair and abusive practices skyrocketed to record levels. The bureau received more than 500,000 complaints in 2020, a 54 percent increase over 2019. Instead of riding to the rescue of desperate victims, the bureau lowered its sights to focus primarily on small-time scammers, and it continued its policy of dramatically reducing fines if the companies demonstrated that they could not afford to pay higher fines. In late March 2020, the bureau issued guidance providing "temporary relief" to financial institutions from many reporting requirements. The guidance disingenuously explained that this bit of deregulation was necessary to free up banking resources to work with customers who were having trouble paying off their loans.[40]

On April 1, the bureau issued guidance for banks, payday lenders, and other consumer creditors on how to comply with the requirements of the recently enacted CARES Act, which required creditors not to report borrowers as delinquent to credit reporting agencies if the borrowers received payment deferrals under the statute. The guidelines went beyond the CARES Act, however, to promise that, during the COVID-19 emergency, the bureau would decline to exercise its supervisory and enforcement powers with respect to the Fair Credit Reporting Act requirement that lenders investigate consumer complaints within thirty to forty-five days. Finally, Director Kraninger assured the financial services industry that the bureau would not prosecute them for "good faith" violations of the CARES Act.[41]

Consumer groups complained that while the bureau was letting banks, debt collectors, and credit bureaus off the hook, it was providing precious little assistance to consumers who were struggling to keep up with their payments and were being targeted by creditors who were "heartless enough to deny them relief." Despite record-setting complaints, the bureau did not undertake a single enforcement action in connection with a COVID-related abuse prior to mid-June 2020.[42]

Department of Labor Enforcement. Trump's Department of Labor used the COVID-19 crisis as an excuse to pull back an Obama admin-istration enforcement policy for violations of wage and hour laws. To provide an incentive to employers who were otherwise inclined to cheat employees, the Obama Labor Department required employers to pay employees double the wages that they owed but had not paid. The double damages rule was high on the hit list of employers at the outset of the Trump administration, but Secretary Alexander Acosta was not inclined to change it. Secretary Eugene Scalia, however, wanted to pull back the policy at the earliest opportunity. In June 2020, the depart-ment announced that it would no longer demand double damages in cases where there was no evidence of bad faith and the employer had no history of prior violations. Critics argued that the middle of a reces-sion brought on by the COVID-19 crisis was an especially bad time to be giving employers an incentive to steal wages from their employees.[43]

The Trump administration took the Republican "compliance assis-tance" approach to enforcement to an extreme not achieved by previous Republican administrations. Instead of vigorously searching out viola-tors of protective laws and forcing them to pay steep penalties for their transgressions, Trump agencies engaged in kumbaya sessions with cor-porate compliance officers who promised to do better in the future. The end result was that benign companies devoted fewer resources to com-pliance and bad actors dodged accountability for the harm they caused to their workers, their customers, their neighbors, and the environment.

CHAPTER 11

IMPEDIMENTS TO DEMOLITION

The previous chapters highlight many successful assaults by the Trump administration on the protective edifice, but they also reveal several failed assaults. This chapter focuses on the impediments that the Trump administration encountered as it hacked away at the edifice.

One of President Donald Trump's earliest deregulatory actions was his high-profile reversal of the Obama administration's denial of a permit for an extension of the Keystone pipeline. This major international artery transports crude oil from the tar sands of Alberta, Canada, eastward across two Canadian provinces before turning south and crossing the entire continental United States to refineries in Port Arthur and Houston, Texas. In 2008, TransCanada Corporation proposed to build a separate leg, called the Keystone XL pipeline, through which it hoped to transport up to 830,000 barrels of crude oil per day from Alberta and the Bakken shale play in Montana, through South Dakota, to its existing facilities in Steele City, Nebraska, from which it could be piped to Illinois or Texas. Such an extensive project required many permits from the federal government and the affected states. In particular, it needed the approval of the State Department to cross the international boundary between the United States and Canada, and that required a finding that the pipeline "would serve the national interest."[1]

Determined to persuade Obama's State Department not to issue the permit, opponents held protests throughout the country, many of which were supported by farmers, ranchers, and even some Tea Party activists. In addition to worrying about the threat that a pipeline breach would pose to the Missouri and Yellowstone Rivers and the aquifers upon which farmers and ranchers depended, the protesters objected to the millions of tons of greenhouse gases that would result from burning the oil that it transported. Pipeline proponents, including the American Petroleum Institute, the U.S. Chamber of Commerce, and four labor unions, touted the jobs that building the pipeline would create and the nation's reduced dependence on oil from the Middle East. In a major victory for the environmental groups and the Native Americans who had for many years opposed the pipeline, Secretary of State John Kerry denied the application in November 2015, finding that it would not serve the national interest.[2]

With the election of Donald Trump, the petroleum industry and the U.S. Chamber of Commerce clamored for rapid approval of the pipeline. Without consulting the State Department staff, President Trump issued a Presidential Memorandum four days after his inauguration inviting TransCanada to apply once again for the permit and directing the State Department to conclude that the existing environmental impact statement, which had been prepared in August 2011, satisfied the National Environmental Policy Act. Two days later, TransCanada filed a new application, and the State Department issued the permit on April 4, 2017. The president proclaimed that it was "going to be an incredible pipeline."[3]

The approval became a rallying cry for opponents of President Trump's "energy dominance" policies. It precipitated a round of protests at the White House and the Trump Hotel in New York. Protesters in Seattle shut down eleven branches of Chase Bank, demanding that the bank refrain from financing the pipeline. Interior Secretary Ryan Zinke called the pipeline protesters "un-American," a characterization that was belied by the fact that 48 percent of respondents to a February 2017 poll opposed building the pipeline, while only 42 percent favored it.[4]

In September 2018, a federal district court in Montana dealt a major blow to the pipeline when it held that the State Department's impact statement was based on obsolete information and that the department had failed to provide an adequate justification for its radical departure from the Obama administration decision. The court issued an injunction prohibiting TransCanada from "engaging in any activity in furtherance of the construction or operation" of the pipeline extension until the department fixed these problems.[5]

President Trump called the decision "a disgrace" and vowed to appeal the case to the Ninth Circuit, where "we're slowly putting new judges." The president apparently believed that his judges would find a way to bend the law to his desires. That court, however, refused to lift the injunction while it considered the merits of the case. In the meantime, the existing Keystone pipeline suffered embarrassing leaks that cast doubt on the company's assurances about the XL extension.[6]

President Trump then attempted to circumvent the judicial process by signing an executive order in April 2019 canceling the delegation of power to the State Department to approve international pipelines, and lodging that power exclusively in himself. He then unilaterally rescinded the 2017 permit and issued what he characterized as a new "presidential permit" allowing construction to proceed without an impact statement. Agreeing with Trump that actions taken by the president himself are not subject to judicial review, the Ninth Circuit dismissed the appeals and ordered the Montana district court to dissolve the injunction.[7]

That action, however, did not end the matter. The indigenous rights and environmental groups returned to the Montana court, this time arguing that the presidential permit violated the Constitution's separation of powers requirements. In a separate action in the same court, they challenged the Corps of Engineers' decision to allow the pipeline to cross numerous streams and rivers in the United States under a single nationwide permit without preparing a separate impact statement or taking into account the pipeline's impact on endangered species. The Rosebud Sioux Tribe and the Fort Belknap Indian Community filed a lawsuit claiming that Trump's presidential permit violated their treaty rights. Environmental groups filed still another lawsuit challenging the Department of the Interior's approval of right-of-way easements across forty-four miles of public land in Montana.[8]

In mid-April 2020, the Montana court vacated the permit on the grounds that the Corps of Engineers did not properly evaluate the pipeline's impact on the pallid sturgeon and the American burying beetle, two endangered species. The Corps of Engineers then shocked the energy industry by suspending all approvals under its nationwide permit for pipeline crossings. That action effectively brought all ongoing pipeline construction projects to a halt as companies faced the prospect of obtaining individual permits to cross every significant body of water their pipelines encountered. Several industry groups petitioned the Ninth Circuit to stay the district court's order, but the appeals court declined. That ruling precipitated a mad scramble to the Supreme Court, which issued a one-paragraph order limiting the district court's injunction to the Keystone XL pipeline.[9]

President Trump's "presidential permit" strategy backfired when President Joe Biden on his first day in office rescinded the permit, effectively killing the pipeline. By then TransCanada had completed ninety miles of the $9 billion pipeline in Canada, but it suspended "advancement of the project" upon learning of Biden's decision. This time, twenty-one Republican attorneys general challenged Biden's order in a Texas federal district court. But it didn't matter, because TransCanada announced in June 2021 that it was canceling the Keystone XL pipeline for good.[10] The determined opposition of environmental groups, local activists, Native American tribes, farmers, ranchers, and blue-state attorneys general throughout Trump's entire four-year term had erected an impenetrable impediment to one of the president's highest priorities.

The Keystone XL pipeline loss was an especially salient example of the difficulties that the Trump administration encountered in its pell-mell rush to demolish the government's protective edifice. The Trump administration discovered that the federal courts insisted that the agencies follow both substantive and procedural law when it attempted to prevent Obama administration regulations from going into effect or to reverse existing regulations. Trump political appointees also encountered resistance from career staff, states, and even companies that had complied with the regulations the administration wanted to repeal. And virtually every Trump assault on the edifice encountered determined political opposition from public interest groups, media pundits, and progressive think tanks. The administration overcame the obstacles most of the time, but it failed on many notable occasions. And the impediments nearly always slowed down the administration's aggressive attempts to deregulate. This alone prevented many initiatives from going into effect.

Legal Impediments to Demolition

Like any autocrat, Donald Trump did not view the law as a serious impediment to his demolition agenda. He assumed that if he issued orders and his appointees in the regulatory agencies carried them out, he would get what he wanted. He soon discovered that federal judges were generally unwilling to aid and abet his attempts to dismantle government institutions and roll back congressionally mandated protections when the agencies did not go about it in the right way. Guided by the language of the Administrative Procedure Act and general principles of administrative law, courts consistently stymied Trump agency attempts to bypass required procedures and analyses, rewrite statutes, and ignore facts in their efforts to obliterate existing protections.[11]

According to the Institute for Policy Integrity at New York University, Trump agencies prevailed in only 17 percent of the cases in which their actions were challenged, compared to a 70 percent win rate for previous administrations. Trump blamed the losses on "Obama judges," but even with Republican-appointed judges, Trump agencies prevailed only 36 percent of the time. For example, the Second Circuit panel of judges that reversed Trump's National Highway Traffic Safety Administration's repeal of the Obama administration's increased penalties for miscreant auto manufacturers was composed of three Trump-appointed judges.[12]

Extending Deadlines. The Trump administration stumbled badly right out of the blocks when agencies followed White House orders to put off the effective dates and compliance dates of more than two dozen recently published Obama administration regulations. In addition to giving the companies subject to the regulations a break, the Trump agencies hoped to give themselves enough time to repeal or revise the regulations before they became effective.[13]

The problem with this rush to deregulate was the agencies' failure to comply with the Administrative Procedure Act, which requires public notice, an opportunity for public comments, and publication of a final rule with a preamble that addresses the public comments and explains the basis for the rule. Both the effective date and the compliance date are legally binding components of the rule that may be changed only through the Act's procedural requirements. Trump agencies strived mightily to avoid those constraints, but reviewing courts rejected nearly all of their attempts.[14]

Notice and Comment. Trump agencies also encountered judicial resistance to hurried attempts to replace Obama administration proposals with Trump administration regulations without public notice.

For example, the Ninth Circuit Court of Appeals set aside the Federal Railroad Administration's attempt to dismiss an Obama administration proposal to require two-person crews for trains, because the agency had failed to provide any notice to the public that it was considering such a move.[15]

Interpreting Statutes. Attempts by Trump agencies to interpret protective statutes to be less protective, often by denying that the statutes empowered them to take protective action, also fared poorly in court. For example, a federal district court in New York vacated a Department of the Interior memorandum concluding that the Migratory Bird Treaty Act did not prohibit unintentional killing of migratory birds. And the Ninth Circuit Court of Appeals rejected the Trump EPA's interpretation of the Toxic Substances Control Act to relieve companies of their obligation to evaluate the risks posed by previous uses of highly toxic chemicals. The Trump administration's interpretation of statutes did prevail in a few cases. For example, a Wyoming district court agreed with the Trump administration that the Bureau of Land Management lacked the authority to regulate methane emissions from oil and gas production facilities to protect the planet from global warming. But the administration's most aggressive attempts to whittle away at the protective edifice by reinterpreting protective laws were doomed to failure.[16]

Justifying Deregulation. In addition to the procedural impediments that the Administrative Procedure Act establishes, an agency action overturning a past rule must pass the Act's "arbitrary and capricious" test. According to the Supreme Court, a rule is arbitrary and capricious if

> the agency has relied on factors which Congress has not intended it to consider, entirely failed to consider an important aspect of the problem, offered an explanation for its decision that runs counter to the evidence before the agency,

or is so implausible that it could not be ascribed to a difference in view or the product of agency expertise.

When an agency wants to reverse a prior administration's approach,
it must supply good reasons for its new position, but it does not necessarily have to demonstrate that the new position is better than the
previous one.[17]

Whereas agencies in previous administrations carefully prepared
extensive documentation and rigorous analysis to back up important
regulations, the Trump agencies gave short shrift to the "reasoned
decision-making" requirements as they rushed to repeal or eviscerate
past regulations. As Georgetown Law professor Lisa Heinzerling put it,
Trump agencies "never got really good at explaining themselves." The
Trump agency actions were often suspect because they were moving
in directions that ran contrary to the relevant statutes. Consequently,
courts routinely found the administration's deregulatory actions to be
arbitrary and capricious.[18]

A good example of the courts' role in impeding poorly justified
Trump administration initiatives is the judicial response to the Department of the Interior's treatment of the sage grouse. Though quite rare,
the sage grouse, an American bird the size of a small chicken with
a huge puffed-out chest and a large turkey-like tail that is known for
its elaborate mating rituals, has an extensive habitat, extending over
165 million acres across eleven Western states. The Obama administration in 2015 reached an accord with ten Western states containing
sage grouse habitat to leave the bird off the endangered species list if
the states worked with federal agencies to create new priority habitat
areas and restrict the activities that could take place there—probably
the most extensive conservation effort in the department's history.[19]

Soon after his confirmation, Trump Interior Secretary Ryan Zinke
created a "Sage-Grouse Review Team" headed by one of his political

appointees to review the 2015 plans with an eye toward increasing state roles and facilitating mineral leasing in the covered areas. The department's Bureau of Land Management then prepared six draft environmental impact statements exploring various options for the birds. But the Environmental Protection Agency staff found that each of the options represented a "major change" in the protections, and it found no scientific basis for any changes.[20]

Without responding to the EPA's concerns, the bureau published a final impact statement and issued a decision providing greater "flexibility" for states to allow increased extractive activity in sage grouse habitat and eliminating nine million acres of priority habitat areas. The bureau concluded that the changes would have no effect on the sage grouse, but it did not provide any data or analysis to support that conclusion. One huge beneficiary of the action was the Independent Petroleum Association of America, a former client of Deputy Secretary David Bernhardt, who played a major role in pushing the changes through.[21]

Environmental groups challenged the action in an Idaho district court. The court found that the net effect of the revisions was "to substantially reduce protections for sage grouse without any explanation that the reductions were justified." The changes ran directly counter to the scientific reports that the agency's scientists had prepared and the EPA staff's scientific input. Importantly, the changes "weakened many of the protections" that the Obama Department of the Interior had relied on in deciding not to list the sage grouse as endangered. In October 2019, the court issued a preliminary injunction prohibiting the bureau from going forward with its rollbacks and reinstating the 2015 plans. Because of this and other judicial interventions, most of the Trump administration's changes to the 2015 compromise never went into effect.[22]

Other Trump administration assaults on the protective edifice were reversed by courts as well: the Ninth Circuit rejected the Department of the Interior's environmental impact statement for a massive oil and gas drilling operation on an artificial island in the Beaufort Sea; an Alaska district court reversed the department's authorization for an oil company to conduct exploration activities in Alaska's Cook Inlet; and a Minnesota district court concluded that the Trump administration's failure to consider worker safety in determining maximum conveyer belt speeds for hog-processing facilities was arbitrary and capricious. Perhaps the most devastating defeat that a Trump administration agency suffered in court was the Ninth Circuit's decision to order the EPA to cancel the tolerances for the pesticide chlorpyrifos after noting that the "EPA's egregious delay exposed a generation of American children to unsafe levels" of the pesticide. The Biden EPA canceled the tolerances in August 2021.[23]

Anti-Backsliding Statutes. Statutory anti-backsliding provisions provided another impediment to the Trump administration's attempts to deregulate. For example, the Mine Safety and Health Act of 1977, which empowers the Mine Safety and Health Administration to write health and safety standards for surface and underground mines, provides that no health or safety standard may "reduce the protection afforded miners by an existing mandatory health or safety standard." At the very end of the Obama administration, the administration extended to metal and nonmetal mining operators its requirement that operators conduct safety examinations before every shift and report every condition that could adversely affect health or safety. The Trump administration modified the rule to allow operators to conduct the required inspection after a shift had commenced and to allow the operator to record only the hazards that it did not promptly attempt to correct. The D.C. Circuit, however, held that the change violated the statutory anti-backsliding provision. The court flatly rejected the Trump administration's familiar mantra that the move would "reduce regulatory burdens without reducing protections." As with nearly all deregulatory moves, this one did reduce regulatory protections because miners were not being protected while examinations were being conducted.[24]

Practical Impediments to Demolition

The Trump administration also encountered many practical impediments to advancing the demolition agenda. Some were self-imposed. For example, Trump's command that federal agencies review every one of tens of thousands of regulations was simply an impossible goal that was accomplished by none of the agencies.[25] Career employees invested in the status quo were another form of brakes on the radical policy reversals the administration sought to implement, many of which ran counter to the statutes that empowered the agencies. Perhaps surprisingly, the Trump administration's attempts to deregulate also encountered resistance from some companies that had already invested in complying with the regulations or that wanted to burnish their public images.

Staff Resistance. Since the late nineteenth century, career civil servants have been protected from dismissal without cause, and in recent years most federal workers have joined unions that have provided additional protections against arbitrary job-related actions by upper-level political appointees. The scientists, engineers, economists, attorneys, and other professionals who do most of the day-to-day work of writing and enforcing regulations are guided by professional norms that demand adherence to laws, respect for facts and data, and a commitment to objectivity. Over time, agency staffs develop methodologies, approaches, and procedures to which they are inclined to adhere. These forces can yield staff resistance to changes desired by upper-level decisionmakers that depart from professional norms, the agency's "standard operating procedures," or the agency's statutes. Career staffers can, without fear of reprisal, publicly contradict the president when he misstates the facts, as the National Park Service famously did when President Trump publicly claimed that his inauguration crowd was larger than Obama's, and as the National Weather Service did when Trump claimed that Hurricane Dorian was threatening Alabama.[26]

Staff resistance to Trump administration deregulatory initiatives was unique in the extent to which civil servants engaged in open acts of what law professor Jennifer Nou calls "civil servant disobedience." After the White House placed restrictions on public communications by federal agencies regarding certain forbidden topics, including climate change, more than a dozen "rogue" versions of the agencies sprung up on Twitter, calling themselves "the Unofficial Resistance team," to spread the forbidden messages. After Interior Secretary Ryan Zinke complained to the National Petroleum Council that 30 percent of the department's seventy thousand employees were "not loyal to the flag," some staffers wore T-shirts that read "30% DISLOYAL" and secretly called themselves "the disloyals." Staff leaks to the media were often effective in thwarting the Trump administration's most extreme deregulatory initiatives. On many occasions, civil servants produced reports that reflected their assessments of the available information even when the reports contradicted the policy preferences of their politically appointed superiors.[27]

The resistance was especially intense at the EPA. The initial reaction of many career staffers to the shock troops that Scott Pruitt brought in to fill upper-level positions was to "hunker down and survive," a strategy involving a certain amount of self-censorship. But some were committed to fulfilling their statutory responsibilities, even if that meant clashing with upper-level political appointees. They were insulted by President Trump's decision to travel to EPA headquarters to sign an executive order requiring the EPA to rescind restrictions on power plant greenhouse gas emissions that dozens of EPA professionals had spent thousands of hours preparing. Employees in the agency's Chicago office took to the streets to protest the Trump administration's climate change reversals, organized a social media campaign, and participated in community forums to tout their efforts to protect the environment despite the administration's deregulatory policies. Responding to a command that employees not use social media, an EPA employee launched an unofficial account that posted tweets criticizing Administrator Scott Pruitt and the Trump White House, which quickly attracted ninety thousand followers.[28]

Conservative activists argued that if a federal employee did not like the direction that the Trump administration was taking, "the solution is for that federal employee to honorably resign, not actively or passively hamper the White House." But the willingness of upper-level Trump appointees to reject settled science led some agency scientists to regard remaining at the agency and doing their jobs to be necessary acts of resistance. When Trump appointees referred industry-suggested rollbacks to the staff, the scientists and engineers replied with analyses showing that no changes in the facts warranted changes in the targeted regulations. They made sure that sound scientific estimates of the adverse effects of the proposed rollbacks appeared in the relevant preambles and technical support documents so that environmental groups challenging the regulations in court could rely on the agency's own estimates. For example, when Trump appointees at the top of the EPA decided not to increase the stringency of the national primary ambient air–quality standard for particulate matter, the staff-written risk assessment estimated that the failure to tighten the standard would result in more than twelve thousand premature deaths per year. Sometimes the resistance was petty, like defacing the posters that were hung in the agency hallways at Pruitt's insistence. Sometimes it was futile, like one staffer's insistence on reinserting the word "climate" into the name of his office every time the Trump people deleted it.[29]

Supporters of the Trump deregulatory initiatives soon came up with a response to staff resistance. A nonprofit "opposition research" organization called America Rising filed twenty Freedom of Information Act requests for emails and other documents written by EPA employees who spoke out against the agency's policies. Calling the operation an "anti-resistance" effort, a vice president of the organization explained that the group was trolling for information that might prove illegal or embarrassing that Republicans could use to undermine the resistors' credibility. One of the targets of the requests accused America Rising of "trying to intimidate and bully us into silence."[30]

Science Advisory Board Resistance. As noted in Chapter 5, EPA Administrator Scott Pruitt attempted to stack the agency's advisory committees with scientists who shared his policy views and by banning scientists who received grants from the EPA. He was largely successful, but a majority of the scientists on the agency's Science Advisory Board remained committed to the scientific data and were not swayed by the political preferences of Pruitt or his successor, Andrew Wheeler. Environmental groups were dubious when Pruitt appointed Michael Honeycutt to chair the board, but they credited him with keeping it focused on the science. It also helped that the board's deliberations were open to the public so that members knew that what they said and did would be visible to their peers in the scientific community. On several occasions, the board became a thorn in the side of the EPA's political leaders as it contradicted their conclusions with references to mainstream scientific literature.[31]

Company Resistance. Industry resistance to changes aimed at widening the scope or increasing the stringency of existing regulation is a well-known phenomenon. Less well known is the tendency of companies that have already complied with regulatory requirements to resist deregulatory policy changes. Having invested resources in complying, these companies are not anxious to have their competitors relieved of requirements with which they already comply. In the case of pocketbook protections, reputable companies benefit from a fair market-place where they do not have to compete with dishonest companies. Capital-intensive companies crave certainty, and they are inclined to resist rapid change, even if it is in a deregulatory direction. Companies that manufacture pollution controls and equipment for renewable energy projects often oppose deregulatory environmental and energy policies.[32]

A good example of company resistance is the reaction of manu-facturers of new diesel truck engines to the Trump EPA's relaxation of air pollution standards for a small but growing niche industry that manufactures "glider kits." A glider kit consists of a new truck chassis with a frame, front axle and wheel, cab, and brakes. Glider assembly companies combine glider kits with refurbished engines and power trains from wrecked or worn-out "donor" trucks to create "glider vehi-cles" that are about 25 percent less expensive than new trucks. In the mid-2010s glider assemblers produced upwards of ten thousand glider vehicles per year.[33]

During the Obama administration, the EPA had a big problem with glider vehicles. Emissions of greenhouse gases and other pollutants from such vehicles were ten to fifty times higher than emissions from trucks coming off the assembly line. So when the EPA issued its Phase 2 standards for new heavy-duty trucks in October 2016, it concluded that glider vehicles came within the statutory definition of "new motor vehicle" and therefore had to comply with the new standards. It did, however, create an exemption allowing glider assemblers to sell up to three hundred glider vehicles per year that did not meet the standards. The agency calculated that the limitations on glider vehicles would pre-vent 350–1,600 premature deaths per year along with many nonfatal respiratory illnesses.[34]

The manufacturers of new engines were comfortable with that result because they knew that they could design new engines to meet the standards. Knowing that the old engines they used could not meet the new emissions limitations and convinced that the production limits would put them out of business, glider assemblers sued the EPA. After the 2016 election, the CEO of the largest glider assembler met with Scott Pruitt to plead its case. Having hosted a major campaign event for Donald Trump, he did not have to remind Pruitt that glider assemblers were generally located in states that voted for the president. In mid-November 2017, the EPA published a proposal to repeal the emissions requirements for all glider vehicles based on the Trump administration's conclusion that glider trucks did not come within the statutory definition of "new motor vehicle."[35]

The large engine manufacturers protested that the glider assemblers were trying to secure a competitive advantage by extending the lives of heavily polluting engines when truckers would otherwise be purchasing new trucks containing much cleaner engines. Worse, the EPA's contention that it lacked authority to regulate glider trucks meant that states could write their own emissions standards for those vehicles, leading to a patchwork of regulations that would be a nightmare for companies selling to a national market. Finally, the manufacturers argued that the regulatory uncertainty caused by the EPA's proposal made it difficult for them to plan for future models. Taken aback by the strong opposition, the agency put the controversial proposal on the back burner for the remainder of the Trump administration.[36]

Several other Trump administration rollbacks encountered resistance from companies within the regulated industry. The major oil companies resisted the Trump EPA's efforts to roll back limits on greenhouse gas emissions from oil and gas development projects, and some auto manufacturing companies opposed the EPA's attempt to roll back Obama administration limitations on greenhouse gas emissions from automobiles. The resistance was not always successful. When the airline industry begged the Federal Aviation Administration to require passengers to wear masks to increase public confidence that air travel was safe, the agency declined. And when National Economic Council Director Gary Cohn warned President Trump that several CEOs of major corporations had signed a statement urging Trump not to withdraw from the Paris Climate Accords, Trump responded that his voters "don't live on Park Avenue."[37]

Political Impediments to Demolition

Political opposition to federal agency actions is nothing new. The Trump administration encountered political opposition from Democrats in Congress, Democratic mayors and state attorneys general, public interest groups, and various progressive media outlets. During President Trump's first two years, the Trump agencies had little to fear from a Congress that was controlled by the Republican Party. As noted earlier, Congress invoked the Congressional Review Act to repeal seventeen Obama administration regulations. Trump administration attempts to dismantle agencies, to roll back regulations, and to give violators a free pass encountered resistance from Democratic members of Congress, but they were powerless to prevent the administration's assault on the protective edifice.

The dynamics changed after the 2018 elections put the Democrats in control of the House of Representatives. The change was even more radical by virtue of the fact that several of the freshman representatives were vigorous supporters of federal environmental, safety, and financial regulation. Rep. Katie Porter (D-Cal.), a student of and co-author with Senator Elizabeth Warren (D-Mass.), for instance, quickly distinguished herself as a powerful advocate for consumers in committee hearings. Employing her comprehensive knowledge of financial services law and clever props that made her critiques obvious to nonexpert observers, she exposed how upper-level officials at the Consumer

Financial Protection Bureau were easing regulations in subtle ways that were wholly inconsistent with the agency's statutes.[38]

The change did not portend more protective legislation, because the Senate remained under the control of free-marketeer Republicans, and President Trump stood ready to veto any legislation that irritated his Fox News–informed populist base. It did, however, put Democrats in control of House committees charged with overseeing government agencies. And they did so with gusto in hearings with titles like "CFPB's Role in Empowering Predatory Lenders: Examining the Proposed Repeal of the Payday Lending Rule," "The Administration's War on a Merit Based Civil Service," "The Devastating Health Impacts of Climate Change," and "Threat to America's Children: The Trump Administration's Proposal to Undermine Protections from Mercury Air Toxics Standards." These hearings gave Trump administration critics a forum to explain to the public the wrongheadedness of the Trump administration's attempts to dismantle agencies, denigrate expertise, and roll back protections. Committee members posed tough questions to Trump administration regulatory officials and demanded information on their deregulatory moves.[39] And the possibility of being the subject of one of these hearings made Trump-appointed agency heads think twice about pushing out ill-considered regulatory rollbacks and policy changes.

States and Cities. States and cities that are adversely affected by deregulatory actions can be powerful political impediments to agency implementation of deregulatory policies. To the (considerable) extent that the regulatory statutes fail to preempt state and local regulations, states and cities are free to enact laws that retain existing regulatory requirements when the federal government deregulates. Attorneys general from blue states can file lawsuits challenging regulatory rollbacks. And state governors can offer politically salient critiques of presidents from their own bully pulpits.

States and cities did step in to provide protections that the Trump administration rolled back or declined to enact. When President Trump withdrew the United States from the Paris Climate Accords, many states with Democratic governors formed the United States Climate Alliance and pledged their states to meeting the Paris goals with or without the federal government. More than three hundred mayors, many from red states, pledged their cities to meeting the same goals. As the EPA dilly-dallied with updating the federal standards for lead in drinking water after the Flint, Michigan, tragedy, several states stepped in with their own protective regulations. Three states proposed to ban the pesticide chlorpyrifos after the EPA withdrew a federal action to limit exposure to that toxic pesticide. Once Trump-appointee Mick Mulvaney took over as head of the Consumer Financial Protection Bureau, several large states beefed up implementation and enforcement of state consumer protection laws.[40]

Although the administration claimed that it supported devolving regulatory authority to the states, in reality it did so only when the states were regulating less stringently than the federal agencies. When the states regulated more stringently, the Trump agencies stepped in to limit state action.[41] Chapter 7 recounted the battle that ensued when the EPA attempted to withdraw California's waiver allowing it to regulate auto emissions more stringently, and Chapter 8 highlighted the fight over the EPA's attempt to take away the states' veto power over federal permits that threatened state water-quality standards.

The preceding pages are filled with examples of Democratic state attorneys general filing lawsuits challenging Trump agency actions and omissions. The attorneys general of New York and California each filed more than one hundred lawsuits against various Trump administration agencies. They did not win all of the time, but they prevailed frequently enough that the mere fact that they sued induced the Trump agencies to follow the law. For example, when the EPA pushed back by two years the effective date of Obama-era regulations protecting farmworkers from the risks of toxic pesticides, a lawsuit filed by three state attorneys general persuaded EPA Administrator Wheeler to begin enforcing the regulations.[42]

The Trump administration often fired back, sometimes launching political and legal attacks on the dissenting cities and states, and sometimes threatening them with retaliatory action. For example, in retaliation for California's opposition to Trump administration policies, the Department of Transportation canceled a $928 billion grant and threatened to require the state to return $2.5 billion that previous administrations had given to the state to help build a high-speed rail system.[43]

Progressive Groups. Public interest groups were another impediment to the Trump administration's deregulatory efforts. Consumer groups including Public Citizen and Americans for Financial Reform, and environmental groups such as WildEarth Guardians, the Center for Biological Diversity, Natural Resources Defense Council, and the Sierra Club had the resources and staff to comment on proposed changes in regulations, generate public opposition to those changes, and challenge final deregulatory action in court. The Natural Resources Defense Council alone sued Trump agencies once every ten days on average during the first two years of President Trump's term. A group of former EPA employees called the Environmental Protection Network offered sophisticated critiques of proposed EPA budget cuts and regulatory rollbacks and served as a conduit for leaks from their former colleagues to the press.[44]

Grassroots groups including Indivisible and MoveOn generated public outcries against deregulatory changes and mobilized support for existing regulatory programs. The groups occasionally practiced civil disobedience, as when members of a group called Extinction Rebellion superglued themselves to various entrances to the Capitol building in July 2019 to protest the 116th Congress's failure to take up legislation declaring climate change to be a national emergency. Activists in the

Sunrise Movement staged loud demonstrations outside House Speaker Nancy Pelosi's office and elsewhere on Capitol Hill to demand stringent "Green New Deal" legislation. And think tanks such as the Center for American Progress, the Center for Progressive Reform, and New York University's Institute for Policy Integrity provided ideas and intellectual support for the resistance.[45]

Academics. Other impediments to the demolition agenda during the Trump administration were professors in academia who were committed to government decision making based on logic and facts. Academic scientists were outspoken in their resistance to the Trump administration's constant denigration of scientists and persistent downplaying of the risks of climate disruption. Despite the historic reluctance of scientists to become involved in politics, concern in the scientific community was so intense that tens of thousands of scientists and supporters of science marched in Washington, D.C., and six hundred other cities in April 2017 in support of government policies based on science, not ideology. More than 420 sociologists issued a public statement early in the Trump administration criticizing the president for appointing climate deniers to his cabinet. Academics pointed out the contradictions in the Trump administration's approaches to regulatory issues. For example, New York University law professor Richard Revesz showed how the administration's frequently expressed desire to return regulatory power to the states was belied by its efforts to restrict state power when the states wanted to regulate more stringently than Trump agencies.[46] While it would be foolish to suggest that Trump or his political appointees were greatly influenced by vocal academics, their message to the public that the Trump administration was abusing science and logic may have influenced some voters in the 2018 and 2020 elections.

In its mad rush to dismantle federal agencies and roll back both recent and long-standing protections, the Trump administration quickly encountered serious obstacles, some of which were easily overcome and some of which were not. Trump appointees could easily ignore the criticisms of academics, progressive pundits, and public interest groups, and they could in fact turn those complaints into political capital with a Trumpian populist base that had been conditioned over the years by Fox News to distrust expertise and despise leftists. But the companies that benefited from the Trump administration's bias in favor of energy infrastructure could not ignore the opposition of a coalition of environmental groups and indigenous peoples that slowed the permitting and construction of pipelines and other major projects.[47] Economics certainly played a role as declining oil prices made massive capital investments in pipelines impractical. But protests and lawsuits played equally important roles in the failure of the Trump administration's infrastructure policy.

Trump appointees could less easily ignore resistance from the staff, science advisory boards, and compliant companies. They soon discovered that it was difficult to accomplish deregulatory goals without staff support and over the objections of outside scientists, even when the administration determined the membership of the advisory committees. Companies that had already sunk capital into meeting regulatory requirements had resources to devote to opposing agency attempts to repeal or replace those requirements.

The most daunting impediment was an independent judiciary that insisted that the Trump agencies follow established statutory requirements and legal norms. Even judges appointed by President Trump were unwilling to tolerate blatant violations of the Administrative Procedure Act's requirement that agencies allow public comment on proposals to change effective dates or other binding requirements of previously issued regulations. They were equally unwilling to allow Trump agencies to pervert the meaning of duly enacted statutes. And they devoted the same "hard look" to deregulatory actions that they devoted to new regulations to ensure that they were supported by evidence and analysis and were not otherwise arbitrary and capricious. Virtually all of the Trump administration's major deregulatory initiatives wound up in court, and many remained there for years. The administration won some of the legal battles, but it lost others, and many remained unresolved at the end of President Trump's term.[48] Georgetown University law professor William Buzbee suggested that the Trump administration was not especially concerned about its losses in court, because it was willing to skirt the relevant legal requirements for the symbolic value to the president's political base of its aggressive pursuit of a demolition agenda.[49] That strategy, however, failed when Trump's appeal to the Trumpian populist base proved insufficient to propel him over the victory line in the 2020 elections.

PART III

THE DEMOLITION AGENDA AT WORK: A CASE STUDY

CHAPTER 12

COVID-19

America's experience with COVID-19 provides a tragic demonstration of the dreadful impact of the demolition agenda on public health. The efforts of the Trump administration to chip away at the protective edifice by defunding government agencies, eliminating essential programs, downplaying risks, easing regulation, and incompetently exercising the regulatory authorities that it belatedly invoked precipitated a public health disaster.

Big government was necessary to address the COVID-19 pandemic.[1] The president and the agencies that served under him had ample regulatory powers to invoke in such emergencies. But the government needed to exercise those powers quickly and effectively, and it needed to be guided by sober assessments of the facts about the coronavirus, its capacity to spread, and the availability of technologies and techniques to stop the spread, to treat its victims, and to defeat the virus with near-universal vaccination. By the time the pandemic hit, the federal agencies were so decimated, the leadership was so reluctant to take decisive action, and the president's populist base was so determined to resist any form of government regulation that disaster was inevitable. Overall, the Trump administration's handling of the COVID-19 crisis provides a morbid but compelling case study in the damage that four years of continuous assault have wrought on protective federal agencies and the people and places they were created to protect.

It would have been difficult enough for a seasoned and competent leader to manage this crisis, but Donald Trump was neither. At the outset, when there was still time to confine the coronavirus and prevent a full-blown pandemic, Trump ignored the advice of expert civil servants and belittled the risks. Once he belatedly recognized the severity of the outbreak, he attempted to project the image of a trusted leader, but his distrust of experts and his dismantling of government agencies proved fatal in a deadly emergency.

Dismantling Preparatory Institutions

The Trump administration was wholly unprepared for the COVID-19 pandemic, but it didn't have to be. The federal government had added institutional protections against pandemics to the protective edifice over the years, but the Trump administration had allowed them to languish. After the swine flu outbreak of 2009, the U.S. Agency for International Development initiated a $200 million project called PREDICT to identify viruses that had the potential to produce pandemics and to train scientists in China and elsewhere on how to detect and respond to those threats. The Trump administration neglected the project and allowed its funding to run out. Dozens of scientists and analysts were laid off three months before the COVID-19 outbreak in Wuhan, China.

In 2016, a task force headed by the National Security Council's Directorate for Global Health Security and Biodefense produced a comprehensive report calling on the White House to prioritize procurement of personal protective equipment in advance of a future pandemic. The recommendation was ignored by the incoming Trump administration. And in 2018, National Security Council Director John Bolton eliminated the directorate and folded it into the office in charge of weapons of mass destruction.

During the Obama administration, an office in the Department of Health and Human Services called the Biomedical Advanced Research and Development Authority had anticipated the need for a rapid ramp-up of N95 mask production in the event of a pandemic. Concluding that rapid mask production as a pandemic loomed on the horizon was preferable to building huge stockpiles of masks that could over time age past their expiration dates, the Biomedical Authority entered into a $45 million contract with a mid-sized mask manufacturer to come up with a machine that could manufacture 1.5 million masks a day in an emergency. The company came up with plans for a machine that satisfied the agency's criteria in 2018, but the Trump administration budget for the Biomedical Authority didn't include money for building a prototype machine, and the project died.[2]

Failing to Heed the Warnings

As the COVID-19 pandemic began to spread across America in mid-March 2020, President Trump denied responsibility for failing to prepare for the pandemic, because "[n]obody knew there would be a pandemic or epidemic of this proportion." That was palpably false. Long before the pandemic struck, Obama administration officials had extensively briefed incoming Trump administration officials on the threat of just such a pandemic. They presented a sixty-nine-page "playbook" for addressing a "pathogen of pandemic potential." The officials who received the briefing from Obama administration officials, however, took no action, and by January 2020 they had been fired by Trump or had otherwise moved on.[3]

In July 2019, the Federal Emergency Management Agency issued a multi-agency report analyzing the risks presented by nine scenarios, one of which was a pandemic caused by a novel strain of influenza virus called the "Crimson Contagion Scenario." The report predicted that the pandemic would require social distancing, which would disrupt utilities, police, fire, and other government services. Business closures would result in widespread loss of services. Hospitals would be quickly overwhelmed, and there would be a shortage of medical supplies and equipment, hospital beds, and healthcare workers. The report was circulated to high-level political appointees in the agencies, who took no action to prepare for the possible pandemic.[4]

President Trump began to receive national security briefings from U.S. intelligence agencies in early January 2020 warning of the global danger presented by an outbreak of a highly transmissible pathogenic virus in Wuhan, China. Although the advisors told him that China was not providing accurate information and was not allowing teams from the U.S. Centers for Disease Control into that country to investigate, Trump declined to press China's president for better data. Instead, he publicly praised China for its "efforts and transparency" and assured the public that "[i]t will all work out well." Both Health and Human Services Secretary Alex Azar and presidential trade advisor Peter Navarro explicitly warned the president in January that a pandemic was on the way and that it would "imperil the lives of millions of Americans." Trump took no action until January 31, when he placed a rather porous ban on travel from China. By then, around 300,000 people had already traveled to the United States from China, and the disease was quietly spreading within the United States. The President's Daily Brief warned of the coming pandemic more than a dozen times in January and February.[5]

Trump later told journalist Bob Woodward that he knew in February that the coronavirus was highly contagious and that it was coming to the United States. He was, however, more concerned with preserving the bustling economy upon which he was basing his reelection bid than he was with heeding warnings from experts from the "deep state." The stock market, not the death count, was his guidepost. Even when the warnings came from senior officials he had appointed, the president was initially inclined to pay more attention to warnings from his economic advisors that if he persuaded the country to shelter in place, a deep recession would follow. Former Health and Human Services Secretary and former Kansas governor Kathleen Sibelius concluded that "[w]e basically wasted two months."[6]

Downplaying the Risks

Instead of rallying the public around the advice of the experts, Trump consistently downplayed the risks that COVID-19 posed to public health and the national economy.[7] The *Washington Post* tabulated more than two hundred separate occasions on which the president downplayed the risks the virus posed. On January 22, Trump told CNBC that the situation was limited to "one person coming in from China" and was therefore "totally under control." On February 2, Trump assured Sean Hannity on Fox News that "[w]e pretty much shut it down coming from China." On February 14, Trump espoused a theory that warmer weather in April would kill the virus, a position that was contradicted by the World Health Organization. By February 20, it was clear that many people in the United States had contracted the disease and that it was spreading within the country, but Trump announced that the incidence of the disease was "going down, not up" and would "be pretty soon at only five people." On February 27, Trump predicted that "one day—it's like a miracle—it will disappear." The president did not let the pandemic get in the way of his holding large rallies, where he stirred up support for his reelection bid by declaring the COVID-19 pandemic the Democrats' "new hoax."[8]

During February and early March, the conservative media and Trump's legions of supporters on the internet echoed Trump's dismissal of the risks posed by the coronavirus. For several critical weeks in late February and early March, popular Fox News commentators Sean Hannity and Laura Ingraham assured viewers that the coronavirus was not a serious threat to the United States. Only Tucker Carlson recognized the threat for what it was, but his focus was mostly on keeping possibly infected Chinese people out of the country. On February 28, Rush Limbaugh told millions of Trumpian populist listeners that COVID-19 "appears far less deadly" than seasonal flu, and he complained that government scientists and the mainstream media "keep promoting panic."[9]

In his efforts to reassure the public, Trump was able to rely on so-called experts who belittled the risks. One paper that was quite influential in the White House was published by the Hoover Institution on March 16 and was written by libertarian law professor Richard Epstein. Relying on his idiosyncratic theory of "evolutionary economics," he predicted that as people died off from the most virulent variations of the virus, they would no longer spread the disease, and less virulent variations would take over. By his calculations, the death toll in the United States would probably not exceed five hundred. A delighted President Trump tweeted: "WE CANNOT LET THE CURE BE WORSE THAN THE PROBLEM ITSELF." As the death toll soared past five hundred, Epstein added a correction that put the maximum death toll at five thousand. A professor of medicine at Stanford Medical School named John Ioannidis at least had medical expertise, but he filled the cable news networks during the spring of 2020 with unsupported reassurances that no more than ten thousand Americans would die of COVID-19.[10]

When administration officials suggested that the future might not be as rosy as the president suggested, they were quickly banished to the bureaucratic equivalent of Siberia. On February 25, a mid-level civil servant at the Centers for Disease Control and Prevention named Nancy Messonnier held a press conference to tell the public that COVID-19 was indeed spreading rapidly throughout the country and that the only question now was "how many people in this country will have this severe illness." Her honest assessment of the issue caused the stock markets to tumble. This threat to Trump's "not a problem" narrative infuriated the president, who wanted to fire Messonnier, and it inspired

Vice President Mike Pence to order Health and Human Services Secretary Alex Azar to prohibit employees from publicly commenting on the pandemic in the future. Assured by the president that COVID-19 was "like a flu," thousands of Americans celebrated Mardi Gras in New Orleans at the end of February and hit the beaches of Florida and Texas during spring break.[11]

The event that focused the nation's attention on the reality of the disease was the National Basketball Association's decision on March 11 to suspend the 2020 season. In a ten-minute Oval Office address on the same day, the president announced that he would be putting restrictions on travel from Europe as well as China. He assured listeners that the government was "cutting massive amounts of red tape to make antiviral therapies available in record time." The president then explained that for the vast majority of Americans the coronavirus risk was "very, very low," but he urged elderly Americans and those with underlying health conditions to be "very, very careful." He stressed that no nation was "more prepared or more resilient than the United States."[12]

The halfhearted speech was out of character, and it did not work. Stock futures plummeted as he spoke. The next day, the stock market suffered its greatest single-day loss since Black Monday in 1987 and then took another dive the next day. Having lost control of the narrative, Trump needed a new one. Now he announced that he "felt it was a pandemic long before it was called a pandemic." On March 17, Trump asked nonessential people to remain at home for fifteen days and limit gatherings to no more than ten people. As the Trump administration pivoted, so did Fox News. The narrative changed from belittling the risk of COVID-19 to portraying Trump as a wartime hero and characterizing criticism of the administration as unpatriotic.[13]

On April 3, the CDC recommended that all Americans wear masks when they left their houses. Yet, when asked whether he would follow the agency's advice, President Trump stressed that it was a voluntary matter and said he was not inclined to wear a mask. This encouraged reckless behavior among his base. As state and local officials began to close schools and impose limits on bars and restaurants in mid-March, they encountered strong resistance from Trump supporters, who quoted the president and conservative pundits to the effect that the COVID-19 threat was a minor one that did not warrant such severe measures.[14]

As the daily briefings by the vice president's pandemic task force attracted large television audiences, President Trump decided to take over the presentations. From that point forward, instead of informative, data-heavy presentations on the status of the disease and efforts to combat it, the briefings turned into the Trump Show, filled with boasting, misinformation, and plugs for ineffective "miracle" cures. But they came to an ignominious end in late April when Trump asked Dr. Deborah Birx on live television whether it might be a good idea to inject a disinfectant like bleach into people as a cure. The task force then went dormant, and Dr. Birx decided that the best use of her time was to fly across the country beseeching governors not to abandon social distancing and mask-wearing policies too quickly.[15]

On April 29, President Trump declared victory. His administration's response to the pandemic had been "a great success story." The country had "crossed a big boundary and much better days are ahead." As states began to relax shutdowns and mask requirements in early May and experts warned of a second spike in the summer, the White House slipped back into denial mode. Trump began to hold large indoor political rallies where masks were not required, but the Trump campaign was careful to have the people who crowded together without masks sign liability waivers. Back in his element, the president at a Tulsa rally added a racist element to his narrative, deriding testing for the "Kung-flu."[16]

Infection, hospitalization, and death rates all predictably shot up during the summer, as a second wave began, reaching more than sixty thousand cases per day in mid-July, even as Vice President Pence penned a sunny op-ed in the *Wall Street Journal* titled "There Isn't a Coronavirus 'Second Wave.'" Trump's political strategists found an expert who would parrot the president's views to give them credibility in Fox News commentator Dr. Scott Atlas. A professor of radiology at Stanford, Atlas had no training in virology or epidemiology, but he confidently espoused his view that the best way to address COVID-19 was to protect the elderly and immune-compromised and allow the disease to spread through the population until the country achieved herd immunity. He was convinced that wearing masks would do little to stop the spread of the disease. His do-nothing message resonated with Trump's base, and Trump soon shuffled Anthony Fauci and Deborah Birx off to the sidelines and elevated Atlas to the public role of scientific expert.[17]

By mid-September, Trump was back to holding large indoor rallies where he mocked Joe Biden for wearing a mask, boasted that the country was defeating the "China virus," and promised the maskless crowds that "we are not shutting the country again." Then, on September 26, the president, who was not feeling well, tested positive for COVID-19. He nevertheless participated in a nationally televised debate with candidate Joe Biden on September 28 without revealing the results of the test. As his condition rapidly deteriorated, on October 2, a military helicopter whisked the president to Walter Reed Medical Center to be treated for COVID-19. When Trump returned to the White House three days later, he quickly removed his mask as he entered the building and later urged his Twitter followers not to fear COVID-19, because he felt better than he did twenty years ago (this despite the fact that, as the *New York Times* reported the following February, Trump was "sicker with Covid-19 in October than publicly acknowledged at the time, with extremely depressed blood oxygen levels at one point and a lung problem associated with pneumonia caused by the coronavirus"). Returning to the campaign trail, he told unmasked crowds that the disease was "disappearing." As the seven-day average of new infections reached an all-time high, public health experts and medical ethicists were flabbergasted by Trump's blatant disregard for the health of his audiences.[18]

The nation experienced an even greater surge of hospitalizations and deaths in the months following the 2020 election. The heads of the CDC and the Food and Drug Administration joined Drs. Fauci and Birx in urging President Trump to use his bully pulpit to urge the 74 million Americans who voted for him to take reasonable precautions to protect themselves and their neighbors. But the lame-duck president would have none of it. Instead, he hosted elaborate holiday parties where maskless guests sipped champagne and listened to the president explain how he had really won the election in a landslide, while the caterers, servers, and military personnel were exposed to the virus.[19]

Failure to Test

The Trump administration had an opportunity to contain the pandemic in late January and February 2020 by testing possible carriers and quarantining those who tested positive. But the administration botched it. Early in his administration, President Trump had named four political appointees to the Centers for Disease Control and Prevention along with Director Robert Redfield to ensure that the agency adhered closely to White House policy. A practicing evangelical Christian, Redfield was a "nice guy," but he lacked the expertise to head the CDC. At the outset of the pandemic, the CDC decreed that a test it had developed for detecting COVID-19 in humans would be the exclusive test for the nation and that samples could be sent to a few select laboratories for analysis. The government inexplicably refused to permit university laboratories to test people returning from China. FDA staffers reported that Health and Human Services Secretary Azar refused to allow the agency to work with university and commercial laboratories to approve more tests because too many positive tests might be inconsistent with President Trump's efforts to play down COVID-19 risks. President Trump later confided to his supporters at a campaign rally that he had instructed his aides to slow down testing because it was yielding too many positive results.[20]

Doctors soon discovered that the CDC test was defective, and it took another two weeks to come up with a new test and get it approved by the FDA. To conserve scarce testing kits, the CDC issued guidelines limiting them to people who had recently traveled to China or had been in contact with someone suffering from the disease. The lack of widespread testing meant that public health officials lost a valuable opportunity to undertake "contact tracing" of people who had come into contact with infected individuals. Throughout the country, infected people were spreading the virus to others, but nobody was testing to see who had the virus. And President Trump was telling the country that "we're testing everybody that we need to test" and "finding very little problem."[21]

It was not until the end of February that the FDA finally allowed any previously certified laboratory to test for COVID-19; the administration effectively wasted the critical month of February. The nation never had enough tests and equipment to mitigate the spread of the disease until it was out of control. A public health expert at Georgetown University, Lawrence Gostin, concluded that the death toll in the United States would have been "dramatically lower" if the country had tested more people in the early weeks of the outbreak and brought about greater social distancing. When asked whether he took responsibility for the testing fiasco, Trump responded: "No. I don't take responsibility at all."[22]

Leadership Failure

As the pandemic overtook the country in March and April, people looked to the federal government for leadership. They discovered severely weakened federal institutions and a president who was wholly unprepared for the task of speaking truthfully to the public about the need to sacrifice short-term convenience and economic well-being for long-term public health and economic progress. Angered by press reports detailing the administration's failure to recognize the seriousness of the situation in February and early March, Trump rejoined that "[e]verything we did was right." In fact, the opposite was true. Good leaders know how to draw on the wisdom and expertise of competent advisors. But over his first three years in office, Trump had created a culture of sycophants where no high-level official was brave enough to tell the president what he needed to know but did not want to hear. Rather than seeking consensus on a strategy to address the pandemic crisis, the White House staff devolved into a circus of warring factions.[23]

When it finally accepted the need to limit large gatherings, to require masks in public places, and to protect essential employees, the Trump administration pushed off responsibility for controlling the spread of the coronavirus to state and local officials. The federal government offered some aid by sporadically providing personal protective equipment, ventilators, and medicines (some of which did not work), and the CDC provided periodic guidance on mitigation measures. But regulations became the responsibility of states and local governments. The Trump administration likewise punted to the states the difficult decision of when to lift restrictions and open things back up. The problem with that approach was that the states lacked the federal government's expertise and financial resources, and individual states were in no position to address what was clearly a national problem.[24]

When Trumpian populists in Minnesota and Michigan staged armed protests against their strict protections, Trump did not back up the CDC and the director of his COVID-19 task force. Instead, he tweeted: "LIBERATE MICHIGAN!" and "LIBERATE MINNESOTA!" In addition to sending a clear message that it was acceptable, even noble, not to wear masks, the president was telling his supporters that it was OK to ignore the CDC and his health advisors. As the election season locked in attitudes about the pandemic, even some patients being treated in intensive care units for COVID-19 mimicked the president in denying that it was any worse than the flu. A California nurse who had treated many COVID-19 patients reported that "[e]very single person I have encountered who was misinformed on COVID-19 referenced the president's dishonesty on Fox News or social media." Journalist Lawrence Wright concluded that Trump "became not a leader but a saboteur."[25]

Failure to Protect Workers

As part of the Trump administration's cowardly attempt to pass off responsibility for protecting public health to state and local officials, the Occupational Safety and Health Administration shirked its statutory responsibility to provide safe workplaces for the millions of employees who did not have the option of sheltering in place and telecommuting, either because they were essential workers or because they feared they would lose their jobs if they did not show up for work. For those workers, the risk that they would become sickened with COVID-19 depended on the precautions that their employers voluntarily took to protect them. Because most workers went home to families or roommates, workplace practices that put workers at risk of contracting COVID-19 put their families at risk as well. Thus, the federal government's failure to protect workers made the pandemic worse for everyone.[26]

Nurses, physicians' assistants, and other healthcare providers in hospitals, doctor offices, clinics, and nursing homes were at greatest risk from the pandemic. The media reported horror stories of nurses having to reuse masks and rig shields out of saran wrap. Meat-packing plants were also prime breeding grounds for the coronavirus. The employees who worked shoulder-to-shoulder on the fast-moving packing lines sliced, deboned, and "gut-snatched" carcasses at such a rapid clip that they did not have time to cover their mouths when they sneezed or wipe their noses afterward. The towns in which they operated became hot spots of COVID-19 infections in rural America. The grocery stores, hardware stores, pharmacies, and other retail establishments that remained open because they provided essential services exposed their employees to the risk of contracting COVID-19 as they performed their daily functions of restocking shelves, working checkout counters, and dealing with abandoned and potentially contaminated shopping carts. Workers who provided public transportation services were particularly at risk of contracting airborne diseases. Bus and subway drivers, pilots and flight attendants, and taxi drivers deserved but received little protection. Workers in packing operations worked shoulder-to-shoulder arranging fresh fruit and vegetables to be placed in containers and shipped to stores and distribution centers. Warehouse workers for companies including Amazon, UPS, Federal Express, and XPO were exposed to the coronavirus on the packages and through interactions with fellow workers.[27]

The federal government agency charged with safety in the workplace had a statutory obligation to write health standards requiring conditions and practices "reasonably necessary or appropriate" to provide healthful employment. In cases where employees were exposed to a "grave danger" from harmful substances or a "new hazard," the Occupational Safety and Health Administration was obliged to issue "emergency temporary standards to take effect immediately." A separate "general duty clause" required every employer to furnish "employment and a place of employment which are free from recognized hazards that are causing or are likely to cause death or serious physical harm to his employees."[28] The Trump administration failed to write regulations protecting workers from the coronavirus, and its meager efforts to enforce the general duty clause left millions of workers at risk.

In response to the swine flu pandemic of 2009–2010, the Obama administration OSHA had put together a pathogen protection standard to protect healthcare workers, but the Trump administration put the project on hold and never got back to it. At the outset of the COVID-19 pandemic, the Trump OSHA received thousands of complaints about the failures of employers to protect workers, and ultimately COVID-19 killed more workers in a shorter period of time than any other health emergency that OSHA had encountered in its fifty-year history. Expecting pressure from Congress to take action, the career staff in OSHA's Health Directorate prepared a draft emergency temporary standard, but Labor Secretary Eugene Scalia killed the initiative.[29]

In early March, the AFL-CIO and affiliated unions petitioned OSHA to issue an Emergency Standard. The unions argued that employers could easily prevent infections in the workplace through feasible techniques like keeping workers six feet apart, providing effective masks, and providing hand sanitizer throughout the workplace. Labor Secretary Scalia responded that an emergency temporary standard was unnecessary because OSHA had ample power to protect workers from COVID-19 through the general duty clause. Scalia explained that because employers were already "implementing measures to protect workers," an emergency standard would "add nothing." The AFL-CIO then sued OSHA in the D.C. Circuit Court of Appeals, but the court declined to intervene.[30]

Instead of issuing regulations, OSHA wrote guidance documents that, by their own terms, "creat[ed] no new legal obligations," and it prepared a poster providing tips on how to prevent the spread of infections. To reinforce the point, President Trump issued an executive order stating that "non-adherence to [COVID-19] guidelines shall not by itself be a basis for enforcement action." The fact that workers continued to die of work-related COVID-19 infections contracted in hospitals, meatpacking plants, warehouses, mass transit vehicles, and other facilities demonstrated that OSHA's guidance documents were not working. (The Biden administration OSHA issued an emergency temporary standard in June 2021, but it was limited to healthcare workers.)[31]

OSHA told the public that the statute's general duty clause provided the tool it needed "to hold employers accountable" if they disregarded appropriate safety practices. But the agency was not using that tool. To invoke the general duty clause, OSHA must prove that a "recognized hazard" is present in the workplace and that "feasible" technologies or work practices are available to abate that hazard. The serious risks that the coronavirus posed to workers were generally recognized hazards that were likely to cause death or serious physical harm, and many technologies and work practices such as wearing masks and plexiglass barriers were easily available to protect workers from infections. Yet when workers at a Georgia poultry-processing plant complained to OSHA about standing shoulder to shoulder on a rapidly moving assembly line without protective barriers or masks and reported that three employees had died of COVID-19, OSHA watched from the sidelines.[32]

Instead of protecting meat-packing plant employees, President Trump issued an executive order invoking the Defense Production Act to require the plants to remain open, even if state or local authorities ordered them closed. The order also purported to shield the companies from liability to workers who contracted COVID-19 on the job and to their families and friends. The president had hesitated to invoke the Defense Production Act to increase supplies of face masks and reagents for testing, but he was eager to use that power to protect the owners of meat production facilities from state and local regulation. By the time that President Trump issued the executive order, twenty packing-plant workers had died of COVID-19 and 6,500 workers had been hospitalized, tested positive for COVID-19, or were quarantined and awaiting results.[33]

From February 2020 through January 2021, OSHA received 57,000 complaints related to COVID-19, but inspected less than 6 percent of the referenced workplaces. And many of the inspections consisted merely of telephone conversations in which the inspector queried the employer about the precautions the employer was taking. A major limitation of OSHA's enforcement capacity was the pitifully small number of inspectors that remained at OSHA after the Trump administration decimated the agency's staff. The 862 federal inspectors working for OSHA at the time of the outbreak constituted the smallest inspectorate in OSHA's history. OSHA inspections suffered a precipitous decline during the first few months of the pandemic. By the end of the year, they were still down 35 percent from the previous year. Trump's OSHA did not issue its first COVID-related citation until July 2020. By the end of the year, OSHA had issued several fines for general-duty-clause violations related to COVID-19 averaging a meager $14,000 per employer. Two of those fines, totaling $29,000, were levied against two of the nation's largest meat-packing companies, whose revenue for the year totaled nearly $65 billion.[34]

Lost Lives and Suffering

The damage that resulted from the Trump administration's failures was apparent in hospitals and cemeteries in every corner of the country. According to a Columbia University study, the country would have saved 36,000 lives by May 3, 2020, if stay-at-home measures, mask wearing, and social distancing had begun a week earlier in March, and 54,000 lives if they had begun two weeks earlier. By mid-December 2020, the disease was killing more than three thousand people a day, most of whom would have been spared had containment measures been taken earlier. The United States accounts for only 4 percent of the world's population, but it suffered 20 percent of the deaths. A panel of thirty-three scientists assembled by the scientific journal *Lancet* calculated that 40 percent of the U.S. deaths would have been avoided if the death rate had been closer to that of its peers in the G7 developed nations. Former FDA commissioner Scott Gottlieb, a Trump appointee, allowed that there was "always going to be" a spread of the coronavirus in the fall and winter, "but it didn't have to be nearly this bad."[35]

The toll was particularly high for the essential workers who did not have the option of sheltering in place. By the end of the Trump administration, over 57,000 workers at meat-packing plants had tested positive for COVID-19 and at least 280 had died. More than 250,000 hospital and nursing home employees had tested positive, and more than 1,700 had died. Among correctional staff at prisons, there were 27,500 positive tests and 74 deaths. Almost 20,000 employees of Amazon tested positive for the virus.[36]

Even after Trump exited the White House, the Trump effect on pandemic deaths and illnesses persisted in Republican governors' refusal to require sensible precautions in the face of a third COVID-19 surge in January and February of 2021, and the adamant refusal of Trumpian populists to get vaccinated. At the time of this writing, COVID-19 has claimed more than 700,000 American victims. It is impossible to know how many of these deaths would have been avoided if President Trump had not dismantled the agencies designed to protect us, disregarded expert opinion, and downplayed the risks. Had he urged Americans to wear masks and encouraged governors to take strong mitigation measures in early February, many anti-government populists and some governors would have ignored him. But if he had not politicized mask wearing and social distancing, many of those victims would still be alive.

PART IV

REBUILDING THE PROTECTIVE EDIFICE

CHAPTER 13

SAVING AND ENHANCING PROTECTIVE GOVERNMENT

Joe Biden's decisive victory in the 2020 presidential election demonstrated that a substantial majority of American voters reject the simplistic appeals to fear and prejudice of Trumpian populism, and it brought an end to the assaults on the protective edifice from within the government.[1] The subsequent election of two Democratic senate candidates in Georgia runoff elections, putting both Houses of Congress under Democratic control, set the table for repairing and enhancing the protective edifice. To achieve long-lasting reform, progressives in and out of government will have to restore public trust in government, reinvigorate the civil service, rebuild damaged protective institutions, and make them better. The rebuilding project will require additional resources, political determination, and time. It will encounter serious roadblocks. But there are good reasons to be optimistic about the future of the protective agencies and regulation in America.

Restoring Trust in Government

The first step in rebuilding the protective edifice is restoring public trust in government. The Republicans' strategy for the last four decades has been to criticize government incessantly when the Democrats are in power and to run it so poorly when Republicans are in power that people lose their faith in government's ability to improve their lives. In the early 1960s, more than 70 percent of Americans said that they

trusted government to do the right thing. By 2019, only 17 percent held
that view. Clearly, restoring trust in government will be no easy task.
It will require strong leadership and activism at the grassroots level
devoted to demonstrating the capacity for ambitious programs backed
by sound science to protect Americans from harm.[2]

The COVID-19 pandemic, which demonstrated the inability of
free-market fundamentalism and disrespect for science to protect
Americans, may have set the nation on the path toward renewal of the
administrative state that the Trump administration was so determined
to deconstruct. While President Trump was in denial mode in the early
months of the pandemic, some state and local governments took strong
regulatory action to limit the spread of the disease. As time went on,
the president reluctantly invoked the Defense Production Act to require
General Motors to build ventilators and to demand that 3M make more
masks for American users, and the shortages were alleviated. This was
as broad and powerful an assertion of regulatory power as any of the
regulations that the Trump administration had spent the prior three
years trying to remove from the books. And Operation Warp Speed,
envisioned by a career civil servant and operationalized by experts in
the government, university laboratories, and the private sector, was
spectacularly successful in making highly effective vaccines available
in record time. The public approved of these assertions of governmental power by a two-to-one margin.[3]

Compelling Narratives and Symbols. Building public trust in government will take compelling narratives that lift up shared values of economic and physical security for all Americans. It should, for example,
be possible to weave a narrative around the need for government action
to prevent the damage caused by climate disruption by focusing on the
awful world we are bequeathing to our children if we do not reduce
greenhouse emissions. Another narrative could focus on the public
lands that our great-grandfathers and the ancestors of indigenous peo-

ples bequeathed to us and our responsibility to preserve them for our great-grandchildren. Progressive activists need to speak the language of solidarity and appeal to the idea of public welfare.[4]

Symbols can be a powerful way to expose the perverse impact of market fundamentalism on communities. Public Citizen's "monopoly man," dressed in the tuxedo and top hat worn by the monopolist featured on the Parker Brothers game "Monopoly," showed up at hearings at Mick Mulvaney's Consumer Financial Protection Bureau as a powerful symbol of the Trump administration's effort to increase profits for financial institutions at the expense of consumers. Progressive activists need to think harder about symbolic representations of the protection that government provides against greedy banks, irresponsible employers, polluters, and plunderers.

Public Participation. Much of the resentment that fuels Trumpian populism is the conviction of millions of Americans that they have no say in determining what the government does. Federal regulators can help build connections between the public and government decisionmakers by offering many opportunities for ordinary people to participate in policy development and implementation. For example, in addition to publishing notices in the *Federal Register* soliciting comments on rulemaking proposals, agencies should reach out to respected voices in rural communities to help explain actions like the Waters of the United States rule, and they should sit down with rural residents to hear their concerns in person. Congress should consider establishing an Office of Public Advocate in regulatory agencies to ensure the engagement of marginalized communities in rulemaking proceedings that affect them. This will take additional resources, but the investment will be worth it if affected people feel that the agency values their input.[5]

Governing Well. The most powerful contribution that the current and future administrations can make toward restoring public trust in government is to govern well. The agencies need to write clear regulations supported by transparent analysis and to enforce those regulations in an evenhanded way that provides the protections to which people and places are entitled under the relevant statutes. President Biden attempted to achieve that goal by appointing experienced policymakers to the upper levels of the agencies. The perception of calm competence that the Biden administration has thus far projected has helped to build public trust. And federal agencies should devote more resources to publicizing success stories in press releases, television interviews, and social media. As good government protects people from the vicissitudes of the marketplace, activists, academics, think tanks, and progressive politicians should give government a shout-out.[6]

Reinvigorating Government Service

The lengthy 2018 government shutdown and the president's obvious contempt for the civil service deeply eroded the long-standing bargain that attracted highly qualified professionals to public service. Civil servants forego the possibility of outsized incomes in return for a degree of job security and attractive benefits, including access to good medical insurance and reasonable working hours (for the most part). Most regulatory agencies experienced a massive exodus of scientists, engineers, lawyers, and other professionals at the outset of the Trump administration. During the first two years of the Trump administration, more than 1,600 scientists left the federal government.[7] The loss of longtime civil servants erased many years' worth of valuable institutional memory that may be irreplaceable. And the constant assault on the civil service by President Trump and Republicans in Congress made it very difficult to recruit talented professionals to fill the vacancies left by the mass exodus. A January 2019 report by the Senior Executives Association warned that the degradation in the workforce had reached the point at which "critical operations might fail" in the event of a major crisis. And that is exactly what happened in the spring of 2020 when the nation was invaded by a silent coronavirus killer.[8]

It is time to show dedicated civil servants a little respect. They do not put their lives on the line every day, but they do make large sacrifices so that the rest of us receive the protections that we need and deserve. They do not deserve the contempt that Republican politicians and the conservative media constantly pour on them. We need leaders with the courage and patience to explain to the public that the civil service is part of this nation's basic infrastructure, just like highways, bridges, and airports.[9]

Congress and the Biden administration should assign a high priority to reviving the "best American traditions of public service as an honorable, even noble calling." The first step in this project is to fill the vacancies left by the Trump administration's purge and the upcoming vacancies attributable to the fact that there are five times as many civil servants over age sixty as under thirty. This will require congressional action to pay or otherwise compensate government professionals at levels that are comparable to professionals in the private sector, and to provide training and other educational opportunities for those professionals. Congress should also expand the existing protections against arbitrarily firing civil servants to other negative actions like reassigning them to do-nothing jobs for which they are unqualified. To ensure high-quality recruits over the long term, law professor Jon Michaels has suggested establishing a program in universities similar to the ROTC program for recruiting military officers.[10]

Over the past half-century, presidents have greatly expanded the number of political appointees in the agencies at the expense of the civil service. Prior to the Reagan administration, for example, career civil servants were routinely promoted to head the Centers for Disease Control and Prevention, and they served across presidential administrations. President Reagan turned this into a political position so that directors changed with changing administrations, and directors felt pressure to please the president or risk being fired. President Trump added six political positions to the Center's organizational structure. Congress and the Biden administration should move in exactly the opposite direction by limiting political appointees to the minimum necessary to provide policy oversight, and they should allow civil servants to play "a central role in defining the public interest and implementing the programs that will achieve it."[11]

President Biden promised to rebuild the civil service. He got off to a good start by repealing the Trump executive orders limiting collective bargaining rights and due process protections for civil servants. In sharp contrast to the Trump administration's hiring freeze, the Biden administration began an aggressive process of staffing up, and the president requested increases in agency budgets to facilitate hiring more people. At his swearing-in ceremony, EPA Administrator Michael Regan, himself a former EPA staffer, told the EPA staff that he was assigning a high priority to ensuring that the agency's career experts were reincorporated into agency decision-making processes, and he expressed a willingness to hire back employees who had left out of frustration during the Trump years.[12]

Rebuilding Government to Make It Better

The Trump administration's assault on government was like a hurricane that leveled a coastal city. The Biden administration is now faced with the dilemma of how to reconstruct the government that the Trump administration so vigorously attempted to demolish. In the process, Biden appointees should try to make government agencies both more effective in providing protection and more resilient to future assaults.[13] While this is not the place for a detailed description of all of the needed reforms, the following thumbnail sketches offer some broad possibilities.

Committing Resources. Rebuilding government will require Congress to appropriate substantially more resources to allow starved federal agencies to staff up to the levels of the Clinton or even the Carter years. It may be necessary to come up with alternative sources of funding such as permit fees, and to allow agencies to keep some or all of the monies paid in fines for violations that the agencies uncover. Congress may need to create new agencies, and it should empower existing agencies to write more protective regulations, provide clearer incentives for companies to behave responsibly, and provide more effective oversight of existing products and technologies.[14]

Fixing Trump-Era Mistakes. A major project for all of the agencies will be to fix the terrible mistakes of the Trump agencies. Some fixes are fairly easy to implement, and some have already taken place. For example, on inauguration day, President Biden signed an executive order rescinding more than a dozen of President Trump's deregulatory executive orders. Similarly, the agencies can rescind internal policies and guidance documents that reflect Trump's deregulatory policies. For example, the Biden Department of Education reversed Secretary DeVos's stingy policy for forgiving student loans and began discharging loans to defrauded students on a wholesale basis, canceling more than $10 billion in federal loans to more than 500,000 students in the first eight months of the administration. Biden's chief of staff also ordered the agencies to stop working on regulations that had not been finalized before Trump left office. And the Department of the Interior moved the Bureau of Land Management's headquarters back to Washington, D.C., where its leaders would have better access to the levers of power.[15]

The Democrat-controlled Congress, however, was reluctant to use the Congressional Review Act to overturn Trump rollbacks. Democrats introduced only six resolutions of disapproval, and Congress passed only three, one of which was to overturn the Trump EPA's rollback of the Obama EPA's standards for methane emissions from oil and gas drilling operations.[16]

Aside from the Congressional Review Act, overturning final Trump administration regulations will be difficult. The White House published a list of 102 regulations and other Trump administration actions that the agencies were required to reexamine and repeal or revise to be consistent with Biden administration policies. For those that remained in litigation, the Biden administration on many occasions successfully requested that courts hold the litigation in abeyance to give the administration a chance to reverse course. This will require the agencies to employ notice-and-comment procedures and to build records that justify undoing Trump administration rollbacks. In cases where events have outrun the rulemaking process, such as the Obama administration's Clean Power Plan, the Biden agencies may have to start over from scratch. Even when things are proceeding smoothly, however, this resource-intensive process can take eighteen to thirty-six months to complete in addition to the time consumed by judicial review.[17]

Reliance on Science. The Trump administration was not interested in scientific information and expertise if it ran counter to President Trump's policy of the moment. On issues ranging from climate change to endangered species to COVID-19, Trump agencies ignored mainstream scientists and promoted fringe scientists whose sometimes bizarre theories were compatible with the administration's deregulatory policies. Decisions based on unsound science yielded bad results. The nation has lost four years of valuable time in reducing greenhouse gases, populations of threatened and endangered species are declining, and more than 700,000 people in the United States have died of COVID-19. The Biden administration must instill a new respect for science and pursue a data-driven approach to regulation that relies on scientific facts when they are available, and errs on the side of safety when faced with scientific uncertainty. It should also establish and enforce scientific integrity standards to ensure that agency scientists do not feel pressure to shape their scientific assessments to fit political goals.[18]

President Biden began that process on inauguration day with an executive order promising to "listen to the science" and to "improve public health and protect the environment." He also created an initiative to prevent "improper political interference in the conduct of scientific research" and "the suppression or distortion of scientific or technological findings." A memo to agency heads instructed them to review their agencies' websites to ensure that they reflected the president's respect for science. To symbolize his commitment to reliance on science in decision making, Biden replaced the portrait of Andrew Jackson in the Oval Office with a portrait of Benjamin Franklin.[19]

The Biden administration should repopulate the key scientific advisory committees with highly qualified, mainstream scientists who have expertise in the relevant areas, do not have strong connections with the regulated industries, and are committed to providing objective scientific advice. Agencies should not bar scientists from advisory committees solely because they receive government funding to support their research. The EPA's new administrator, Michael Regan, took an important step in this direction when he fired all of the members of the agency's two most important advisory committees and replaced most of them with scientists chosen through a competitive process that considered nominees "in a way that return[ed] the agency to its standard process of incorporating a balanced group of experts."[20]

Judicious Permitting. It is time for a more judicious approach to granting access to our collective resources. The burden of proof should be on the permit applicant to demonstrate that the permitted activities meet the regulatory criteria, and factual assertions should be supported by sound data and analysis. Some resources are so sensitive that

permits for activities that might threaten them should be banned altogether. President Biden got off to an excellent start with the appointment of Deb Haaland to be the first Native American Secretary of the
Interior. A strong supporter of green initiatives and environmental justice, Haaland quickly revoked twelve Trump administration orders and
issued an order prioritizing climate change. Soon after the inauguration, President Biden issued an executive order imposing a moratorium
on fossil fuel leasing on federal lands pending a "comprehensive review
and reconsideration" of the department's fossil fuel program. But a federal district court in Louisiana enjoined the department from implementing the moratorium.[21]

The Biden administration has not, however, attempted to undo existing permits for large projects. For example, the Biden administration
defended in court the Trump administration's approval of Conoco-
Phillips' massive Willow oil and gas drilling project, which was projected to pull more than 300,000 barrels of oil a day for thirty years
from the National Petroleum Reserve in Northwest Alaska. And to
the great chagrin of Native American and environmental activists, the
Biden administration told a court that it did not support draining the
controversial Dakota Access pipeline while the Corps of Engineers
completed an environmental impact statement.[22]

The Biden administration should initiate a rulemaking to reinstate
long-standing environmental impact statement regulations and make
them even more protective. The Council on Environmental Quality
should enhance its interagency coordination role to ensure that environmental justice becomes an integral part of agency thinking about
projects that significantly impact the human environment.[23] Agencies
that had adopted the guidelines of Trump's council should return to
their previous procedures.

President Biden got off to a good start by appointing Brenda Mallory,
a former general counsel to the council and director of regulatory policy

at the Southern Environmental Law Center, to head the council. Biden's ambitious infrastructure bill emphasized green energy projects, but it was ambiguous about the role that environmental reviews would play in permitting those projects. And the administration has not been in a hurry to revoke or revise Trump's changes to the environmental impact statement regulations.[24]

Forceful Enforcement. The Biden agencies should focus on strict enforcement rather than "compliance assistance" so as to hold violators accountable and to give companies a powerful incentive to comply with the law. Violations of the law must have consequences that go beyond being merely a cost of doing business. And enforcement should be completely free of political interference. For unrepentant scofflaws, criminal sanctions should be invoked far more frequently. This will require a dramatic change in attitude as well as additional resources to beef up agency enforcement operations.[25]

The Biden administration has shown encouraging signs of putting a renewed emphasis on strict enforcement. The Justice Department quickly withdrew a number of Trump administration memoranda related to regulatory enforcement, including the Trump-era prohibition on using supplemental environmental projects in environmental litigation. Responding to a Biden executive order, the Occupational Safety and Health Administration issued a new "national emphasis program" focusing inspections on "high-hazard" industries and on individual companies that posed a high risk of contracting COVID-19. Reversing a Trump administration policy, the Consumer Financial Protection Bureau issued an interpretive rule confirming that it did have the power to supervise military lenders to protect military families from predatory tactics, and the agency reinstated the program. The Department of Education reestablished the aggressive student loan enforcement unit that the Trump administration had abolished in 2018. Even before the inauguration, career attorneys in the EPA and the Justice Department picked up the pace at which they pursued enforcement cases against polluters. In the spring of 2021, the EPA shut down a refinery in the Virgin Islands that posed a serious threat to largely minority neighboring communities.[26]

Focus on the Vulnerable. Environmental justice demands that agencies pay particular attention to the complaints of vulnerable communities and ensure that they receive the same protection as well-off communities in the exurbs far removed from major industrial plants. Executive Order 12,898, which dates back to the Clinton administration but was ignored by the Trump administration, requires agencies to take environmental justice considerations into account in writing regulations and issuing permits. The Biden administration should focus on fence-line communities and other communities that are disproportionately affected by pollution in regulating emissions of harmful pollutants into the nation's air and water and siting coal ash and hazardous waste disposal facilities.[27]

When it comes to climate change, all Americans are vulnerable to more violent hurricanes, droughts, wildfires, and other calamities brought on by global warming. As with much pollution, however, climate disruption disproportionally affects the poorest and most vulnerable people, who lack sufficient resources to adapt or to rebuild after climate change–caused natural disasters. Heat waves hit communities of color harder than they do white communities in both urban and rural settings. Poor and minority communities are more likely to be found in flood-prone areas than are white and high-income populations.[28]

President Biden received a mandate to take action to mitigate climate disruption. According to exit polls, 74 percent of Biden voters said that climate change was "very important" to their vote. Under orders from President Biden, the United States officially re-entered the Paris agreement in mid-February 2021. And Biden vowed to make up for four lost years. Among other things, he set a goal of making half of new automobile production consist of fully electric or plug-in hybrid vehicles by 2030. So long as the filibuster remains an option for Republican senators, however, climate change legislation is unlikely. The administration will therefore have to use its authorities under existing statutes. As it plans for climate resiliency, it should provide a place at the table for representatives of long-neglected vulnerable communities to ensure that they are protected from rising sea levels, fiercer storms, and wilder wildfires.[29]

Ordinary consumers are a vulnerable population because they do not have the time or the energy to become fully informed about the products and services that they purchase. Millions of low- and moderate-income families do not have enough income to pay for basic necessities. In addition, the COVID-19 pandemic threw many comfortably middle-class families into financial distress. All of these families are vulnerable to payday lenders and other scam artists who are skilled at extracting money from desperate people. Student borrowers are vulnerable to abusive tactics by student loan collectors. The Consumer Financial Protection Bureau should make a special effort to protect the most vulnerable consumers—traditionally underserved minority consumers and the elderly—and ensure that they or their representatives are heard when the agency is making important regulatory decisions.[30]

One elegant solution to the payday lending problem is to enact legislation empowering the U.S. Postal Service to make loans of up to $1,000 to people in need of a short-term loan at interest rates slightly higher than the Treasury Department pays on Treasury bonds. In 2018, Senator Kirsten Gillibrand (D-N.Y.) introduced a bill to do just that. The Treasury Department could start the ball rolling by loaning the Postal Service the initial funds, or Congress could appropriate the funds. Because it would not be attempting to extract obscene profits from desperate borrowers, the Postal Service could charge much lower interest rates, and it would be required to ensure that borrowers had the wherewithal to pay back the loans at the end of the loan periods. Best of all, the thirty thousand post offices around the country would make it easy for low-income residents of "bank deserts" to find a lender of last resort other than a private payday lender.[31]

Some animal species are especially vulnerable because they are nearing extinction. On his first day in office, President Biden signed an executive order requiring the Department of the Interior to review the Trump administration's endangered species and migratory bird regulations.[32] The department should complete the review with regulations repealing those regulations.

The Trump administration endangered vulnerable places of pristine beauty and cultural value, and the new administration got off to a good start in reversing Trump-era directives. On inauguration day, President Biden signed an executive order imposing a temporary moratorium on all further lease-related activity within the Alaska National Wildlife Refuge. The order also directed the Department of the Interior to review the boundaries of the Bears Ears National Monument and the Grand Staircase-Escalante National Monument with an eye toward restoring their original pre-Trump boundaries. In June 2021, the department "suspended" the existing Arctic Refuge leases for as long as it took for it to determine whether they were lawfully granted by the Trump administration, and it recommended that President Biden reinstate the original boundaries for the two national monuments. In the same month, the Forest Service announced that it would be revising or repealing the Tongass exemption from the roadless area rule. In July, the service announced that it would end large-scale timber sales in the entire Tongass Forest, and it promised to focus instead on resilience, wildlife management, and habitat improvement. And in October 2021, Biden announced that he would restore the original boundaries to Bears Ears and Grand Staircase-Escalante. President Biden should also consider designating new national monuments, including the proposed Great Bend of the Gila River National Monument in the Sonoran Desert, which would protect vulnerable petroglyphs and other sacred sites.[33]

Impediments to Progressive Reform

Reformers who want to rebuild and enhance the protective edifice will, of course, encounter many impediments, the most profound of which is Donald Trump's continuing appeal to millions of Trumpian populists and his resulting domination of the Republican Party. Trump has made a career out of fomenting distrust of institutions that have gotten in the way of his commercial and political interests. It will be exceedingly difficult for the Biden administration and its allies to rebuild public trust in government institutions when Trump continues to insist that the 2020 election was stolen and that he is the only legitimate president. Free marketeers and business Republicans will continue to support Trump or his successor, and they will continue to make deregulation a cornerstone of Republican policy no matter who wins the nomination.[34]

A Trump Judiciary. With free-market fundamentalists, including Neil Gorsuch, Brett Kavanaugh, and Amy Coney Barrett, on the bench, lawyers for regulated companies may find it easier to persuade reviewing courts that agency actions are inconsistent with authorizing statutes or are arbitrary and capricious under the Administrative Procedure Act. At the same time, lawyers for public interest groups will find it harder to persuade courts to force agencies to fulfill their statutory obligations to write protective regulations. Worse, the federal courts are likely to employ expansive definitions of property rights and corporate free speech rights to challenge as unconstitutional government efforts to protect consumers, workers, neighbors, and the environment from preventable harm. The Court's power to decide what the Constitution says is the ultimate hedge against democratic exercises of legislative power.[35]

Companies and trade associations will dependably challenge all Biden administration regulations that add to their costs. Any nationally significant regulatory action undertaken by the Biden administration will also attract federal lawsuits by more than twenty Republican attorneys general. And a brand new organization called America First Legal, headed by former White House aide Stephen Miller, promises to use the legal system to overturn Biden administration regulatory initiatives.[36]

It may be difficult for Biden agency initiatives to survive judicial review in a federal judiciary that includes 230 Trump-appointed judges. In many situations, the challenger to a regulation can choose the court that will hear the challenge. Opponents of Biden administration regulations will rush to their favorite district court or to the Fifth Circuit Court of Appeals, a court that is heavy with Republican appointees. As of this writing, Republican attorneys general have already successfully petitioned a Trump appointee to the federal court for the Western District of Louisiana to issue a nationwide preliminary injunction against the Biden moratorium on oil and gas leasing on federal lands, thereby forcing lease sales to continue.[37]

Polarization. None of the three groups that make up the demolition crew—free marketeers, business Republicans, and Trumpian populists—came away from the 2020 elections "chastened or sobered." Trumpian populists, in particular, were convinced that the deep state had prevailed by stealing the election. The "#StopTheSteal" movement that sprang to life even before Biden was declared the victor was a festering boil that burst on January 6 with the assault on the Capitol. The United States remains a deeply polarized nation in which partisan posturing and ad hominem attacks are the order of the day.[38]

Donald Trump has been quite successful in exploiting these divisions and "making them larger." Under Trump, the Republican Party has gone beyond polarization to foment raw tribalism in its Trumpian populist base. The result is a huge divide between Trumpian populists who distrust government and progressives who believe that government should play a large role in protecting vulnerable people and places. In a polarized political environment where compromise is nearly impossible, legislative solutions to pressing problems are exceedingly rare and administrative solutions require intense effort through long time horizons. This situation is not likely to change any time soon.[39]

Resistance from the Demolition Crew. The demolition crew did not simply fade into the background of American politics after the 2020 elections. Free-market fundamentalists had to concede that government intervention was necessary to stem the economic losses caused by the COVID-19 pandemic, but they referred to the forgivable loans to companies as necessary "restitution" for the restrictions that governments placed on public gatherings and the consequential loss of economic opportunities for the companies. Free-market funders will continue to finance conservative think tanks and litigation groups. The Competitive Enterprise Institute's Myron Ebel observed that it was "much easier to stop stuff than it is to get stuff done." The head of the American Energy Alliance boasted that groups like his could tie up Biden administration initiatives for years in court with the expectation of victory in a Supreme Court with a 6–3 majority of conservative Republican appointees.[40]

Some business Republicans appeared to pull away from the coalition after President Trump fomented an attack on the Capitol to prevent Congress from certifying Joe Biden's victory. The American Petroleum Institute, the National Association of Manufacturers, and the U.S. Chamber of Commerce all condemned the actions. It was not long, however, before companies and trade associations returned to contributing to Republicans who had voted against certifying the Biden victory. The Chamber of Commerce supported the forgivable loans to businesses during the pandemic, but it did not support other big government programs. Having taken hundreds of billions in federal largess, business Republicans will continue to invoke the myth that regulations kill jobs to advocate more deregulation.[41]

The Trumpian populists' angry rejection of government intervention during the COVID-19 pandemic, despite the overwhelming scientific evidence that it would stem the progress of the coronavirus, is a strong indication that they continue to believe free-marketeer myths. They did not accept stay-at-home orders, social distancing, mask wearing, and the other pandemic precautions, because they valued their individual freedom over their responsibilities to their friends and neighbors. Despite the success of the Trump administration's Operation Warp Speed, a large percentage of Trumpian populists refused to take the vaccine, and that resulted in a fourth surge of infections, hospitalizations, and deaths among the unvaccinated in the summer of 2021. Trumpian populists will enthusiastically continue to follow the exhortations of Donald Trump and conservative media pundits to oppose Biden administration regulatory programs.[42]

Conservative News Media. Conservative news outlets ranging from talk radio stations to Fox News to the Drudge Report have for decades lobbed grenades at the protective edifice. Right-wing pundits routinely used government agencies as punching bags as they railed against government experts and "job-killing" regulations. They constantly emphasized economic freedom as a meta-value that should trump other policy considerations. And they were strong proponents of the privatization of public resources. Their skill at converting free-marketeer think-tank reports into language accessible to their viewers and at stoking fear of cultural displacement in white rural and working-class Americans made them ideal progenitors of Trumpian populism.[43]

The conservative news media are, if anything, more powerful today than they were at the outset of the Trump administration. Although Trump has had many disputes with Fox News and some of its commentators, they do not disagree about the desirability of reducing the size and power of the federal government. And new media outlets like Newsmax and One America News Network have sprung up to tell Trumpian populists how to think about current events while being careful not to irritate Trump.[44] Given their ability to stir up populist anger and resentment, conservative media outlets represent a formidable impediment to rebuilding the protective edifice.

Writing New Laws. Intense polarization makes it very difficult to enact legislation of any kind because there is little room for compromise. The prospects for protective legislation are further dimmed by the makeup of the Senate and the continuing vitality of the filibuster. Senators representing only 17 percent of the U.S. population have the power to stop most bills from going forward. As a practical matter, this means that any major legislation must gain the assent of politicians representing rural America. And lobbyists for many industries are constantly monitoring the legislative process to ensure that Congress does not enact protective legislation that their clients oppose. Disgraced former lobbyist Jack Abramoff, who was imprisoned for violating lobbying restrictions, remarked that "Washington . . . is the same swamp it used to be, but they rearranged the alligators and the lily pads." If legislation is required in order to implement needed reforms, it may be necessary to eliminate the Senate filibuster.[45]

Reasons for Optimism

Despite the difficulties that lie ahead for leaders who want to use the power of government to protect people and the planet from profiteers, polluters, and plunderers, there are reasons to be optimistic. Free-market fundamentalism lost much of its persuasive power during the

Great Recession of 2009, and the COVID-19 pandemic of 2020 clearly revealed the need for collective action to address common problems. Public support for government protections remains strong. Although Trumpian populism is still attractive to a great many mostly male, mostly white Americans, changing demographics and changing attitudes suggest that avid Trumpian populists will constitute a diminishing minority of U.S. voters.[46]

Opinion polls consistently conclude that the public strongly supports government regulation and the protections that it provides. In a January 2021 poll of 1,156 likely voters, 58 percent of respondents believed that government should prioritize protecting people's health and safety even if it comes at the expense of economic growth, and only 38 percent believed that it should prioritize economic growth. In the same poll, 54 percent of respondents believed that we needed more regulation of business practices of large banks, while only 17 percent believed that we should have less regulation. And a 2016 poll found that a majority of Trump voters were opposed to reducing the power of many federal agencies, including the Food and Drug Administration and the Consumer Financial Protection Bureau.[47]

The Trump administration did not have an affirmative regulatory agenda for the future. It was content to destroy the agencies without giving much thought to what would replace them. President Trump promised to continue to dismantle the agencies and repeal regulations if he was reelected. Although free marketeers were happy with that program, it was intensely unappealing to people who expected the government to protect them. Although regulation was not the only issue in the 2020 election, climate change was featured throughout the campaign. The fact that Joe Biden won by more than 7 million votes suggests that a majority of voters rejected Trump's assault on the protective edifice.[48]

The election of Donald Trump inspired thousands of college-educated mothers and grandmothers in suburbia to become politically active at the local level. They won local elections in 2018, and they made substantial contributions to the Democratic takeover of the House of Representatives in that year, and to the Biden victory and takeover of the Senate in 2020. Historian Lara Putnam and sociologist Theda Skocpol believe that this activism represents a "shift in long-standing trends" in political participation. These women are likely to remain a vital force in future elections.[49]

Trump placed prominent climate change deniers in powerful positions throughout the government, but they were unable to change the government's approach to climate science to any significant degree. Despite pressure from conservative activists to assemble scientists for a ludicrous "red team–blue team" debate over the extent to which human activities are responsible for global warming, Trump's political advisors prevented EPA and White House economic advisor William Happer from putting the idea into practice. August scientific bodies and the courts prevented Trump agencies from ignoring the effects of their actions on climate disruption. The Obama EPA's endangerment finding remains in effect, and the Department of the Interior has begun to take the climate effects of burning the fuels produced by oil and gas leases into account when deciding whether to offer federal lands for leasing. The federal agencies responsible for preparing the congressionally required national climate assessments continued to issue reports containing dire warnings about the damage to the planet that would occur if greenhouse gas emissions were not greatly reduced. Although the nation made little lasting progress in reducing greenhouse gas emissions during the Trump administration, the scientific predicate for regulating those emissions remains in place. More important, many corporations, including those whose products and activities are major contributors to greenhouse gas emissions, now recognize the critical need to bring them down.[50]

There is some evidence that the funders of free-market think tanks and Trumpian populist activist groups are having second thoughts about the wisdom of demolishing government institutions. In May 2019, the Koch network renamed itself "Stand Together," and Charles Koch terminated Freedom Partners, the entity that had funded much of the network's past political work. The "investors" were now "partners" in a "philanthropic community." The group would still focus on building a strong economy, which would require more deregulation, but it also wanted to help neighborhoods deal with poverty and addiction and to make members of society more tolerant of one another. Charles congratulated Joe Biden on his victory and promised to try to work with the Biden administration on issues upon which they could find agreement. This turned off some partners who were interested in remaining players in electoral politics. But many remained in the fold.[51]

Robert and Rebekah Mercer shut down their hedge fund, Renaissance Technologies, in May 2018. By mid-2019, they had drastically cut back on their contributions to conservative politicians and right-wing causes. A disappointed Republican strategist complained: "Crickets. They're gone."[52]

This decline in support caused a significant disruption in some of the groups that had been prominent warriors in the assaults on the protective edifice. For example, the loss of support from the Mercers and major oil companies attempting to improve their public images forced the Heartland Institute to lay off more than half of its staff in early 2020.[53] It remains to be seen whether other conservative think tanks and activist groups will suffer similar fates. But the apparent reduction in financial support for government-bashing groups from big-money contributors is an encouraging sign for supporters of government protections.

The decision by major oil companies to cut off support for anti-regulatory groups like the Heartland Institute was part of a broader trend in corporate America to reduce support for radical Republican politicians and Trumpian populist activist groups. The Chamber of Commerce's adamant opposition to all federal regulation gradually softened during the Trump administration. By mid-2019, the Chamber's official stance was that climate change was a "real threat" and that "humans contributed to it." The Chamber initiated a leadership change in 2019 when Suzanne Clark became its president, and she became the CEO upon Thomas Donohue's retirement in February 2021. The Chamber endorsed thirty Democratic House candidates, twenty-three of whom supported greenhouse gas regulation, during the 2020 elections. After President Biden was elected, the Chamber endorsed rejoining the Paris Climate Accords and supported market-based climate change legislation.[54]

In August 2019, the Business Roundtable attempted to burnish corporate America's image by drafting a "statement of corporate purpose" that committed its 180 corporate signatories to "creating economic opportunity for all of their stakeholders: customers, employees, suppliers, communities and shareholders." It also revised its principles for corporate governance to include a commitment to sustainable business practices. And in September 2020, the Roundtable endorsed putting a price on carbon dioxide emissions to combat climate disruption.[55]

This is not to suggest that business Republicans have become supporters of protective regulation in general. But these developments indicate that at least some of them can be persuaded to accept necessary regulation, and that they are increasingly wary of forming coalitions with Trumpian populists who have little respect for the rule of law and the legal institutions that are a critical precondition to a properly functioning marketplace.

The demographics of rural America are beginning to change as young college-educated people return to the land to operate farms that grow organic products for booming markets for local food. The number of farmers between the ages of twenty-five and thirty-four grew by 2.2 percent between 2007 and 2012, and most of these new farmers were not offspring of existing farmers. They are better educated and tend to be more progressive than farmers who grew up on the land. Former Deputy Agriculture Secretary Kathleen Merrigan believes that a "sea change" is coming in American agriculture as more young people become farmers. Following an influx of immigrants to rural areas, around 10 million rural Americans are people of color, and they are not Trumpian populists. They can be persuaded to support progressive policies, including worker safety and health regulation, pollution controls, and consumer protection regulation.[56]

Fundamentalist Christianity is on the decline nationwide, as is Christianity in general. In fact, the decline in church membership among millennials has been driven by an "allergic reaction" to the politicization of religion by the religious right. White evangelical Christians declined from 23 percent of the population in 2006 to 14.5 percent in 2021. Membership in the Southern Baptist Church decreased to its lowest level since the Reagan administration. Only half of the children raised in the Southern Baptist Church at the turn of the century remained members as adults.[57]

Not all evangelical Christians are Trump zealots. A group called Red Letter Christians, a reference to Bibles that print Jesus' words in red letters, believe that too many evangelical leaders have been wooed away from Jesus' teachings by Donald Trump. They cannot abide Trump's denigration of immigrants, his racism, and his obvious preference for the rich over the poor. Leaders of national evangelical and Baptist organizations met with Mick Mulvaney in February 2019 to urge him not to rescind the Consumer Financial Protection Bureau's regulations on payday lending. They viewed the usurious interest rates that payday lenders charge as sinful. Similarly, many young evangelicals cannot comprehend the opposition of the aging leaders of the movement to regulatory action combatting climate change.[58]

On the same day that voters in South Dakota elected Donald Trump by a margin of almost 30 percent, they enacted a referendum placing a 36 percent cap on interest on short-term and vehicle title loans by a margin of 52 percent, thereby effectively killing the payday lending industry in that state. This remarkable accomplishment was attributable to a strong populist appeal to voters from South Dakotans for Responsible Lending, the South Dakota AARP, various religious groups, and Steve Hickey, a longtime Republican legislator and pastor.

The South Dakota experience suggests that progressives can reach rural and white working-class Americans on issues that are close to their own experiences without appealing to resentments against "the others." Rural and white working-class Americans are concerned about their safety and the safety of their children and grandchildren. Conservative pundits and Republican politicians have focused those concerns on real risks posed by terrorists and criminals and imagined risks posed by immigrants and Antifa. But progressives should be able to focus them on the real threats posed by tainted food, unsafe workplaces, polluted air, and contaminated drinking water. If they can pierce the din of conservative media, progressives might even persuade farmers and urban workers of the urgent need to reduce climate disruption before it turns the world into a far less hospitable place. If rural and white working-class populists generally support governmental programs like Social Security and Medicare that assist everyone, they can perhaps be persuaded to support regulatory programs that likewise benefit everyone.[59]

The Pelerin Palace hotel, where the first meeting of Friedrich Hayek's Mont Pelerin Society took place in December 1946, was restored in the 2010s and converted into twenty-four ultra-luxury condominiums for occupation by wealthy folks who could afford to live in "the most expensive property in Switzerland."[60] It stands in all of its elegant

excess as an altogether fitting symbol for the free-market fundamentalist ideology that coalesced there seventy-five years ago and continues to
attract adherents who are untroubled by the wide disparities in wealth
that free markets have produced and that enable some to live in palaces
while most struggle to keep their heads above water.

The free marketeers and business Republicans struck a Faustian
bargain with Donald Trump and his populist following: Trump would
aggressively pursue the demolition agenda, and they would acquiesce
in his self-dealing and anti-democratic, misogynistic, and racist behavior. They were delighted with the Trump administration's unprecedented assault on regulatory agencies and the resulting easing of regulatory
restrictions. While the media focused on Trump's daily tweets, his
appointees in the regulatory agencies were demolishing the institutions
that protect Americans from a wide variety of risks. A spokesman for
the U.S. Chamber of Commerce concluded that the Trump administration's "[r]educing rules—and avoiding new ones—[was] a big win for
American business."[61]

Because of the Trump administration's abysmal record in court,
many of its deregulatory initiatives were overturned or were delayed
long enough for the Biden administration to revise or revoke them. But
the Trump administration successfully defended many of its deregulatory actions. Some of the adverse effects of the Trump administration
actions survived judicial review, and the consequences of its failure to
regulate things like greenhouse gas emissions, workplace heat levels,
slaughterhouse wastes, student loan servicers, and threats to endangered species will continue into the foreseeable future.[62]

According to many scientists, global emissions of greenhouse gases
during the Trump administration crossed a tipping point past which the
most damaging effects of global warming are now unavoidable. In May
2020, carbon dioxide levels in the atmosphere reached 417 parts per
million, the highest level in human history. According to an estimate

by scientists at the Lawrence Berkeley Laboratory, the Clean Power Plan, which the Trump administration repealed, would have contributed 15 percent of the greenhouse gas reductions needed to meet the goal of the Paris Accords. The reductions in emissions attributable to the automobile standards that the Trump administration repealed would have contributed another 8 percent. The carbon dioxide that entered the atmosphere because of these rollbacks will linger there for centuries.[63]

The Biden administration has taken some important steps toward repairing the edifice, but the effort will take much time and many resources.[64] The 2022 elections will play a critical role in determining the success of the Biden administration's efforts. Off-year elections in the past have derailed efforts by Democratic presidents to advance protective legislation and regulation. President Bill Clinton's plans to "reinvent" government to make regulation more effective were interrupted by the 1994 elections, in which militantly anti-government Republicans running on a "Contract with America" took over the House of Representatives and made Newt Gingrich its Speaker. Instead of bold new regulatory initiatives, the Clinton administration attempted to co-opt the radical deregulatory reforms that Congress was considering with deregulatory initiatives of its own. And Clinton declared that "the era of big government is over." Similarly, President Barack Obama's ambitious plans to control greenhouse gas emissions and to implement the Dodd–Frank Act and the Food Safety Modernization Act were waylaid by the 2010 off-year elections in which the Tea Party helped return the House of Representatives to Republican control. The Obama administration beat a hasty retreat, and the flow of protective regulations slowed to a trickle until after President Obama prevailed in the 2012 election.[65] If the Republican Party regains control of the House or the Senate or both in the 2022 elections, free marketeers, business Republicans, and Trumpian populists will take up the demolition agenda once again, and the Biden administration will find it very difficult to repair the protective edifice, and virtually impossible to put much-needed additional protections into place.

Despite a serious setback in the 2020 elections, the demolition agenda remains alive and well in free-marketeer think tanks and academic centers, in populist activist groups, and in many corporations and trade associations. The Trump administration's assaults on the protections that federal agencies provide demonstrated that those protections cannot be taken for granted. It took enormous political effort, often generated during crises following catastrophic failures of unregulated markets, to put those protections in place. Their fate will depend on how American voters value them in the future.

ACKNOWLEDGMENTS

As always, I am indebted to many people and institutions for making this book possible. The Joe R. and Teresa Lozano Long Endowed Chair in Administrative Law at the University of Texas School of Law supported my summer research and a semester sabbatical. My always upbeat assistant, Dottie Lee, provided administrative support. My colleagues at the University of Texas School of Law provided critical guidance at the book's formative stage at one of our drawing board luncheons, and Professors Jane Cohen and Mechele Dickerson provided detailed comments. Thanks to my cousin, Ben Thomas, for reviewing the entire manuscript with a keen eye to detail. I am deeply grateful to Gary Bass, formerly of the Bauman Foundation and a pillar of the public interest community, for introducing me to Diane Wachtell of The New Press, who did a marvelous job of guiding me in my attempt to document the Trump administration's assaults on the protective edifice in a way that I hope is accessible to the general public. Finally, I thank my wife, Cathy, for holding down the fort and being a continuing source of inspiration.

NOTES

The notes that follow will employ the following abbreviations:

New York Times—NYT

Wall Street Journal—WSJ

Washington Post—WP

Introduction

1. The Jennifer Zeleny story is drawn from Bethany McLean, "How Wells Fargo's Cutthroat Corporate Culture Allegedly Drove Bankers to Fraud," *Vanity Fair*, May 31, 2017; Michael Corkery & Stacy Cowley, "Wells Fargo Killing Sham Account Suits by Using Arbitration," *NYT*, December 6, 2016.

2. "Arbitration in America," *Hearings Before the Senate Judiciary Committee*, 116th Cong. (April 2, 2019) (testimony of Prof. Myriam Gilles, Benjamin N. Cardozo School of Law, Yeshiva University) [hereinafter Gilles Testimony]; Sylvan Lane, "Wells Fargo to Pay $575 Million in 50-State Settlement over Sales Practices," *The Hill*, December 28, 2018.

3. Deborah R. Hensler, et. al., *Class Action Dilemmas* (2000), at 4–6, 50, 84, 89, 109; Edward F. Sherman, "Consumer Class Actions: Who Are the Real Winners?" 56 *Maine L. Rev.* 223 (2004), at 223–24, 231–33.

4. Richard Cordray, *Watchdog* (2020), at 193 (closed doors, consumers unaware); Bureau of Consumer Financial Protection, "Arbitration Agreements," 82 *Fed. Reg.* 33,210 (July 19, 2017), at 33,227; Gilles Testimony (unfair to consumers, accountability); Martha McCluskey, et al., "Regulating Forced Arbitration in Consumer Services" (Center for Progressive Reform, May 2016), at 19–20 (arbitrators incentive, secrecy).

5. Cordray, *Watchdog*, at 194 (class action limitation, accountability); "Examining the CFPB's Proposed Rulemaking on Arbitration: Is It in the Public Interest and for the Protection of Consumers," *Hearing Before the Subcommittee on Financial Institutions and Consumer Credit of the House Committee on Financial Services*, 114th Cong. (May 18, 2016) (testimony of F. Paul Bland, Jr., Public Justice) (13 percent); Gilles Testimony (considerable perversion); Ted Mermin, "Cordray Takes on Wall Street with Consumer Protection Rule," *San Francisco Chronicle*, July 11, 2017 (Posner quote).

6. U.S.C. § 1639c(e)(1).

7. Bureau of Consumer Financial Protection, "Arbitration Agreements," 82 *Fed. Reg.* 33,210 (July 19, 2017).

8. Evan Weinberger, "Trump Officially Kills CFPB Arbitration Rule," *Law 360*, November 1, 2017; Andrew Ackerman & Yuka Hayashi, "Lobbying Beats Back New

Rule for Banks," *WSJ*, October 27, 2017; Jessica Silver-Greenberg, "Sparing Banks, Senate Repeals Litigation Rule," *NYT*, October 25, 2017, at A1; Elizabeth Dexheimer, "Wall Street Lobbyists Descend on Obscure Senator Before Big Vote," *BNA Daily Report for Executives*, September 1, 2017; Michael Macagnone, "House Passes Repeal of CFPB Arbitration Rule," *Law 360*, July 25, 2017.

9. Jimmie E. Gates, "Legally Blind Woman's Case Sent to Arbitration," *Jackson Clarion-Ledger*, April 5, 2018, at A5.

10. I detail four assaults on federal regulation in *Freedom to Harm*. Thomas O. McGarity, *Freedom to Harm* (2013).

11. Michael Wolff, *Fire and Fury* (2018), at 133 (Bannon quote).

12. Donald Trump, "Remarks by President Trump on Deregulation," December 14, 2017, https://www.whitehouse.gov/briefings-statements/remarks-president-trump-de regulation.

Chapter 1: The Protective Edifice

1. Industrial Union, *AFL-CIO v. American Petroleum Inst.*, 448 U.S. 607 (1980) (OSHA benzene standard); Environmental Protection Agency, "Bailey Waste Disposal, Bridge City, TX Cleanup Activities," cumulis.epa.gov/supercpad/cursites /csitinfo.cfm?id=0602911; Environmental Protection Agency," Star Lake Canal, Port Neches, TX Cleanup Activities," cumulis.epa.gov/supercpad/cursites/csitinfo .cfm?id=0605043.

2. "Voluntary Evacuation Order Issued Days After Texas Blast," *E&E News*, December 5, 2019; Kiah Collier, "Texas Chemical Plant Rocked by Multiple Explosions Was Declared High Priority Violator by EPA," *Government Executive*, December 2, 2019; Jacob Dick, et al., "Port Neches Rocked by Explosion," *Austin American-Statesman*, November 28, 2019, at A4.

3. Jacob S. Hacker & Paul Pierson, *Winner-Take-All Politics* (2010), at 113–14; Mancur Olson, *The Logic of Collective Action* (1971), at 11–22.

4. "Verses About Usury," Serata.com, https://sarata.com/bible/verses/about/usury .html.

5. Rena Steinzor & Sidney Shapiro, *The People's Agents* (2010), at 196 (quote).

6. Steinzor & Shapiro, *People's Agents*, at 196–97; Jennifer Nou, "Taming the Shallow State," *Notice & Comment*, February 28, 2017.

7. Steinzor & Shapiro, *People's Agents*, at 197.

8. Alexander Nazaryan, *The Best People* (2019), at 9 (quote); Anne Applebaum, "The Trump White House Is Destroying Our Civil Service," *WP*, August 3, 2018.

9. Brink Lindsey, "Free Markets and Limited Government Reconsidered" (Niskanen Center, June 23, 2020); Allie Gottlieb, "Is Regulation Good for Business?" *Regulatory Review*, December 9, 2019 (quoting Richard Cordray, former Director, CFPB) (clear rules); Sarah Conly, "Three Cheers for the Nanny State," *NYT*, March 24, 2013, at A21 (quote).

Chapter 2: The Demolition Crew

1. R.M. Hartwell, *A History of the Mont Pelerin Society* (1995), at 26–27, 31–32 (quotes); Fredrich von Hayek, *The Road to Serfdom* (50th Anniversary ed. 1994), at xlii, 16; Alfred S. Regnery, *Upstream* (2008), at 27. The description of the Mont Pelerin Society is drawn from Donald T. Critchlow, *The Conservative Ascendancy* (2007); Alan Ebenstein, *Friedrich Hayek: A Biography* (2001); Regnery, *Upstream*; Hartwell, *A History*; The Mont Pelerin Society Homepage, www.montpelerin.org/home.cfm.

2. Critchlow, *Conservative Ascendency*, at 16, 31; Ebenstein, *Friedrich Hayek*, at 144; Hartwell, *A History*, at 26–27; Christopher Leonard, *Kochland* (2019), at 42 (elitist); Dieter Plehwe, "Introduction," in *The Road From Mont Pelerin* (Philip Mirowski & Dieter Plehwe, eds., 2009), at 15.

3. Hartwell, *A History*, at xii, 64; Regnery, *Upstream*, at 31 (quote).

4. Fred Block & Margaret R. Somers, *The Power of Market Fundamentalism* (2014), at 2–3, 24–25; Milton Friedman & Rose Friedman, *Free to Choose* (1979), at 2; Nancy MacLean, *Democracy in Chains* (2017), at 66, 104–05, 143–45 (public goods); Thomas O. McGarity, "The Expanded Debate over the Future of the Regulatory State," 63 *U. Chi. L. Rev.* 1463 (1996), at 1485.

5. Critchlow, *Conservative Ascendency*, at 105 (credibility), 120 (oppose regulation); Trudy Lieberman, *Slanting the Story: The Forces That Shape the News* (2000), at 37 (credibility), 149 (packaging); John Micklethwait & Adrian Wooldridge, *The Right Nation* (2004), at 167–68 (packaging); Michael Pertschuk, *Revolt Against Regulation* (1982), at 63 (firepower), 64 (dehumanizing quote); Note, "The Political Activity of Think-Tanks: The Case for Mandatory Contributor Disclosure," 115 *Harv. L. Rev.* 1502 (2002) (nondisclosure).

6. David Brock, *The Republican Noise Machine* (2004), at 61 (on message); John B. Judis, *The Paradox of American Democracy* (2001), at 129 (public trust); MacLean, *Democracy in Chains*, at 36 (reframed); Jane Mayer, *Dark Money* (2016), at 89 (public trust); David M. Ricci, *The Transformation of American Politics* (1993), at 180 (reframed).

7. Nina J. Easton, *Gang of Five* (2000), at 17, 75, 85–87, 161, 276, 365; Coral Davenport, "A Night with Grover," *National Journal*, September 15, 2012, at 3.

8. Ross Gelbspan, *The Heat Is On* (1997), at 64–70 (CEI); Jacob S. Hacker & Paul Pierson, *Off Center* (2005), at 129 (Club for Growth); Jimmy Tobias, "The US Lawyers Rolling Back Wildlife Protection One Species at a Time," *The Guardian*, October 21, 2019 (Pacific Legal Foundation); David Callahan, "The Think Tank as Flack," *Washington Monthly*, November 1999 (CEI); The Club for Growth, Homepage, www.clubforgrowth.org/join-now-3/?gclid=EAIaIQobChMIgO6e_sju7gIV5PbjBx3uxgr DEAAYASAAEgJjI_D_BwE.

9. John J. Miller, *A Gift of Freedom* (2006), at 7.

10. Micklethwait & Wooldridge, *Right Nation*, at 78; Daniel Schulman, *Sons of Wichita* (2014), at 3, 98, 215, ch. 5; Leonard, *Kochland*, at 157–87; Mayer, *Dark Money*, at 3, 88; Kenneth P. Vogel, *Big Money* (2014), at 13; Taylor Lincoln, "A Key Cog in Charles Koch's Master Plan" (Public Citizen, June 3, 2019), at 43.

11. Scot Waldman, "Meet the 'Dead Industrialists' Funding Climate Denialism," *E&E News*, June 26, 2020.

12. Jacob S. Hacker & Paul Pierson, *American Amnesia* (2016), at 135 (oppose regulation); Salena Zito & Brad Todd, *The Great Revolt* (2019), at ch. 6 (referring to Business Republicans as "Rotary Reliables").

13. Alyssa Katz, *The Influence Machine* (2015), at xiii, 27, 64, 78 (biggest gorilla); Pertschuk, *Revolt Against Regulation*, at 58 (reaction to 70s); Sheryl Gay Stolberg, "Pugnacious Builder of the Business Lobby," *NYT*, June 1, 2013, at B1 (Donahue); Julie Kosterlitz & Peter H. Stone, "Enterprise Retooled," *National Journal*, February 20, 2010, at 40 (beacon); Elizabeth Williamson, "Climate Issues Divide U.S. Chamber of Commerce, Big Members," *WSJ*, April 17, 2008; Tom Hamburger, "Chamber of Commerce Vows to Punish Anti-Business Candidates," *Los Angeles Times*, January 8, 2008, at A1; U.S. Chamber of Commerce, "About the U.S. Chamber of Commerce," https://www.uschamber.com/about/about-the-us-chamber-of-commerce.

14. Hacker & Pierson, *American Amnesia*, at 203; Pertschuk, *Revolt Against Regulation*, at 57; Judis, *Paradox*, at 121–22.

15. Jill Varshay, "Manufacturers' Lobby Savors New Visibility," *Congressional Quarterly*, February 28, 2005, at 497; National Association of Manufacturers, "About the NAM," https://www.nam.org/about/.

16. Tim Alberta, *American Carnage* (2019), at 136; Katz, *Influence Machine*, at xv.

17. Alberta, *American Carnage*, at 34; Richard Cordray, *Watchdog* (2020), at 26; John B. Judis, *The Populist Explosion* (2016), at 58; Jeff Nesbit, *Poison Tea* (2016), at 25; Reece Peck, *Fox Populism* (2019), at 1; Joseph E. Stiglitz, *People, Power, and Profits* (2019), at 113–14.

18. Bryan T. Gervais & Irwin L. Morris, *Reactionary Republicanism* (2018), at 1; Mayer, *Dark Money*, at 167–68; Anne Nelson, *Shadow Network* (2009), at 157 (DeVos); Nesbit, *Poison Tea*, at 24–25 (tobacco industry), 42–43; Schulman, *Sons of Wichita*, at 272 (grasstops); Jonathan Mahler, "All the Right People," *NYT Magazine*, June 24, 2018 (Heritage Action); Alex Kotch, "Documents Reveal a Powerful, Secretive Foundation's Blueprint for Spreading Right-Wing Ideology, State by State," Moyers & Company, May 11, 2017; Jane Mayer, "The Reclusive Hedge Fund Tycoon Behind the Trump Presidency," *New Yorker*, March 27, 2017 (Mercers); Alex Shephard, "The D.C. Think Tank Behind Donald Trump," *New Republic*, February 22, 2017 (Heritage Action).

19. Alberta, *American Carnage*, at 55 (flags); Leonard, *Kochland*, at 434; Mayer, *Dark Money*, at 181; Peck, *Fox Populism*, at 5 (Fox News); Vogel, *Big Money*, at 46 (hired organizers); Kate Zernike, *Boiling Mad* (2010), at 42–43 (fiscal responsibility quote); "Free Gas! Americans for Prosperity Tries to Buy Public's Support with an Offer Few Can Refuse," *Alternet*, October 16, 2012.

20. Alberta, *American Carnage*, at 6 (taking sides); Gervais & Morris, *Reactionary Republicanism*, at 5, 65, 216–17 (power wains); Michael Wolff, *Fire and Fury* (2018), at 163 (Trump co-opts); Brad Bannon, "What Happened to the Tea Party," *The Hill*, August 14, 2018; Jane Coaston, "In 2018, the Tea Party Is All in for Trump," *Vox*, May 16, 2018; Seth McLaughlin, "Tea Party Pushed to Trump's Shadow at CPAC," *Washington Times*, February 21, 2018; Michael Grunwald, "How the GOP Learned

to Stop Worrying and Love Spending," *Politico*, October 26, 2017 (fiscal responsibility); Deana A. Rohlinger & Leslie Bunnage, "Did the Tea Party Movement Fuel the Trump-Train?" *Social Media & Society*, April–June, 2017; Jonathan Raban, "Telling It Like It Is, and Winning," *NYT*, January 8, 2017, at SR7 (taking sides).

21. Zito & Todd, *Great Revolt*, at 246; Tory Newmyer, "Koch Network Announces Plan to Oppose Trump Tariffs," *WP*, June 4, 2018; Kate Ackley, "Capitol Cash Machines," *Congressional Quarterly*, July 6, 2015.

22. Binyamin Appelbaum, *The Economists' Hour* (2019), at 14; David Frum, *Trumpocracy* (2018), at 215–17; Schulman, *Sons of Wichita*, at 309; Katherine Stewart, *The Power Worshipers* (2019), at 41 (quoting Ralph Drolinger, Capitol Ministries); Vogel, *Big Money*, at 130, 143; Zito & Todd, *Great Revolt*, at 242; Zernike, *Boiling Mad*, at 9.

23. Alberta, *American Carnage*, at 418–19, 496; Eric Boehm, "Yes, There Are Libertarians in Pandemics," *Reason*, March 10, 2020.

24. Appelbaum, *Economists' Hour*, at 324; Leonard, *Kochland*, at 561; Nelson, *Shadow Network*, at 188; Zito & Todd, *Great Revolt*, at 9; Charles Koch, "Trump's Policies Must Not Benefit Only Big Businesses Like Mine," *WP*, April 27, 2017.

25. Katz, *Influence Machine*, at 237; Zito & Todd, *Great Revolt*, at 243.

26. Gervais & Morris, *Reactionary Republicanism*, at 10, 125; David Brooks, "The G.O.P. Is Rotting," *NYT*, December 8, 2017, at A29; Jennifer Steinhauer & Jonathan Weisman, "In the DeMint Era at Heritage, a Shift from Policy to Politics," *NYT*, February 24, 2014, at A1.

27. Alberta, *American Carnage*, at 38; Joshua Green, *Devil's Bargain* (2017), at 106; Judis, *Populist Explosion*, at 70–71; Stolberg, "Pugnacious Builder," at B1.

28. Green, *Devil's Bargain*, at xv; Brody Mullins & Alex Leary, "Washington's Biggest Lobbyist Gets Shut Out," *WSJ*, May 3, 2019, at A1.

29. Stiglitz, *People, Power, and Profits*, at 175.

30. Appelbaum, *Economists' Hour*, at 14–15 (common ground); Jacob S. Hacker & Paul Pierson, *Let Them Eat Tweets* (2020), at 142 (common ground), 144 (judges); Leonard, *Kochland*, at 536 (judges), 561 (Koch support); Kathleen Hall Jamieson & Joseph N. Capella, *Echo Chamber* (2008), at 60 (Fox News); Stewart, *Power Worshipers*, at 120–21 (common ground); Adam Davidson, "Made in Austria," *NYT Magazine*, August 21, 2012, at 18 (Hayekians).

31. Alberta, *American Carnage*, at 261 (Trump's populist appeals); Gervais & Morris, *Reactionary Republicanism*, at 168 (Trump's populist appeals); Nelson, *Shadow Network*, at 209–10 (religious right); Cliff Sims, *Team of Vipers* (2019), at 45 (trust in mainstream media); Stiglitz, *People, Power, and Profits*, at 14–15 (business Republicans); Zito & Todd, *Great Revolt*, at 6, 11–12 (Trump pitches message); Matea Gold, "The Mercers and Stephen Bannon: How a Populist Power Base Was Funded and Built," *WP*, March 17, 2017.

32. Alberta, *American Carnage*, at 394 (electoral votes); Zito & Todd, *Great Revolt*, at 3 (counties), 172 (Catholic voters); Katie Glueck, "Trump's Shadow Transition Team," *Politico*, November 22, 2018 (evangelicals); Brian Bennett & Justin Worland, "Beyond the Base," *Time*, October 22, 2018, at 30 (college-educated voters); Jerome

W. Peters, "In a Backlash to the Backlash, Republican Voters Embrace Trump," *NYT*, June 23, 2018, at A1 (wealthy voters); Christopher Sebastian Parker, "The Real Reason Trump Won: White Fright," *The Conversation*, November 17, 2016 (Tea Party votes).

33. Alberta, *American Carnage*, at 7 (Trump took credit); Frum, *Trumpocracy*, at 41–42 (large checks); Amanda Taub, "Partisanship as Tribal Identity: Voting Against One's Economic Interests," *NYT*, April 13, 2017, at A10.

34. James Hohmann, "As Trumpism Coopts CPAC, the Reagan Era Ends," *WP Daily 202*, February 24, 2020 (star); Jeremy W. Peters, "A 'Never Trump' Coalition's New Point of View: Never Mind, He's Fine," *NYT*, October 6, 2019, at Y15; Rachael Bade, "Trump's Takeover of GOP Forces Many House Republicans to Head for the Exits," *WP*, September 22, 2019; Tim Alberta, "Trump's Takeover of Conservativism is Complete and Total," *Politico*, February 25, 2018 (2016 CPAC); Jonathan Martin & Jeremy W. Peters, "Critics Give Way as the G.O.P. Tilts to Trump's Orbit," *NYT*, October 26, 2017, at A1; Jay Caruso, "The Republican Dilemma," *The Atlantic*, June 4, 2017 (mute); David Weigel & Robert Costa, "Trump's America Will Be On Vivid Display at Annual Conservative Gathering," *WP*, February 21, 2017 (2017 CPAC).

35. Alberta, *American Carnage*, at 2 (89 percent); Frum, *Trumpocracy*, at 47–48; Scott Wong, "Trump Keeps Tight Grip on GOP," *The Hill*, March 18, 2019 (2018 elections); Robert Costa, "'We're Not Going to Turn on Our Own': Republicans Rally Around Trump as Threats Mount," *WP*, March 2, 2019 (2018 elections); Brian Bennett & Justin Worland, "Beyond the Base," *Time*, October 22, 2018, at 30 (Luntz quote); Shawn Zeller, "It's Trump's Party Now," *Congressional Quarterly*, April 16, 2018; Alberta, "Trump's Takeover."

Chapter 3: Appointing Toxic Leaders

1. Anne Nelson, *Shadow Network* (2019), at 206 (wrecking ball quote).

2. Executive Order 13770, 82 *Fed. Reg.* 9333 (January 28, 2017); Jacob S. Hacker & Paul Pierson, *Let Them Eat Tweets* (2020), at 153 (fierce deregulators), 156 (waivers); Robert Kuttner, *The Stakes* (2020), at 56 (regulated industries); Alexander Nazaryan, *The Best People* (2019), at xi (best people quote), xiii (waivers), 74 (Heritage Foundation); Evan Osnos, "Trump vs. the 'Deep State,'" *The Atlantic*, May 21, 2018 (Heritage Foundation, Americans for Prosperity); Scott Waldman, "Survey: Most Enviro Officials Tied to Fossil Fuel Industry," *E&E News*, April 12, 2017; Geof Koss, "McConnell Brushes Off Ethics Warning," *E&E News*, January 9, 2017; Jamelle Bouie, "Government by the Worst Men," *Slate*, November 18, 2016 (kakistocracy).

3. Michael Lewis, *The Fifth Risk* (1018), at 32 (waste of time), 37 (briefing papers); Nazaryan, *Best People*, at 25 (toilet paper).

4. Nazaryan, *Best People*, at 152 (transfer), 153 (attorney general), 156 (energy industry favorite); Niina Heikkinen, "Koch Industries Involved in Pruitt's Confirmation," *E&E News*, April 26, 2017 (Koch Industries); Robin Bravender, "From 'The Possum' to EPA Boss," *E&E News*, January 4, 2017 (education); Coral Davenport, "E.P.A. Workers Fight to Stop Confirmation," *NYT*, February 17, 2017, at A1; Brady Dennis, "Scott Pruitt, Longtime Adversary of EPA, Confirmed to Lead the Agen-

cy," *WP*, February 17, 2017; Niina Heikkinen, "Protesters Make Last Stand Against Pruitt," *E&E News*, February 1, 2017; Kevin Bogardus, "Enviros, Industry Ready for Battle Over Pruitt," *E&E News*, January 17, 2017 (support); Kevin Bogardus & Geof Koss, "Groups Intensify Ideological Battle Over Pruitt," *E&E News*, January 12, 2017 (environmental groups); Mike Soraghan, "Pruitt Dismantled Environmental Unit in Okla," *E&E News*, December 16, 2016; Eric Lipton, "Energy and Regulators on One Team," *NYT*, December 7, 2014, at A1 (cut and paste, Republican Attorneys General Association).

5. Nazaryan, *Best People*, at 158 (Heritage Foundation); Kevin Bogardus, "Ex-Hill Aide, Vocal Trump Ally Returns to EPA in Key Role," *E&E News*, March 16, 2020 (Inhofe infantry quote); Sean Reilly, "Lobbyist to Join EPA Air Office as Senior Advisor," *E&E News*, October 30, 2019 (NAM); Steve Eder & Hiroko Tabuchi, "E.P.A. Chief's Ethics Woes Have Echoes in His Past," *NYT*, April 22, 2018, at A1 (barred banker, law partner); Robin Bravender, "Top Aide to Pruitt Is Leaving," *E&E News*, April 5, 2018 (Republican Attorneys General Association); Kevin Bogardus, "Pruitt's Political Deputies Accumulate Power," *E&E News*, July 14, 2017.

6. Kevin Bogardus, "Pruitt to Tout 'Back to Basics,'" *E&E News*, December 7, 2017; Alex Guillen & Emily Holden, "What EPA Chief Scott Pruitt Promised—And What He's Done," *Politico*, November 21, 2017; Alex Guillen, "The Radical Idea Behind Trump's EPA Rollbacks," *Politico*, June 18, 2017; Coral Davenport, "Nominee Appears Poised to Cut E.P.A. with a Scalpel, Not a Cleaver," *NYT*, February 6, 2017, at A12 (scalpel).

7. Zack Colman, "Emails Show Pruitt Networking with Key Trump Allies," *E&E News*, May 11, 2018; Jennifer A. Dlouhy, "How Conservative Activists Saved Scott Pruitt's Job—For Now," *Bloomberg Law*, April 12, 2018; Brady Dennis & Juliet Eilperin, "Fancy Dinners, Far Flung Speeches: Calendars Detail EPA Chief's Close Ties to Industry," *WP*, December 3, 2017; Eric Lipton & Lisa Friedman, "On Busy Calendar, E.P.A. Chief Puts Interests of Industries First," *NYT*, October 3, 2017, at A1; Scott Waldman, "Pruitt Finds Friendly Media Outlets to Tell His Story," *E&E News*, May 17, 2017.

8. Christopher Leonard, *Kochland* (2019), at 557–58 (obsessed); Kevin Bogardus & Sean Reilly, "Pruitt Swept Office for Surveillance Devices—Documents," *E&E News*, December 19, 2017; Juliet Eilperin & Brady Dennis, "At EPA, Guarding the Chief Pulls Agents from Pursuing Environmental Crimes," *WP*, September 20, 2017; Kevin Bogardus, "Investigators Probe Threats to Pruitt," *E&E News*, September 14, 2017; Lisa Friedman & Coral Davenport, "Spending to Protect Former E.P.A. Chief Soared to $3.5 Million," *NYT*, September 4, 2018, at A18; Niina Heikkinen, "Investigators Brought in Millions. Now They're Guarding Pruitt," *E&E News*, May 12, 2017.

9. Nazaryan, *Best People*, at 159–64 (office décor, travel); Coral Davenport, Lisa Friedman & Maggie Haberman, "Mired in Scandal, Pruitt Is Forced to Exit E.P.A. Post," *WP*, July 5, 2018, at A1 (Oklahoma flights); Brady Dennis & Juliet Eilperin, "Scott Pruitt Steps Down as EPA Head After Ethics, Management Scandals," *WP*, July 5, 2018 (restaurant); Kevin Sullivan, Juliet Eilperin & Brady Dennis, "Lobbyist Helped Arrange Scott Pruitt's $100,000 Trip to Morocco," *WP*, May 1, 2018; Philip Bump, "A New Call for Investigating Pruitt—After Trump Already Offered His Verdict," *WP*, April 9, 2018 (own nickel); Eric Roston, "Security Detail Added $30K More

to EPA Chief's Italy Trip," *Bloomberg Law*, March 21, 2018; Kevin Bogardus, "Dems Question Security Reasons for Pruitt's First-Class Travel," *E&E News*, February 20, 2018; Alex Guillen, "Pruitt's Security Threat? A Passenger Shouting 'You're F---ing Up the Environment,'" *Politico*, February 15, 2018; Juliet Eilperin & Brady Dennis, "First-Class Travel Distinguishes Scott Pruitt's EPA Tenure," *WP*, February 11, 2018.

10. Eric Lipton, et al., "Getting Favors for Pruitt and Family Was Part of Job, Aides Say," *NYT*, June 15, 2018, at A1; Julie Hirschfeld Davis & Lisa Friedman, "Chief of Staff Advised a Resistant President to Fire the E.P.A.'s Chief," *NYT*, April 7, 2018, at A15 (changed locks); Jennifer A. Dlouhy & Susan Decker, "Pruitt's Family Stayed at Lobbyist's $50-A-Night Condo," *Bloomberg/BNA Daily Report for Executives*, April 3, 2018 (door); Kevin Bogardus, "More Questions About Pruitt's Condo," *E&E News*, April 2, 2018; Brad Plumer & Eric Lipton, "Head of E.P.A. Rented Residence from Wife of an Energy Lobbyist," *NYT*, March 31, 2018, at A11.

11. Nazaryan, *Best People*, at 168 (errands); Eric Lipton, et al., "Getting Favors" (billionaire); Juliet Eilperin, et al., "EPA Chief Scott Pruitt Tapped Aide, Donors to Help Wife Land Job at Conservative Group," *WP*, June 13, 2018; Juliet Eilperin, Josh Dawsey & Brady Dennis, "Pruitt Enlisted Security Detail in Picking Up Dry Cleaning, Moisturizing Lotion," *WP*, June 8, 2018; Juliet Eilperin, Josh Dawsey & Brady Dennis, "Scott Pruitt Had Aide Do Various Personal Tasks, Including Hunt for a Used Trump Hotel Mattress," *WP*, June 4, 2018 (mattress).

12. Nazaryan, *Best People*, at 172 (reports); Lisa Friedman, Eric Lipton & Coral Davenport, "As Pruitt Fell, Allies in E.P.A. Were Leaving," *NYT*, July 6, 2018 (interest in power); Brady Dennis & Juliet Eilperin, "Scott Pruitt Steps Down as EPA Head After Ethics, Management Scandals," *WP*, July 5, 2018 (federal inquiries, resignation); Anthony Adragna & Emily Holden, "Republicans Losing Patience with Scandal-Scarred Pruitt," *Politico*, June 6, 2018; Eric Lipton, Kenneth P. Vogel & Lisa Friedman, "Officials at E.P.A. Raised Concerns and Were Ousted," *NYT*, April 6, 2018, at A1 (rallied to defense).

13. Nazaryan, *Best People*, at 176 (arcade game), 177 (Tonto, no cattle quote), 178 (Montana Senate), 182–83 (education, navy); Elizabeth Kolbert, "The Damage Done by Trump's Department of the Interior," *New Yorker*, January 22, 2018 (special flag); Juliet Eilperin, "Trump Taps Montana Congressman Ryan Zinke as Interior Secretary," *WP*, December 13, 2016 (Roosevelt Republican); Kenneth P. Vogel, Maggie Severns & Rachael Bade, "Trump Selects Zinke as Interior Secretary," *Politico*, December 13, 2016.

14. Nazaryan, *Best People*, at xxviii (eighteen investigations), 187 (mid-level positions); 188–89 (travel), 195 (Halliburton deal); Juliet Eilperin, Josh Dawsey & Daryl Fears, "Interior Secretary Zinke Resigns Amid Investigations," *WP*, December 15, 2018; Jimmy Tobias, "The Zinke Effect: How the US Interior Department Became a Tool of Big Business," *The Guardian*, November 12, 2018 (checklist quote); Adam Aton, "IG Report Says Zinke Dispensed Perks," *E&E News*, October 18, 2018.

15. Tim Alberta, *American Carnage* (2019), at 222 (House Freedom Caucus); Justin Miller, "The Freedom Caucus's Man on the Inside," *American Prospect* (Fall, 2017), at 58 (cut regulations); Robert O'Harrow, Jr., Shawn Boburg & Renae Merle, "How Trump Appointees Curbed a Consumer Protection Agency Loathed by the GOP," *WP*, December 4, 2018 (inexperienced, high salaries); Catherine Rampell, "How Mick

Mulvaney Is Dismantling a Federal Agency," *WP*, January 25, 2018 (goal quote); Michael Grunwald, "Mick the Knife," *Politico*, September 1, 2017 (free-market fundamentalist); Michael D. Shear, "Trump Picks Mick Mulvaney, South Carolina Congressman, as Budget Director," *NYT*, December 16, 2016.

16. Pipeline and Hazardous Materials Safety Administration, "Pipeline Safety: Safety of Underground Natural Gas Storage Facilities," 85 *Fed. Reg.* 8104 (February 12, 2020), at 8105 (storing natural gas); Linda Chiem, "DOT Finalizes Eased Hours-of-Service Rule for Truckers," *Law 360*, May 14, 2020; Charles S. Clark, "Transportation Dept. Rebuts Report that Secretary Failed to Divest Stock," *Government Executive*, May 29, 2019; "Transport Safety Rules Sidelined Indefinitely Under Trump as Part of a Sweeping Retreat in Regulations," *CNBC*, February 26, 2018 (Eisner quote); Blake Sobczak, "DOT Rolls Back Rules for Oil Train Brakes," *E&E News*, December 6, 2017; Jeremy W. Peters & Maggie Haberman, "For Transportation, Trump Picks a Washington Insider," *NYT*, November 30, 2016, at A14 (Chao background).

17. Eric Lipton & Michael Forsythe, "Inspector Faults Chao for Misuse of Cabinet Post," *NYT*, March 4, 2021, at A1; Alex Gangitano, "Chao Letter to Trump Cites Wednesday's 'Events at the US Capitol' as Reason for Resignation," *The Hill*, January 8, 2021; Hannah Knowles, "Transportation Secretary Elaine Chao Faces Investigation over 'Troubling' Ethics Allegations," *WP*, September 17, 2019; Tucker Doherty & Tanya Snyder, "Chao Created Special Path for McConnell's Favored Projects," *Politico*, June 10, 2019; Michael Forsythe, et al., "A Cabinet Official, a Firm and a 'Bridge' to Beijing," *NYT*, June 2, 2019, at A1; Ted Mann & Brody Mullins, "Transportation Secretary Fails to Relinquish Shares," *WSJ*, May 29, 2019.

18. Julie Zausmer, "Rick Perry, Under Scrutiny for His Ukraine Trip, Says Trump Is God's 'Chosen One,'" *WP*, November 25, 2019 (chosen one quote); Mehdi Hasan, "Donald Trump Ushers in a New Era of Kakistocracy: Government by the Worst People," *Austin American-Statesman*, January 20, 2017 (Perry education, Moniz, Chu, Dancing); Philip Bump, "Trump's Cabinet Picks Are Often in Direct Conflict with the Agencies They May Lead," *WP*, December 13, 2016 (lapse of memory).

19. Rebecca Beitsch, "Trump Administration Rolls Back Efficiency Standards for Showerheads, Washers and Dryers," *The Hill*, December 15, 2020; Keith Goldberg, "Energy Dept. Faces New Bulb Efficiency Fight in 2nd Circ.," *Law 360*, February 25, 2020; Christa Marshall & Hannah Northey, "Political Hire Tapped for No. 2 Efficiency Post," *E&E News*, February 18, 2020; Lesley Clark, "Rick Perry Joins Board of Dakota Access Developer," *E&E News*, January 6, 2020; Kelsey Brugger, "Perry: Dems Live in a 'Fantasy World' on Climate Change," *E&E News*, August 15, 2019.

20. Masha Gessen, *Surviving Autocracy* (2020), at 19 (destroyed Detroit schools), 43 (investment in companies); Nazaryan, *Best People*, at 214 (childhood), 215 (Amway, religious schools), 217 (generous supporters); Nelson, *Shadow Network* (2019), at 69 (church), 70 (investments in groups), 73 (deeply dysfunctional quote); Katherine Stewart, *The Power Worshipers* (2019), at 188 (generous supporters); Mark Binelli, "The Michigan Experiment," *NYT Magazine*, September 10, 2017, at 53; Andy Kroll, "Meet the New Kochs: The DeVos Clan's Plan to Defund the Left," *Mother Jones*, January 21, 2014 (destroying unions).

21. Gessen, *Surviving Autocracy*, at 20; Nazaryan, *Best People*, at 50, 214, 219; Tim Alberta, "The Education of Betsy DeVos," *Politico*, November/December 2017.

22. Nazaryan, *Best People*, at 214 (aid private schools); Jim Lardner, "Mapping Corruption," *American Prospect*, (March/April 2020), at 14 (ideologues); Laura Meckler, "Betsy DeVos Emerges a Trump Cabinet Survivor," *WP*, April 28, 2019; Kate Wagner, "Betsy DeVos's Summer Home Deserves a Special Place in McMansion Hell," *Vox*, August 6, 2018; Offices of Senator Elizabeth Warren and Representative Katherine Clark, "DeVos Watch, Year One: Failing America's Students" (February 2018), at 4 (Schmoke); Patricia Cohen, "DeVos Adviser Is Tied to Firm Under Scrutiny," *NYT*, March 18, 2017, at A1 (Eitel).

23. Lewis, *Fifth Risk*, at 92 (other hires), 112 (Clovis); Marc Heller, "From Watermelon Delivery Boy to Trump's Pick for USDA," *E&E News*, February 6, 2017; Chris Mooney & John Wagner, "Trump Picks Sonny Perdue for Agriculture Secretary," *WP*, January 18, 2017.

24. Katie Thomas, "F.D.A. Nominee, Paid Millions by Industry, Will Recuse Himself if Needed," *NYT*, March 30, 2017, at A13; Laurie McGinley & Carolyn Y. Johnson, "Trump to Select Scott Gottlieb, a Physician with Deep Drug-Industry Ties, to Run the FDA," *WP*, March 10, 2017.

25. Nazaryan, *Best People*, at 94–96 (low public profile); Lisa Friedman, "New Energy Secretary Fits Trend: Cabinet Dominated by Lobbyists," *WP*, October 18, 2019; Lance Williams, "Recording Reveals Oil Industry Execs Laughing at Trump Access," *Reveal*, March 23, 2019 (access); Jennifer A. Dlouhy & Jesse Hamilton, "Ex-Industry Lobbyists Win Top Jobs in Agencies They Once Fought," *Bloomberg/BNA, Environment Reporter*, December 21, 2017.

26. Keith Goldberg, "Hunton, Greenberg Traurig Alums Tapped for EPA, DOE Posts," *Law 360*, February 13, 2020 (Benevento); Lisa Friedman, "New Energy Secretary Fits Trend: Cabinet Dominated by Lobbyists," *WP*, October 18, 2019; "Senate Confirms EPA Waste Chief Peter Wright in Party-Line Vote," *Inside EPA*, July 19, 2019 (187 sites); Kevin Bogardus, "Ex-Chemical Industry Official Joins Agency," *E&E News*, July 18, 2019; Zack Colman & Alex Guillen, "Documents Detail Multimillion-Dollar Ties Involving EPA Official, Secretive Industry Group," *Politico*, February 20, 2019 (Wehrum); Abby Smith & Amena H. Saiyid, "Ethics Rules Can't Corral EPA Air Chief from Advancing Policies," *Bloomberg Law*, September 20, 2018 (many lawsuits); Christine Powell, "4 Things to Know About the New EPA Chief," *Law 360*, July 9, 2018; Coral Davenport, "Steady Hand in Washington, Known for Quietly Whittling Away at the Rulebook," *NYT*, July 5, 2018, at A13; Kevin Bogardus, "Right Thrilled as Trump Taps Former Coal Lobbyist for Top Post," *E&E News*, October 6, 2017.

27. Juliet Eilperin, "Zinke's #2 Has So Many Potential Conflicts of Interest He Has to Carry a List of Them All," *WP*, November 19, 2018; Coral Davenport & Nicholas Fandos, "Strolling Though Parks. Rolling Back Regulations," *NYT*, July 26, 2017, at A11; Brittany Patterson, "Meet the Man Deciding the Department of the Interior's Future," *E&E News*, November 17, 2016.

28. *Bullock v. Bureau of Land Management*, 489 F.Supp.3d 1112 (D. Mont. 2020); Scott Streater, "Critics Celebrate Pendley Ouster, But He's Still in Charge," *E&E News*, August 17, 2020; Michael Doyle, "BLM Honcho Reveals Long Recusal List," *E&E News*, September 25, 2019; Bobby Magill, "'Trumpian' BLM Chief Expected to Open Development Floodgates," *Bloomberg Law*, July 30, 2019.

29. Lesley Clark, "Brouillette and Climate: Is DOE Changing Course?" *E&E News*, March 5, 2020 (work on quote); Lesley Clark, Jeremy Dillon & Hannah Northey, "Meet the 'Hill Creatures,' Brouillette's Inner Circle," *E&E News*, January 9, 2020; Lisa Friedman, "Senate Confirms Dan Brouillette to Lead Energy Department," *NYT*, December 2, 2019; Lesley Clark & Jeremy Dillon, "5 Takeaways from Dan Brouillette Hearing," *E&E News*, November 15, 2019; Kelsey Brugger, "Secretary Brouillette? Here's What to Know," *E&E News*, October 21, 2019.

30. Braden Campbell, "Acosta Departure Paves Way for Pro-Biz Shift at DOL," *Law 360*, July 12, 2019; Anzish Mirza, "10 Things You Didn't Know About Alexander Acosta," *U.S. News & World Report*, February 24, 2017; Burgess Everett, "Labor Nominee Puzder Withdraws," *Politico*, February 15, 2017; Bryce Covert, "Charges Filed Against Trump's Labor Secretary Pick's Company over Wage Theft and Sexual Harassment," *Think Progress*, January 26, 2017.

31. Mark Sherman, Kevin Freking & Jill Colvin, "Labor Nominee Scalia Dislikes Regulations," *Austin American-Statesman*, July 20, 2019, at A2; Editorial, "Gene Scalia's Winning Record," *WSJ*, July 20, 2019, at A16; David Harrison & Andrew Ackerman, "Labor Pick Scalia Fought Regulations on Businesses," *WSJ*, July 20, 2019, at A6; Noam Scheiber & Glenn Thrush, "For Labor Dept., a Conservative Who Long Battled Unions," *NYT*, July 16, 2019, at A19 (lobbyists and ideologues); Suzy Knimm, "Senate Confirms Trump's Controversial Pick to Lead Mine Safety," *ABC News*, November 15, 2017; Dylan Brown, "Coal Exec Faces Questions About Murray Ties, Violations," *E&E News*, September 18, 2017 (MSHA); Vin Gurrieri, "Trump Taps SC Agency Head to Lead DOL Wage and Hour Unit," *Law 360*, September 4, 2017 (lobbyists and ideologues).

32. Andy Pasztor & Andrew Tangel, "Former Delta Official to Be Nominated to Lead FAA," *WSJ*, March 20, 2019; Shaun Courtney, "Trump Picks Safety Agency's Deputy to Be Administrator," *Bloomberg Law*, April 6, 2018 (King); "Transport Safety Rules Sidelined Indefinitely Under Trump as Part of a Sweeping Retreat in Regulations," CNBC, February 26, 2018 (Rosen).

33. David Mora, "Update: We Found a 'Staggering' 281 Lobbyists Who've Worked in the Trump Administration," *ProPublica*, October 18, 2018; Eric Lipton & Danielle Ivory, "How the Spoils Were Doled Out to Trump Campaign Workers and Allies," *NYT*, March 8, 2018, at A18 (conservative think tanks, Koch brothers).

Chapter 4: Dismantling Agencies

1. David Frum, *Trumpocracy* (2018), at 100–01; Philip Wallach, "On Deregulation, Trump Has Achieved Little," *National Review*, December 19, 2019.

2. Massimo Calabresi, "Inside Donald Trump's War Against the State," *Time*, March 20, 2017, at 27, 28.

3. U.S.C. § 5491(b)(1), (c)(3) (inefficiency clause), § 5497(a)(2)(C) (reasonably necessary clause), 5512(b)(2)(A) (FSOC oversight); Patricia A. McCoy, "Inside Job: The Assault on the Structure of the Consumer Financial Protection Bureau," 103 *Minnesota L. Rev.* 2543 (2019), at 2547 (immune to lobbying); David C. John, "How to Protect Consumers in the Financial Marketplace: An Alternate Approach" (Heritage

Foundation, September 8, 2009), at 1 (objections); Suzanna Andrews, "The Woman Who Knew Too Much," *Vanity Fair*, November 2011 (objections).

4. McCoy, "Inside Job," at 2550–51.

5. McCoy, "Inside Job," at 2605 (court challenges); Gary Rivlin & Susan Antilla, "No Protection for Protectors," *The Intercept*, November 18, 2017 (criticism); Joe Nocera, "The Travails of Ms. Warren," *NYT*, July 22, 2011 (crippling); Binyamin Appelbaum, "Former Ohio Attorney General to Head New Consumer Agency," *NYT*, July 17, 2011 (lobbyists).

6. Richard Cordray, *Watchdog* (2020), at 34–35 (Cordray recruits); Ylan Q. Mui, "Consumer Agency Pick Cordray Lost Some, Won Some," *WP*, July 27, 2011 (Ohio AG); Devin Roose, "He'll Take Consumer Protection for $1,000, Alex," *NYT*, July 18, 2011 (Cordray resume).

7. Cordray, *Watchdog*, at 90–92 (evidence-based approach, years to complete); McCoy, "Inside Job," at 2561 (qualitative insights); Stacy Cowley, "Consumer Protection Director Braces for a Reckoning," *NYT*, November 25, 2016, at B1 (complaints); Alan Zibel, "Regulator Tightens Compensation Rules for Mortgage Lenders," *WSJ*, January 18, 2013; Nick Timiraos & Alan Zibel, "Rules Set for Home Lenders," *WSJ*, January 10, 2013; Prentiss Cox, Jose Quinonez & William Bynum, "Why We Must Not Gut Consumer Protections," *Minneapolis Star-Tribune*, June 9, 2017 (aggressive protector).

8. Cordray, *Watchdog*, at 66 (portal), 67 (bullhorn quote); George Cahlink, "Judgment Day Is Coming," *Congressional Quarterly*, November 1, 2015, at 14, 16 (650,000 complaints).

9. Jane Mayer, *Dark Money* (2016), at 292–93 (think tank articles); Jake Halpern, "Will Guys with Guns Replace U.S. Regulators?" *NYT*, November 27, 2016, at SR3 (Trump complaint); Cowley, "Reckoning" (rogue agency quote).

10. Noah Millman, "How the GOP Swiped the Mantle of Populism from Democrats," *The Week*, April 5, 2017 (CFPB popular); Ken Cuccinelli, "Reforming CFPB Isn't Enough. Eliminate It" (FreedomWorks, January 23, 2017).

11. Executive Order 13,772, 82 *Fed. Reg.* 9965 (February 3, 2017) § 2; Editorial, "Playing Tricks with Dodd-Frank," *NYT*, June 17, 2017, at A22 (consumer lending increase); Gregory Roberts, "Treasury Report Says Key CFPB Enforcement Tool Should Remain," *Bloomberg/BNA Daily Report for Executives*, June 14, 2017; Alan Rapoport & Matthew Goldstein, "Trump Plan Would Cut Dodd-Frank," *NYT*, June 13, 2017, at B1 (Treasury Dept. report).

12. Cordray, *Watchdog*, at 184 (fire Cordray); Nicholas Confessore, "Get Cash Now from the Poor," *NYT Magazine*, April 21, 2019, at 30 (Trump persuaded); Joseph Lawler, "One of Trump's Top Court Candidates Would Be Trouble for the CFPB," *Washington Examiner*, July 9, 2018 (Cordray remains); Marta Tellado, "Consumer Reports CEO: We All Have a Stake in the Future of the CFPB," *The Hill*, December 7, 2017 (polls); Renae Merle, "Richard Cordray Is Stepping Down as Head of Consumer Financial Protection Bureau," *WP*, November 15, 2017 (torrid pace).

13. U.S.C. § 3345(a)(2) (Vacancies Reform Act); 12 U.S.C. § 5491(b)(5) (Dodd–Frank Act); Michael Grunwald, "Trump Wants to Dismantle Elizabeth Warren's Agency,"

Politico, December 5, 2017 (total disaster quote); Spencer S. Hau & Thomas Heath, "Federal Judge Rules That Trump's Choice Can Remain at Head of Consumer Watchdog Bureau," *WP*, November 28, 2017; Katie Rogers, "Two 'Acting Directors,' and One Skeptical Judge," *NYT*, November 28, 2017, at A1 (Trump appointee); Sylvan Lane, "Two Directors Battle for Control of Consumer Bureau," *The Hill*, November 27, 2017 (Mulvaney message); Tara Siegel Bernard, "Agency Picked a New Leader. So Did Trump," *NYT*, November 25, 2017, at A1 (donuts, messages to staff, consternation); Evan Weinberger, "CFPB Director Cordray to Resign After Turbulent Tenure," *Law 360*, November 15, 2017.

14. McCoy, "Inside Job," at 2545 (dismantling); Robert O'Harrow, Jr., Shawn Boburg & Renae Merle, "How Trump Appointees Curbed a Consumer Protection Agency Loathed by the GOP," *WP*, December 4, 2018 (Mulvaney quote); Nancy Cook, "What Do We Think About Mick? Trump Narrows Down Chief of Staff Search," *Politico*, July 24, 2018 (White House official quote); Jalan Rappaport, "Mulvaney, in First Report to Congress, Urges Weakening of Consumer Bureau," *NYT*, April 3, 2018, at A10; Kate Berry, "It 'Would Stab a Knife' into CFPB: Critics React to Mulvaney Proposal," *American Banker*, April 2, 2018 (consumer group, industry critics); Renae Merle & Tracy Jan, "Trump Is Systematically Backing Off Consumer Protections, to the Delight of Corporations," *WP*, March 6, 2018; Grunwald, "Trump Wants to Dismantle" (banks, mortgage market doing well).

15. O'Harrow, Boburg & Merle, "How Trump Appointees Curbed" (spokesperson quote, shirk responsibilities); Jesse Eisinger, "The CFPB's Declaration of Dependence," *ProPublica*, February 15, 2018 (freeze on data collection); Chris Bruce, "Consumer Bureau Wants Feedback on Supervisory Revamp," *Bloomberg BNA Banking Daily*, February 15, 2018; Renae Merle & Thomas Heath, "Even Before Court Victory, Trump's Pick to Lead Consumer Watchdog Began Reshaping Agency," *WP*, November 29, 2017; Renae Merle, "Trump's Pick for Consumer Watchdog Bureau Orders Freeze on Hiring and Rulemaking," *WP*, November 27, 2017.

16. Jolina C. Cuaresma, "Commissioning the Consumer Financial Protection Bureau," 31 *Loyola Consumer L. Rev.* 102 (2019), at 165, n.310 (outdated quote); McCoy, "Inside Job," at 2577 (no additional monies), 2583–84 (three regulations).

17. O'Harrow, Boburg & Merle, "How Trump Appointees Curbed" (supervisory powers); Lalita Clozel, "CFPB to Prioritize Business Costs," *WSJ*, May 11, 2018, at B10; Danielle Douglas-Gabriel, "Federal Consumer Watchdog Plays Down Changes to Its Student Protection Unit," *WP*, May 10, 2018 (protests); Glen Thrush & Stacy Cowley, "Mulvaney Demotes Student Loan Unit in Consumer Bureau Reshuffle," *NYT*, May 9, 2018, at B4; Jon Hill, "Mulvaney Cuts CFPB Fair Lending Office's Enforcement Power," *Law 360*, February 1, 2018.

18. Cuaresma, "Commissioning," at 1 (undercut quote); Evan Weinberger, "New Tone, Old Policies at CFPB Under Kraninger," *Bloomberg Law*, June 18, 2019 (morale); Confessore, "Get Cash Now," at 30 (shocked); O'Harrow, Boburg & Merle, "How Trump Appointees Curbed" (more efficient quote, career official complaints).

19. Allied Progress, "Press Release: Group Launches Campaign Pressing Trump on CFPB Director, Releases Poll Showing President's Shortlist Is Deeply Unpopular," February 12, 2018 (2018 poll); Gary Rivlin & Susan Antilla, "No Protection for Protectors," *The Intercept*, November 18, 2017 (2016 poll); Americans for Financial

Reform, "Press Release: How Americans View Wall Street and Financial Regulation," April 2017 (2017 poll).

20. McCoy, "Inside Job," at 2579; David Lazarus, "'Unqualified' and 'Dangerous' Trump Appointee Set to Take Over Consumer Agency," *Los Angeles Times*, December 4, 2018; Alan Rappeport, "Consumer Bureau Pick to Face Grilling over Her Inexperience," *NYT*, July 18, 2018, at B1; Glenn Thrush, "White House Confirms That Mulvaney Deputy Is Pick to Lead Consumer Bureau," *NYT*, June 16, 2018 (free marketeer).

21. Cuaresma, "Commissioning," at 151 (top priority, lower priority); Americans for Financial Reform, "Kraninger Lets Industry 'Drive the Agenda' at CFPB," February 6, 2020; Lauren E. Willis, "CFPB Head Misguided in Reliance on Consumer Education," *The Hill*, September 7, 2019.

22. U.S. Constitution, art. II, § 1, § 3; *PHH Corp. v. CFPB*, 839 F.3d 1 (D.C. Cir. 2016); Cuaresma, "Commissioning," at 140–42 (Chamber of Commerce).

23. *Seila Law, LLC v. Consumer Financial Protection Bureau*, 140 S.Ct. 2183 (2020) (no basis quote); Editorial, "Its Director May Now Be Subject to Political Winds, but the CFPB Is Here to Stay," *WP*, July 2, 2020 (great relief); Brent Kendall & Andrew Ackerman, "Consumer Agency Ordered to Revamp," *WSJ*, June 30, 2020, at A1 (refuse to defend); Jon Hill, "CFPB Defender Says Constitutional Case 'Remarkably Weak,'" *Law 360*, January 15, 2020 (Clement appointment); Kate Berry, "Kraninger's Stance on CFPB Constitutionality Puts Rules in Limbo," *American Banker*, October 1, 2019 (realignment).

24. Kate Berry, "CFPB's Kraninger Resigns Just as Biden Takes Office," *American Banker*, January 20, 2021; Brent Kendall & Andrew Ackerman, "Consumer Agency Ordered to Revamp," *WSJ*, June 30, 2020, at A1 (industry promise).

25. Evan Osnos, "Trump vs. the 'Deep State,'" *The Atlantic*, May 21, 2018 (turkey farm quote).

26. Department of the Interior, Office of the Inspector General, "Reassignment of Senior Executives at the U.S. Department of the Interior," Report No. 2017-ER-061 (April 2018), at 7 (specialists' belief), 9 (227 employees); Andrew Restuccia, "Federal Workers Spill on Life in Trump's Washington," *Politico*, March 30, 2018 (civil servant reaction); Adam Federman, "The Plot to Loot America's Wilderness," *The Nation*, December 4–11, 2017 (twenty-seven scientists); Kellie Lunney, "Zinke Advances Overhaul as He Questions Loyalty of Workers," *E&E News*, September 26, 2017 (Zinke quote).

27. Coral Davenport & Roni Caryn Rabin, "E.P.A. Places the Head of Its Office of Children's Health on Leave," *NYT*, September 26, 2018, at A16.

28. Kevin Bogardus & Ariel Wittenberg, "'Opportunity to Strike': Inside Kids' Health Office Shake-Up," *E&E News*, August 29, 2019 (Etzel claim, Wheeler meeting, budget); Davenport & Rabin, "E.P.A. Places" (pesticide position); "Suspended Children's Health Office Chief Returns to EPA in New Role," *Inside EPA*, April 12, 2019; "Wheeler Seeks to Affirm Children's Health Commitment After Etzel Removal," *Inside EPA*, October 5, 2018, at 2 (photo op).

29. Executive Order 13,781, 82 *Fed. Reg.* 13,959 (March 13, 2017) § 1; Kellie Lunney, "Document Reveals Ambitious Reorganization Timeline," *E&E News*, February 2, 2018 (Western governors); Ari Natter & Jennifer A. Dlouhy, "Interior Department Proposes a Sweeping Reorganization," *Bloomberg/BNA, Environment & Energy Report*, January 11, 2018 (industry view); Juliet Eilperin & Darryl Fears, "Interior Plans to Move Thousands of Workers in the Biggest Reorganization in Its History," *WP*, January 10, 2018 (Zinke plan); Cheryl Bolen, "OMB Tells Federal Agencies to Start Reorganizing," *Bloomberg/BNA Energy & Climate Report*, April 12, 2017.

30. Government Accountability Office, "Bureau of Land Management: Agency's Reorganization Efforts Did Not Substantially Address Key Practices for Effective Reforms" (March 6, 2020); Ben LeFebre, "Trump Administration to Move Environmental Review Staff to States," *Politico*, September 25, 2019; Juliet Eilperin & Steven Mufson, "New BLM Headquarters to Share a Building with a Chevron Corporate Office," *WP*, September 21, 2019; Scott Strater, "BLM Move Could Leave Skeleton Crew in D.C.," *E&E News*, July 16, 2019; Juliet Eilperin & Lisa Rein, "Interior to Move Most of Bureau of Land Management's D.C. Staff Out West as Part of Larger Reorganization Push," *WP*, July 15, 2019.

31. Scott Streater, "Trump: BLM Leaders Should Live 'In the Great American West,'" *E&E News*, February 21, 2020 (reduction campaign quote); John Freeman & James R. Skillen, "Moving Bureau of Land Management Headquarters to Colorado Won't Be Good for Public Lands," *Government Executive*, January 8, 2020 (get rid of employees); Eric Katz, "Interior to Offer Buyouts to Employees Tapped for Relocation, as Some Already Head for Exits," *Government Executive*, November 6, 2019 (move children, morale); Judy Fahys, "What the BLM Shake-Up Could Mean for Public Lands and Their Climate Impact," *Inside Climate News*, October 8, 2019 (think tanks); Juliet Eilperin & Lisa Rein, "Interior to Move Most of Bureau of Land Management's D.C. Staff Out West as Part of Larger Reorganization Push," *WP*, July 15, 2019 (chilling effect, institutional memory, cost per employee).

32. Juliet Eilperin, "Trump Officials Moved Most Bureau of Land Management Positions Out of D.C. More Than 87 Percent Quit Instead," *WP*, January 28, 2021 (41 moved, 287 retired); Jennifer Yachnin, "Activists Stage 'Unwelcoming Committee' at BLM HQ," *E&E News*, January 2, 2020 (unwelcoming committee); Eric Katz, "Interior to Offer Large Relocation Incentive to Employees Who Move Out West," *Government Executive*, September 12, 2019 (relocation bonus).

Chapter 5: Denigrating Expertise

1. Katherine Eban, "'Really Want to Flood NY and NJ': Internal Documents Reveal Team Trump's Chloroquine Master Plan," *Vanity Fair*, April 24, 2020 (Ellison app); Tanya Monnay, "'Dark Money' Groups Pushed Trump to Back Unproven COVID-19 Treatment" (Center for Responsive Politics, April 8, 2020); Yasmeen Abutaleb, Laurie McGinley & Josh Dawsey, "Oracle to Partner with Trump Administration to Collect Data on Unproven Drugs to Treat Covid-19," *WP*, March 24, 2020; Thomas M. Burton, "FDA Says Wider Testing of Drugs Is Risky," *WSJ*, March 19, 2020, at A6 (bypass); Christopher Rowland, Carolyn Y. Johnson & Laurie McGinley, "Trump

Calls Anti-Malarial Drug a 'Game Changer' for Coronavirus, but the FDA Says It Needs Study," *WP*, March 19, 2020 (Bayer promise).

2. Katz, Marshall & Banks, "Addendum to the Complaint of Prohibited Personnel Practice and Other Prohibited Activity by the Department of Health and Human Services Submitted by Dr. Rick Bright" [Rick Bright Whistleblower Complaint], at 39–40; Jonathan Rockoff & Brianna Abbott, "Health Experts Warn About Virus Drugs' Outlook," *WSJ*, March 25, 2020, at B5 (two studies); Noah Weiland & Maggie Haberman, "Oracle Is Enlisted by the White House to Aid in the Study of Unproven Drugs," *NYT*, March 25, 2020, at A9 (shot of inspiration quote); Abutaleb, McGinley & Dawsey, "Oracle to Partner" (options, Hahn, Redfield, and Fauci opposition).

3. Stephanie Busari & Bukola Adebayo, "Nigeria Records Chloroquine Poisoning After Trump Endorses It for Coronavirus Treatment," *CNN World*, March 23, 2020 (FDA press release); Katie Thomas & Denise Grady, "Embrace of a Drug Goes Against Science," *NYT*, March 21, 2020, at A13 (Fauci caution); Rowland, Johnson & McGinley, "Trump Calls Antimalarial Drug" (game-changer quote, approved quote, so great quote).

4. Joe Parkinson & David Gauthier-Villars, "Trump Sparks Run on Two Drugs," *WSJ*, March 24, 2020, at A9 (run on drugs); Thomas & Grady, "Embrace of a Drug" (what the hell quote, other drug uses); Christopher Rowland, "As Trump Touts an Unproven Coronavirus Treatment, Supplies Evaporate for Patients Who Need Those Drugs," *WP*, March 23, 2020 (doctors prescribe).

5. Brian Stelter, *Hoax* (2020), at 308 (five hundred times); Paul Farhi, "For Fox News Hosts, the Hydroxychloroquine Controversy Is Fuel for the Culture War," *WP*, April 11, 2020.

6. Rick Bright Whistleblower Complaint, at 42.

7. Rick Bright Whistleblower Complaint, at 43; Elizabeth Y. McCuskey, "FDA in the Time of COVID-19," *Administrative and Regulatory Law News*, Spring 2020, at 7, 9; John Lauerman, "U.S. Allows Emergency Use of Drug Trump Backed Against Virus," *Bloomberg Law*, March 30, 2020.

8. Josh Dawsey, "'What Do You Have to Lose?': Inside Trump's Embrace of a Risky Drug Against Coronavirus," *WP*, April 7, 2020 (Trump meeting, Giuliani); Jonathan Swan, "Scoop—Inside the Epic White House Fight over a Virus Drug," *Axios Sneak Peek*, April 5, 2020 (White House determination); Rowland, Johnson & McGinley, "Trump Calls Antimalarial Drug" (anecdotal evidence).

9. Rick Bright Whistleblower Complaint, at 44 (flood New Jersey quote, do it anyway); Dawsey, "'What Do You Have to Lose?'" (rush to hospitals); Denise Grady & Andrea Kannapell, "Trump Urges Use of Drug Yet Unproven," *NYT*, April 5, 2020, at A10 (clean out lungs quote).

10. Annie Karni & Katie Thomas, "President Says He Takes Drug Deemed a Risk," *NYT*, May 19, 2020, at A1; Peter Baker, Katie Rogers & David Enrich, "Trump's Promotion of Drug Divides the Experts," *NYT*, April 7, 2020, at A1 (what have you got quote); Rebecca Ballhaus & Jared S. Hopkins, "President's Push of Certain Drugs Defies Experts," *WSJ*, April 7, 2020, at A4 (Trump advocacy); Emily Goodin, "Trump Refuses to Let Dr. Tony Fauci Answer About Anti-Malarial as a Coronavirus Treatment," *London Daily Mail*, April 5, 2020 (29 million doses).

11. Aaron Blake, "FDA's Hydroxychloroquine Reversal Raises Even Bigger Questions About Trump's Role in Pushing for the Drug," *WP*, June 15, 2020; Editorial, "The Results Are In. Trump's Miracle Drug Is Useless," *WP*, May 18, 2020 (two studies); Jane C. Timm, "Trump Says He's No Longer Taking Hydroxychloroquine," *NBC News*, May 25, 2020; Emily Kopp, "States Weigh What to Do with Millions of Malaria Pills," *Roll Call*, May 7, 2020 (doctors quit prescribing); Food and Drug Administration, "Coronavirus (COVID-19); Update: FDA Reiterates Importance of Close Patient Supervision for 'Off-Label' Use of Antimalarial Drugs to Mitigate Known Risks, Including Heart Rhythm Problems," April 24, 2020; Jared S. Hopkins, "Antimalarial Drug Draws New Analysis, But Doesn't Fully Protect," *WSJ*, April 20, 2020, at A7 (five dozen people); Jeremy Page, "Chinese Doctors Question Sought-After Drug," *WSJ*, April 10, 2020, at A16; Hannah Osborne, "French Hospital Stops Hydroxychloroquine Treatment for COVID-19 Patient over Major Cardiac Risk," *Newsweek*, April 8, 2020.

12. Sheryl Gay Stolberg, "Mad Scramble to Stock Millions of Malaria Pills, Likely for Naught," *NYT*, June 17, 2020, at A7 (stuck with millions); Michael M. Grynbaum, "Stars of Fox News Promoted a Malaria Drug for Weeks. No Longer," *NYT*, April 23, 2020, at A9; Michael D. Shear & Maggie Haberman, "Stand on Drug Led to Ouster, Official Says," *NYT*, April 23, 2020, at A1 (cronyism quote).

13. Philip Rucker & Carol Leonnig, *A Very Stable Genius* (2020), at 12 (histrionics); Joseph E. Stiglitz, *People, Power, and Profits* (2019), at 20 (base); Michael Wolff, *Fire and Fury* (2018), at 114 (Trump on expertise).

14. Brittany Patterson, "Meet the Climate Guy Who Quit Interior," *E&E News*, February 6, 2018; Darryl Fears, "Interior Department Whistleblower Resigns; Bipartisan Former Appointees Object to Zinke's Statements," *WP*, October 6, 2017; Brittany Patterson, "Scientist on Adaptation Reassigned to Job with 'No Duties,'" *E&E News*, July 20, 2017; Joel Clement, "I'm a Scientist. I'm Blowing the Whistle on the Trump Administration," *WP*, July 19, 2017.

15. Reece Peck, *Fox Populism* (2019), at 43, 151–52 (anecdote); Stiglitz, *People, Power, and Profits*, at 164 (undermine civil service); Lisa Rein, et al., "How Trump Waged War on His Own Government," *WP*, October 29, 2020; Andrew Restuccia, "Federal Workers Spill on Life in Trump's Washington," *Politico*, March 30, 2018 (deep state quote); Joe Davidson, "Trump Labor Adviser's Plan for Cutting Federal Compensation, Potentially Even Paid Holidays," *WP*, December 17, 2017; Lisa Rein, "Trump Has a Plan for Government Workers. They're Not Going to Like It," *WP*, November 21, 2016 (easier to fire).

16. Donald Trump, "Memorandum for the Heads of Executive Departments and Agencies," 82 *Fed. Reg.* 8493 (January 25, 2017) (long-term plan); Lydia Wheeler, "Federal Workers on Edge over Trump Call for Firing Power," *The Hill*, February 1, 2018 (State of the Union, union president); "White House Memo Encourages Early Retirements from EPA, Agencies," *Inside EPA*, April 14, 2017, at 13; Alan Rappeport, "Agencies Still Told to Cut as Hiring Freeze Is Lifted," *NYT*, April 12, 2017, at A12; Lisa Rein & Damian Paletta, "White House Tells Agencies to Come Up With a Plan to Shrink Their Workforces," *WP*, April 11, 2017.

17. *American Federation of Government Employees v. Trump*, 929 F.3d 748 (D.C. Cir. 2019); Executive Order 13,836, 83 *Fed. Reg.* 25,329 (May 25, 2018); Executive

Order 13,837, 83 *Fed. Reg.* 25,335 (May 25, 2018); Executive Order 13,839, 83 *Fed. Reg.* 25,343 (May 25, 2018); Eric Katz, "Claiming Trump Has 'Declared War,' Feds Rally to Fight Back Against Executive Orders," *Government Executive*, July 25, 2018; Kevin Bogardus, "Union Leaders Gird for Trump's Executive Orders," *E&E News*, June 13, 2018 (critics); Lisa Rein, "Largest Federal Employees Union Sues Trump over 'Official Time' Rollback," *WP*, May 31, 2018; Joe Davidson, "Trump's Orders Show Unwavering Attack on Federal Unions, Employees," *WP*, May 29, 2018; Lisa Rein, "Trump Takes Aim at Federal Bureaucracy with New Executive Orders Rolling Back Civil Service Protections," *WP*, May 25, 2018 (think tanks, news pundits).

18. Lisa Rein, "As Remote Work Rises at U.S. Companies, Trump Is Calling Federal Employees Back to the Office," *WP*, January 12, 2020; Eric Katz, "Trump Administration Calls for Fewer Performance Awards, Stricter Rating System for Feds," *Government Executive*, July 15, 2019; Eric Wagner, "White House Opposes Senate Pay Raise Proposal," *Government Executive*, July 24, 2019 (pay increase); Joe Davidson, "Trump Thanks Federal Employees with $143.5 billion in Retirement Cuts," *WP*, May 9, 2019; Noam Scheiber, "Trump Moves to Freeze Federal Workers' Wages," *NYT*, August 30, 2018, at B4; Danielle Nichole Smith, "Trump Axes 2019 Pay Hikes for Civilian Federal Employees," *Law 360*, August 30, 2018 (serious economic conditions quote).

19. Michael Lewis, *The Fifth Risk* (2018), at 50 (exodus); Alexander Nazaryan, *The Best People* (2019), at 157 (civil servant concerns, exodus); Adam Aton, "Biden Climate Team Says It Underestimated Trump's Damage," *E&E News*, January 6, 2021 (unfilled positions, ground up quote); Brady Dennis, Juliet Eilperin & Andrew Ba Tran, "With a Shrinking EPA, Trump Delivers on His Promise to Cut Government," *WP*, September 8, 2018 (more money, numbers, institutional memory); Lisa Rein & Andrew Ba Tran, "How the Trump Era Is Changing the Bureaucracy," *WP*, December 30, 2017 (6 percent); Lisa Friedman, Marina Affo & Derek Kravitz, "E.P.A. Officials, Disheartened by Agency's Direction, Leave in Droves," *NYT*, December 23, 2017, at A16 (not replaced).

20. Hiroko Tabuchi, "A Trump Insider Embeds Climate Denial in Scientific Research," *NYT*, March 2, 2020 (Goklany); Juliet Eilperin & Dino Grandoni, "Unlike Those in the Resistance, Certain Career Officials' Stars Have Risen Under Trump," *WP*, March 26, 2018.

21. Executive Order 13,957, 85 *Fed. Reg.* 67,631 (October 21, 2020) § 4 (quote); Eric Wagner, "Biden Signs Executive Order Killing Schedule F, Restoring Collective Bargaining Rights," *Government Executive*, January 22, 2021; Lisa Rein, "Trump's 11th-Hour Assault on the Civil Service by Stripping Job Protections Runs Out of Time," *WP*, January 18, 2021; Erich Wagner, "The Legal Theories at the Heart of Trump's Order Politicizing the Civil Service," *Government Executive*, November 3, 2020 (firestorm); Hailey Konath, "Trump Gives Agencies More Power to Hire, Fire Fed. Workers," *Law 360*, October 22, 2020 (profound rearrangement); Lisa Rein & Eric Yoder, "Trump Issues Sweeping Order for Tens of Thousands of Career Federal Employees to Lose Civil Service Protections," *WP*, October 22, 2020 (expert estimates).

22. Department of the Interior, "Order No. 3369, Promoting Open Science," September 28, 2018; Environmental Protection Agency, "Strengthening Transparency

in Regulatory Science; Proposed Rule," 83 *Fed. Reg.* 18,768 (April 30, 2018), at 18,773–74.

23. Jeremy Berg et al., "Joint Statement on EPA Proposed Rule and Public Availability of Data," *Science* (April 30, 2018) (not every case quote); Thomas O. McGarity & Wendy E. Wagner, "Deregulation Using Science Strategies," 68 *Duke L. J.* 1719 (2019), at 1768–69 (harder to take action); Danny Hakim & Eric Pipton, "Once-Trusted Studies Are Scorned by Trump's E.P.A.," *NYT*, August 25, 2018.

24. Environmental Protection Agency, "Strengthening Transparency in Pivotal Science Underlying Significant Regulatory Actions and Influential Scientific Information; Final Rule," 86 *Fed. Reg.* 469 (January 6, 2021); Stephen Lee, "EPA Officially Nixes Trump's Science Transparency Regulation," *Bloomberg Law*, May 26, 2021; Eric Katz, "Interior Reverses Trump Science Policy, Vows to Free Career Staff from Political Interference," *Government Executive*, March 5, 2021; Chris Mindock, "Trump 'Secret Science' Rule Killed by Montana Court," *Law 360*, February 1, 2021; Lisa Friedman, "New E.P.A. Policy Puts Limits on Use of Science," *NYT*, January 5, 2021, at A16.

25. Nathan Cortez, "Information Mischief Under the Trump Administration," 94 *Chicago-Kent L. Rev.* 315 (2019), at 326–30, 332–35 (Trump administration prevention); Gretchen T. Goldman, et al., "Ensuring Scientific Integrity in the Age of Trump," 355 *Science* 696 (February 17, 2017); Albert C. Lin, "President Trump's War on Regulatory Science," 43 *Harv. Env. L. Rev.* 247 (2019), at 266–70 (Trump administration prevention); "Ensuring Scientific Integrity in the Age of Trump," 355 *Science* 696 (February 17, 2017) (virtue of dissemination); Helena Bottemiller Evich, "'It Feels Like Something Out of a Bad Sci-Fi Movie,'" *Politico*, August 5, 2019 (Department of Agriculture); Rein, et al., "How Trump Waged War" (scientists throughout government); Dylan Brown, "Dems Question Interior over Scrapped Mining Study," *E&E News*, February 12, 2019 (Department of the Interior); Coral Davenport, "How Much Has 'Climate Change' Been Scrubbed from Federal Websites? A Lot," *NYT*, January 10, 2018; Jason Samenow, "I Worked on the EPA's Climate Change Website. Its Removal Is a Declaration of War," *WP*, June 22, 2017.

26. McGarity & Wagner, "Deregulation," at 1778–79 (brake on politicization); Union of Concerned Scientists, "Abandoning Scientific Advice," (January 2018) (important vehicle quote); Memorandum to Members of the Chartered SAB and SAB Liaisons from Alison Cullen re: Preparations for Chartered Science Advisory Board (SAB) Discussions of EPA Planned Agency Actions and Their Supporting Science in the Fall 2017 Regulatory Agenda, dated May 18, 2018, at 4–6 (blew the whistle).

27. "EPA Advisory Committees: How Science Should Inform Decisions," *Hearings Before the Subcommittee on Investigations and Oversight and the Subcommittee on Environment of the House Committee on Science, Space, and Technology*, 116th Cong. (July 16, 2019), at 25–28 (testimony of J. Alfredo Gomez, Government Accountability Office); Ibid., at 41 (testimony of Thomas A. Burke, Johns Hopkins University) [Burke Testimony] (manipulate science); Ibid., at 49 (testimony of Deborah L. Swackhamer, University of Minnesota) (manipulate science); McGarity & Wagner, "Deregulation," at 1760–61 (cleared out); Scott Waldman, "Scientist Who Rejects Warming Named to Advisory Panel," *E&E News*, February 1, 2019 (conservative think tanks).

28. Burke Testimony, at 40 (no restrictions on industry scientists); Bruce Rolfsen, "DOL Advisory Panel Nominees Face New Conflict-of-Interest Review," *Bloomberg Law*, November 6, 2020; Stephen Lee, "EPA's New Science Advisory Board Head Wants to Sidestep Policy," *Bloomberg Law*, October 16, 2020 (Science Advisory Board); Rebecca Beitsch, "Shuffles of EPA's Science Advisers, Elevates Those with Industry Ties," *The Hill*, October 14, 2020; Marianne Lavelle, "How a Contrarian Scientist Helped Trump's EPA Defy Mainstream Science," *Inside Climate News*, May 28, 2020 (largest funders); Sean Reilly, "GOP Lawmakers, Industry Had EPA's Ear on Advisory Panels," *E&E News*, May 24, 2018 (agency scientists); E. Scott Pruitt," Strengthening and Improving Membership on EPA Federal Advisory Committees," October 31, 2017 (Pruitt directive).

29. *Physicians for Social Responsibility v. Wheeler*, 956 F.3d 634 (D.C. Cir. 2020), at 644–48; Sean Reilly, "Regan Names New Science Advisers After Firing Trump's Picks," *E&E News*, August 3, 2021 (Biden administration change); Sylvia Carignan, "At Least Seven Members Removed from EPA Science Advisory Board," *Bloomberg Environment & Energy Report*, November 3, 2017 (trade associations); Jon Meadows, "FreedomWorks Foundation Supports Pruitt Curbing Conflicts of Interests at EPA" (FreedomWorks, October 31, 2017) (activist groups).

30. Masha Gessen, *Surviving Autocracy* (2020), at 26–27 (broader tendency); Lin, "President Trump's War," at 261–65 (broader tendency); Michael Doyle, "Internal Doc: Trump Admin Overrode Scientist on Owl Habitat," *E&E News*, May 7, 2021; Josh Dawsey, "'What Do You Have to Lose?': Inside Trump's Embrace of a Risky Drug Against Coronavirus," *WP*, April 7, 2020.

31. Christopher Leonard, *Kochland* (2019), at 559 (lacked justification); Natasha Geiling, "Scott Pruitt Was Even More Selfish and Vengeful Than We Thought," *New Republic*, October 26, 2020 (operations officer quote); Coral Davenport, Lisa Friedman & Maggie Haberman, "Mired in Scandal, Pruitt Is Forced to Exit E.P.A. Post," *WP*, July 5, 2018, at A1 (demote employees); Restuccia, "Federal Workers Spill," *Politico*, March 30, 2018 (morale); Rachel Leven, "A Behind-the-Scenes Look at Scott Pruitt's Dysfunctional EPA" (Center for Public Integrity, November 9, 2017) (frozen out); Coral Davenport, "E.P.A. Chief Voids Obama-Era Rules in Blazing Start," *NYT*, July 2, 2017, at A1 (political appointees, frozen out).

32. Josh Dawsey, "Pruitt Survived Months of Controversy by Preserving His Relationship with Trump," *WP*, July 5, 2018 (OMB determination); Emily Holden, "Pruitt Faces Another Probe for Employee Retaliation Allegations," *Politico*, June 24, 2018 (employees reassigned); Coral Davenport & Eric Lipton, "Staff Tells of Rampant Secrecy at Pruitt's E.P.A.," *NYT*, August 12, 2017, at A1 (escorted, cell phones, stocked with leftists quote); "Total Cost for Pruitt's Phone Booth Was Closer to $43K," *E&E News*, March 14, 2018, 2017.

33. Ricardo Torres, "Foxconn, State Agree to New Deal; Foxconn Expecting to Hire Up to 1,454 by 2025," *Milwaukee Journal Sentinel*, April 21, 2021; Lisa Friedman, "E.P.A. Experts Objected to 'Misleading' Agency Smog Decision, Emails Show," *NYT*, May 24, 2019; Michael Hathorne, "EPA Chief Pruitt Overrules Staff, Gives Wisconsin's Walker, Foxconn Big Break on Smog," *Chicago Tribune*, May 2, 2018.

34. Lewis, *Fifth Risk*, at 49 (DOE); Nazaryan, *Best People*, at 186 (figure out quote); Josh Dawsey, "In Speech, Mulvaney Says Republicans Are Hypocritical on Deficits,"

WP, February 19, 2020 (CFPB); Nicholas Confessore, "Get Cash Now from the Poor," *NYT Magazine*, April 21, 2019, at 30 (CFPB).

35. Eric Katz, "Trump Has Slashed Jobs at Nearly Every Federal Agency; Biden Promises a Reversal," *Government Executive*, November 19, 2020 (every department and agency); Lisa Rein, et al., "How Trump Waged War"; Brad Plumer & Coral Davenport, "Science Under Attack: How Trump Is Sidelining Researchers and Their Work," *NYT*, December 28, 2019; Andrew Restuccia, "Federal Workers Spill," *Politico*, March 30, 2018 (numbers, morale).

Chapter 6: Stepping on the Brake

1. The story of Cullum Owings's death is drawn from Steve Owings, "Message from Our Co-Founder, Road Safe America," https://roadsafeamerica.org/about-us-042219/message-from-our-co-founder/.

2. The chronology is drawn from Road Safe America, "Road Safe America Timeline," https://roadsafeamerica.org/about-us-042219/timeline.

3. National Highway Traffic Safety Administration, "Federal Motor Carrier Safety Administration, Motor Vehicle and Carrier Safety Standards, Parts and Accessories Necessary for Safe Operation; Speed Limiting Devices," 81 *Fed. Reg.* 61,942 (September 7, 2016); Alan Levin, "Killer-Truck Fix Hits Roadblock in Trump's Quest to Cut Rules," *Bloomberg Law*, July 5, 2017 (agency predictions); Tom Krisher, "Safety Advocates Fear Truck Speed Limiter Rule Could Stall Under Trump," *CBS Detroit*, December 19, 2016 (physics, trucker opposition).

4. Joan Lowy & Tom Krisher, "Safety Rules Getting Sidelined in Regulations Purge," *Austin American-Statesman*, March 9, 2018, at A18.

5. Keith B. Belton & John D. Graham, "Trump's Deregulation Record: Is It Working?" 71 *Admin. L. Rev.* 803 (2019), at 830; Eric Lipton, "Scott Pruitt Is Slowly Strangling the EPA," *Vox News*, January 30, 2018.

6. Reince Priebus, "Memorandum for the Heads of Executive Departments and Agencies; Regulatory Freeze Pending Review," 82 *Fed. Reg.* 8346 (January 24, 2017); Lisa Ellman, "Trump's Freeze on Regulations Could Cause Major Delays for Commercial Drones," *The Hill*, January 31, 2017; Josh Gerstein, "Agencies Interpret Trump Regulatory Freeze Broadly," *Politico*, January 24, 2017 (withdrawals).

7. Executive Order No. 13,771, 82 *Fed. Reg.* 9339 (February 3, 2017) § 2(a), (c); Memorandum for Regulatory Policy Officers at Executive Departments and Agencies and Managing and Executive Directors of Certain Agencies and Commissions from Dominic J. Mancini re: Interim Guidance Implementing Section 2 of the Executive Order of January 30, 2017, Titled "Reducing Regulation and Controlling Regulatory Costs," dated February 2, 2017, at 4 (exemption).

8. Comment, "One for the Price of Two: The Hidden Costs of Regulatory Reform Under Executive Order 13,771," 70 *Ad. L. Rev.* 491 (2018), at 500 (too many rules); "Industry Urges OMB to Prioritize EO's Cost Savings over '2–1' Rule Repeal," *Inside EPA*, March 17, 2017, at 1; Arianna Skibell, "Reformers Dust Off Plans to Kill Stale Rules," *E&E News*, February 7, 2017 (praise); Robb Mandelbaum, "Trump's Regula-

tion Order: What It Means for Small Businesses," *Forbes*, January 31, 2017 (drive growth quote).

9. "Regulatory Reform Task Forces Check-In," *Joint Hearing Before the Subcommittee on Government Operations and the Subcommittee on Healthcare, Benefits and Administrative Rules of the House Committee on Oversight and Government Reform*, 115th Cong. (October 24, 2017) (testimony of James Goodwin, Center for Progressive Reform), at 83 (capital costs); Michael A. Livermore, "Polluting the EPA's Long Tradition of Economic Analysis," 70 *Case Western L. Rev.* 1063 (2020), at 1078 (ignore benefits); Peter M. Shane, "The Obscure—But Crucial—Rules the Trump Administration Has Sought to Corrupt," *The Atlantic*, December 4, 2019 (inconsistent with statute); Amy Sinden, "Chamber's Brief Lays Bare Crackpot Theory at Heart of Two-for-One Order," *CPR Blog*, June 15, 2017 (net benefits); Thomas McGarity et al., "Trump's New 'Regulatory Czar'" (Center for Progressive Reform, April 2017), at 2 (triple work).

10. Environmental Protection Agency, "Review of the National Ambient Air Quality Standards for Particulate Matter," 85 *Fed. Reg.* 82,684 (December 18, 2020), at 82,689–91; Sean Reilly, "EPA Advances Soot Rule Despite COVID-19 Concerns," *E&E News*, November 5, 2020 (12,000 premature deaths); Coral Davenport, "White House Rejects New Emissions Rules Despite Covid-19 Link," *NYT*, April 15, 2020, at B3.

11. Executive Order 13,990, 86 *Fed. Reg.* 7037 (January 25, 2021); White House, "Fact Sheet: List of Agency Actions for Review," January 20, 2021; Michael Phillis, "EPA Says Stricter Particulate Matter Controls Not Needed," *Law 360*, December 7, 2020.

12. Patrick McGeehan, "Failure to Test for Sleep Apnea Is Cited as the Root Cause of 2 Train Crashes," *NYT*, February 7, 2018, at A22; Ashley Halsey III, "Plan to Test Drivers for Sleep Apnea Is Scrapped," *WP*, August 9, 2017, at A3.

13. McGeehan, "Failure to Test"; Halsey, "Plan to Test" (truckers object); Alan Levin, "Trump Halts U.S. Effort to Combat Truckers' Sleep Disorders," August 4, 2017 (notice).

14. Andrea Ball, "Worked to Death," *Austin American-Statesman*, October 27, 2019, at A1.

15. Fatima Hussein & Bruce Rolfsen, "OSHA Heat Protection Rule Lags While Record Temperatures Rise," *Bloomberg Law*, July 6, 2021; Public Citizen, "Workers Left Behind Under Trump's OSHA" (August 30, 2018), at 14 (risks, preventive measures, OSHA refusal); Georgina Gustin, "Heat Wave Safety: 130 Groups Call for Protections for Farm, Construction Workers," *Inside Climate News*, July 17, 2018 (statistics, climate change, farmworkers).

16. Ariel Wittenberg, "Biden in Hot Seat to Protect Workers from Warming," *E&E News*, January 22, 2021 (Trump failure); Public Citizen, "Workers Left Behind"; Bruce Rolfsen, "Worker Safety Advocates Press OSHA to Prevent Heat Stress on the Job," *Bloomberg/BNA Occupational Safety & Health Reporter*, July 17, 2018.

17. Environmental Protection Agency, "Clean Water Act Hazardous Substances Spill Prevention; Final Rule," 84 *Fed. Reg.* 46,100 (September 3, 2019) (EPA response); "The Administration's Priorities and Policy Initiatives Under the Clean Water Act,"

Hearings Before the Subcommittee on Water Resources and the Environment of the House Committee on Transportation and Infrastructure, 116th Congress (September 18, 2019) (testimony of Pamela Nixon, People Concerned About Chemical Safety) (Freedom Industries spill); Courtney Columbus, "Green Groups Sue EPA over Lack of Spill Regs," *E&E News*, March 22, 2019; "Environmentalists Threaten New Suit to Force CWA Spill Prevention Rule," *Inside EPA*, December 21, 2018 (language of section 311).

18. Clark Mindock, "EPA Faces Suit over Slaughterhouse Pollution Standards," *Law 360*, August 4, 2020 (pollution); Marc Heller, "Groups Sue over Slaughterhouse Rules," *E&E News*, December 18, 2019 (pollution, environmental group arguments); Nina Lakhani, "EPA Sued for Allowing Slaughterhouses to Pollute Waterways," *The Guardian*, December 18, 2019 (numbers, EPA denial).

19. Maya Earls, "Reinstate Endangered Species Protections for Beetle, Suit Says," *Bloomberg Law*, March 25, 2021; Maya Earls, "Oregon Timber Sales Draw Lawsuit over Threat to Owl Habitat," *Bloomberg Law*, January 15, 2021; Michael Doyle, "Greens Sue to Restore Gray Wolf Protections," *E&E News*, January 14, 2021; Catrin Einhorn, "Monarch Butterflies Face Threat but Don't Make Endangered List," *NYT*, December 16, 2020, at A14; Maya Earls, "Wildlife Agency Sued Again to Force Wolverine Protection," *Bloomberg Law*, December 15, 2020; Michael Doyle, "Judge Greenlights Lawsuit over Houston Toad," *E&E News*, August 21, 2020; Clark Mindock, "9th Circ. Says Yellowstone Grizzlies Can't Be Isolated, Delisted," *Law 360*, July 8, 2020; Pamela King, "Lawsuit: Trump Officials 'Twiddling Their Thumbs' on Backlog," *E&E News*, February 27, 2020 (listing comparison, moral failure quote, CBD lawsuit); Tamara Ward, "Citing Sea Turtles, Court Faults Trump Fishing Exemptions," *E&E News*, January 6, 2020; Pamela King, "Greens Sue over Red Wolf Recovery Plan," *E&E News*, November 20, 2019; Dylan Brown, "Greens Sue to Save Nev. Wildflower from Exploration," *E&E News*, October 31, 2019; Michael Doyle, "Court Pressure Gets Results for Bumblebee," *E&E News*, September 25, 2019; Michael Phillis, "Enviros Say Alaska Oil & Gas Seismic Tests Will Harm Whales," *Law 360*, September 5, 2019.

20. Jacob S. Hacker & Paul Pierson, *American Amnesia* (2016), at 300.

21. Jolina C. Cuaresma, "Commissioning the Consumer Financial Protection Bureau," 31 *Loyola Consumer L. Rev.* 102 (2019), at 152 (20 percent); Dave Boyer, "Mulvaney Scrutinizing 125 CFPB Cases Opened by Liberal Predecessor," *Washington Times*, November 30, 2017 (freeze).

22. Richard Cordray, *Watchdog* (2020), at 6 (student loans, numbers); "A $1.5 Trillion Crisis: Protecting Student Borrowers and Holding Student Loan Servicers Accountable," *Hearings Before the House Financial Services Committee*, 116th Cong. (September 10, 2019) (testimony of Seth Frotman, Student Borrower Protection Center), at 3 [hereinafter Frotman testimony] (not evenly distributed); Hua Hsu, "Unsettled," *New Yorker*, September 9, 2019; Josh Mitchell, "The Long Road to the Student Debt Crisis," *WSJ*, June 8, 2019, at C1 (for-profit colleges).

23. Cordray, *Watchdog*, at 7–8 (deeply in debt); Frotman testimony (struggle); Student Borrower Protection Center, "A Year Without Action" (December 11, 2018), at 4 (default rates); Diana Hembree, "New Report Finds Student Debt Burden Has 'Disas-

trous Domino Effect' on Millions of Americans," *Forbes*, November 1, 2018 (survey, people in sixties).

24. Cordray, *Watchdog*, at 7 (students get behind); Seth Frotman, "Every Tool at Its Disposal: The Case for a Student Loan Servicing Rulemaking," 31 *Loyola Consumer L. Rev.* 551 (2019), at 555–60, 563 (DoEd student loan responsibility, improper capitalization); Josh Mitchell & Michelle Hackman, "Education Department Criticized on Loan Servicers," *WSJ*, February 15, 2019, at A4 (servicers activities, inspector general); Stacy Cowley, "New York Attorney General Opens Inquiry on Student Debt," *NYT*, July 20, 2017, at B3 (irresponsible loan servicers).

25. Frotman, "Every Tool," at 567–68 (regulatory agenda), 573–76 (CFPB authority); Isaac Boltansky & Lukas Davaz, "Takeaways from CFPB's Spring 2018 Rulemaking Agenda" (Compass Point Research & Trading, May 10, 2018) (scrapped project).

26. Environmental Protection Agency, "Control of Air Pollution from Airplanes and Airplane Engines: GHG Emission Standards and Test Procedures; Final Rule," 86 *Fed. Reg.* 2136 (January 11, 2021); Clark Mindock, "EPA Finalizes Aircraft GHG Emissions Standards," *Law 360*, January 4, 2021; Maxine Joselow, "12 Attorneys General Blast 'Empty' EPA Airplane Rules," *E&E News*, October 20, 2020; Renee Martin-Nagle, "EPA's Proposed Aircraft Emissions Standard Maintains Status Quo," *Bloomberg Law*, October 7, 2020 (Trump administration); Coral Davenport, "E.P.A. Proposes Standards for Aviation Emissions That Airlines Already Meet," *NYT*, July 23, 2020, at B6 (industry behest); Juan Carlos Rodriguez, "EPA Floats Long-Awaited Aircraft GHG Emissions Standards," *Law 360*, July 22, 2020 (environmental groups); David Schultz, "How Will Trump Handle Climate Regulation? Watch the Skies," *Bloomberg/BNA Climate & Energy Report*, January 6, 2017 (NAM).

27. Cordray, *Watchdog*, at 168 (debt collectors), 169 (70 million Americans, debt collection mills); Bureau of Consumer Financial Protection, "Debt Collection Practices (Regulation F): Proposed Rule with Request for Public Comment," 84 *Fed. Reg.* 23,274 (May 21, 2019) [CFPB Debt Collection Proposal], at 23,276 ($11.5 billion industry, three varieties); Lauren Saunders & Martha Bergmark, "A Cancer Survivor Paid an Old Debt, but Collectors Garnished Her Wages Anyway," *Business Insider*, September 6, 2019 (fail to document).

28. Cordray, *Watchdog*, at 10 (harassing), 11 (time passes); CFPB Debt Collection Proposal, at 23,277 (credit reporting agencies, new round of communications); American Civil Liberties Union, "A Pound of Flesh: The Criminalization of Private Debt" (February 2018), at 4 (arrest warrants).

29. CFPB Debt Collection Proposal, at 23,278–79.

30. Cordray, *Watchdog*, at 171 (no proposal); Renae Merle, "Could Debt Collectors Send You Texts, Emails? Consumer Groups Fear CFPB May Allow It," *WP*, April 17, 2019 (zombie debt); Evan Weinberger, "CFPB Could Avoid Fight with New Debt Collection Plan," *Law 360*, June 9, 2017 (regulations necessary).

31. Jon Hill, "CFPB Finishes Disclosure-Focused Regs for Debt Collectors," *Law 360*, December 18, 2020 (final rule description); Jon Hill, "CFPB Adopts Long-Awaited Rules on Debt Collection Industry," *Law 360*, October 30, 2020 (final rule description, consumer group reaction).

32. McGarity et al., "Regulatory Czar," at 2.

Chapter 7: Shifting into Reverse

1. Keith B. Belton & John D. Graham, "Trump's Deregulation Record: Is It Working," 71 *Admin. L. Rev.* 803 (2019), at 844 (previous presidents); Joseph Goffman, "Reconstruct an Administrative Agency," *Environmental Forum*, November/December, 2018, at 40; Bethany A. Davis Noll & Richard L. Revesz, "Regulation in Transition," 104 *Minn. L. Rev.* 1 (2019) (more aggressive); Telia Buford, "What It's Like Inside the Trump Administration's Regulatory Rollback at the EPA," *ProPublica*, December 18, 2017 (top priority); Helaine Olen, "Stymied on Many Fronts, Trump Chips Away at Obama's Legacy Whenever Possible," *WP*, November 27, 2017; C. Ryan Barber & Cheryl Miller, "The Fog of Regulatory War," *National Law Journal*, April 2017, at 17, 18 (maybe more quote).

2. Noll & Revesz, "Regulation in Transition," at 37–41; Lisa Heinzerling, "Unreasonable Delays: The Legal Problems (So Far) of Trump's Deregulatory Binge," 12 *Harv. L. & Policy Rev.* 13 (2018).

3. William W. Buzbee, "Deregulatory Splintering," 94 *Chicago-Kent L. Rev.* 439 (2019), at 442 (neglecting to engage, departure from administrative law); Nadja Popovich, Livia Albeck-Ripka & Kendra Pierre-Louis, "78 Environmental Rules on the Way Out Under Trump (and 11 Rules Reinstated After Challenges)," *NYT*, December 27, 2018, at F12.

4. Executive Order No. 13,777, 82 *Fed. Reg.* 12,285 (February 24, 2017) §§ 2, 3(d)–(e); Danielle Ivory & Robert Faturechi, "Secrecy and Suspicion Surround Administration's Deregulation Teams," *NYT*, August 8, 2017, at A14; Danielle Ivory & Robert Faturechi, "The Deep Industry Ties of Trump's Deregulation Teams," *NYT*, July 11, 2017, at A1; Ariena Skibell, "Clean Power Plan Foe Picked to Lead Deregulation Task Force," *E&E News*, April 4, 2017.

5. Ross Gelbspan, *The Heat Is On* (1997), at 3–4, 33 (free-market think tanks); Jane Mayer, *Dark Money* (2016), at 213 (Fox News, religious right preachers); Kate Zernike, *Boiling Mad* (2010), at 37 (Tea Party); Aaron M. McCright & Riley E. Dunlap, "The Politicization of Climate Change and Polarization in the American Public's Views of Global Warming, 2001–2010," 52 *Sociological Quarterly* 155 (2011), at 179 (litmus test); Riley E. Dunlap, Aaron M. McCright & Jerrod H. Yarosh, "The Political Divide on Climate Change: Partisan Polarization Widens in the U.S.," *Environment*, September/October 2016, at 6 (Republican environmentalists, deep chasm); Clare Foran, "Donald Trump and the Triumph of Climate-Change Denial," *The Atlantic*, December 25, 2016 (38 percent of Republicans); John M. Broder, "Skepticism on Climate Change Is Article of Faith for Tea Party," *NYT*, October 21, 2010, at A1 (industry funded, Fox News, religious right preachers); Jim Tankersley, "U.S. Chamber Shrugs Off Defections," *Los Angeles Times*, October 9, 2009, at A17 (Chamber of Commerce).

6. Christopher Leonard, *Kochland* (2019), at 557 (views match those of base); Peter Baker, "No One Will Say If Trump Denies Climate Science," *NYT*, June 3, 2017, at A1 (not a believer quote); David Schultz, Dean Scott & Andrew Childers, "Only Constant in Trump's Approach to Climate Is Inconsistency," *BNA Energy & Climate Rept.*, April 28, 2017 (inconsistent); John Schwartz, "Trump's Climate Views: Combative, Conflicting and Confusing," *NYT*, March 11, 2017 (full-page ad, global warming

tweet, coal-fired plants quote); Juliet Eilperin, "Trump Says 'Nobody Really Knows' If Climate Change Is Real," *WP*, December 11, 2016 (open mind quote).

7. Scott Waldman & Niina Heikkinen, "Pruitt Suggests Warming Can Help Humans," *E&E News*, February 7, 2018; Scott Waldman, "Study Details Climate Change in Zinke's Backyard," *E&E News*, May 11, 2017; Geof Koss, "Perry Touts Carbon Cuts in Hill Hearings," *E&E News*, January 11, 2017.

8. "Critical Mission: Former Administrators Address the Direction of the EPA," *Hearings Before the Subcommittee on Oversight and Investigations of the Committee on Energy and Commerce*, 116th Cong. (June 11, 2019) (testimony of Gina McCarthy) (talking points); Maxine Joselow, "Another Agency Axes Climate Webpages," *E&E News*, December 18, 2018 (Department of Transportation); Chris Mooney, "EPA's Climate Change Website Went Down a Year Ago for 'Updating.' It's Still Not Back," *WP*, May 4, 2018; Sharon Zhang, "The National Park Service Has Scrubbed 92 Documents About Climate Change from Its Website," *New Republic*, December 22, 2017; Christa Marshall, "Agency Axes 'Clean Energy' from Tech Websites," *E&E News*, May 30, 2017 (Department of Energy); Arianna Skibell, "Trump Orders Freeze, Pledges Energy Reforms," *E&E News*, January 23, 2017 (White House web page).

9. Jean Chemnick & Emily Holden, "Inside the 'Dirty' Fight to Leave the Paris Deal," *E&E News*, July 7, 2017 (Rose Garden speech); Mark Landler, Brad Plumer & Linda Qiu, "A Long List of Economic Burdens, Bolstered by Dubious Data," *NYT*, June 2, 2017, at A1 (Pittsburgh quote).

10. U.S.C. § 7521; *Coalition for Responsible Regulation v. EPA*, 684 F.3d 102 (D.C. Cir. 2012), at 120–23; Environmental Protection Agency, National Highway Traffic Safety Administration, "Light-Duty Vehicle Greenhouse Gas Emission Standards and Corporate Average Fuel Economy Standards; Final Rule," 75 *Fed. Reg.* 25,324 (May 9, 2010); Environmental Protection Agency, "Endangerment and Cause or Contribute Findings for Greenhouse Gases Under Section 202(a) of the Clean Air Act," 74 *Fed. Reg.* 66,496 (December 15, 2009); Margaret Kriz, "Power Player," *National Journal*, January 31, 2009, at 17 (collaborate).

11. Environmental Protection Agency and Department of Transportation, "2017 and Later Model Year Light-Duty Vehicle Greenhouse Gas Emissions and Corporate Average Fuel Economy Standards; Final Rule," 77 *Fed. Reg.* 62,624 (October 15, 2012), at 62,785; Nora Macaluso, "Automakers Support New Fuel Standards but Push for Midterm Review, 'Check-ins,'" *Bloomberg BNA Environment Reporter*, January 20, 2012; Neela Banerjee, "U.S. Seeks to Double Average Gas Mileage by 2025," *Los Angeles Times*, November 17, 2011.

12. Environmental Protection Agency, "Final Determination on the Appropriateness of the Model Year 2022–2025 Light-Duty Vehicle Greenhouse Gas Emissions Standards Under the Midterm Evaluation" (January 2017); Bill Vlasic, "E.P.A. Affirms Goals for Fuel Economy, but Trump Is Likely to Challenge Them," *NYT*, January 14, 2017, at B1 (consumer purchases); Keith Laing, "Carmakers Eye Favorable Regulations Under Trump," *Detroit News*, November 11, 2016.

13. John Voelcker, "Reading Between the Lines of Trump's Speech to Detroit Auto Industry," *Christian Science Monitor*, March 18, 2017 (bailout); Bill Vlasic, "Trump

Moves to Kill Mileage Rule in Step to End 'Assault' on Carmakers," *NYT*, March 16, 2017, at A14 (assault quote).

14. National Highway Traffic Safety Administration, U.S. Environmental Protection Agency, "The Safer Affordable Fuel-Efficient (SAFE) Vehicles Rule for Model Years 2021–2026 Passenger Cars and Light Trucks," 83 *Fed. Reg.* 42,986 (August 24, 2018), at 42,999 (freeze standards, withdraw California waiver); Coral Davenport & Lisa Friedman, "Science Panel Staffed with Trump Appointees Says E.P.A. Rollbacks Lack Scientific Rigor," *NYT*, December 31, 2019; Brady Dennis, Michael Laris & Juliet Eilperin, "Trump Administration to Freeze Fuel-Efficiency Requirements in Move Likely to Spur Legal Battle with States," *WP*, August 2, 2018 (staff quotes); Maxine Joselow & Zack Colman, "Ex-Staffer: Trump Team Steamrolled EPA on Auto Proposal," *E&E News*, August 2, 2018 (staff quotes).

15. Juan Carlos Rodriguez, "Ford, Other Automakers Ink Emissions Deal with California," *Law 360*, August 17, 2020; Keith Goldberg, "Trump Admin. Weakens Obama-Era Vehicle Emissions Rules," *Law 360*, March 31, 2020 (Volvo) ; Matthew Perlman & Bryan Koenig, "DOJ Defends Emissions Deal Probe, but Is It Blowing Smoke?" *Law 360*, September 25, 2019; Maxine Joselow, "Trump Admin Says Calif. Deal with Automakers Broke Law," *E&E News*, September 6, 2019 (bogus).

16. National Highway Traffic Safety Administration and Environmental Protection Agency, "The Safer Affordable Fuel-Efficient (SAFE) Vehicles Rule Part One: One National Program," 84 *Fed. Reg.* 51,310 (September 27, 2019); Ethan N. Elkind, "Trump's Flawed Rollback of Fuel Economy Rules," *Regulatory Review*, May 18, 2020 (easily met); Robinson Meyer, "Trump's New Auto Rollback Is an Economic Disaster," *The Atlantic*, April 13, 2020 (jobs); Maxine Joselow, "Trump's Car Rule Would Cause More Pollution Deaths," *E&E News*, April 2, 2020; Margaret Talbot, "Scott Pruitt's Dirty Politics," *New Yorker*, April 2, 2018 (leaden feeling quote).

17. Environmental Protection Agency, "Proposed Settlement Agreement, Clean Air Act Citizen Suit," 75 *Fed. Reg.* 82,392 (2010).

18. Environmental Protection Agency, "Standards of Performance for Greenhouse Gas Emissions from New, Modified, and Reconstructed Stationary Sources: Electric Utility Generating Units," 80 *Fed. Reg.* 64,510 (October 23, 2015), at 64,512 (Table 1), 64,513; Amy Poszywak, "Clean Power Plan Impact, Though Significant, Is Likely Years Out, Analysts Say," *SNL Electric Utility Report*, August 24, 2015 (little practical relevance).

19. *American Lung Association v. EPA*, 985 F.3d 914 (D.C. Cir. 2021), at 937 (generator shifting); Environmental Protection Agency, "Carbon Pollution Emission Guidelines for Existing Stationary Sources: Electric Utility Generating Units," 80 *Fed. Reg.* 64,662 (October 23, 2015), at 64,669, 64,787, 64,795, 64,804.

20. Adam Liptak & Coral Davenport, "Justices Deal Blow to Obama Effort on Emissions," *NYT*, February 10, 2016, at A1 (stay); "At Deadline, Critics File Host of New Challenges to Power Plant GHG Rules," *Inside EPA*, December 23, 2015.

21. Executive Order 13,783, 82 *Fed. Reg.* 16,093 (March 31, 2017) § 4(b) (quote); Brady Dennis & Juliet Eilperin, "Trump Signs Order at the EPA to Dismantle Environmental Protections," *WP*, March 28, 2017.

22. *American Lung Association v. EPA*, 985 F.3d 914 (D.C. Cir. 2021), at 944–45 (EPA position); U.S. Environmental Protection Agency, "Repeal of the Clean Power Plan; Emission Guidelines for Greenhouse Gas Emissions from Existing Electric Utility Generating Units; Revisions to Emission Guidelines Implementing Regulations," 84 *Fed. Reg.* 32,520 (July 8, 2019), at 32,524, 32,537, table 1, 32,553, 32,568–69.

23. American Lung Ass'n v. EPA, 985 F.3d 914 (D.C. Cir. 2021); Greg Stohr, "Supreme Court Will Consider Curbing EPA Climate Change Power," *Bloomberg Law*, October 29, 2021.

24. U.S. Environmental Protection Agency, "Oil and Natural Gas Sector: Emission Standards for New, Reconstructed, and Modified Sources; Final Rule," 81 *Fed. Reg.* 35,824 (June 3, 2016), at 35,830, 35,836, 35,838, table 3, 35,840, 35,844–46; Rebecca Elliott, "The Leaks That Threaten the Clean Image of Natural Gas," *WSJ*, August 10, 2019, at B4.

25. Bureau of Land Management, "Waste Prevention, Production Subject to Royalties and Resource Conservation," 81 *Fed. Reg.* 83,008 (November 18, 2016); U.S. Environmental Protection Agency, "Oil and Natural Gas Sector: Emission Standards for New, Reconstructed, and Modified Sources; Final Rule," 81 *Fed. Reg.* 35,824 (June 3, 2016).

26. *Wyoming v. Department of the Interior*, 493 F. Supp.3d 1046 (D. Wyo. 2020); *California v. Bernhardt*, 472 F. Supp.3d 573 (N.D. Cal. 2020); Environmental Protection Agency, "Oil and Natural Gas Sector: Emission Standards for New, Reconstructed, and Modified Sources Review; Final Rule," 85 *Fed. Reg.* 57,398 (September 14, 2021), at 57,019, 57,034, 57,040; Bureau of Land Management, "Waste Prevention, Production Subject to Royalties, and Resource Conservation; Rescission or Revision of Certain Requirements; Final Rule," 83 *Fed. Reg.* 49,184 (Sept. 28, 2018), at 49,186–88; Coral Davenport, "Senate Revives Methane Rules Trump Reversed," *NYT*, April 29, 2021, at A1.

27. Lisa Rein, et al., "How Trump Waged War on His Own Government," *WP*, October 29, 2020 (industry happy, political appointees); Scott Waldman, "Trump Riffs on Modern Appliances, and Pundits See a Pattern," *E&E News*, January 24, 2020.

28. Todd C. Frankel, "Trump's Big Policy Win: Stronger Showers, Faster Dishwashers. It's Something Almost No One Asked For," *WP*, December 30, 2020 (toilets); Rebecca Beitsch, "Energy Department Proposes Showerhead Standards Rollback After Trump Complains," *The Hill*, October 12, 2020 (Trump quote); Waldman, "Trump Riffs" (academic research).

29. Department of Energy, "Energy Conservation Program: Definition of Showerhead," 86 *Fed. Reg.* 38,594 (July 22, 2021); Rebecca Beitsch, "Trump Administration Rolls Back Efficiency Standards for Showerheads, Washers and Dryers," *The Hill*, December 15, 2020 (final rule); Lesley Clark, "Trump Showerhead Battle Escalates," *E&E News*, October 16, 2020 (opposition, Trump quote); Beitsch, "Department Proposes" (previous rule, 70 percent, proposal, consumer groups).

30. Rebecca Tan, "Trump Blamed Energy-Saving Bulbs for Making Him Look Orange. Experts Say Probably Not," *WP*, September 13, 2019; Robert Walton, "DOE Move to Weaken Light Bulb Efficiency Standards Could Cost Consumers $12B," *Utility Dive*, February 7, 2019; Scott Waldman, "Trump Tries to Dim Efficiency Gains in

Bulbs," *E&E News*, February 7, 2018; Christa Marshall, "Industry Launches Assault on Obama's Lightbulb Rules," *E&E News*, May 5, 2017.

31. Department of Energy, "Energy Conservation Program: Establishment of a New Product Class for Residential Dishwashers," 85 *Fed. Reg.* 68,723 (October 30, 2020); Hiroko Tabuchi, "Warriors Against Environmental Rules Champion the Dishwasher," *NYT*, September 17, 2019, at A17 (twenty-five power plants); Kelsey Brugger, "DOE Rescinds Standards for Power-Sipping Lightbulbs," *E&E News*, September 4, 2019; Robert Walton, "DOE Proposal to Roll Back Lightbulb Efficiency Puts Billions in Energy Savings on the Line," *Utility Dive*, May 15, 2019 (electric companies); C. Barry Edison Sloane & J. Heywood Edison Sloane, "Thomas Edison Would Not Be Happy," *NYT*, April 11, 2019, at A27; Robert Walton, "DOE Move to Weaken Light Bulb Efficiency Standards Could Cost Consumers $12B," *Utility Dive*, February 7, 2019 (consumer groups).

32. Environmental Protection Agency, "Chlorpyrifos; Order Denying PANNA and NRDC's Petition to Revoke Tolerances," 82 *Fed. Reg.* 16,581 (April 5, 2017) [Chlorpyrifos Petition Denial], at 16,583; Sharon Lerner, "Poison Fruit," *The Intercept*, January 14, 2017 (chlorpyrifos description).

33. U.S.C. § 346a(b)(2)(A)(i)–(ii); Environmental Protection Agency, "Chlorpyrifos; Tolerance Revocations," 80 *Fed. Reg.* 69,080 (November 6, 2015), at 69,080, 69,090; Brady Dennis, "Trump EPA Declines to Ban Pesticide that Obama Had Proposed Outlawing," *WP*, March 29, 2017.

34. Chlorpyrifos Petition Denial; Eric Lipton, "Why Has the E.P.A. Shifted on Toxic Chemicals? An Industry Insider Helps Call the Shots," *NYT*, October 21, 2017 (Hamnet story); "Pruitt Met with Dow CEO Before Rejecting Pesticide Ban," *E&E News*, June 28, 2017 (meeting with lobbyists).

35. *League of United Latin American Citizens v. Regan*, 996 F.3d 673 (9th Cir. 2021) (egregious delay quote); White House, "Fact Sheet: List of Agency Actions for Review," January 20, 2021; Brady Dennis & Juliet Eilperin, "Trump Has Kept This Controversial Pesticide on the Market. Now Its Biggest Manufacturer Is Stopping Production," *WP*, February 6, 2020 (largest manufacturer, other manufacturers); Tiffany Stecker, "Trump EPA's Neurotoxic Pesticide Decision Back in Court," *Bloomberg Law*, August 7, 2019; Adam Alington, "California to Ban Pesticide Chlorpyrifos," *Bloomberg Law*, May 8, 2019; Ellen M. Gilmer, "Court Orders EPA to Respond to Chlorpyrifos Concerns," *E&E News*, April 19, 2019.

36. Ian Austen, "A Runaway Train Explosion Killed 47, but Deadly Cargo Still Rides the Rails," *NYT*, July 16, 2019.

37. Pipeline and Hazardous Materials Safety Administration, "Hazardous Materials: Enhanced Tank Car Standards and Operational Controls for High-Hazard Flammable Trains," 80 *Fed. Reg.* 26,664 (May 8, 2015), at 26,646, Table 1, 26,650; Linda Chiem, "DOT's Brake, Competitive Switching Proposals in Doubt," *Law 360*, October 19, 2017; Eric T. Schneiderman, "Press Release, A.G. Schneiderman, Fellow AGs to Trump Administration: Close Loophole Allowing Trains to Carry Explosive Crude Oil Through Our Communities," May 22, 2017 (bomb trains quote).

38. Fixing America's Surface Transportation Act of 2015, Pub. L. No. 114-94 (December 4, 2015) § 7311(c); Pipeline & Hazardous Materials Administration, "Removal of

Electronically Controlled Pneumatic Brake System Requirements for High Hazard Flammable Unit Trains; Final Rule," 83 *Fed. Reg.* 48,393 (September 25, 2018); U.S. Department of Transportation, "Electronically Controlled Pneumatic Braking Regulatory Impact Analysis" (December 2017), at 6–7; Letter from Earthjustice to Document Management System, Department of Transportation, re: Administrative Appeal of the Final Rule "Hazardous Materials: Removal of Electronically Controlled Pneumatic Brake Systems for High-Hazard Flammable Unit Trains," October 25, 2018 (no public comment, bomb train increase, administrative appeal).

39. Sara Toth Stubb, "The Future of Meat," *Congressional Quarterly Researcher*, September 25, 2020 (injuries); Thomas Gremillion & Deborah Berkowitz, "Risking Food Safety, USDA Plans to Let Slaughterhouses Self-Police," *The Hill*, September 17, 2019 (workers description); Kimberly Kindy, "Pork Industry Soon Will Have More Power over Meat Inspections," *WP*, April 3, 2019 (rapid-motion disorders); Center for Progressive Reform, "Comments on the Proposed Rule, Modernization of Swine Slaughter Inspection," April 30, 2018, at 2 (job description).

40. Department of Agriculture, Food Safety and Inspections Service, "Modernization of Swine Slaughter Inspection; Final Rule," 84 *Fed. Reg.* 52,300 (October 1, 2019), at 52,314–15.

41. *United Food & Commercial Workers Union, Local No. 663 v. USDA*, 451 F. Supp.3d 1040 (D. Minn. 2020).

42. Executive Order 13,650, 78 *Fed. Reg.* 48,029 (August 7, 2013); U.S. Environmental Protection Agency, "Accidental Release Prevention Requirements: Risk Management Programs Under the Clean Air Act," 82 *Fed. Reg.* 4,594 (January 13, 2017) [Obama EPA Risk Management Regulations], at 4,595–96; U.S. Chemical Safety Board, "Investigation Report, West Fertilizer Company Fire and Explosion" (January 2016) (explosion description).

43. Obama EPA Risk Management Regulations, at 4,595–96.

44. *Air Alliance of Houston v. EPA*, 906 F.3d 1049 (D.C. Cir. 2018), at 1065; U.S. Environmental Protection Agency, "Accidental Release Prevention Requirements: Risk Management Programs Under the Clean Air Act; Further Delay of Effective Date," 82 *Fed. Reg.* 13,968 (March 16, 2017); "EPA Imposes Obama-Era RMP Rule Mandates Despite Looming Rollback," *Inside EPA*, December 7, 2018, at 2 (immediately effective); "Chemical Manufacturers Cite CRA Bid in Call for EPA to Delay RMP Rule," *Inside EPA*, February 17, 2017; "Industries Weigh Options for Reversing EPA Facility Safety Rule Revisions," *Inside EPA*, January 13, 2017, at 3 (motion to reconsider).

45. U.S. Environmental Protection Agency, "Accidental Release Prevention Requirements: Risk Management Programs Under the Clean Air Act; Final Rule," 84 *Fed. Reg.* 69,834 (December 19, 2019), at 69,836–37; Fatima Hussein, "Spate of Texas Chemical Accidents Leads to Investigation, Suits," *Bloomberg Law*, February 6, 2020; Michael Phillis, "States Enter Fight Against Chemical Safety Rule Rollbacks," *Law 360*, January 29, 2020; Peter Hayes, "Steelworkers Challenge Rule Easing Chemical Safety," *Bloomberg Law*, January 9, 2020; "Facing Likely Suit, EPA Previews Defense As It Rolls Back Obama RMP Rule," *Inside EPA*, November 29, 2019 (industry groups delighted, $88 million); Juliet Eilperin, "Trump Administration Scales Back Safety Rules Adopted After Deadly Chemical Explosion," *WP*, November 21, 2019.

46. Alexander Nazaryan, *The Best People* (2019), at xxxiv (past Republicans); Juliet Eilperin, Brady Dennis & John Muyskens, "Trump Rolled Back More Than 125 Environmental Safeguards. Here's How," *WP*, November 10, 2020.

47. 33 U.S.C. §§ 1311(a), 1362(7); *Rapanos v. United States*, 547 U.S. 715 (2006).

48. *Rapanos v. United States*, 547 U.S. 715 (2006).

49. U.S. Department of Defense, U.S. Environmental Protection Agency, "Clean Water Rule: Definition of 'Waters of the United States,'" 80 *Fed. Reg.* 37,054 (June 29, 2015), at 37,055–56, 37,060.

50. *Georgia v. Wheeler*, 418 F. Supp.3d 1336 (S.D. Ga. 2019); *Texas v. EPA*, 389 F. Supp.3d 497 (S.D. Tex. 2019); U.S. Department of Defense, U.S. Environmental Protection Agency, "Intention to Review and Rescind or Revise the Clean Water Rule," 82 *Fed. Reg.* 12,532 (March 6, 2017) (challenges); Ellen M. Gilmer & Ariel Wittenberg, "Judge Puts WOTUS on Ice in Texas, La., Miss.," *E&E News*, September 12, 2018; Ariel Wittenberg, "Long Slog Likely If Trump EPA Attempts WOTUS Do-Over," *E&E News*, February 10, 2017 (Pruitt representation); Timothy Cama, "Obama Vetoes GOP Attempt to Block Water Rule," *The Hill*, January 19, 2016; Jenny Hopkinson, "Obama's Water War," *Politico*, May 27, 2015 (industry complaints, environmental groups complaints).

51. Executive Order 13,778, 82 *Fed. Reg.* 12,497 (March 3, 2017) §§ 2–3; Ariel Wittenberg, "Farm Bureau Floats 'Rubber Duck Test' in Bid to Sink WOTUS," *E&E News*, February 2, 2018 (float quote); "Teed Off: Critics Say Trump Water Rule Helps His Golf Links," Associated Press, March 5, 2017.

52. U.S. Department of Defense, U.S. Environmental Protection Agency, "The Navigable Waters Protection Rule: Definition of 'Waters of the United States'; Final Rule," 85 *Fed. Reg.* 22,250 (April 21, 2020), at 22,340–41; U.S. Department of Defense, U.S. Environmental Protection Agency, "Revised Definition of 'Waters of the United States'; Proposed Rule," 84 *Fed. Reg.* 4,154 (February 14, 2019), at 4,155, 4,173; Letter to Andrew R. Wheeler from Michael Honeycutt, re: Commentary on the Proposed Rule Defining the Scope of Waters Federally Regulated Under the Clean Water Act, dated October 16, 2019 (Science Advisory Board).

53. Coral Davenport, "Judge Rejects Trump-Era Rule on Water Pollution That Biden Had Started to Undo," *NYT*, September 1, 2021, at A19; Hannah Northey, "Trump Rule Imperils More Than 40,000 Waterways," *E&E News*, March 19, 2021; Bobby Magill, "Biden Swings Waters Pendulum with Final Resolution Still Elusive," *Bloomberg Law*, January 29, 2021; Maya Earls, "Trump Water Rule Faces New Challenge from Environmental Groups," *Bloomberg Law*, June 25, 2020; Ellen M. Gilmer, "Business Groups, Landowners Mobilize to Defend Trump Water Rules," *Bloomberg Law*, May 22, 2020.

54. U.S.C. §§ 1532(19), 1539(a)(1)(B),1536(a)(2); Department of the Interior, "Final Report: Review of the Department of the Interior Actions That Potentially Burden Domestic Energy," 82 *Fed. Reg.* 50,532 (November 1, 2017), at 50,546 (list).

55. U.S.C. §§ 1536(a)(2), 1536(b)(4); 50 C.F.R. § 402.14(a) (consultation requirement); Department of the Interior, Final Report, at 50,546 (delay).

56. Department of the Interior, Fish and Wildlife Service, "Endangered and Threatened Wildlife and Plants; Regulations for Designating Critical Habitat," 85 *Fed. Reg.* 82,376 (December 18, 2020); Department of the Interior & Department of Commerce, "Endangered and Threatened Wildlife and Plants; Regulations for Listing Species and Designating Critical Habitat," 84 *Fed. Reg.* 45,020 (August 27, 2019), at 44,754; Lisa Friedman, "U.S. Significantly Weakens Endangered Species Act," *NYT*, August 12, 2019, at A1 (quoting David J. Hayes, NYU Law School) (time horizon).

57. Juan Carlos Rodriguez, "Feds Will Reconsider Trump's Endangered Species Act Rules," *Law 360*, June 4, 2021; Sylvia Carignan, "Critical Habitat Protection Rules Targeted by Conservationists," *Bloomberg Law*, January 14, 2021; Daryl Fears, "The Trump Administration Weakened Endangered Species Act Rules. Today 17 State Attorneys General Sued over It," *WP*, September 25, 2019; Juan Carlos Rodriguez, "Trump Admin. Weakens Endangered Species Protections," *Law 360*, August 12, 2019 (bulldozer quote).

58. Robert L. Glicksman, "Trump's Policies Blasting at the Foundations of Conservation in Public Land Law," *The Hill*, July 17, 2018.

59. Ryan Zinke, "Final Report Summarizing Findings of the Review of Designations Under the Antiquities Act" (August 24, 2017) (recent decades); Sarah Krakof, "Public Lands, Conservation, and the Possibility of Justice," 53 *Harv. Civil Rights–Civil Liberties L. Rev.* 213 (2018), at 213; Rebecca Robinson & Stephen Strom, "Views from the Colorado Plateau: The Bears Ears in Two Histories," *Terrain*, August 4, 2016.

60. U.S.C. § 320301(a); Hope M. Babcock, "Rescission of a Previously Designated National Monument: A Bad Idea Whose Time Has Not Come," 37 *Stanford Env. L. J.* 3 (2017), at 11 (crime); John C. Ruple, "The Trump Administration and Lessons Not Learned from Prior National Monument Modifications," 43 *Harv. Env. L. Rev.* 1 (2019), at 10 (proclamations).

61. Barack Obama, "Proclamation No. 9558 of December 28, 2016," 82 *Fed. Reg.* 1,139 (January 5, 2017), at 1,143–44; Krakof, "Public Lands," at 244 (intense negotiations).

62. Krakof, "Public Lands," at 251, 254.

63. Donald J. Trump, "Proclamation 9681 of December 4, 2017," 82 *Fed. Reg.* 58,081 (December 8, 2017), at 58,084–85; Donald J. Trump, "Remarks on Signing Proclamations Affecting Prior Designations Under the American Antiquities Act of 1906 in Salt Lake City, Utah," December 4, 2017; Jennifer Yachnin, "Bears Ears Listed Among World's Most Endangered Sites," *E&E News*, October 31, 2019; Darryl Fears & Juliet Eilperin, "Trump Officials Say a New Plan Will Protect Bears Ears," *WP*, July 27, 2019 (plan); Jennifer Yachnin, "Former Monument Acres Open to Mining Claims," *E&E News*, February 2, 2018.

64. Joshua Partlow, "Tourists and Looters Descend on Bears Ears as Biden Mulls Protections," *WP*, April 8, 2021; Bobby Magill, "Utah Monuments Cases Stayed as Biden Ponders Broader Protections," *Bloomberg Law*, March 8, 2021; Jennifer Yachnin, "Allies: Trump Fixed Past Excesses When He Shrank Sites," *E&E News*, June 10, 2020; Jennifer Yachnin, "Foes Say Trump Misused Law Like 'Dirty, Clean Handkerchief,'" *E&E News*, January 10, 2020.

65. Consumer Financial Protection Bureau, "Payday, Vehicle Title, and Certain High-Cost Installment Loans; Final Rule," 82 *Fed. Reg.* 54,472 (November 17, 2017), at 54,474; Anjali Tsui & Alice Wilder, "How Payday Lenders Spent $1 Million at a Trump Resort—and Cashed In," *ProPublica*, June 5, 2019 (12 million); Karl Racine, "State AGs Must Fill the CFPB Void, but That's Not Enough," *Law 360*, April 27, 2018 (borrowers).

66. Richard Cordray, *Watchdog* (2020), at 198–99, 201 (interest rates); Daniel Karon, "CFPB's Payday Loan Protections Protect Big Business Too," *Law 360*, February 2, 2018 (lenders bank on); Stacy Cowley, "Payday Lenders Face Tough New Restrictions by Consumer Agency," *NYT*, October 6, 2017, at B1 (McDonald's).

67. Bureau of Consumer Financial Protection, "Payday, Vehicle Title, and Certain High-Cost Installment Loans: Final Rule," 82 *Fed. Reg.* 54,472 (November 17, 2017) [Payday Lending Rule], at 54,472–74; Cordray, *Watchdog*, at 201 (Dodd–Frank Act); Elizabeth Warren, "Republicans Remain Silent as Mulvancy's CFPB Ducks Oversight," *WSJ*, March 29, 2018 (massive record).

68. Nicholas Confessore & Stacy Cowley, "Trump Appointees Manipulated Agency's Payday Lending Research, Ex Staffer Claims," *NYT*, April 29, 2020, at A1; Renae Merle, "Payday Lenders Discussed Raising Money for Trump's Campaign to Fend Off Regulation, Audio Reveals," *WP*, October 29, 2019; Allied Progress, "Press Release: Payday Lenders Host High-Dollar Trump Fundraiser Featuring VP Mike Pence," October 7, 2019; Evan Weinberger, "CFPB Expected to Cut Payday Repayment Tests in Rule Overhaul," *Bloomberg Law*, October 19, 2018 (staff unwillingness); Kate Berry, "CFPB Signals Plan to Kill Payday Rule," *American Banker*, January 16, 2018.

69. Payday Lending Rule; Evan Weinberger, "CFPB Looks to Revive Payday Loan 'Ability to Repay' Standard," *Bloomberg Law*, March 24, 2021; Jon Hill, "Advocates Sue to Undo CFPB's Rollback of Payday Rule," *Law 360*, October 29, 2020; Katie Buehler, "Trade Groups Seek Quick Win in CFPB Payday Rule Challenge," *Law 360*, September 28, 2020.

70. Milton Friedman, *Capitalism and Freedom* (1962), at ix; Naomi Klein, *The Shock Doctrine* (2007), at 6, 15; Kelsey Brugger, "Trump May Ease Regulations During Pandemic," *E&E News*, April 21, 2020 (Heritage Foundation, NAM); Toluse Olorunnipa, "Trump Forges Ahead with Broader Agenda Even as Coronavirus Upends the Country," *WP*, April 9, 2020.

71. Rachel Augustine Potter, "How Trump Uses a Crisis: Repeal Rules While Nobody Is Looking," *WP*, June 10, 2020; Emily Holden, "Trump Dismantles Environmental Protections Under Cover of Coronavirus," *The Guardian*, May 14, 2020; Kate Berry, "CFPB Rulemaking Engine Churns on Through Coronavirus," *American Banker*, April 15, 2020; Cheryl Bolen, "Trump Pressured to Halt Regulatory Agenda Except for Virus Rules," *Bloomberg Law*, April 2, 2020 (deny requests to slow down); Lisa Friedman, "President Presses Forward with Regulatory Rollbacks," *NYT*, March 26, 2020, at A24 (no slippage); Ellen Knickmeyer, "Trump Agencies Push Rollbacks as Pandemic Rages," *E&E News*, March 25, 2020.

72. Executive Order 13,924, 85 *Fed. Reg.* 31,353 (May 22, 2020) §§ 1, 4, 7; Cheryl Bolen, "Trump Spring Regulatory Agenda Back on Track After Virus Pause," *Bloomberg Law*, June 18, 2020 (six hundred standards); Jean Chemnick, "Trump Uses Virus

to Permanently Suspend Rules on Industry," *E&E News*, May 20, 2020 (CEI suggestion, administration reached out).

73. Liz Essley, "Trump's Favorite Weapon in the Coronavirus Fight: Deregulation" (Center for Public Integrity, June 30, 2020) (Amber Sahagun tragedy, quote); Jennifer Smith, "U.S. Suspends Truck-Driving Limits to Speed Coronavirus Shipments," *WSJ*, March 14, 2020, at A1.

74. Charlotte McCary, Iliana Paul & Derek Sylvan, "Policy Shifts in a Pandemic" (Institute for Policy Integrity, March 2021), at 3 (pipeline safety extension); Heather Richards, "Interior Flagged Projects to Expedite During Pandemic," *E&E News*, September 2, 2020.

75. Laura Reiley, "FDA Rolls Back Food Rules for 5th Time During Pandemic," *WP*, May 27, 2020; Joyce Hanson, "FDA Relaxes Food-Labeling Rules During COVID-19 Crisis," *Law 360*, April 7, 2020.

76. Valerie Strauss, "Federal Judge Halts Betsy Devos's Controversial Rule Sending Coronavirus Aid to Private Schools," *WP*, August 23, 2020; Alayna Treene, "Former Education Secretaries Step into the Leadership Void," *Axios*, June 13, 2020; Erica L. Green, "DeVos Funnels Relief to Revive Stalled Agenda," *NYT*, May 16, 2020, at A1.

77. *Center for Biological Diversity v. Bernhardt*, 946 F.3d 553 (9th Cir. 2019); Cliff Sims, *Team of Vipers* (2019), at 108 (table set); Eric Lipton & Binyamin Appelbaum, "Regulatory Leashes Coming Off Wall St., Gun Sellers and More," *NYT*, March 6, 2017, at A1 (most aggressive); Mike Debonis, "Hill Republicans Move Full Speed Ahead with Push to Slash Obama-Era Rules," *WP*, January 17, 2017 (Roadmap to Repeal); Daren Bakst & James Gattuso, "Stars Align for the Congressional Review Act" (Heritage Foundation Issue Brief, December 16, 2016) (first order of business); Center for Progressive Reform, "CRA by the Numbers," undated, http://www.progressivereform.org/CRA_numbers.cfm (16 regulations eliminated).

78. H.J. Res. 69, 115th Cong. (April 3, 2017) (inhumane tactics rule); Office of Surface Mining Reclamation and Enforcement, "Congressional Nullification of the Stream Protection Rule Under the Congressional Review Act," 82 *Fed. Reg.* 54,924 (November 17, 2017) (stream protection rule); Michael McAuliff, "Congress Just Repealed Rules to Keep Guns from the Mentally Ill," *HuffPost*, February 15, 2017.

79. Nazaryan, *Best People*, at 102 (coverage overwhelmed); David Jordan & Nia Prater, "Deadline Passes on Law Trump Used to Reverse Obama-Era Regulations," *McClatchy News Service*, May 10, 2017 (quoting James Goodwin, CPR) (no hearings, debates).

80. "Transport Safety Rules Sidelined Indefinitely Under Trump as Part of a Sweeping Retreat in Regulations," *CNBC*, February 26, 2018.

Chapter 8: Sophisticated Sabotage

1. Thomas O. McGarity, David Bollier & Sidney Shapiro, *Sophisticated Sabotage* (2004); Binyamin Appelbaum & Jim Tankersley, "With Red Tape Losing Its Grip, Firms Ante Up," *NYT*, January 2, 2018, at A1 (Hartl quote); "CPR Fears Pruitt's

'Sophisticated Sabotage' Could Hinder EPA for Years," *Inside EPA*, December 1, 2017, at 1.

2. Occupational Safety and Health Administration, "Improve Tracking of Workplace Injuries and Illnesses," 81 *Fed Reg.* 29,623 (May 12, 2016); Bruce Rolfsen, "OSHA Injury Electronic Reporting Backed by Science Advisers," *Bloomberg/BNA Occupational Safety & Health Reporter*, January 9, 2018; Juliet Eilperin, "OSHA Suspends Rule Requiring Firms to Report Injury and Illness Data Electronically," *WP*, May 17, 2017 (encourage safer workplaces); Daniel R. Flynn, "OSHA Update—May 1, 2017: Regulatory Delay, Continued Enforcement, and Recent OSHRC Decisions," *National Law Review*, May 1, 2017.

3. Occupational Safety and Health Administration, "Tracking of Workplace Injuries and Illnesses; Final Rule," 84 *Fed. Reg.* 380 (January 25, 2019); Bruce Rolfsen, "Federal Safety Agencies at Odds on Reporting Worker Injuries," *Bloomberg/BNA Occupational Safety & Health Reporter*, October 1, 2018 (NIOSH); Letter to Deputy Assistant Secretary Loren E. Sweatt from Center for Progressive Reform, re: OSHA NPRM on Tracking of Workplace Injuries and Illnesses, dated September 28, 2018, at 1 (worker advocates); Bruce Rolfsen, "OSHA Seeks to Lift Injury Report Requirement for Big Companies," *Bloomberg/BNA Occupational Safety & Health Reporter*, July 26, 2018.

4. Bruce Rolfsen, "Trump Worker Safety Rule Appealed by 6 States' Attorneys General," *Bloomberg Law*, January 25, 2021; Bruce Rolfsen, "Industry Groups Renew Court Fight over Worker Injury Reporting," *Bloomberg Law*, March 19, 2019; Fatima Hussein & Sam Pearson, "Labor Department Fights to Keep Company Injury Data Private," *Bloomberg Law*, March 14, 2019 (Public Citizen challenge).

5. Bureau of Safety and Environmental Enforcement, "Oil and Gas and Sulfur Operations in the Outer Continental Shelf—Blowout Preventer Systems and Well Control; Final Rule," 81 *Fed. Reg.* 25,888 (April 29, 2016); Bureau of Safety and Environmental Enforcement, "History," https://www.bsee.gov/who-we-are/about-us/history; Bob Cavnar, *Disaster on the Horizon* (2010), at 13, 93; Milo C. Mason, "Where's Macondo? Where's BAST? DOI's Offshore Rules," *Natural Resources and Environment* (Fall 2018), at 50 (environmental groups); Jim Vines, et al., "BSEE Listened to Industry in Well Control Rule Revisions," *Law 360*, June 25, 2018 (vast improvement).

6. Executive Order 13,795, 82 *Fed. Reg.* 20,815 (May 3, 2017) §§ 2, 7 (quotes); Edward Klump, "This Interior Official Sees 'National Bias' Against Oil, Gas," *E&E News*, May 23, 2018; Dylan Brown, "La. Official, Industry Board Member to Head BSSE," *E&E News*, May 22, 2017.

7. Bureau of Safety and Environmental Enforcement, "Oil and Gas and Sulfur Operations in the Outer Continental Shelf—Blowout Preventer Systems and Well Control Revisions; Final Rule," 84 *Fed. Reg.* 21,908 (May 15, 2019), at 21,913; Ted Mann, "When Safety Rules on Oil Drilling Were Changed, Some Staff Objected. Those Notes Were Cut," *WSJ*, February 26, 2020, at A1 (not important quote); David S. Hilzenrath, "Interior's Rollback Includes Surprise Gift to Oil Industry" (Project on Government Oversight, May 14, 2019) (safe margin example); Keith Goldberg, "DOI Rolls Back Post-Deepwater Blowout Safety Regs," *Law 360*, May 2, 2019; David Hilzenrath, "When All Hell Breaks Loose: Years After Deepwater Horizon, Offshore Drilling Hazards Persist" (Project on Government Oversight, December 6,

2018) (wish list); Eric Lipton, "Targeting Rules 'Written with Human Blood,'" *NYT*, March 11, 2018, at A1.

8. Department of Energy, "Energy Conservation Program for Appliance Standards: Procedures for Use in New or Revised Energy Conservation Standards and Test Procedures for Consumer Products and Commercial/Industrial Equipment; Proposed Rule," 86 *Fed. Reg.* 18,901 (April 12, 2021); Department of Energy, "Energy Conservation Program for Appliance Standards: Procedures for Use in New or Revised Energy Conservation Standards and Test Procedures for Consumer Products and Commercial/Industrial Equipment; Final Rule," 85 *Fed. Reg.* 8,626 (February 14, 2020), at 8,680–81; Juan Carlos Rodriguez, "Energy Department Hit with Suits Challenging Efficiency Rule," *Law 360*, April 14, 2020; Lesley Clark, "DOE Overhaul of Efficiency Standards Program Draws Fire," *E&E News*, January 17, 2020; Department of Energy, "Press Release: Department of Energy Issues Final 'Process Rule' Modernizing Procedures in the Consideration of Energy Conservation Standards," January 15, 2020; Dino Grandoni, "Trump Wants to Make Dishwashers Great Again. The Energy Department Has a New Rule for That," *WP Energy 202*, January 17, 2020; Christa Marshall, "DOE Unveils Efficiency Plan That Critics Call a 'Disaster,'" *E&E News*, February 8, 2019 (step further).

9. *Zero Zone, Inc. v. Department of Energy*, 832 F.3d 654, 677–78 (7th Cir. 2016); Interagency Working Group on Social Cost of Greenhouse Gases, United States Government, "Technical Support Document—Technical Update of the Social Cost of Carbon for Regulatory Impact Analysis—Under Executive Order 12866" (August 2016); Chelsea Harvey, "Scientists Have a New Way to Calculate What Global Warming Costs. Trump's Team Isn't Going to Like It," *WP*, January 12, 2017 (NAS Report); Hannah Hess, "Panel Suggests Reforms for Social Cost of Carbon," *E&E News*, January 11, 2017 (150 times).

10. Executive Order 13,783, 82 *Fed. Reg.* 16,093 (March 31, 2017) §§ 3(c), 5(b); Chelsea Harvey, "Trump Team's Wonky CO_2 Calculation Is a Big Deal," *E&E News*, October 25, 2017 ($1 per ton); Ellen M. Gilmer & Pamela King, "Trump's 'Energy Independence' Order: Where Do Things Stand?" *E&E News*, October 24, 2017; Hannah Hess, "OIRA Works Quietly on Updating Social Cost of Carbon," *E&E News*, June 15, 2017 (less precautionary).

11. Doyle Elizabeth Canning, "Zeroing Out Climate Change: A 'Hard Look' at Trump's Social Cost of Carbon," 48 *Environmental Law Reporter* 10,479 (June 2018) (MAGA math); Richard Richels, et al., "The Trump Administration Cooks the Climate Change Numbers Once Again," *The Hill*, July 18, 2020 (limits to U.S. inappropriate); Lisa Friedman, "Nonpartisan Report Says Trump's Climate Metrics Undervalue the 'Social Cost of Carbon,'" *NYT*, July 15, 2020, at A19 (quoting Dr. Michael Greenstone, University of Chicago) (economic reality); John Lee, "The Social Cost of Carbon and Its Impact on Environmental Law," *Law 360*, January 30, 2018 (make world suffer); Harvey, "Trump Team's Wonky CO_2 Calculation (short-sighted).

12. Executive Order 13,771, 82 *Fed. Reg.* 9339 (February 3, 2017).

13. Michael A. Livermore, "Polluting the EPA's Long Tradition of Economic Analysis," 70 *Case Western L. Rev.* 1,063 (2020), at 1,073–74; Joseph E. Aldy, et al., "Co-benefits and Regulatory Impact Analysis: Theory and Evidence from Federal Air Quality Regulations" (National Bureau of Economic Research, July 2020) (econo-

mists agree); Scott Waldman, "To Topple Climate Rules, Officials Erase Air Pollutants," *E&E News*, October 5, 2018 (quoting former EPA administrator William Reilly).

14. "Limited EPA Mercury Data May Bolster Industry Challenge to Utility MACT," *Inside EPA*, January 6, 2012 (co-benefits value); Cathy Cash, "EPA Sticks to Guns on Mercury Rule; Industry Finds Agency Efforts for Flexibility Unsatisfying," *Electric Utility Week*, January 2, 2012, at 1 (costs).

15. Environmental Protection Agency, "National Emission Standards for Hazardous Air Pollutants: Coal-and Oil-Fired Electric Utility Steam Generating Units—Reconsideration of Supplemental Finding and Residual Risk and Technology Review," 84 *Fed. Reg.* 2,670 (February 7, 2019), at 2,675–78; Thomas O. McGarity, *Pollution, Politics and Power* (2019), at 307 (all plants complied); Caroline Cecot, "Deregulatory Cost-Benefit Analysis and Regulatory Stability," 68 *Duke L. J.* 1,593 (2019), at 1,626 (benefits nonexistent); Juliet Eilperin & Brady Dennis, "The EPA Is About to Change a Rule Cutting Mercury Pollution. The Industry Doesn't Want It," *WP*, February 17, 2020.

16. Environmental Protection Agency, "National Emissions Standards for Hazardous Air Pollutants: Coal- and Oil-Fired Electric Steam Generating Units—Reconsideration of Supplemental Finding and Residual Risk and Technology Review," 85 *Fed. Reg.* 31,286 (May 22, 2020); Sean Reilly, "EPA Rolls Back Basis for Power Plant Toxic Emissions Rule," *E&E News*, April 16, 2020 (set precedent).

17. Cecot, "Deregulatory Cost-Benefit Analysis," at 1,625 (criticism); Richard L. Revesz, "Trump Shows His Cards on Environmental Protections—Or a Lack Thereof," *The Hill*, April 30, 2020; Lisa Friedman, "E.P.A. Proposal Puts Costs Ahead of Health Gains," *NYT*, December 28, 2018, at A1 (quoting Ann Weeks, Clean Air Task Force) (criticism); Coral Davenport & Lisa Friedman, "E.P.A. Aims to Revalue Human Health in Its Review of Mercury Rules," *NYT*, September 9, 2018, at A15 (Krupnick quote).

18. Sean Reilly, "EPA Moves to Dump Trump's Cost-Benefit Rule," *E&E News*, April 5, 2021 (lead political appointee); "Top Trump Officials Vow to Intensify Implementation of Deregulatory Agenda," *Environmental Policy Alert*, July 31, 2019 (lock in quote); Abby Smith, "Industry Clamors for EPA's Ear on Revising Cost-Benefit Reviews," *Bloomberg Energy & Climate Report*, May 9, 2018.

19. Environmental Protection Agency, "Increasing Consistency and Transparency in Considering Benefits and Costs in the Clean Air Act Rulemaking Process," 85 *Fed. Reg.* 84,130 (December 23, 2020), at 84,156; Sean Reilly, "Cost-Benefit Rule Slashes EPA Regulatory Power," *E&E News*, December 9, 2020 (Wheeler quote).

20. Environmental Protection Agency, "Rescinding the Rule on Increasing Consistency and Transparency in Considering Benefits and Costs in the Clean Air Act Rulemaking Process; Interim Final Rule," 86 *Fed. Reg.* 26,406 (May 14, 2021); Dawn Reeves, "Critics Eye Applied Challenges as EPA Rescinds Trump Cost-Benefit Rule," *Inside EPA*, June 8, 2021 (biding time).

21. U.S.C. § 4332(2)(C); Council on Environmental Quality, "Update to the Regulations Implementing the Procedural Provisions of the National Environmental Policy

Act; Final Rule," 85 *Fed. Reg.* 43,304 (July 16, 2020), at 43,306 (no substantive outcome, 100 to 150 EISs).

22. Kelsey Brugger, "Companies Pressure White House on NEPA Guidelines," *E&E News*, November 22, 2019; Tiffany Middleton, "What Is an Environmental Impact Statement?" ABA Teaching Legal Docs, December 17, 2018, https://www.americanbar.org/groups/public_education/publications/teaching-legal-docs/teaching-legal-docs--what-is-an-environmental-impact-statement-/ (500 EISs); "Keystone Ruling Offers Fresh Rebuke of Reasoning Behind Trump Rollbacks," *Inside EPA*, November 16, 2018, at 27 (quoting Michael Gerrard, Columbia University) (environmental groups response); Pamela King, "Where Does Keystone XL Go from Here," *E&E News*, November 13, 2018; Nick Sobczyk, "Koch Network Weigh In on NEPA Rollback," *E&E News*, August 10, 2018.

23. Rebecca Teitsch, "Trump Finalizes Rollback of Bedrock Environmental Law NEPA," *The Hill*, July 15, 2020 (Trump quote); Heather Richards, "NEPA Rewrite Could Thwart Climate Fight Against Drilling," *E&E News*, January 10, 2020 (Trump administration projects); Lisa Friedman, "Trump's Move Against Landmark Environmental Law Caps a Relentless Agenda," *NYT*, January 9, 2020 (Neumayr acknowledgment).

24. Council on Environmental Quality, "Update to the Regulations Implementing the Procedural Provisions of the National Environmental Policy Act; Final Rule," 85 *Fed. Reg.* 43,304 (July 16, 2020) [CEQ Update Rule], at 43,331; Adam Aton, "How Trump Agencies' NEPA Reviews Lowball Climate Impacts," *E&E News*, October 9, 2019 (cumulative impacts).

25. CEQ Update Rule, at 43,351, 43,375; Lisa Friedman, "Trump Rule Would Exclude Climate Change in Infrastructure Planning," *NYT*, January 3, 2020.

26. CEQ Update Rule, at 43,335.

27. Niina H. Farah, "Trump NEPA Rules Begin After Court Denies Freeze," *E&E News*, September 14, 2020; Lisa Friedman, "Trump Guts Bedrock Law of Environmental Policy," *NYT*, July 20, 2020, at A17 (applause); Justin Sink, Jennifer A. Dlouhy & Jennifer Jacobs, "Trump's Infrastructure Approval Overhaul Seen Helping Polluters," *Bloomberg Law*, July 16, 2020 (environmental and environmental justice groups, giveaway quote, increase controversy); Rebecca Beitsch, "Critics Warn Trump's Latest Environmental Rollback Could Hit Minorities, Poor Hardest," *The Hill*, January 12, 2020.

28. "The President's Imposition of New Environmental Mitigation Regulations," *Hearings Before the Subcommittee on Oversight and Investigations of the House Committee on Natural Resources*, 114th Congress (February 24, 2016) (testimony of Michael Bean, DoI) [Bean Testimony] (popular vehicle, mitigation banks); David Schultz & Alan Kovski, "Zinke Preparing to Reshape Interior Through Personnel," *Bloomberg/BNA Daily Environment Report*, June 21, 2017 (compensatory mitigation).

29. Barack Obama, "Presidential Memorandum: Mitigating Impacts on Natural Resources from Development and Encouraging Related Private Investment," November 3, 2015 §§ 1, 3(b); Bean Testimony.

30. Memorandum to Assistant Directors and All Field Office Officials from Deputy Director for Policy and Programs, re: Compensatory Mitigation, dated July 24, 2018; Michael Doyle, "Trump Admin Torpedoes Obama-Era Mitigation Goal," *E&E News*, July 27, 2018; Schultz & Kovski, "Zinke Preparing" (Trump dim view; rescissions).

31. Kelsey Brugger, "Republican Governors Turn on Zinke Plan," *E&E News*, January 15, 2019; Juan Carlos Rodriguez, "BLM Wildlife Protection Shift Opens Door to Lawsuits," *Law 360*, July 26, 2018 (environmental groups); Greg Zimmerman, "What's Interior Secretary Zinke's Beef with 'Compensatory Mitigation,'" *WestWise*, June 30, 2017 (mystified observers).

32. U.S.C. § 1341(a), (d); *PUD No. 1 of Jefferson County v. Washington Department of Ecology*, 114 S.Ct. 1900 (1994).

33. Competitive Enterprise Institute, "CEI Leads Coalition to Comment in Support of EPA's Proposed Rule Updating Regulations on Water Quality Certification," October 22, 2019; Kelsey Brugger, Ariel Wittenberg & Hannah Northey, "What's in Trump's Energy Orders?" *E&E News*, April 9, 2019 (industry complaints).

34. Executive Order 13,868, 84 *Fed. Reg.* 15,495 § 3(c) (April 15, 2019); Clifford Krauss, "Trump Moves to Fast-Track Oil and Gas Pipelines," *NYT*, April 10, 2019, at B4.

35. Ariel Wittenberg & Kelsey Brugger, "EPA Focused on 4 Projects in Crafting State Permit Rule," *E&E News*, August 20, 2019 (very rare, 132 days); "States Fault Premise, Process for EPA Plan to Change CWA 401 Policy," *Inside EPA*, May 31, 2019, at 1; Juan Carlos Rodriguez, "Trump Moves to Speed Up Energy Projects," *Law 360*, April 10, 2019 (environmental groups).

36. Environmental Protection Agency, "Clean Water Act Section 401 Certification Rule," 85 *Fed. Reg.* 42,210 (July 13, 2020), at 42,215, 42,229, 42,285; Lisa Friedman, "E.P.A. Limits States' Power to Oppose Energy Projects," *NYT*, June 2, 2020, at A22 (run out the clock quote); "Corps Limits States' Time for CWA 401 Reviews as EPA Limits Scope," *Inside EPA*, August 16, 2019, at 1.

37. *PUD No. 1 of Jefferson County v. Washington Department of Ecology*, 114 S.Ct. 1900 (1994); "Western States Question EPA's Legal Power to Change CWA 401 Rule," *Inside EPA*, September 20, 2019, at 3; Maxine Joselow, "How Republicans Shifted Gears on Calif. Car Emissions," *E&E News*, May 8, 2018 (Whitehouse quote).

38. In re Clean Water Act Rulemaking, 2021 WL 4924844 (N.D. Cal. 2021); Victoria McKenzie, "Trump-Era Clean Water Rule Hit with Death Blow," *Law 360*, October 22, 2021); Pamela King, "Trump Water Regulation to Remain Pending Biden Review," *Bloomberg Law*, August 3, 2021; Brad Plumer, "E.P.A. to Restore Influence of States over Energy Projects," *NYT*, May 28, 2021; Steven Mufson, "Trump Signs Executive Orders Seeking to Speed Up Oil and Gas Projects," *WP*, April 10, 2019 (pipelines continue to leak).

39. *Bauer v. DeVos*, 325 F. Supp.3d 74 (D.D.C. 2018), at 80 (Corinthian collapse, borrower defense rule); Stacy Cowley, "Unclear Path for Defrauded Students," *NYT*, November 11, 2018, at B1 (350,000 students and graduates, 100,000 claims).

40. Hannah Albarazi, "Alsup Baffled by Feds' Fight with Students over Loan Relief," *Law 360*, October 24, 2019 (servicers' actions); Stacy Cowley, "Students Duped by Colleges Lose Automatic Loan Reprieve," *NYT*, August 30, 2019, at B6 (180,000 claims); Cowley, "Unclear Path" (different approach, one position).

41. Stacy Cowley, "DeVos Tries Again to Cut Debt Relief for Students Who Were Misled," *NYT*, December 10, 2019, at B1 (original formula); Mike LaSusa, "De Vos Hit with $100K Contempt Fine in Student Loan Row," *Law 360*, October 24, 2019.

42. Sarah Butrymowicz & Meredith Kolodner, "Shutdowns Lift For-Profit Colleges," *NYT*, June 18, 2020, at B1; Stacy Cowley, "DeVos Tries Again to Cut Debt Relief for Students Who Were Misled," *NYT*, December 10, 2019, at B1 (second formula, slap quote); Danielle Douglas-Gabriel, "Education Secretary Betsy DeVos Rolls Out New Method for Approving Student Debt Relief Claims," *WP*, December 10, 2019.

43. Environmental Protection Agency, "Pollutant-Specific Significant Contribution Finding for Greenhouse Gas Emissions from New, Modified, and Reconstructed Stationary Sources: Electric Utility Generating Units, and Process for Determining Significance of Other New Source Performance Standards Source Categories," 86 *Fed. Reg.* 2,542 (January 13, 2021), at 2,542–43; Jennifer Hijazi, "Appeals Court Scraps Trump Rule That Limited Emission Regulation," *Bloomberg Law*, April 5, 2021; Jean Chemnick, "Trump EPA Aims to Tie Biden's Hands with Rulemaking Surprise," *E&E News*, January 12, 2021.

Chapter 9: Promiscuous Permitting

1. Dylan Brown, "Mine Fight Fueled by Fears of a New Gold Rush," *E&E News*, October 25, 2019.

2. U.S. Environmental Protection Agency, "Proposed Determination of the U.S. Environmental Protection Agency Region 10 Pursuant to Section 404(c) of the Clean Water Act, Pebble Deposit Area, Southwest Alaska" (July 2014), at ES-2 [EPA Proposed Determination] (description of project); "EPA Pebble Settlement Leaves Toughest Issues Unresolved," *Greenwire*, May 17, 2017 (untapped reserves).

3. EPA Proposed Determination, at ES-1 (unparalleled quote, description of Bristol Bay); Bill Weir, "A Hot Debate Is Brewing in Alaska These Days over What Is Worth More, the Gold in the Ground or the Gold in the Water," *CBS This Morning*, August 25, 2017 (salmon runs).

4. Dylan Brown, "Meet the Salmon Scientist at the Center of the Pebble Fight," *E&E News*, November 11, 2019 (citing a study of water pollution from surface mines); Kim Heacox, "Trump's EPA Wants to Put a Toxic Mine in Pristine Alaska," *The Guardian*, April 22, 2019 (tailings impoundments); Weir, "Hot Debate" (sulfuric acid).

5. Brown, "Salmon Scientist" (Halford description, community concerns); Tim Bradner, "Analysis: Breaking Down the Pebble Debate," *Mat-Su Valley Frontiersman*, April 18, 2019 (wealthy businessman); Elwood Brehmer, "Bristol Bay Study Stands, but EPA Moves to Halt Its Finding," *Alaska Journal of Commerce*, July 19, 2017 (referendum).

6. Executive Order 13,807, 82 *Fed. Reg.* 40,463 (August 15, 2017) § 5 (infrastructure); Executive Order 13,783, 82 *Fed. Reg.* 16,093 (March 31, 2017) § 2 (energy independence); Executive Order 13,766, 82 *Fed. Reg.* 8,657 (January 30, 2017) (expediting environmental reviews); "Does It Take 10 Years to Get a Permit to Build a Road, as Donald Trump Said," PolitiFact, January 30, 2018.

7. EPA Proposed Determination, at ES-5 (scientists' conclusion); Editorial, "The Pebble Mine Victory," *WSJ*, May 17, 2017, at A18 (first time).

8. U.S. Environmental Protection Agency, "Proposal to Withdraw Proposed Determination to Restrict the Use of an Area as a Disposal Site; Pebble Deposit Area, Southwest Alaska," 82 *Fed. Reg.* 33,123 (July 19, 2017); Bradner, "Breaking Down" (meeting); Drew Griffin, "EPA Head Met with a Mining CEO—and Then Pushed Forward a Controversial Mining Project," *CNN Wire*, September 22, 2017; "EPA Pebble Settlement Leaves Toughest Issues Unresolved," *Greenwire*, May 17, 2017 (condemnation).

9. Sophia Morris, "EPA Lifts Restrictions on Pebble Mine Project," *Law 360*, July 30, 2019 (would not be expected quote); "Where EPA Foresees Devastation, the Army Doesn't," *Greenwire*, February 27, 2019 (different approaches); "Pebble Unveils Revised Mining Plan," *Greenwire*, October 5, 2017 (formal application).

10. "The Pebble Mine Project: Process and Potential Impacts," *Hearings Before the Subcommittee on Water Resources and Environment of the House Committee on Transportation and Infrastructure*, 116th Cong. (October 25, 2019) (testimony of Richard K. Borden, Midgard Environmental Services), at 3 (wastewater); Brown, "New Gold Rush" (CEO admission).

11. U.S. Environmental Protection Agency, "Notification of Decision to Withdraw Proposed Determination to Restrict the Use of an Area as a Disposal Site; Pebble Deposit Area, Southwest Alaska," 84 *Fed. Reg.* 45,749 (August 30, 2019); Scott Bronstein, et al., "EPA Dropped Salmon Protection After Trump Met with Alaska Governor," *CNN Wire*, August 9, 2019.

12. Dino Grandoni, "How Pebble Mine Opponents Used Fox News to Push Trump to Delay the Alaska Project," *WP Energy 202*, August 24, 2020; James Marshall, "Trump Whisperer Tucker Carlson Takes on Pebble Mine," *E&E News*, August 17, 2020; Michael D. Shear & Henry Fountain, "It's Trump Jr. vs. Trump Sr. over Alaskan Mineral Mine," *NYT*, August 6, 2020, at A19; Ariel Wittenberg, "Trump: 'I'll Take a Look' at Pebble Mine," *E&E News*, August 6, 2020.

13. James Marshall, "Alaska to Appeal Pebble Mine Permit Denial," *E&E News*, January 11, 2021; Joyce Hanson, "Northern Dynasty to Fight Rejection of Pebble Mine Permit," *Law 360*, December 17, 2020; Steven Frank & Jennifer A. Dlouhy, "U.S. Rejects Controversial Alaska Pebble Gold, Copper Mine," *Bloomberg Law*, November 25, 2020; Juliet Eilperin, "Alaska Mining Executive Resigns a Day After Being Caught on Tape Boasting of His Ties to GOP Politicians," *WP*, September 23, 2020; Henry Fountain, "Tape Casts Doubt on Alaska Mine Plan," *NYT*, September 22, 2020, at A13; James Marshall & Ariel Wittenberg, "Green Sting: Pebble Execs Brag About Influence in Secret Tape," *E&E News*, September 22, 2020; James Marshall, "Biden Comes Out Against Pebble Mine," *E&E News*, August 10, 2020.

14. *Standing Rock Sioux Tribe v. Corps of Engineers*, 205 F. Supp.3d 4 (D.C. Cir. 2016), at 7, 113–14 (description of pipeline); Mike Soraghan, "Trail of Spills Haunts Dakota Access Developer," *E&E News*, May 26, 2020 (history of leaks); Sandy Tolan, "What's Next for the Dakota Access Pipeline," *The Nation*, December 6, 2016 (nearly completed).

15. Saul Elbein, "The Seventh Generation," *NYT Magazine*, February 5, 2017, at 25 (description of protest).

16. *Standing Rock Sioux Tribe v. Corps of Engineers*, 205 F. Supp.3d 4 (D.C. Cir. 2016), at 7, 119; Soraghan, "Trail of Spills" (Trump stock); Maxine Joselow, "5 Things to Know About the Company Building Dakota Access," *E&E News*, January 27, 2017.

17. *Standing Rock Sioux Tribe v. Corps of Engineers*, 255 F. Supp.3d 101 (D.D.C. 2017), at 119–20; Donald J. Trump, "Memorandum for the Secretary of the Army, re: Construction of the Dakota Access Pipeline," 82 *Fed. Reg.* 8,661 (January 30, 2017).

18. Alan Kovski, "Dakota Access Pipeline Ready to Open for Business," *Bloomberg/BNA Energy & Climate Report*, May 3, 2017; Cecelia Smith-Schoenwalder, "Hundreds March to White House in Pipeline Protest," *E&E News*, March 10, 2017; Mark Berman, "Dakota Pipeline Protest Camp: Ten Arrested, Dozens More Believed to Remain After Evacuation Deadline," *WP*, February 22, 2017; Steven Mufson & Juliet Eilperin, "Trump Seeks to Revive Dakota Access, Keystone XL Oil Pipelines," *WP*, January 24, 2017 (protesters left).

19. *Standing Rock Sioux Tribe v. Corps of Engineers*, 282 F. Supp.3d 91 (D.D.C. 2017), at 101.

20. *Standing Rock Sioux Tribe v. Corps of Engineers*, 440 F. Supp.3d 1 (D.D.C. 2020), at 16–26; Mike Lee, "Pipeline Expansion Sparks Battles in 3 States," *E&E News*, November 14, 2019; Keith Goldberg, "Tribe Calls Corps' Redo of DAPL Enviro Review 'A Sham,'" *Law 360*, August 16, 2019.

21. *Standing Rock Sioux Tribe v. Corps of Engineers*, 471 F. Supp.3d 71 (D.D.C. 2020); Ellen M. Gilmer, "Dakota Access Shutdown to Cause Harm, Government Lawyers Warn," *Bloomberg Law*, November 23, 2020 (three years); Collin Eaton & Christopher M. Matthews, "Judge Orders Pipeline Shut Down, Citing Faulty Environmental Permit," *WSJ*, July 7, 2020, at B2 ($2 billion); Jacey Fortin & Lisa Friedman, "Dakota Pipeline Is Ordered Shut Down During Environmental Review," *NYT*, July 7, 2020, at B5 (taxes and royalties); Ellen M. Gilmer, "Anti-Pipeline Playbook Snags Biggest Victories Yet," *Bloomberg Law*, July 7, 2020 (first time, conventional wisdom).

22. *Standing Rock Sioux Tribe v. U.S. Corps of Engineers*, 985 F.3d 1032 (D.C. Cir. 2021); Gregory Wallace & Keith Goldberg, "DC Judge Won't Shut Down Dakota Access Pipeline," *Law 360*, May 21, 2021; Mike Soraghan, "Dakota Access CEO Gives $10 Million to Boost Trump," *E&E News*, September 23, 2020; Ellen M. Gilmer, "Trump Administration Joins Dakota Access Pipeline Appeal," *Bloomberg Law*, July 13, 2020.

23. Bureau of Land Management, "Who We Are, What We Do," https://www.blm .gov/about/our-mission; Adam Aton, "Public Lands Spew 25% of U.S. Emissions—USGS," *E&E News*, November 27, 2018 (emissions).

24. Department of the Interior, "Secretarial Order 3338, Discretionary Programmatic Environmental Impact Statement to Modernize the Federal Coal Program," January 15, 2016; Department of the Interior, "Press Release, Secretary Jewell Offers Vision for Balanced, Prosperous Energy Future," March 17, 2015; Michael C. Blumm & Oliver Jamin, "The Trump Public Lands Revolution: Redefining 'The Public' in Public Land Law," 48 *Envtl. L.* 311 (2018) (three-year expectation).

25. Executive Order 13,783 § 6; White House, "Fact Sheet, President Donald Trump: Putting Coal Country Back to Work," February 16, 2017; Department of the Interior, "Secretarial Order 3348"; James Marshall, "Biden Admin to Review Federal Coal Leasing Program," *E&E News*, August 17, 2021; Coral Davenport, "Federal Judge Says Biden Cannot Pause New Leases for Drilling on Public Lands," *NYT*, June 16, 2021, at A13; Dylan Brown, "Coal Leasing Sputters Despite Trump's Promises," *E&E News*, March 3, 2020 (withdrawn applications); Pamela King, "2 Years After Trump's Energy Order: What Remains," *E&E News*, March 27, 2019 (little impact); Gilmer & King, "Trump's 'Energy Independence' Order" (demand plummeted).

26. Konnath, "Biden's DOI Can't Get Suit" (leases, pending leases); Bobby Magill, "Interior Order Revokes Trump Moves on Coal Leasing Moratorium," *Bloomberg Law*, April 16, 2021; Timothy Egan, "We Are Squandering Our Children's Inheritance for Oil," *NYT*, March 29, 2019, at A26; Darryl Fears & Juliet Eilperin, "The Trump Administration Is Opening Millions of New Acres to Drilling—and That's Just a Start," *WP*, March 15, 2019; Eric Lipton & Hiroko Tabuchi, "Trump Fracking Boom Imperils Landscape of American West," *NYT*, October 27, 2018, at A1.

27. Heather Richards, "Opposition Grows to BLM Auction Near Arches, Bears Ears," *E&E News*, July 16, 2020; Juliet Eilperin & Darryl Fears, "Oil and Gas Companies Want to Drill Within a Half-Mile of Utah's Best-Known National Parks," *WP*, March 18, 2020; Miranda Green, "Zinke's Drilling Agenda to Outlast Tenure," *The Hill*, December 27, 2018 (changed approach); Rachel Leven, "Drilling Overwhelms Agency Protecting America's Lands" (Center for Public Integrity, November 13, 2018) (skip environmental reviews); Eric Lipton & Hiroko Tabuchi, "Trump Fracking Boom Imperils Landscape of American West," *NYT*, October 27, 2018, at A1 (National Park Service).

28. Kelsey Brugger, "Protesters Outnumber Bidders at Some Lease Sales," *E&E News*, December 14, 2018; Eric Lipton & Hiroko Tabuchi, "For Lease: Land to Drill On, Dirt Cheap," *NYT*, November 27, 2018, at B1 ($1.50 per acre, noncompetitive leases, locked-up land); Georgiana Gustin, "Oil and Gas Drilling on Federal Land Headed for Faster Approvals, Zinke Says," *Inside Climate News*, July 6, 2017 (glut).

29. *Dine Citizens Against Ruining Our Environment v. Bernhardt*, 923 F.3d 831 (10th Cir. 2019); *Citizens for a Healthy Community v. BLM*, 377 F. Supp. 1223 (D. Colo. 2019) (greenhouse gas omission); *WildEarth Guardians v. Zinke*, 368 F. Supp.3d 41 (D.D.C. 2019) (greenhouse gas omission); Niina H. Farah, "Judge Orders BLM to Redo NEPA Reviews for Oil Leases," *E&E News*, December 15, 2020; Eric Lipton, "Trump Unlocks Federal Lands in a Final Rush," *NYT*, December 12, 2020, at A1; Niina H. Farah, "Judge Strikes Down 'Sloppy and Rushed' BLM Climate Review," *E&E News*, November 16, 2020; Niina H. Farah, "Judge Tosses 287 Interior Leases over NEPA Review," *E&E News*, May 4, 2020; Morgan Conley, "BLM Ordered to Rethink Approval of Mont. Drilling Leases," *Law 360*, May 1, 2020; Heather Richards, "Judge

Hands Climate Analysis Back to BLM," *E&E News*, December 12, 2019; Juliet Eilperin, "Facing Democratic Resistance, Interior Secretary Promotes Oil and Gas Drilling," *WP*, May 10, 2019 (downstream emissions); Brittany Patterson, "Greens Resist Trump with Lawsuits on CO2," *E&E News*, February 8, 2018. But see Clark Mindock, "Judge Backs Climate Impact Reviews for Oil and Gas Leases," *Law 360*, August 19, 2020.

30. U.S. Fish and Wildlife Service, "Refuge Features," https://www.fws.gov/refuge /arctic/refuge_features.html.

31. Margaret Kriz Hobson, "Alaska Natives Battle over ANWR," *E&E News*, February 19, 2019 (tribes at odds); Henry Fountain & Steve Eder, "Thirst for Oil Threatens Arctic Refuge," *NYT*, December 2, 2018, at A1.

32. "Oil and Gas Exploration and Development in the Arctic Coastal Plain," *Hearings Before the Senate Energy and Natural Resources Committee*, 115th Congress (November 2, 2017) (testimony of Greg Sheehan, Fish and Wildlife Service).

33. Blumm & Jamin, "Trump Public Lands Revolution," at 352 (tax bill rider); Steven Mufson, "Companies Take First Steps to Drill for Oil in Arctic National Wildlife Refuge," *WP*, June 1, 2018 (four decades, lease sale requirement).

34. Heather Richards & Niina H. Farah, "3 Issues May Thwart Trump's ANWR Plan," *E&E News*, August 18, 2020 (lack of staff input); Jennifer Dlouhy, "Trump Plans Arctic Drilling Rights Sale in Likely 2020 Clash," *Bloomberg Law*, August 17, 2020 (least protective, buffer zones); Juliet Eilperin, "Trump Finalizes Drilling Plan for Arctic National Wildlife Refuge," *WP*, August 1, 2020 (option selected); Heather Richards, "'There Is Not a Climate Crisis,' BLM Says in Refuge Docs," *E&E News*, September 25, 2019; Adam Aton, "Drilling Could Cause Extinctions in a Warming ANWR—Agency," *E&E News*, September 13, 2019 (debatable assumption); Bobby Maggill, "Long-Term Damage, Extinctions Likely with Arctic Refuge Drilling," *Bloomberg Law*, September 13, 2019 (extinction); Steven Mufson & Juliet Eilperin, "Trump Administration Opens Huge Reserve in Alaska to Drilling," *WP*, September 13, 2019 (description of selected option).

35. Coral Davenport, Henry Fountain & Lisa Friedman, "U.S. Suspends Drilling Leases in Arctic Lands," *NYT*, June 2, 2021, at A1; Heather Richards, "Executive Order Will Pause All ANWR Oil Activities," *E&E News*, January 20, 2021; Heather Richards, "Ex-Trump Official 'Disappointed' by ANWR Sale He Championed," *E&E News*, January 7, 2021 ($14.4 million); Juliet Eilperin & Steven Mufson, "Trump Auctions Drilling Rights to Arctic National Wildlife Refuge on Wednesday," *WP*, January 6, 2021 (banks opt out); Jennifer A. Dlouhy, "Big Oil Skips Trump's Last-Minute Arctic Drilling-Rights Auction," *Bloomberg Law*, January 6, 2021; Clark Mindock, "Trump Admin. Cuts Arctic Lands Planned for Oil Auction," *Law 360*, December 21, 2020 (expedite).

36. Bobby Magill, "Grim Prospects for Drilling on Arctic Leases Despite Trump Push," *Bloomberg Law*, January 21, 2021 (lawsuits); Juliet Eilperin & Steven Mufson, "Trump Auctions Drilling Rights to Arctic National Wildlife Refuge on Wednesday," *WP*, January 6, 2021 (2024 auction); Jennifer A. Dlouhy, "Big Oil Skips" (must obtain permits); John Podesta, "Trump Wants to Spoil Alaska's Pristine Environment. We Can't Let That Happen," *WP*, September 13, 2019 (dwindling fleet).

37. Alaska Wilderness League, "Tongass National Forest, Why to Love This Place," https://www.alaskawild.org/places-we-protect/tongass-national-forest/ (Tongass description, 8 percent sequestration); Brendan Jones, "We Need the Tongass Now More Than Ever," *WP*, August 29, 2019 (Roosevelt); Marc Heller, "These Alaska Natives Want to Upend Trump's Pro-Timber Rule," *E&E News*, August 14, 2019 (endangered species, salmon).

38. *Wyoming v. USDA*, 661 F.3d 1209 (10th Cir. 2011); United States Department of Agriculture, "2001 Roadless Rule," https://www.fs.usda.gov/roadmain/roadless/2001rule (roadless area rule description); Marc Heller, "Trump Administration Moves to Ease Tongass Restrictions," *E&E News*, August 30, 2018 (9.3 million acres).

39. Heller, "Trump Administration Moves to Ease."

40. Coral Davenport, "Trump Administration Releases Plan to Open Tongass Forest to Logging," *NYT*, September 26, 2020, at A11 (capacity to absorb carbon dioxide); Brendan Jones, "We Need the Tongass" (no sense); Heller, "These Alaska Natives" (recreational value, mineral extraction).

41. Juliet Eilperin, "Trump Administration Proposes Expanding Logging in Alaska's Tongass National Forest," *WP*, October 15, 2019; Heller, "These Alaska Natives" (meeting).

42. Marc Heller, "Old or Young Growth? Tongass Logging at a Crossroads," *E&E News*, October 7, 2019 (young growth, limited harvests); Marc Heller, "More Tongass Logging Could Cost Taxpayers Money—Report," *E&E News*, October 1, 2019 ($30 million cost); Juliet Eilperin & Josh Dawsey, "Trump Pushes to Allow Logging in Alaska's Tongass National Forest," *WP*, August 27, 2019 (opponents).

43. Juliet Eilperin, "Trump to Stop Protections from Tongass National Forest, One of the Biggest Intact Temperate Rainforests," *WP*, October 28, 2020 (finalized proposal); Coral Davenport, "Trump Administration Releases Plan to Open Tongass Forest to Logging," *NYT*, September 26, 2020, at A11 (critics).

44. Juliet Eilperin, "Biden Administration Proposes Sweeping Protections for Alaska's Tongass National Forest," *WP*, July 15, 2021; Bobby Magill, "Trump-Era Roadless Rule to Be Scrapped for Alaska Forest," *Bloomberg Law*, June 11, 2021; Maya Earls, "Tongass National Forest's Opening to Logging Draws Tribes' Suit," *Bloomberg Law*, December 24, 2020.

45. Bobby Magill, "Oil, Gas Industry Stockpiled Drilling Leases Before Biden 'Pause,'" *Bloomberg Law*, January 28, 2021; Heather Richards, "Drillers Amass BLM Permits Challenging Biden's Climate Plan," *E&E News*, January 12, 2021; Juliet Eilperin & Dino Grandoni, "Biden Vowed to Ban New Drilling on Public Lands. It Won't Be Easy," *WP*, November 19, 2020 (4 million acres).

Chapter 10: Failure to Enforce

1. The Jennifer Riordan story is drawn from Michael Laris, "'It Appeared That We Had Time': How the FAA Missed a Chance to Save Jennifer Riordan," *WP*, December 2, 2019; Zach Wichter, "Inspections Must Use Ultrasound," *NYT*, April 21, 2018, at A15; Zach Wichter, "Similar Type of Failure Worried Regulators in '16," *NYT*,

April 20, 2018, at A15; Connor Shine, "Why Some Fan Blade Inspections Still Aren't Required After Similar 2016 Southwest Airlines Engine Failure," *Dallas Morning News*, April 19, 2018; Evan Hooper, "Southwest, Engine Manufacturer Disagreed on Time Needed to Inspect Fan Blades," *Dallas Business Journal*, April 19, 2018.

2. Lori Aratani, Michael Laris & Ian Duncan, "Lax FAA Oversight Allowed Southwest to Put Millions of Passengers at Risk, IG Says," *WP*, February 11, 2020; Andy Pasztor & Alison Sider, "Safety Lapses Found at Southwest," *WSJ*, January 31, 2020, at B1 (IG quote).

3. Pub. L. 94-163, 89 Stat. 871 (December 22, 1975); 49 U.S.C. § 32912 (civil penalties); National Highway Traffic Safety Administration, "Civil Penalties; Final Rule," 84 *Fed. Reg.* 36,007 (July 26, 2019) [NHTSA Repeal Rule], at 36,009, 36,016.

4. Pub. L. 114-74, § 701, 129 Stat. 584, at 599–600; NHTSA Repeal Rule, at 36,012.

5. NHTSA Repeal Rule, at 36,009, 36,012, 36,015–20.

6. *New York v. National Highway Traffic Safety Administration*, 974 F.3d 87 (2d Cir. 2020); National Highway Traffic Safety Administration, "Civil Penalties," 86 *Fed. Reg.* 3,016 (January 14, 2021); Maxine Joselow, "15 States Sue over Trump Delay of Higher Automaker Fines," *E&E News*, February 17, 2021; Maxine Joselow, "Lawsuit Targets Trump Rule Delaying Fines for Automakers," *E&E News*, January 25, 2021; Maxine Joselow, "Trump Admin Delays Higher Fines for Auto Polluters," *E&E News*, January 14, 2021 (locked in quote); Timothy Cama, "Trump Admin to Reconsider Penalties for Car Efficiency Violations," *The Hill*, July 11, 2017 (Sierra Club quote).

7. The Ray Hatfield story is drawn from Tim Loh, "As Trump Sings Coal's Praises, Mine Fatalities Are on the Rise," *Bloomberg/BNA Energy & Climate Report*, August 4, 2017; Bill Estep, "Eastern Kentucky Coal Mine Death Blamed on Safety Lapses," *Lexington Herald-Leader*, July 17, 2017; "MSHA: Mine Where Miner Killed Cited for Past Violations," *Appalachian News-Express*, February 3, 2017.

8. AFL-CIO, "Death on the Job: The Toll of Neglect" (April 2019), at 34 (compliance assistance); Timothy Cama, "Coal Mining Deaths Double in 2017," *The Hill*, January 2, 2018; Dylan Brown, "Coal Exec Faces Questions About Murray Ties, Violations," *E&E News*, September 18, 2017 (United Mine Workers); "Coal Mine Deaths Surge, Putting Feds and Miners at Odds," *CBS News*, August 3, 2017 (no citations).

9. U.S.C. § 654(a)(1) (general duty clause); Rena Steinzor & Sidney Shapiro, *The People's Agents* (2010), at 20 (small penalties); AFL-CIO, "Death on the Job," at 3 ($7,761); Jim Morris, "Death in the Trenches" (Center for Public Integrity, December 14, 2017) (criminal penalties).

10. Deborah Berkowitz, "Worker Safety in Crisis: The Cost of a Weakened OSHA" (National Employment Law Project, April 30, 2020) (suspended hires); AFL-CIO, "Death on the Job" (inspector ratio, 165 years), at 16; Ben Penn, "Inside Scalia's Pro-Industry Revamp of Labor Agency Enforcement," *Bloomberg Law*, November 4, 2020; Michael Graebell, Bernice Young & Maryam Jameel, "Millions of Essential Workers Are Being Left Out of COVID-19 Workplace Safety Protections," *ProPublica*, April 16, 2020 (862 inspections).

11. Christina L. Lyons, "Worker Safety," *Congressional Quarterly*, May 4, 2018, at 291, 392 (75 percent, past experience); Sam Pearson, "Republicans Urge More Worker

Safety Compliance Help for Companies," *Bloomberg Law*, February 7, 2018 (compliance assurance).

12. AFL-CIO, "Death on the Job," at 19–20 (homepage, buried fatalities report); Morris, "Death in the Trenches" (Michaels quote, Duke report); Alex Leary, "Trump Administration Pushes to Deregulate with Less Enforcement," *WSJ*, June 23, 2019 (discard Obama); Sam Pearson, "Worker Fatalities List Moved Off OSHA Website Home Page," *Bloomberg/BNA Occupational Safety and Health Reporter*, August 29, 2017; Alexandra Berzon, "OSHA Cuts Down Fatality Reporting in the Workplace," *WSJ*, August 28, 2017, at B6 (press releases, Chamber of Commerce complaint); Paul Feldman, "OSHA Under Trump Is Tight-Lipped—Democratic Senators Demand to Know Why," *Working in These Times*, May 30, 2017 (discourage employers); Carla J. Gunnin, "OSHA Issues First Enforcement Action Press Release Since Start of Trump Administration," *National Law Review*, April 20, 2017.

13. Charles Piller, "FDA Enforcement Actions Plummet Under Trump," *Science*, July 2, 2019.

14. Mike Soraghan, "PHMSA Staff Concerned About Agency-Industry Ties—IG," *E&E News*, January 19, 2021 (35 percent); Mike Soraghan, "No Penalties for 90% of Pipeline Blasts," *E&E News*, November 15, 2018 (rarely assessed, Elliott quote); Laura LaValle & Hana Vizcarra, "GAO Report May Impact PHMSA Pipeline Safety Inspections," *Law 360*, September 21, 2017 (PHMSA responsibility); Zoe Schlanger, "The US Has One Inspector for Every 5,000 Miles of Pipeline—Or Twice the Length of the Country, Each," *Quartz*, March 10, 2017.

15. Karen Brulliard & William Wan, "Caged Raccoons Drooled in 100-Degree Heat. But Federal Enforcement Has Faded," *WP*, August 22, 2019.

16. Brulliard & Wan, "Caged Raccoons" (quoting William Stokes).

17. Juan Carlos Rodriguez, "EPA Focus on Compliance over Enforcement Stirs Questions," *Law 360*, January 31, 2019 (inadequate resources); Alex Guillen & Emily Holden, "What EPA Chief Scott Pruitt Promised—and What He's Done," *Politico*, November 21, 2017 (enforcement suffered); James Hoffman, "How EPA Chief Scott Pruitt Wants to Redefine 'Environmentalism,'" *WP Daily 202*, November 17, 2017; Paul Stinson, "States Should Be Front Line of Enforcement, EPA Official Says," *Bloomberg/BNA Energy & Climate Report*, August 4, 2017; "Critics Fear EPA Budget Will Spur State Race to the Bottom on Enforcement," *Inside EPA*, April 28, 2017, at 1 (signal to states).

18. Mike Soraghan, "EPA Allows Producers to Self-Report Violations," *E&E News*, April 1, 2019 (self-reporting program); Juan Carlos Rodriguez, "EPA Focus on Compliance over Enforcement Stirs Questions," *Law 360*, January 31, 2019 (attorney quote); Mike Soraghan, "Trump's EPA Turns to Less Punitive Responses to Pollution," *E&E News*, June 11, 2018 (National Compliance Initiative).

19. Office of the Inspector General, U.S. Environmental Protection Agency, "Resource Constraints, Leadership Decisions, and Workforce Culture Led to a Decline in Federal Enforcement" (May 13, 2021), at 41 (company inclinations); David Coursen, "Reversing Rollbacks in the Post-Trump Era Is Not Enough," *The Hill*, December 7, 2020 (fewer enforcement actions, fewer criminal referrals, prosecutions down).

20. U.S. Environmental Protection Agency, "Supplemental Environmental Projects Policy 2015 Update (March 15, 2015)," at 1 (definition of SEPs, civil penalty reduction); Memorandum to Regional Administrators from Cynthia Giles re: Issuance of the 2015 Update to the 1998 U.S. Environmental Protection Agency Supplemental Environmental Projects Policy, March 10, 2015 (popular with EPA staff); Kenneth T. Kristl, "Making a Good Idea Even Better: Rethinking the Limits on Supplemental Environmental Projects," 31 *Vt. L. Rev.* 217, 218 (2007), at 222 (history of SEPs); Patrice L. Simms, "Leveraging Supplemental Environmental Projects: Toward an Integrated Strategy for Empowering Environmental Justice Communities," 47 *Env. Rept.* 10,511 (2017), at 10,521 (most cases settled); Comment, "Environmental Remediation Through Supplemental Environmental Projects and Creative Negotiation: Renewed Community Involvement in Federal Enforcement," 26 *B.C. Environmental Affairs L. Rev.* 189 (1998), at 212 (popular with local communities); Note, "Supplemental Environmental Projects: A Bargain for the Environment," 12 *Pace Env'l L. Rev.* 789 (1995), at 809 (popular with violators). For an extended analysis of the advantages, disadvantages, and legality of SEPs, see Thomas O. McGarity, "Supplemental Environmental Projects in Complex Environmental Litigation," 98 *Tex. L. Rev.* 1405 (2020).

21. John Braithwaite, *Restorative Justice & Responsive Regulation* (2002), at 11 (defining restorative justice); Steven Bonorris, "Environmental Enforcement in the Fifty States: The Promise and Pitfalls of Supplemental Environmental Projects," 11 *Hastings W.-NW. J. Envtl. L. & Policy* 185 (2005), at 204 (opportunity to experiment, environmental justice); Comment, "Environmental Remediation," at 223 (individual circumstances); Note, "Supplemental Environmental Projects," at 809 (beyond EPA's power).

22. Memorandum from Jean E. Williams, Deputy Assistant Attorney General to ENRD Section Chiefs and Deputy Section Chiefs, re: Withdrawal of Memoranda and Policy Documents, February 4, 2021 (Biden withdrawal); Memorandum from Jeffrey Bossert Clark, Assistant Attorney General to ENRD Deputy Assistant Attorneys General and Section Chiefs (March 12, 2020); Juan Carlos Rodriguez, "Feds' New Settlement Policy May Imperil Restoration Projects," *Law 360*, June 15, 2017 (chilling effect).

23. U.S.C. §§ 703(a) (statutory language); *NRDC v. Dept. of the Interior*, 397 F. Supp.3d 430 (S.D.N.Y. 2019), at 435 (traditional definition of "take," Obama solicitor memorandum); Michael Doyle, "Bird Deaths Showcase Dilemma over Migratory Treaty Law," *E&E News*, July 26, 2019 (many prosecutions); Michael Doyle, "Dem Presses Zinke over Mixed Signals on Migratory Birds," *E&E News*, December 4, 2018 (BP agreement).

24. *NRDC v. Dept. of the Interior*, 397 F. Supp.3d 430 (S.D.N.Y. 2019), at 436 (Jorjani memorandum), 442 (refusal to prosecute); Elizabeth Shogren, "Trump's Choice for Interior Department Secretary Had Big Role in Eliminating Bird Protections," *Reveal*, February 12, 2020 (Bernhardt, Jorjani roles).

25. Darryl Fears & Juliet Eilperin, "A Controversial Trump Legal Opinion Weakened a Law to Protect Birds. Now It Might Be Made Permanent," *WP*, January 30, 2020 (hundreds of thousands of birds); Lisa Friedman, "A Trump Policy 'Clarification' All But Ends Punishment for Bird Deaths," *NYT*, December 24, 2019 (efforts canceled);

Connor Ferrall, "The Trump Administration Takes Aim at Migratory Birds," *Regulatory Review*, November 6, 2019; Juan Carlos Rodriguez, "DOI Can't Shake Lawsuit over Flip on Migratory Bird Kills," *Law 360*, August 1, 2019.

26. Bobby Magill, "Billion Birds at Risk as U.S. Pushes Final Rule Ahead of Biden," *Bloomberg Law*, November 27, 2020 (EIS prediction); Lisa Friedman, "Trump Administration Moves to Relax Rules Against Killing Birds," *NYT*, January 30, 2020, at A1 (proposal).

27. *Natural Resources Defense Council, Inc. v. U.S. Dept. of the Interior*, 2020 WL 4605235 (August 11, 2020); Department of the Interior, Fish and Wildlife Service, "Regulations Governing Take of Migratory Birds," 86 *Fed. Reg.* 1,134 (January 7, 2021); Maxine Joselow, "Biden Officials Finalize a Rule Making It Harder to Kill Birds, Reversing Trump," *WP*, September 29, 2021; Juliet Eilperin & Sarah Kaplan, "Trump Officials Move to Relax Rules on Killing Birds," *WP*, November 27, 2020 (pursued rulemaking); Juan Carlos Rodriguez, "Feds' Weakening of Migratory Bird Protections Vacated," *Law 360*, August 11, 2020.

28. U.S.C. §§ 5563(a), 5564(a), 5565(a)(2); Jolina C. Cuaresma, "Commissioning the Consumer Financial Protection Bureau," 31 *Loyola Consumer L. Rev.* 102 (2019), at 103–04 (Cordray actions); Lisa J. Servon, "Will Trump Kill the CFPB?" *American Prospect*, July 7, 2017 (TransUnion, Equifax actions); Gary Rivlin, "On Money," *NYT Magazine*, April 23, 2017, at 18 (Bank of America, Citibank; Honda, Toyota); Craig Holman, "The Wolves of Wall Street Are Out," *The Hill*, April 5, 2017 (student loans).

29. Yuka Hayashi, "Lawsuits Are 'Last Resort' for CFPB," *WSJ*, July 27, 2018, at A2 (shift to collaboration); Mick Mulvaney, "The CFPB Has Pushed Its Last Envelope," *WSJ*, January 24, 2018, at A19 (focus on quantifiable harm); Dave Boyer, "Mulvaney Scrutinizing 125 CFPB Cases Opened by Liberal Predecessor," *Washington Times*, November 30, 2017.

30. Cuaresma, "Commissioning," at 149 (11 cases); Robert Schmidt & Jesse Hamilton, "Wall Street Frets over a Revived CFPB Trump Left Toothless," *Bloomberg Law*, December 9, 2020 (mass exodus); Nicholas Confessore, "Get Cash Now from the Poor," *NYT Magazine*, April 21, 2019, at 30 (Mulvaney requirement, micromanagement); Robert O'Harrow, Jr., Shawn Boburg & Renae Merle, "How Trump Appointees Curbed a Consumer Protection Agency Loathed by the GOP," *WP*, December 4, 2018 (Blankenstein quote and salary, Blankenstein controversy).

31. Minority Staff of the Senate Committee on Banking, Housing, and Urban Affairs, "Consumers Under Attack: The Consumer Financial Protection Bureau Under Director Kraninger" (March 2020), at 13 (Blankenstein in charge; no discrimination actions); Brad Karp, Roberto Gonzalez & Hilary Oran, "What CFPB Policy Shift Means for Scrutiny of Abusive Acts," *Law 360*, March 25, 2021 ("abusive" policy statement); Rachel Rodman & Kendra Wharton, "Key Takeaways from CFPB's Year-End Enforcement Flurry," *Law 360*, January 26, 2021 (lame-duck activity); Eamonn K. Moran, "How Far Left Will CFPB Swing in 2021?" *American Banker*, December 30, 2020 (2020 cases); Robert Schmidt & Jesse Hamilton, "Wall Street Frets over a Revived CFPB Trump Left Toothless," *Bloomberg Law*, December 9, 2020 (major bank enforcement); Al Barbarino, "CFPB Sanctions Payday Lender $1.4 Million over 'Deceptive' Tactics," *Law 360*, April 2, 2020 (Cordray initiation); Lauren E. Willis, "CFPB Head Misguided in Reliance on Consumer Education," *The Hill*, September 7,

2019 (education); Alex Leary, "Trump Administration Pushes to Deregulate with Less Enforcement," *WSJ*, June 23, 2019, at A1 (2019 cases); Jim Saksa, "CFPB to Focus on Protecting Consumers, Not Enforcing Laws on Financial Institutions," *Roll Call*, April 17, 2019.

32. Minority Staff of the Senate Committee on Banking, Housing, and Urban Affairs, "Consumers Under Attack," at 19–20 (rarely sought restitution); Tory Newmyer, "Consumer Financial Protection Bureau, Muzzled Under Trump, Prepares to Renew Tough Industry Oversight," *WP*, January 27, 2021 ($700 million); Kate Berry & Neil Haggerty, "Dems Unload on CFPB's Kraninger: 'You Are Absolutely Worthless,'" *American Banker*, October 16, 2019 (Enova International); Evan Weinberger, "New Tone, Old Policies at CFPB Under Kraninger," *Bloomberg Law*, June 18, 2019 (ability to pay); Linda Jun & Christine Hines, "Watchdog Agency Must Pick a Side: Consumers or Scammers," *The Hill*, June 11, 2019 (Kraninger discount); Confessore, "Get Cash Now," at 53 (payday lender prosecution); O'Harrow, Boburg & Merle, "How Trump Appointees Curbed" (lower penalties).

33. Minority Staff of the Senate Committee on Banking, Housing, and Urban Affairs, "Consumers Under Attack," at 6 (Military Lending Act); Christopher L. Peterson, "Mission in Action? Consumer Financial Protection Bureau Supervision and the Military Lending Act" (Consumer Federation of America, November 1, 2018), at 5–7 (shops); Gideon Weissman & Ed Mierzwinski, "Protecting Those Who Serve" (US PIRG, June 2017), at 1, 7–8 (prime targets, readiness, security clearances); Americans for Financial Reform, "Servicemembers, Veterans and Their Families" (June 21, 2017) (Cordray actions).

34. Patricia A. McCoy, "Inside Job: The Assault on the Structure of the Consumer Financial Protection Bureau," 103 *Minnesota L. Rev.* 2,543 (2019), at 2,591 (pulled examiners); Peterson, "Mission in Action," at 13 (overrule staff, only when complaint filed); Jon Hill, "CFPB Accuses Fintech LendUp of Military Lending Violations," *Law 360*, December 4, 2020 (two enforcement actions); Weinberger, "New Tone, Old Policies"; Kate Berry, "Pentagon, Others Baffled by CFPB Plan to Cease Military Lending Exams," *American Banker*, October 11, 2018.

35. U.S. Department of Labor, Office of the Inspector General, "COVID-19: MSHA Faces Multiple Challenges in Responding to the Pandemic" (July 24, 2020), at 2; Valerie Bauman & Lydia Wheeler, "Government Works to Match Health Rules to Rapid Virus Response," *Bloomberg Law*, March 31, 2020 (allow hospitals to treat).

36. Executive Order 13,924, 85 *Fed. Reg.* 31,353 (May 22, 2020) § 5; Memorandum for the Deputy Secretaries of Executive Departments and Agencies from Paul J. Ray, re: Implementation of Section 6 of Executive Order 13924, dated August 31, 2020, at 2, 4; Kelsey Brugger, "How Conservative Ideology Could Hamstring Enforcement," *E&E News*, September 14, 2020 (due process, restatements of demands).

37. Memorandum to All Governmental and Private Sector Partners from Susan Parker Bodine, re: COVID-19 Implications for EPA's Enforcement and Compliance Assurance Program, dated March 26, 2020, at 3, 5; Kelsey Brugger, "EPA Enforcement Move Meets API Wish List—and Then Some," *E&E News*, April 1, 2020.

38. Ellen Knickmeyer, et al., "Thousands Allowed to Bypass Environmental Rules in Pandemic," *AP News*, August 24, 2020 (AP analysis); Grant Gilezan, "End of EPA

Virus Policy Poses Challenges for Cos.," *Law 360*, September 8, 2020; Sean Reilly, "Study of Emissions and Virus Deaths Implicates EPA Policy," *E&E News*, July 17, 2020; Hailey Konnath, "EPA Plans to End Controversial COVID-19 Enforcement Policy," *Law 360*, June 30, 2020; Kevin Bogardas, "Watchdog Questions Pandemic Enforcement Policy," *E&E News*, June 18, 2020; "Polluted US Areas Are Among Worst-Hit by Coronavirus—Putting People of Color Even More at Risk," *The Guardian*, April 14, 2020.

39. Kevin Stawicki, "FDA to Restart On-Site Inspections Paused for Virus," *Law 360*, July 10, 2020; Kyle Bagenstose, "Coronavirus Is Testing America's Food Safety Net," *Austin American-Statesman*, May 12, 2020, at A1 (no in-person inspections, inspections declined, recalls declined); Gosia Wozniacka, "Critical Food and Farm Rules Have Been Rolled Back Amid Pandemic," *Civil Eats*, April 14, 2020 (for-cause inspections); Jack Queen, "FDA Warns More CBD Sellers About Bogus COVID-19 Claims," *Law 360*, April 8, 2020.

40. Consumer Financial Protection Bureau, "Press Release: CFPB Annual Complaint Report Highlights More Than a Half-Million Complaints Received in 2020," March 24, 2021 (complaints, disingenuous explanation); Tory Newmyer, "Consumer Financial Protection Bureau, Muzzled Under Trump, Prepares to Renew Tough Industry Oversight," *WP*, January 27, 2021 (small-time scammers); Evan Weinberger, "CFPB Penalties Decline as Enforcement Actions Go Small," *Bloomberg Law*, August 14, 2020 (affordability policy); Andrew Keshner, "Consumer Complaints to the CFPB Are Skyrocketing as the Coronavirus Outbreak Continues," *Market Watch*, July 19, 2020; Jon Hill, "CFPB Halts Some Reporting Reqs, Eyes Exam Scheduling," *Law 360*, March 26, 2020 (guidance).

41. Newmyer, "Muzzled Under Trump" (good faith); Jon Hill, "CFPB Issues Credit Reporting Guidance Amid Pandemic," *Law 360*, April 1, 2020.

42. Colin Medwick & Michela Zonta, "Protecting American Consumers in Crisis" (Center for American Progress, July 27, 2020) (no enforcement action); Hill, "Credit Reporting Guidance" (consumer groups' complaint).

43. Ben Penn, "Virus Link to 'Double Damages' Rollback Skewered by Obama Alums," *Bloomberg Law*, June 26, 2020 (Obama policy, critics' complaints); Ben Penn, "DOL Pulls Back from Use of 'Double Damages' in Wage Cases," *Bloomberg Law*, June 25, 2020.

Chapter 11: Impediments to Demolition

1. Executive Order 13,337, 69 *Fed. Reg.* 25,299 (2004); *Indigenous Environmental Network v. Department of State*, 2017 WL 5632435 (November 22, 2017).

2. *Indigenous Environmental Network v. Department of State*, 2017 WL 5632435 (November 22, 2017); Juliet Eilperin, "Obama Allies' Interests Collide over Keystone Pipeline," *WP*, October 16, 2011.

3. *Indigenous Environmental Network v. Department of State*, 2017 WL 5632435 (November 22, 2017) (new application); "Presidential Memorandum for the Secretary of State, the Secretary of the Army, and the Secretary of the Interior, January 24, 2017," 82 *Fed. Reg.* 8,663 (January 30, 2017); Marianne Lavelle, "Keystone XL Pipe-

line Foes Rev Up Fight Again After Trump's Rubber Stamp," *Inside Climate News*, March 25, 2017 (Trump quote); Manuel Quinones, "Solar 'Disappointed' at Chamber Rhetoric," *E&E News*, March 21, 2017.

4. Rebecca Elliott, Vipal Monga & Miguel Bustillo, "Once Revived, Pipeline Plan Stalls Again," *WSJ*, November 10, 2018, at B3 (rallying cry); Mike Lee, "'Ideology' Behind Protests 'Simply Un-American'—Zinke," *E&E News*, October 2, 2018; "Protesters Shut Down Chase Bank Branches in Seattle," *E&E News*, May 9, 2017; Lavelle, "Keystone XL Pipeline Foes" (protests); Hannah Northey, "Public Divided over KXL, Dakota Access—Poll," *E&E News*, February 22, 2017.

5. *Indigenous Environmental Network v. Dept. of State*, 347 F. Supp.3d 561 (D. Mont. 2018), at 582, 584, 591.

6. Pamela King, "Appeals Court Keeps Pipeline on Ice," *E&E News*, March 18, 2020; Keith Goldberg, "What to Know After Court Dumps Keystone XL Approval," *Law 360*, November 9, 2018 (Trump quote); Mitch Smith & Julie Bosman, "Keystone Pipeline Leaks 210,000 Gallons of Oil in South Dakota," *NYT*, November 16. 2017.

7. Executive Order No. 13,867, 84 *Fed. Reg.* 15,491 (April 15, 2019); "Presidential Permit," March 29, 2019, https://www.whitehouse.gov/presidential-actions/presidential-permit/; Halley Konnath, "9th Circ. Kills Keystone XL Challenge in Light of New Permit," *Law 360*, June 6, 2019.

8. Ellen M. Gilmer, "Keystone XL Faces New Legal Challenge over Federal Land Crossing," *Bloomberg Law*, July 14, 2020; Andrew Westney, "Tribes Say Trump Violated Treaties by OKing Keystone XL," *Law 360*, July 29, 2019; Peter Hayes, "Keystone Pipeline Permit Challenged as Unconstitutional," *Bloomberg Law*, April 8, 2019.

9. Mike LaSusa, "Justices Limit Voiding of Water Permit to Keystone Pipeline," *Law 360*, July 6, 2020; Ellen M. Gilmer, "Fast-Track Permits Stay Blocked for Keystone XL, Other Pipes," *Bloomberg Law*, May 28, 2020 (9th Circuit); Hannah Northey, "Energy Projects in Chaos After Permit Shutdown," *E&E News*, April 27, 2020; David Simpson, "Enviros Get Army Corps' XL Pipeline Permit Remanded," *Law 360*, April 15, 2020.

10. Brady Dennis & Steven Mufson, "Keystone XL Pipeline Developer Pulls Plug on Controversial Project," *WP*, June 9, 2021; Dave Simpson, "21 AGs Sue Biden Admin. over XL Pipeline Permit Revocation," *Law 360*, March 17, 2021; Michael Phillis, "Biden Scraps Keystone XL Pipeline Permit on Day 1," *Law 360*, January 20, 2021.

11. Robert L. Glicksman & Emily Hammond, "The Administrative Law of Regulatory Slop and Strategy," 68 *Duke L. J.* 1651 (2019), at 1653–54; Margot Sanger-Katz, "For Trump Administration, It Has Been Hard to Follow the Rules on Rules," *NYT*, January 22, 2019; Oliver Milman, "'Sloppy and Careless': Courts Call Out Trump Blitzkrieg on Environmental Rules," *The Guardian*, February 20, 2018 (quoting Professor Richard Revesz, NYT School of Law).

12. Bethany A. Davis-Noll & Christine Pries, "The Administration's Record in the Courts," *The Hill*, November 3, 2020 (IPI study); Lisa Friedman & John Schwartz, "A Second Term Could Make Trump's Environmental Rollback Stick," *NYT*, September 25, 2020, at A13 (Second Circuit panel); Fred Barbash, "The Real Reason the

Trump Administration Is Constantly Losing in Court," *WP*, March 19, 2019 (Trump quote).

13. Keith B. Belton & John D. Graham, "Trump's Deregulation Record: Is It Working," 71 *Admin. L. Rev.* 803 (2019), at 853–54; Bethany A. Davis Noll & Alec Dawson, "Deregulation Run Amok" (Institute for Policy Integrity, November 2018); Jennifer A. Dlouhy & Alan Levin, "Trump Tests Legal Limits by Delaying Dozens of Obama's Rules," *Bloomberg/BNA, Environment Reporter,* July 14, 2017; Bethany A. Davis Noll, "Stealth Repeal: Trump's Strategy to Roll Back Regulations Through Delay," *The Hill,* May 2, 2017 (time to repeal).

14. 5 U.S.C. § 553; Glicksman & Hammond, "Regulatory Slop," at 1670; Lisa Heinzerling, "Unreasonable Delays: The Legal Problems (So Far) of Trump's Deregulatory Binge," 12 *Harv. J. L. & Policy* 13 (2018); Ellen M. Gilmer, "Trump Environmental Record Marked by Big Losses, Undecided Cases," *Bloomberg Law,* January 11, 2021.

15. *Transportation Division of the International Association of Sheet Metal, Air, Rail and Transportation Workers v. Federal Railroad Administration,* 988 F.3d 1170 (9th Cir. 2021).

16. *Safer Chemicals, Healthy Families v. EPA,* 943 F.3d 397 (9th Cir. 2019), at 424 (toxic chemicals); *Wyoming v. Department of the Interior,* 493 F. Supp.3d 1046 (D. Wyo. 2020) (methane emissions); *Natural Resources Defense Council, Inc. v. U.S. Dept. of the Interior,* 2020 WL 4605235 (August 11, 2020) (migratory birds); Timothy Puko, "Judge Restores Obama Ban on Oil, Gas Drilling Off Alaska," *WSJ,* April 14, 2019, at A3.

17. 5 U.S.C. § 706(2)(C); *FCC v. Fox Television Stations, Inc.,* 556 U.S. 502 (2009) (changed position); *Motor Vehicle Manufacturers Ass'n v. State Farm Mutual Auto Ins. Co.,* 463 U.S. 43 (1983), at 43 (quote).

18. Pamela King & Jeremy F. Jacobs, "What Trump's Dismal Deregulatory Record Means for Biden," *E&E News,* January 11, 2021 (Heinzerling quote); Friedman & Schwartz, "Second Term" (courts' findings); Amanda Reilly & Sean Reilly, "Court Losses Pile Up for EPA," *E&E News,* August 13, 2018 (quoting Patrice Simms, Earthjustice) (opposite direction); Richard Revesz, "Pruitt Exemplified How Partisanship Hinders Policymaking," *Slate,* July 10, 2018 (short shrift); Stuart Shapiro, "Trump's Deregulatory Record Doesn't Include Much Actual Deregulation," *Government Executive,* May 14, 2018 (short shrift, courts' findings).

19. *Western Watersheds Project v. Schneider,* 417 F. Supp. 3d 1319 (D. Idaho 2019), at 1326 (Obama accord); Hiroko Tabuchi, "Trump Fracking Boom Imperils Landscape of American West," *NYT,* October 27, 2018 (sage grouse description); Brittany Patterson, et al., "Former Zinke Backers Dismayed by Department's Direction," *E&E News,* November 27, 2017 (most extensive conservation effort); Eric Lipton & Jeremy Dillon, "On the Brink," *Congressional Quarterly,* March 13, 2017, at 30 (sage grouse description).

20. *Western Watersheds Project v. Schneider,* 417 F. Supp. 3d 1319 (D. Idaho 2019), at 1327 (six draft EISs); Department of the Interior, "Order No. 3353, Greater Sage-Grouse Conservation and Cooperation with Western States," June 7, 2017 (Zinke order, EPA staff); Jimmy Tobias, "The Zinke Effect: How the US Interior Department Became a Tool of Big Business," *The Guardian,* November 12, 2018 (head of groups).

21. *Western Watersheds Project v. Schneider*, 417 F. Supp. 3d 1319 (D. Idaho 2019), at 1328 (no analysis); Coral Davenport, "Drilling Plan Threatens 9 Million Acres of Sage Grouse Habitat," *NYT*, December 6, 2018, at A1 (beneficiary); Scott Streater, "BLM's Long-Awaited Revisions Emphasize State 'Flexibility,'" *E&E News*, December 6, 2018.

22. *Western Watersheds Project v. Schneider*, 417 F. Supp. 3d 1319 (D. Idaho 2019), at 1327–28, 1332, 1335; Hannah Pugh, "Can Conservation by Consensus Save the Sage Grouse?" *Regulatory Review*, June 10, 2021 (changes never went into effect).

23. *Center for Biological Diversity v. Bernhardt*, 982 F.3d 723 (9th Cir. 2020) (Beaufort Sea); *United Food and Commercial Workers Union, Local No. 663 v. USDA*, 2021 WL 1215865 (D. Minn. 2020), at 23 (belt speeds); Juan Carlos Rodriguez, "EPA Bans Chlorpyrifos Use on Food in Win for Green Groups," *Law 360*, August 18, 2021; Brady Dennis, "Federal Court Rules EPA Must Ban Pesticide Linked to Harm in Children—or Prove It Is Safe," *WP*, April 29, 2021 (chlorpyrifos); Niina H. Farah, "Court Finds Alaska Oil Project Would Harm Beluga Whales," *E&E News*, April 1, 2021 (Cook Inlet).

24. 30 U.S.C. §§ 811(a); *United Steel v. Mine Safety and Health Administration*, 925 F.3d 1279 (D.C. Cir. 2019), at 1282, 1283–85.

25. Belton & Graham, "Trump's Deregulation Record," at 846.

26. Susan Milligan, "The Bureaucracy Strikes Back," *U.S. News*, October 25, 2019; Christopher Flavelle & Benjamin Main, "Washington Bureaucrats Are Quietly Working to Undermine Trump's Agenda," *Bloomberg Politics*, December 18, 2017.

27. David Frum, *Trumpocracy* (2018), at 171 (leaks); Jennifer Nou, "Civil Servant Disobedience," 94 *Chicago-Kent L. Rev.* 349 (2019), at 351–52 (reports); Evan Osnos, "Trump vs. the 'Deep State,'" *The Atlantic*, May 21, 2018 (T-shirts); Mindy Weisberger, "'Rogue' Science Agencies Defy Trump Administration on Twitter," *Scientific American*, January 27, 2017; Steve Gorman, "Defying Trump, Twitter Feeds for U.S. Government Scientists Go Rogue," *Reuters*, January 26, 2017.

28. Alexander Nazaryan, *The Best People* (2019), at 160 (hunker down); Marianne Lavelle, "The Resistance: In the President's Relentless War on Climate Science, They Fought Back," *Inside Climate News*, December 27, 2020 (self-censorship); Michael Hawthorne, "EPA Employees Targeted by Trump Defend Their Role: 'We're Here to Protect Public Health,'" *Chicago Tribune*, April 27, 2017 (Chicago protests); Kevin Bogardus, "'I Walk Among My Colleagues Like a Zombie in a Bad Dream,'" *E&E News*, March 30, 2017 (insulted); Kevin Bogardus & Robin Bravender, "Snarky Twitter Activists, Fearful Feds Wage War on Trump," *E&E News*, January 26, 2017 (unofficial account).

29. Nazaryan, *Best People*, at 164 (defacing); Lavelle, "The Resistance" (reinserting climate); Coral Davenport, "For Environmental Rollbacks, Devils Lurk in the Details," *NYT*, March 31, 2020, at A19 (agency's own estimates, particulate matter example); Sharon Lerner, "EPA Staffers Are Being Forced to Prioritize Energy Industry's Wish List, Says Official Who Resigned in Protest," *The Intercept*, August 3, 2017 (analyses); Evan Halper, "At Trump's EPA, Going to Work Can Be an Act of Defiance," *Los Angles Times*, April 4, 2017 (acts of resistance); Fred Lucas, "Rogue Fed-

eral Bureaucrats Threaten Trump's Agenda," *Daily Caller*, February 5, 2017 (quoting Neil Siefring, Hilltop Advocacy) (conservative activist quote).

30. Eric Lipton & Lisa Friedman, "E.P.A. Staff Fears Effort to Target Emails of Critics," *NYT*, December 18, 2017, at A1 (quote); Eric Lipton & Lisa Friedman, "Media Advisor for E.P.A. Investigated Its Workers," *NYT*, December 16, 2017, at A16.

31. Lavelle, "The Resistance."

32. Patricia A. McCoy, "Inside Job: The Assault on the Structure of the Consumer Financial Protection Bureau," 103 *Minnesota L. Rev.* 2,543 (2019), at 2,605 (dishonest companies); David Roberts, "Many Businesses Oppose Trump's Deregulatory Agenda. Here's Why," *Vox*, August 30, 2019 (crave certainty); Niina Heikkinen, "Another Industry Group Asks Agency to Regulate Carbon," *E&E News*, September 21, 2017 (invested resources); Russell Gold & Lynn Cook, "Bold Move May Have Limited Impact," *WSJ*, June 2, 2017 (pollution controls).

33. Environmental Protection Agency, "Repeal of Emission Requirements for Glider Vehicles, Glider Engines, and Glider Kits," 82 *Fed. Reg.* 53,442 (November 16, 2017); Congressional Research Service, "Glider Kit, Engine, and Vehicle Regulations" (September 10, 2018); Camille von Kaenel, "Foes of Obama Truck Rules Hope for Sympathy from Trump Team," *E&E News*, August 3, 2017.

34. Environmental Protection Agency and Department of Transportation, "Greenhouse Gas Emissions and Fuel Efficiency Standards for Medium- and Heavy-Duty Engines and Vehicles—Phase 2," 81 *Fed. Reg.* 73,478 (October 25, 2016), at 73,518; Office of the Inspector General, Environmental Protection Agency, "EPA Failed to Develop Required Cost and Benefit Analyses and to Assess Air Quality Impacts on Children's Health for Proposed Glider Repeal Rule Allowing Used Engines in Heavy-Duty Trucks" (December 5, 2019) [EPA IG Glider Truck Report], at 3; Juliet Eilperin, "EPA Plans to Repeal Emission Standards for Truck Components," *WP*, October 23, 2017.

35. Environmental Protection Agency, "Repeal of Emission Requirements for Glider Vehicles, Glider Engines, and Glider Kits," 82 *Fed. Reg.* 53,442 (November 16, 2017), at 53,444; EPA IG Glider Truck Report, at 3 (Pruitt meeting); Camille von Kaenel, "When Trump's Deregulation Is at Odds with Industry," *E&E News*, August 28, 2017 (campaign event); Camile von Kaenel, "EPA Gives Reprieve to Big Rigs," *E&E News*, August 18, 2017; von Kaenel, "Foes of Obama Truck Rules" (manufacturers comfortable); Christine Powell, "DC Circ. Pumps Brakes on Heavy Duty Truck Rule," *Law 360*, May 8, 2017 (assemblers sue).

36. Abby Smith, "EPA Plan to Kill Glider Truck Limits in Limbo Amid GOP Pressure," *Bloomberg Environment & Energy Report*, October 17, 2018; Juliet Eilperin, "EPA Plans to Repeal Emission Standards for Truck Components," *WP*, October 23, 2017 (large manufacturers protest); "Truck, Engine Makers Raise Fears on EPA Review of Heavy Duty Trucks," *Inside EPA*, August 25, 2017, at 24 (state regulations); von Kaenel, "Foes of Obama Truck Rules" (uncertainty).

37. Bill Saporito, "Is Walmart the New C.D.C.?" *NYT*, July 25, 2020, at A22 (masks); Jennifer A. Dlouhy, "Trump Gives Businesses Deregulation Whether They Want It or Not," *Bloomberg Law*, August 30, 2019 (oil and gas, auto manufacturing); Juliet

Eilperin & Toluse Olorunnipa, "'He Gets to Decide': Trump Escalates His Fight Against Climate Science Ahead of 2020," *WP*, February 28, 2019 (Park Avenue quote).

38. David Dayen, "Congress's New Progressives Take on the Banks," *American Prospect* (Spring 2019), at 25 (Porter description); Neil Haggerty & Kate Berry, "The Next Elizabeth Warren? How Katie Porter Is Shaking Up House Banking Panel," *American Banker*, October 14, 2019 (powerful advocate, comprehensive knowledge); Ellen M. Gilmer, "Environmental Litigation Reform Going on the Back Burner," *E&E News*, November 27, 2018 (dynamics changed).

39. House Committee on Oversight and Reform, "Past Hearings," https://oversight .house.gov/legislation/hearings?page=1 (hearing titles); George Cahlink & Kellie Lunney, "Committee Emerges as Active Front in Climate Push," *E&E News*, April 2, 2019 (forum).

40. Kate Berry, "In Rebuke of CFPB, States Look to Get Tough on Debt Collectors," *American Banker*, January 16, 2020; Brady Dennis & Juliet Eilperin, "States Aren't Waiting for the Trump Administration on Environmental Protections," *WP*, May 19, 2019 (chlorpyrifos); Benjamin Storrow, "States Focus on Chemicals Linked to Warming When Feds Won't," *E&E News*, April 4, 2019 (states stepped in); David Schultz, "Flint Water Woes Spur States to Act on Lead as EPA Struggles," *Bloomberg Law*, March 25, 2019; "Midwestern States' Strict Environmental Policies Fight Trump Deregulation," *Inside EPA*, February 22, 2019; Lizette Alvarez, "Mayors, Sidestepping Trump, Vow to Fill Void on Climate Change," *NYT*, June 27, 2017, at A9.

41. Stephen Lee, "Wheeler, Bernhardt Tout Virtues of Giving Power to States," *Bloomberg Law*, July 17, 2019 (administration claims); Maxine Joselow, "Trump Targets Blue States with Rules and Actions—Critics," *E&E News*, April 12, 2019 (quoting Jody Freeman, Harvard Law School).

42. Malathi Nayak, "California's 100th Trump Suit Targets Environmental Rollback," *Bloomberg Law*, August 28, 2020 (California attorney general lawsuits); Adam Allington, "EPA Abandons Plans to Roll Back Farmworker Pesticide Protections," *Bloomberg Law*, January 29, 2019; Amanda Reilly, "In Schneiderman's Wake, Battle Against Trump Continues," *E&E News*, May 8, 2018 (New York attorney general lawsuits).

43. Toluse Olorunnipa, "'This Is What I Am Fighting': Trump Tries to Cast U.S. Cities as Filthy and Crime-Ridden in Attempt to Sway 2020 Voters," *WP*, July 2, 2019 (fired back); Annie Karni & Jennifer Medina, "U.S. May Wrest Billions for Rail for California," *NYT*, February 19, 2019, at A1.

44. Natural Resources Defense Council, "How NRDC Sues the President," March 13, 2018, https://www.nrdc.org/stories/how-nrdc-sues-president; Alexander C. Kaufman, "Former EPA Employees Are So Worried About Trump's Plans, They Formed Their Own Alt-EPA," *Huffington Post*, June 15, 2017; Neela Banerjee, "EPA Veterans Mobilize to Defend Agency's Work, Bracing for Trump's Impact," *Inside Climate News*, February 15, 2017.

45. Celia Wexler, "Dept. of Fine Print: How the Center for Progressive Reform Works for Change," *Blue Tent*, December 13, 2020; Maxine Joselow, "What's Next After Super-Gluing Yourself to the Capitol," *E&E News*, August 2, 2019; Mark K. Matthews, "Climate Protesters Target Democrats—Again," *E&E News*, December 10,

2018 (Sunrise movement); Jason Plautz & Ben Geman, "A Bruised Liberal Power-house Faces an Uncertain Future," *National Journal*, November 28, 2016 (Center for American Progress).

46. Elle Rothermich, "EPA, Explain Yourself," *Regulatory Review*, January 5, 2021 (Revesz); Ben Santor, "I'm a Climate Scientist. And I'm Not Letting Trickle-Down Ignorance Win," *WP*, July 15, 2017; Jeel Achenbach, Ben Guarino & Sarah Kaplan, "Why People Are Marching for Science," *WP*, April 21, 2017; John H. Cushman, Jr., "Tens of Thousands March for Science and Against Threats to Climate Research," *Inside Climate News*, April 22, 2017; Amy Harmon & Henry Fountain, "For Scientists, a Political Test," *NYT*, February 7, 2017, at D1 (reluctance); Zahara Hirji, "Trump's Choices 'Detrimental to the Planet and People,' Environmental Sociologists Say," *Inside Climate News*, February 3, 2017; Debra Kahn, "Scientists Fearing Trump 'Lobotomy' Clamor to Speak Out," *E&E News*, January 27, 2017.

47. Paul H. Tice, "Trump Hasn't Solved the Pipeline Crisis," *WSJ*, October 9, 2019.

48. Gilmer, "Trump Environmental Record."

49. William W. Buzbee, "Agency Statutory Abnegation in the Deregulatory Playbook," 68 *Duke L. J.* 1,509 (2019), at 1,516.

Chapter 12: COVID-19

1. Gerald F. Seib & John McCormick, "Coronavirus Means the Era of Big Government Is Back," *WSJ*, April 27, 2020, at A1; Phillip Rucker & Robert Costa, "Commander of Confusion: Trump Sows Uncertainty and Seeks to Cast Blame in Coronavirus Crisis," *WP*, April 3, 2020 (quoting Senator Kamala Harris).

2. Abigail Tracy, "How Trump Gutted Obama's Pandemic-Preparedness Systems," *Vanity Fair*, May 1, 2020 (eliminated directorate); Jon Swaine, "Federal Government Spent Millions to Ramp Up Mask Readiness, but That Isn't Helping Now," *WP*, April 4, 2020 (BARDA contract); Emily Baumgaertner & James Rainey, "Trump Administration Ended Pandemic Early-Warning Program to Detect Coronaviruses," *Los Angeles Times*, April 2, 2020 (PREDICT, scientists laid off); Tom Hamburger, "Inside America's Mask Crunch: A Slow Government Reaction and an Industry Wary of Liability," *WP*, April 2, 2020 (task force); Beth Cameron, "I Ran the White House Pandemic Office. Trump Closed It," *WP*, March 13, 2020 (task force).

3. Lawrence Wright, "The Plague Year," *New Yorker*, January 4 & 11, 2021, at 20, 24 (playbook); David E. Sanger, et al., "Warnings of Pandemic Last Year Went Unheeded," *NYT*, March 20, 2020, at A1 (nobody knew quote, Obama briefing, no action).

4. Wright, "Plague Year," at 20, 24–25 (Crimson Contagion); Thomas Frank, "Disaster Agency Foresaw Killer Virus Months Before COVID-19," *E&E News*, April 9, 2020 (Crimson Contagion).

5. Michael Lewis, *The Premonition* (2021), at 179 (300,000); Greg Miller & Ellen Nakashima, "President's Intelligence Briefing Book Repeatedly Cited Virus Threat," *WP*, April 27, 2020; Eric Lipton, et al., "Despite Timely Alerts, Trump Was Slow to Act," *NYT*, April 12, 2020, at A1 (Azar); Maggie Haberman, "Trade Adviser Warned White House in January of Risks of a Pandemic," *NYT*, April 6, 2020 (Navarro quote,

no action); Shane Harris, et al., "U.S. Intelligence Reports from January and February Warned About a Likely Pandemic," *WP*, March 20, 2020 (Trump quote).

6. Josh Dawsey, Felicia Sonmez & Paul Kane, "Trump Acknowledges He Intentionally Downplayed Deadly Coronavirus, Says Effort Was to Reduce Panic," *WP*, September 9, 2020 (Woodward); Eric Lipton, et al., "Despite Timely Alerts, Trump Was Slow to Act," *NYT*, April 12, 2020, at A1 (initial inclination); Michael Biesecker, "US 'Wasted' Months Before Preparing for Coronavirus Pandemic," *AP*, April 5, 2020.

7. Peter Sullivan, "Dire Projections Put New Focus on Trump Coronavirus Response," *The Hill*, April 2, 2020.

8. Lewis, *Premonition*, at 216 (miracle quote); Aaron Blake & J.M. Rieger, "The 201 Times Trump Has Downplayed the Coronavirus Threat," *WP*, November 3, 2020 (two hundred occasions); Linda Qui, Bill Marsh & Joy Huang, "The President vs. the Experts: How Trump Downplayed the Coronavirus," *NYT*, March 20, 2020, at A13 (Trump quotes); Anne Gearan, Seung Min Kim & Erica Warner, "Trump Administration Tries to Play Down the Health and Economic Risks of the Coronavirus," *WP*, February 28, 2020 (new hoax quote).

9. Jeremy W. Peters, "Pro-Trump Media's Virus Pivot: From Alarm to Denial to Blame," *NYT*, April 2, 2020, at A1 (Limbaugh); Ben Smith, "How Fox Got the Virus So Wrong: Start with Its C.E.O.," *NYT*, March 23, 2020 (Hannity, Ingraham, Carlson).

10. Lewis, *Premonition*, at 295 (Ioannidis); Andy Slavitt, *Preventable* (2021), at 91 (Trump tweet); James Chotiner, "The Contrarian Coronavirus Theory That Informed the Trump Administration," *New Yorker*, March 30, 2020 (evolutionary economics); Richard A. Epstein, "Addendum to Coronavirus Perspective," *Defining Ideas*, March 24, 2020; Josh Dawsey, et al., "Trump Weighs Restarting Economy Despite Warnings from U.S. Public Health Officials," *WP*, March 23, 2020; Richard A. Epstein, "Coronavirus Perspective," *Defining Ideas*, March 16, 2020 (Epstein).

11. Lewis, *Premonition*, at 225 (markets, Azar prohibition); Slavitt, *Preventable*, at 52 (Trump wanted to fire); Nicholas Kristof, "Trump's Deadly Search for a Scapegoat," *NYT*, April 16, 2020, at A22 (Mardi Gras, spring break); Qui, Marsh & Huang, "President vs. the Experts" (Messonnier quote).

12. Slavitt, *Preventable*, at 21 (NBA); Eric Lipton, et al., "Despite Timely Alerts"; Donald Trump, "Remarks by President Trump in Address to the Nation," March 11, 2020 (Trump quotes).

13. Slavitt, *Preventable*, at 76 (Trump requests, stock market); Greg Sargent, "Fox News Watchers Still Think the Media Hyped Coronavirus," *WP*, April 2, 2020; Katie Rogers, "Trump Now Claims He Always Knew the Coronavirus Would Be a Pandemic," *NYT*, March 17, 2020 (Trump quote); Philip Bump, "Trump Offered a Few Proposals in Response to the Coronavirus Outbreak—and a Number of Self-Defenses," *WP*, March 11, 2020 (speech didn't work); Gabriel Sherman, " 'He's Definitely Melting Down over This': Trump, Germaphobe in Chief, Struggles to Control the COVID-19 Story," *Vanity Fair*, March 9, 2020 (new narrative).

14. Slavitt, *Preventable*, at 129 (reckless behavior); Yasmeen Abutaleh, et al., "The Inside Story of How Trump's Denial, Mismanagement and Magical Thinking Led to the Pandemic's Dark Winter," *WP*, December 19, 2020 (CDC recommendation, no

mask); Rucker & Costa, "Commander of Confusion (quoting Dayton, Ohio, mayor Nan Whaley) (strong resistance).

15. Slavitt, *Preventable*, at 137, 146–47 (dormant task force, Birx travel); Meridith McGraw & Sam Stein, "It's Been Exactly One Year Since Trump Suggested Injecting Bleach. We've Never Been the Same," *Politico*, April 23, 2021 (press briefings stop); Katie Rogers, "Dire Warnings as President Pushes Sham Cures," *NYT*, April 25, 2020, at A1.

16. Astead W. Herndon, "A Safe Space for Believers," *NYT*, June 22, 2020, at A1 (Kung flu quote); Morgan Chalfant, "White House Officials Downplay Chance of COVID-19 'Second Spike,'" *The Hill*, June 12, 2020; Felicia Sanmez, "Trump's Tulsa Campaign Rally Sign-Up Page Includes Coronavirus Liability Disclaimer," *WP*, June 12, 2020; Peter Baker, "Trump and Kushner Boast of Success in Recasting Administration's Response," *NYT*, April 30, 2020, at A8 (success story quote, big boundary quote).

17. Slavitt, *Preventable*, at 148 (infection rates, Atlas credentials); Wright, "Plague Year," at 20, 50 (masks); Abutaleh, et al., "Inside Story" (populist base, sidelines); Mike Pence, "There Isn't a Coronavirus 'Second Wave,'" *WSJ*, June 17, 2020, at A19.

18. Mark Meadows, *The Chief's Chief* (2021), at 150–61; Noah Weiland, et al., "Trump Was Sicker Than Acknowledged with Covid-19," *NYT*, February 12, 2021, at A1; Gina Kolata & Roni Caryn Rabin, "'Don't Be Afraid of Covid' Comment Has Public Health Experts Livid," *NYT*, October 6, 2020, at A10; Toluse Olorunnipa & Josh Dawsey, "Trump Returns to White House, Downplaying Virus That Hospitalized Him and Turned West Wing into a 'Ghost Town,'" *WP*, October 5, 2020 (disappearing quote); Josh Dawsey, Ashley Parker & Colby Itkowitz, "Trump Tests Positive for Coronavirus, Plans to Go to Walter Reed Hospital, Two Officials Say," *WP*, October 2, 2020; Adam Nagourney & Jeremy W. Peters, "Trump and His Base Minimize Virus Ahead of Election," *NYT*, September 22, 2020, at A15 (not shutting quote).

19. Abutaleh, et al., "Inside Story."

20. Lewis, *Premonition*, at 176 (CDC refusal); Slavitt, *Preventable*, at 49 (Redfield, CDC decree, Azar refusal); Herndon, "Safe Space" (slow down testing).

21. Wright, "Plague Year," at 36 (Trump quote); Brett Murphy & Letitia Stein, "Feds Sidelined, Misled Scientists About Virus Tests," *Austin American-Statesman*, March 29, 2020, at A8 (doctors discovered, virus spread); Michael D. Shear, et al., "Testing Blunders Cost Vital Month in U.S. Virus Fight," *NYT*, March 29, 2020, at A1 (CDC guidelines, lack of testing).

22. Wright, "Plague Year," at 34 (never enough tests); Abutaleh, et al., "Inside Story" (wasted February); Peter Sullivan, "Dire Projections Put New Focus on Trump Coronavirus Response," *The Hill*, April 2, 2020 (Gostin quote); Joanne Hawana, Aaron Josephson & Ben Zegarelli, "What FDA Has Done So Far in Response to COVID-19," *Law 360*, March 31, 2020; Haley Sweetland Edwards, "Opportunity Cost," *Time*, March 30, 2020 (Trump quote).

23. Slavitt, *Preventable*, at 83–85, 121 (culture of sycophants); Wright, "Plague Year," at 38 (warring factions); Abutaleh, et al., "Inside Story" (quoting Anita Cicero, Johns Hopkins Center for Health Security) (leadership with empathy); Aaron Blake, "Trump's Propaganda-Laden, Off-the-Rails Coronavirus Briefing," *WP*, April 14,

2020 (Trump quote); Peter Baker & Maggie Haberman, "Trump Is Faced with Crisis Too Big for Big Talk," *NYT*, March 22, 2020, at A1 (wholly unprepared).

24. Lewis, *Premonition*, at 225 (responsibility for regulation); Slavitt, *Preventable*, at 113–14 (opening up, problem).

25. Slavitt, *Preventable*, at 123–24 (Trump tweet, OK to ignore); Wright, "Plague Year," at 20, 57 (saboteur quote); Diana Falzone, " 'It's the Trump Bubble': The Right Has Created a Wave of COVID Patients Who Don't Believe It's Real," *Vanity Fair*, November 19, 2020.

26. Maria Perez, "Workers Are Getting Sick and Dying, but OSHA Won't Crack Down on Businesses That Fail to Follow COVID-19 Guidelines," *Milwaukee Journal Sentinel*, April 15, 2020 (families at risk). For a comprehensive analysis of the Trump administration's failure to protect workers from COVID-19 risks, see Thomas O. McGarity, Michael C. Duff & Sidney Shapiro, "Protecting Workers in a Pandemic" (Center for Progressive Reform, June 2020).

27. Noam Scheiber & Michael Corkery, "Pork Plant Workers Say They Can't Cough Safely," *NYT*, April 24, 2020, at B3; Noam Scheiber, "OSHA Cedes Worker Care to Employers," *NYT*, April 23, 2020, at B1 (packing plants); "The Epicenter," *NYT Magazine*, April 19, 2020, at 25; Campbell Robertson & Robert Gebeloff, "How Millions of Women Became the Most Essential Workers in America," *NYT*, April 18, 2020, at A1 (healthcare providers); Zach Montague, "Grocer's Ailing Workers in the Capital Highlight the Risks Facing Others," *NYT*, April 16, 2020, at A8; Caitlin Dickerson & Miriam Jordan, "South Dakota Meat Plant Is Now Country's Biggest Coronavirus Hot Spot," *NYT*, April 15, 2020, at A1; Yvette Cabrera, "Essential but Exposed," *Grist*, April 4, 2020; Hamburger, "Inside America's Mask Crunch" (horror stories); Rachel Abrams & Jessica Silver-Greenberg, " 'Terrified' Package Delivery Employees Are Going to Work Sick," *NYT*, March 21, 2020, at A1; AFL-CIO, A Petition to Secretary Scalia for an OSHA Emergency Temporary Standard for Infectious Disease, March 6, 2020 (transportation workers).

28. 29 U.S.C. §§ 652(8); 654(a)(1), 655(c), 661, 667.

29. Ian Kullgren & Bruce Rolfsen, "Virus Worker Safety Rule Tests Biden After Trump DOL Nixed Draft," *Bloomberg Law*, March 23, 2021 (staff draft); In re American Federation of Labor and Congress of Industrial Organizations, Emergency Petition for a Writ of Mandamus, and Request for Expedited Briefing and Disposition, April 18, 2020, at 9 (COVID-19 killed more workers); Peter Whoriskey, Jeff Stein & Nate Jones, "Thousands of OSHA Complaints Filed Against Companies for Virus Workplace Safety Concerns, Records Show," *WP*, April 16, 2020; Emily Schwing, "How OSHA Has Failed to Protect America's Workers from COVID-19," *Government Executive*, April 7, 2020 (Obama OSHA).

30. In re American Federation of Labor and Congress of Industrial Organizations, 2020 WL 3125324 (D.C. Cir. 2020); Braden Campbell, "AFL-CIO Sues to Make Labor Dept. Issue Virus Safety Rule," *Law 360*, May 18, 2020; Kevin Stawicki, "AFL-CIO Chief Keeps Up Attack on DOL's Pandemic Response," *Law 360*, May 8, 2020 (Scalia quote); Bruce Rolfsen, "OSHA Virus Emergency Regulation Not Needed, Labor Chief Says," *Bloomberg Law*, April 24, 2020; AFL-CIO, "Petition to Secretary Scalia."

31. Occupational Safety and Health Administration, "Occupational Exposure to COVID-19; Emergency Temporary Standard," 86 *Fed. Reg.* 32,376 (June 21, 2021) (Biden administration emergency temporary standard); Occupational Safety and Health Administration, "Guidance on Preparing Workplaces for COVID-19" (March 2020), at ii; Aliza Karetnick, Brian D. Pedrow & Elizabeth Schilken, "Doctrine of Primary Jurisdiction—an Ace for Dismissing Covid-19 Suits?" *Bloomberg Law,* June 11, 2020 (Trump executive order); Deborah Berkowitz, "Worker Safety in Crisis: The Cost of a Weakened OSHA" (National Employment Law Project, April 30, 2020) (workers continue to die); Dave Jamieson, "Trump Administration Tells Employers Not to Worry About Recording COVID-19 Cases," *Huffington Post,* April 13, 2020 (poster); David Michaels, "One Thing We Can Do to Protect Frontline Workers," *Politico,* April 7, 2020 (guidance unenforceable).

32. *SeaWorld v. Perez,* 748 F.3d 1202 (D.C. Cir. 2014), at 1207 (OSHA burden of proof); Josh Fidelson, "Inspectors Hit 45-Year Low at Agency Key to Reopening Workplaces," *Bloomberg Law,* April 28, 2020 (OSHA quote); Scott Gottlieb & Stephen Ostroff, "Keep Workers Healthy on the Job," *WSJ,* April 20, 2020, at A17 (generally recognized hazards); Whoriskey, Stein & Jones, "Thousands of OSHA Complaints" (Georgia plant).

33. 50 U.S.C. App. § 2157 (liability shield); Executive Order 13,917, 85 *Fed. Reg.* 26,313 (May 1, 2020); Editorial, "Why Trump Ordering Meat Plants to Stay Open Is Worrisome," *WP,* April 30, 2020; Jen Skernitt & Lydia Mulvany, "U.S. Food-Worker Deaths Reach 20 as Thousands See Virus Impact," *Bloomberg Law,* April 28, 2020 (numbers).

34. Alexandra Berzon, Shalini Ramachandran & Coulter Jones, "How OSHA Fell Short in the Pandemic," *WSJ,* March 5, 2021, at A1 (inspection numbers); Bruce Rolfsen, "OSHA Inspector Numbers Increase for First Time in Trump's Term," *Bloomberg Law,* November 27, 2020 (35 percent); Ben Penn, "Inside Scalia's Pro-Industry Revamp of Labor Agency Enforcement," *Bloomberg Law,* November 4, 2020 (decline, several fines), Kimberly Kindy, "More Than 200 Meat Plant Workers in the U.S. Have Died of COVID-19. Federal Regulators Just Issued Two Modest Fines," *WP,* September 13, 2020 ($654 billion); Tom Hals, "U.S. Hits Nursing Home Operator with First Coronavirus Workplace Citation," *Reuters,* July 22, 2020; Donovan Slack, Dennis Wagner & Dan Keemahill, "Coronavirus at Work: Safety Inspectors Reviewing Scores of Employee Hospitalizations, Deaths," *USA Today,* May 1, 2020 (phone inspections); Michael Graebell, Bernice Young & Maryam Jameel, "Millions of Essential Workers Are Being Left Out of COVID-19 Workplace Safety Protections," *ProPublica,* April 16, 2020 (862 inspectors).

35. Slavitt, *Preventable,* at 5 (20 percent of deaths); Leslie Kaufman, "Trump EPA Actions Caused Thousands of Deaths, Lancet Finds," *Bloomberg/BNA Environment & Energy Report,* February 10, 2021 (40 percent); Abutaleh, et al., "Inside Story" (3,000 deaths, Gottlieb quote); James Glanz & Campbell Robertson, "Lockdown Delays Cost at Least 36,000 Lives, Data Suggest," *NYT,* May 21, 2020, at A1 (Columbia study).

36. Timothy Noah, "Is Biden Ditching His Promise to Protect Workers from Covid-19," *New Republic,* April 14, 2021 (meatpacking plants); Sharon Lerner, "How Trump Gutted OSHA and Workplace Safety Rules," *The Intercept,* October 20, 2020

(hospital and nursing homes); Bruce Rolfsen, "OSHA's Low Fines Won't Protect Workers from Virus, AFL-CIO Says," *Bloomberg Law*, October 6, 2020 (correctional staff); Matt Day, Spencer Soper & Josh Eidelson, "Amazon Says Almost 20,000 Workers Had COVID-19 in Six Months," *Bloomberg Law*, October 2, 2020.

Chapter 13: Saving and Enhancing Protective Government

1. "Presidential Election Results: Biden Wins," *CNN*, November 3, 2020 (decisive victory).

2. Jacob S. Hacker & Paul Pierson, *American Amnesia* (2016), at 197; Robert Kuttner, *The Stakes* (2020), at 43 (public cynicism); Alexander Nazaryan, *The Best People* (2019), at xxxii (run it poorly); Dan Balz, "Crisis Exposes How America Has Hollowed Out Its Government," *WP*, May 17, 2020 (poll).

3. Andy Slavitt, *Preventable* (2021), at 114–15 (Operation Warp Speed); David Dayen, "Mind the Trust Gap," *American Prospect*, March/April, 2020, at 4 (leadership and activism); Gerald F. Seib & John McCormick, "Coronavirus Means the Era of Big Government Is Back," *WSJ*, April 27, 2020, at A1 (public approval).

4. Masha Gessen, *Surviving Autocracy* (2020), at 223.

5. Yascha Mounk, "America Is Not a Democracy," *The Atlantic*, March 2021, at 81, 83 (no say); Robert Bonnie, Emily Pechar Diamond & Elizabeth Rowe, "Understanding Rural Attitudes Toward the Environment and Conservation in America" (Nicholas Institute, Duke University, February 2020), at 6–7 (additional resources).

6. Maria De Benedetto, Nicola Lupo & Nicoletta Rangone, "Taking Trust in Government Seriously," *Regulatory Review*, January 25, 2021 (clear regulations); Michael Tomasky, "The Greatest Story Never Told," *Democracy Journal*, Winter 2012, at 125 (shout-out); Rebecca Beitsch & Morgan Chalfant, "Biden Builds Team to Get Aggressive on Regs," *The Hill*, December 27, 2020; Brett Samuels, "Biden Looks to Career Officials to Restore Trust, Morale in Government Agencies," *The Hill*, November 28, 2020; John Kamensky, "Where Are the Stories About Government's Vital Work," *Government Executive*, February 25, 2019.

7. Emily Badger, Quoctrung Bui & Alicia Parlapiano, "Federal Work Force Grew Smaller, and Unhappier, Under Trump," *NYT*, February 4, 2021, at A14 (civil servant understanding).

8. Badger, Bui & Parlapiano, "Work Force Grew Smaller" (assault); Brad Plumer & Coral Davenport, "Science Under Attack: How Trump Is Sidelining Researchers and Their Work," *NYT*, December 28, 2019 (irreplaceable); Dan Diamond, Lisa Rein & Juliet Eilperin, "Trump Left Behind a Damaged Government. Here's What Biden Faces as He Rebuilds It," *WP*, February 6, 2021 (exodus); Molly Jahn, Gregory Treverton & David A. Bray, "A Government by Too Few," *Time*, February 4, 2019, at 17 (SEA report); Shawn Zeller, "Civil Servants on the Brink," *Congressional Quarterly*, February 4, 2019 (SEA report); Robert M. Tobias, "It's Back to Work, but Not Back to Normal," *Government Executive*, January 28, 2019 (benefits); Paul C. Light, "The Government Shutdown Could Become a Government Breakdown," *WP*, January 18, 2019 (bargain); Todd C. Frankel, Taylor Telford & Danielle Paquette, "The Shutdown

Threatens the Promise of Government Jobs—and a Way of Life," *WP*, January 15, 2019 (bargain, difficult to hire).

9. Donald F. Kettl & Paul Verkuil, "Reconstructing the Administrative State," *Government Executive*, January 28, 2019 (show respect); Paul R. Verkuil, "Why Government Professionals Matter," *Regulatory Review*, December 4, 2017 (large sacrifices, need for leaders).

10. Rena Steinzor & Sidney Shapiro, *The People's Agents* (2010), at x (best traditions quote, pay at comparable levels); K. Sabeel Rahman, "Reconstructing the Administrative State in an Era of Economic and Democratic Crisis," 131 *Harv. L. Rev.* 1672 (2018), at 1680 (provide training); Jon Michaels, "Revitalize the Bureaucracy," in *Rethinking Admin Law: From APA to Z* (American Constitution Society 2019), at 9, 11 (expand protections, ROTC suggestion); Eric Katz, "Republicans Take First Shots at Slashing Individual Federal Employees' Salaries," *Government Executive*, July 27, 2017 (five times as many).

11. Lewis, *Premonition*, at 290 (CDC); Steinzor & Shapiro, *People's Agents*, at 195 (quote); Michaels, "Revitalize the Bureaucracy," at 9, 14–15 (expanded political appointees).

12. Executive Order 14,003, 86 *Fed. Reg.* 7,231 (January 27, 2021); Lisa Rein, "The Federal Government Puts Out a 'Help Wanted' Notice as Biden Seeks to Undo Trump Cuts," *WP*, May 21, 2021; Brady Dennis & Dino Grandoni, "New EPA Administrator: 'Science Is Back,'" *WP*, March 15, 2021 (willing to hire back); Eric Katz, "Biden Tells Public Servants They Are the 'Lifeblood of Democracy,'" *Government Executive*, March 12, 2019 (Biden promise); Stephen Lee, "Regan Pledges During Swearing-In to Mend EPA Staff Relationships," *Bloomberg Law*, March 11, 2021.

13. Gessen, *Surviving Autocracy*, at 81–82, 225.

14. Thomas O. McGarity, *Freedom to Harm* (2013), at 219, 270–77.

15. Executive Order 13,992, 86 *Fed. Reg.* 7,049 (January 25, 2021); Rachel Frazin, "Interior Reverses Trump, Moves BLM Headquarters Back to DC," *The Hill*, September 17, 2021; Stacy Cowley, "Broadening Debt Aid for Students," *NYT*, September 13, 2021; Jon Hill, "Biden Freezes Late Trump Regs for White House Review," *Law 360*, January 20, 2021; Stephen Lee & Bobby Magill, "Biden to Move Fast to Strike Down Trump's Environmental Agenda," *Bloomberg Law*, November 9, 2020 (rescind policies).

16. S. J. Res. No. 14, 117th Cong. (2021); Mark Febrizio, "Biden Is Using Multiple Mechanisms to Reverse Trump's Regulatory Agenda" (George Washington University Regulatory Studies Center, April 21, 2021) (six resolutions).

17. White House, "Fact Sheet: List of Agency Actions for Review," January 20, 2021 (list of 102 regulations); Pamela King, "Courts Freeze Trump Rule Litigation," *E&E News*, February 9, 2021; Pamela King, "If Biden Axes Trump Regs, Courts Will Need Explanations," *E&E News*, November 9, 2020; Lee & Magill, "Biden to Move Fast" (start over); Rachel Frazin, "Biden Would Face Hurdles Undoing Trump Environmental Rollbacks," *The Hill*, October 7, 2020 (18–36 months).

18. Preet Bharara, et al., "National Task Force on Rule of Law & Democracy Proposals for Reform" (Brennan Center for Justice 2019), at 7.

19. Executive Order 13,990, 86 *Fed. Reg.* 7,037 (January 25, 2021) § 1; Joe R. Biden, Jr., "Memorandum re: Restoring Trust in Government Through Scientific Integrity and Evidence-Based Policymaking," 86 *Fed. Reg.* 8,845 (February 10, 2021); Kelsey Brugger, "Biden Brings Science Back to the Oval Office," *E&E News*, January 29, 2021.

20. Sean Reilly, "Regan Names New Science Advisers After Firing Trump's Picks," *E&E News*, August 3, 2021; Juan Carlos Rodriguez, "EPA Purges Scientific Advisory Boards," *Law 360*, March 31, 2021 (quote); Romesh Ratnesar, "Democracy Needs a Good Bureaucracy," *Business Week*, November 16, 2020 (Biden administration should populate).

21. *Louisiana v. Biden*, 2021 WL 2446010 (W.D. La. June 15, 2021); Juan Carlos Rodriguez, "Haaland Nixes Trump-Era DOI Orders in Climate Push," *Law 360*, April 16, 2021; Nicholas Kusnetz & Judy Fahys, "Biden's Pause of New Federal Oil and Gas Leases May Not Reduce Production, but It Signals a Reckoning with Fossil Fuels," *Inside Climate News*, January 27, 2021; Michael Doyle, "Biden Taps N.M. Rep. Deb Haaland for Interior Secretary," *E&E News*, December 17, 2020.

22. Lisa Friedman, "Biden Administration Defends Huge Alaska Oil Drilling Project," *NYT*, May 27, 2021, at A1; Hannah Northey & Jeremy P. Jacobs, "Dakota Access Decision Snarls Biden's Equity Progress," *E&E News*, May 5, 2021.

23. Robert Verchick, "Biden Plans to Pick Brenda Mallory to Lead the White House Council on Environmental Quality. Here's What She Can Do to Boost Public Protections," *Center for Progressive Reform Blog*, December 17, 2020.

24. Kelsey Brugger, "What Biden's Infrastructure Plan Could Do for Permitting," *E&E News*, April 2, 2021; Neela Banerjee & Rebecca Hersher, "Biden to Nominate Brenda Mallory to Run Council on Environmental Quality," *National Public Radio,* December 17, 2020.

25. Rena Steinzor, *Why Not Jail?* (2014) (criminal sanctions); Environmental Protection Network, "Resetting the Course of EPA" (August 2020), at 14 (free of political interference, beef up resources).

26. Memorandum from Jean E. Williams, Deputy Assistant Attorney General to ENRD Section Chiefs and Deputy Section Chiefs, re: Withdrawal of Memoranda and Policy Documents, February 4, 2021; Patricia A. McCoy, "Inside Job: The Assault on the Structure of the Consumer Financial Protection Bureau," 103 *Minnesota L. Rev.* 2,543 (2019), at 2,591 (Trump military loan policy); Danielle Douglas-Gabriel, "Education Dept. Revives Student-Aid Enforcement Unit Gutted by DeVos," *WP*, October 10, 2021; Jon Hill, "CFPB Reverses Trump-Era Military Lending Exam Policy," *Law 360*, June 16, 2021; Jennifer Hijazi, "Biden EPA Sends Early Signal of Tough Pollution Enforcement," *Bloomberg Law*, May 28, 2021 (refinery); Al Barbarino, "OSHA Rolls Out Biden-Ordered Virus Protection Program," *Law 360*, March 12, 2021; Ellen M. Gilmer, "DOJ's Rapid Rollback of Trump Policies Marks Environmental Reset," *Bloomberg Environment & Energy Report*, February 5, 2021; Noam Scheiber, "Biden Orders OSHA to Issue New Guidelines to Protect Workers from Coronavirus," *NYT*, January 22, 2021, at B6; Pamela King, "How Biden Might Change Environmental Enforcement," *E&E News*, November 12, 2020 (DOJ, EPA enforcement).

27. Executive Order 12,898, 59 *Fed. Reg.* 7,629 (February 16, 1994); Sharon Lerner, "When Pollution Is a Way of Life," *NYT*, June 22, 2019, at SR9 (environmental justice); Ronald White, "Life at the Fenceline" (Environmental Justice Health Alliance, Coming Clean & Campaign for Healthier Solutions, September 2018), at 1–2.

28. Thomas Frank, "Heat Waves Hit Small Towns of Color Harder Than White Ones," *E&E News*, July 14, 2021; Dino Grandoni, "Biden Stokes Hope Among Climate Scientists," *WP* Energy 202, January 29, 2021 (disproportionately impacts); Daniel Cusick, "Past Racist Practice Fuels Climate Woes Today—Research," *E&E News*, January 21, 2020; Daniel Cusick, "Poor and Minorities More Likely to Be Inundated," *E&E News*, December, 19, 2017.

29. Dino Grandoni & Brady Dennis, "Biden Calls for Half of New Cars to Be Electric or Plug-In Hybrids by 2030," *WP*, August 5, 2021; Lesley Clark, "Granholm Talks Climate, Grid and 'Slighted' Scientists," *E&E News*, April 15, 2021 (quoting Shalanda Baker, DOE) (place at the table); Jean Chemnick, "U.S. Reenters Climate Accord in Sprint for New CO_2 Goals," *E&E News*, February 19, 2021; Dino Grandoni & Brady Dennis, "U.S. Officially Rejoins Paris Accord, Vowing to Make Up for Lost Time," *WP*, February 19, 2021 (lost years); Brianna Jackson & Kellie Lunney, "Biden to Roll Back Trump's Environmental Agenda," *Bloomberg Law*, November 9, 2020 (mandate, exit polls).

30. Namratha Somayajula, "Biden Administration Should Restore, Strengthen Consumer Protections," *The Hill*, November 20, 2020 (middle-class families); Diane Thompson, "Consumer Financial Protection Bureau Leaders Should Focus on Racial and Economic Inequality," *Working Economics Blog*, October 13, 2020; Barbara Van Kerkhove & Ruhi Maker, "Too Big to Fail . . . Too Poor to Bank: How Mainstream Financial Services Can Help Low-Income Working Families Succeed" (Empire Justice Center, September 16, 2018), at 3 (basic necessities); Jeff Sovern, Ann L. Goldweber & Gina M. Calabrese, "Why We Need to Save the Consumer Financial Protection Bureau," *The Conversation*, July 10, 2017 (vulnerability).

31. Daniel Marans, "Kirsten Gillibrand Unveils a Public Option for Banking," *Huffington Post*, April 25, 2018.

32. Michael Doyle, "Interior to Set a New Course for ESA," *E&E News*, January 20, 2021.

33. Executive Order 13,990, 86 *Fed. Reg.* 7,037 (January 25, 2021) §§ 3, 4; Coral Davenport, "Biden to Restore Protections That Trump Stripped from 3 National Monuments," *NYT*, October 8, 2021, at A14; Heather Richards, "Biden Admin Restores Tongass Protections Trump Stripped," *E&E News*, July 15, 2021; Coral Davenport, "Haaland Urges the Restoration of Three Protected Sites," *NYT*, June 15, 2021, at A17; Bobby Magill, "Trump-Era Roadless Rule to Be Scrapped for Alaska Forest," *Bloomberg Law*, June 11, 2021; Coral Davenport, Henry Fountain & Lisa Friedman, "U.S. Suspends Drilling Leases in Arctic Lands," *NYT*, June 2, 2021, at A1; Heather Richards, "Executive Order Will Pause All ANWR Oil Activities," *E&E News*, January 20, 2021; Jennifer Yachnin, "How Biden Could Expand National Monuments," *E&E News*, December 7, 2020.

34. Jacob S. Hacker & Paul Pierson, *Let Them Eat Tweets* (2020), at 211 (continued support from business Republicans and free marketeers); Lisa Lerer, "From His

Resort, Trump Has G.O.P. in an Iron Grip," *NYT*, May 9, 2021, at A1; Michael Scherer, "State and Local GOP Committees Attack Any Republicans Who Dare Turn on Trump," *WP*, February 10, 2021 (populists will support Trump); Audra D. S. Burch & Campbell Robertson, "Division, Distrust and Dissatisfaction: A Bleak New Morning in America," *NYT*, November 5, 2020, at F8 (rebuild trust).

35. Juan Carlos Rodriguez, "Biden's Green Overhaul Will Have to Clear Trump's Judiciary," *Law 360*, March 18, 2021.

36. Rob Bluey, "Trump Allies to Counter Left, Block Biden by Going to Court," *Daily Signal*, April 26, 2021 (America First Legal); Thomas Catenacci, "Republican Attorneys General Plan to Create Legal Roadblocks for Biden Agenda," *Daily Signal*, April 12, 2021; Thomas Frank, "A Biden Win Wouldn't Mean a Slam-Dunk for Climate—Experts," *E&E News*, October 16, 2020 (quoting Barry Rabe, University of Michigan) (companies will challenge).

37. *Louisiana v. Biden*, 2021 WL 2446010 (W.D. La., June 15, 2021); Bob Van Voris, "Biden Agenda Faces GOP Legal Attacks and Skeptical Trump Judges," *Bloomberg Law*, November 10, 2020 (230 judges); Pamela King, "How 200 Trump Judges Could Shape Environmental Policy," *E&E News*, June 24, 2020.

38. Alan I. Abramowitz, *The Great Alignment* (2018), at 117 (deeply polarized); Kathleen Hall Jamieson & Joseph N. Capella, *Echo Chamber* (2008), at 246 (ad hominem attacks); Matthew Rosenberg, Jim Rutenberg & Nick Corasaniti, "Frenzied Rush of Falsehoods from the Top," *NYT*, November 6, 2020, at A1 ("StopTheSteal" movement); Michael Gerson, "This Election Was a Reflection of Who We Are as a Country," *WP*, November 5, 2020 (chastened and sobered quote).

39. Abramowitz, *Great Alignment*, at 1–2; Hacker & Pierson, *Tweets*, at 8, 172, 208, 267 (tribalism, huge divide, not likely to change); Joseph E. Stiglitz, *People, Power, and Profits* (2019), at xix (making larger quote).

40. Scott Waldman, "Trump Welcomed Climate Deniers. What Now for Them?" *E&E News*, December 22, 2020 (Ebel quote, American Energy Alliance boast); William A. Galston, "The 'Trump Bump' Is Already Over," *WSJ*, April 8, 2020, at A17 (restitution).

41. Darragh Roche, "List of Companies That Have Resumed Donations to GOP Election Objectors," *Newsweek*, July 16, 2021; Dino Grandoni, "Business Leaders Once Allied with Trump Now Condemn Him for Stoking Violence," *WP* Energy 202, January 7, 2021; Seib & McCormick, "Era of Big Government Is Back" (quoting Scott Reed, U.S. Chamber of Commerce).

42. Slavitt, *Preventable*, at 4 (valued individual freedom); Apoorva Mandavilli & Benjamin Mueller, "Delta Variant Widens Gulf Between 'Two Americas': Vaccinated and Unvaccinated," *NYT*, July 15, 2021, at A1; Joshua Green, "Trumpism Isn't Going Away," *Bloomberg Businessweek*, November 9, 2020 (populists will follow); Seib & McCormick, "Era of Big Government Is Back" (angry rejection).

43. Reece Peck, *Fox Populism* (2019), at 38, 94, 170, 187.

44. Jason Zengerle, "OutFoxed," *NYT Magazine*, January 17, 2021, at 7; David Folkenflik, "Newsmax Rises on Wave of Resentment Toward Media—Especially Fox News," *NPR*, November 30, 2020.

45. Hacker & Pierson, *Tweets*, at 206 (17 percent); Jamieson & Capella, *Echo Chamber*, at 246 (very difficult to enact); Nazaryan, *Best People*, at 67, 70 (lobbyists, Abramoff); Eric Mogilnicki & Drey Samuelson, "It's Beyond Time to Retire the Filibuster," *WP*, September 7, 2020.

46. Naomi Klein, *This Changes Everything* (2014), at 465 (Great Recession); Reid Wilson, "Increasingly Active Younger Voters Liberalize US Electorate," *The Hill*, May 15, 2021.

47. James Godwin & Ethan Winter, "Building a Progressive Regulatory Agenda" (Data for Progress, Center for Progressive Reform, January 2021), at 3, 8 (January 2021 poll); Nikita Vladimirov, "Poll: Trump Voters More Supportive of Federal Spending Than Other Conservatives," *The Hill*, December 20, 2016 (2016 poll).

48. Katy Stech Ferek, "More EPA Rule Cuts Vowed if Trump Wins," *WSJ*, September 4, 2020, at A3; Philip Wallach, "On Deregulation, Trump Has Achieved Little," *National Review*, December 19, 2019 (content to destroy); Jenna Johnson, Juliet Eilperin & Ed O'Keefe, "Trump Is Finding It Easier to Tear Down Old Policies Than to Build His Own," *WP*, June 4, 2017 (no affirmative agenda).

49. Lara Putnam & Theda Skocpol, "Middle America Reboots Democracy," *Democracy Journal*, Summer 2018, at 51 (mothers and grandmothers, shift quote); Erin Delmore, "This Is How Women Voters Decided the 2020 Election," *NBC News*, November 13, 2020; William H. Frey, "Biden's Victory Came from the Suburbs," *Brookings*, November 13, 2020.

50. Clifford Krauss, "The Chief of Exxon Mobil Changes Tone on Emissions," *NYT*, March 4, 2021, at B3; Ted Mann & Timothy Puko, "Carbon Pricing Gains Traction," *WSJ*, March 2, 2021, at A6; Kylie Mohr & Maxine Joselow, "Auto Trade Group Supports Biden Net-Zero Goals," *E&E News*, February 2, 2021; Marianne Lavelle, "The Resistance: In the President's Relentless War on Climate Science, They Fought Back," *Inside Climate News*, December 27, 2020 (red team-blue team, endangerment finding, climate assessments).

51. James Hohmann, "The Koch Network Is Reorganizing Under a New Name and with New Priorities," *WP*, May 20, 2019.

52. "Darkness, Darkness—The Mercers Are Disappointed in Trump," *Down with Tyranny Blog*, June 20, 2019.

53. Alexander C. Kaufman, "Pro-Trump Climate Denial Group Lays Off Staff Amid Financial Woes, Ex-Employees Say," *Huffington Post*, March 7, 2020.

54. Brody Mullins, "Key Business Group Names Woman CEO for the First Time," *WSJ*, February 10, 2021, at A5; Nick Sobczyk, "Chamber Shifts on Climate, Supports Market-Based Policy," *E&E News*, January 20, 2021; Shane Goldmacher & Nick Corasaniti, "The Donor Class Pressures Republicans Still Backing Trump," *NYT*, January 14, 2021, at A16 (broader trend); Joseph Winters, "Why Did the World's Biggest Business Lobby Endorse 23 Climate Candidates?" *Grist*, September 22, 2020; Nick Sobczyk & Geof Koss, "Chamber Changes Tune on Climate, but Dems Remain Skeptical," *E&E News*, June 11, 2019 (real threat quote).

55. Nick Sobczyk, "Business Roundtable Calls for a Price on Carbon," *E&E News*, September 16, 2020; Jamie Dimon, "How to Save Capitalism," *Time*, February 3, 2020

(quote); "Grappling with Internal Splits, Industry Groups Try to Shift GHG Stance," *Inside EPA*, November 1, 2019, at 1 (revised principles).

56. LaTosha Brown, "The Untapped Power of Rural Voters," *NYT*, June 9, 2019, at A23 (10 million); Caitlin Dewey, "A Growing Number of Young Americans Are Leaving Desk Jobs to Farm," *WP*, November 23, 2017.

57. Anne Nelson, *The Shadow Network* (2019), at 266 (Southern Baptists); "Declining Christianity Leads to Dramatic US Religious Realignment, CRC Study Finds" (Cultural Research Center, Arizona Christian University, June 8, 2021) (decline); Adam Gabbatt, "'Allergic Reaction to US Religious Right' Fueling Decline of Religion, Experts Say," *The Guardian*, April 5, 2021 (quoting Prof. David Campbell, Notre Dame University).

58. Nicholas Confessore, "Get Cash Now from the Poor," *NYT Magazine*, April 21, 2019, at 30 (Mulvaney meeting); Meera Subramanian, "Generation Climate: Can Young Evangelicals Change the Climate Debate," *Inside Climate News*, November 21, 2018.

59. Salena Zito & Brad Todd, *The Great Revolt* (2018), at 209 (concern for children's safety); Charla Rios, Diane Standaert & Yasmin Farahi, "The Sky Doesn't Fall" (Center for Responsible Lending, January 2020) (South Dakota vote); Molly Ball, "Donald Trump's Forgotten Man," *Time*, February 26, 2018, at 24 (progressives can reach).

60. The Restoration of Pelerin Palace, http://www.lucidmotion.co.uk/pelerin-palace -restoration-film/; PropGOLuxury.com; DuParc Kempinski—The Most Expensive Property in Switzerland, July 9, 2010, https://www.propgoluxury.com/en /propertynews/vaud/1008-du-parc-kempinski.html.

61. Renae Merle & Tracy Jan, "Trump Is Systematically Backing Off Consumer Protections, to the Delight of Corporations," *WP*, March 6, 2018 (big win quote); "Transport Safety Rules Sidelined Indefinitely Under Trump as Part of a Sweeping Retreat in Regulations," *CNBC*, February 26, 2018 (quoting Dan Bosch, American Action Forum) (delighted); David A. Graham, "Trump Has Quietly Accomplished More Than It Appears," *The Atlantic*, August 2, 2017.

62. Ellen M. Gilmer, "Trump Environmental Record Marked by Big Losses, Undecided Cases," *Bloomberg Law*, January 11, 2021 (successful defenses); Pamela King & Jeremy F. Jacobs, "What Trump's Dismal Deregulatory Record Means for Biden," *E&E News*, January 11, 2021 (many initiatives overturned).

63. Coral Davenport, "Trump's Environmental Legacy May Be Lasting Harm to the Climate," *NYT*, November 10, 2020 (tipping point, 417 ppm, 1.8 billion); Sharon Lerner, "As the West Burns, the Trump Administration Races to Demolish Environmental Protections," *The Intercept*, September 19, 2020 (linger for centuries); Marianne Lavelle, "Trump Repeal of Climate Rules Means U.S. Paris Target Now Out of Reach," *Inside Climate News*, March 20, 2017 (Berkeley estimate).

64. Chris Morran, "The Government Donald Trump Left Behind," *Government Executive*, January 31, 2021.

65. Thomas O. McGarity, *Freedom to Harm* (2013), at 76–78, 288–90; William J. Clinton, "State of the Union Address," January 23, 1996 (Clinton quote).

ABOUT THE AUTHOR

Thomas O. McGarity is the William Powers Jr. and Kim L. Heilbrun Chair in Tort Law at the University of Texas at Austin School of Law, and the past president of the Center for Progressive Reform. He is the author of *Pollution, Politics, and Power*; *Freedom to Harm*; and *The Preemption War*, among other books. He lives in Austin, Texas.

PUBLISHING IN THE PUBLIC INTEREST

Thank you for reading this book published by The New Press. The New Press is a nonprofit, public interest publisher. New Press books and authors play a crucial role in sparking conversations about the key political and social issues of our day.

We hope you enjoyed this book and that you will stay in touch with The New Press. Here are a few ways to stay up to date with our books, events, and the issues we cover:

- Sign up at www.thenewpress.com/subscribe to receive updates on New Press authors and issues and to be notified about local events
- www.facebook.com/newpressbooks
- www.twitter.com/thenewpress
- www.instagram.com/thenewpress

Please consider buying New Press books for yourself; for friends and family; or to donate to schools, libraries, community centers, prison libraries, and other organizations involved with the issues our authors write about.

The New Press is a 501(c)(3) nonprofit organization. You can also support our work with a tax-deductible gift by visiting www.thenewpress.com/donate.